WOMEN AND CHILDREN FIRST

THE WELLCOME INSTITUTE SERIES IN THE HISTORY OF MEDICINE

Edited by W.F. Bynum and Roy Porter,
The Wellcome Institute

WOMEN AND CHILDREN FIRST

INTERNATIONAL MATERNAL AND INFANT WELFARE 1870–1945

Edited by
**Valerie Fildes, Lara Marks
and Hilary Marland**

London and New York

First published in 1992
by Routledge
11 New Fetter Lane, London EC4P 4EE

Simultaneously published in the USA and Canada
by Routledge
a division of Routledge, Chapman and Hall Inc.
29 West 35th Street, New York, NY 10001

Typeset by LaserScript, Mitcham, Surrey
Printed and bound in Great Britain
by Biddles Ltd, Guildford and King's Lynn

British Library Cataloguing in Publication Data
A catalogue record for this book is available from the British Library.

Library of Congress Cataloging in Publication Data

Women and children first: international maternal and infant welfare,
1870–1945/edited by Valerie Fildes, Lara Marks, and Hilary Marland.
p. cm. – (The Wellcome Institute series in the history of medicine; 4)
Includes bibliographical references and index.
1. Maternal health services – History – 20th century. 2. Maternal
health services – History – 19th century. 3. Infant health services –
History – 20th century. 4. Infant health services – History – 19th
century. 5. Maternal and infant welfare – Government policy.
I. Fildes, Valerie A. II. Marks, Lara, 1963– . III. Marland, Hilary.
IV. Series.
[DNLM: 1. Child Health Services – history. 2. Health Policy –
history. 3. Infant Welfare – history. 4. Maternal Health Services –
history. 5. Maternal Welfare – history. WA 11.1 W872]
RG940.W66 1992
362.1'982'009–dc20
DNLM/DLC
for Library of Congress 92-7627
CIP

ISBN 0–415–08090–8

For the mothers and children of the Third World

Contents

Contents

Illustrations

Tables

Illustrations

Figures

Illustrations

Plates

Contributors

Cynthia Comacchio is assistant professor at the Department of History, Wilfred Laurier University, Waterloo, Ontario. She received her masters degree at York University, Toronto, Ontario, and her doctorate in Canadian History at the University of Guelph, Ontario. Her research interests include childhood and the family, gender and class. She has published articles on maternal and child welfare in rural Canada, marriage, and class analysis, and is working on a book on maternal and child welfare in Ontario, 1914–1940.

Valerie Fildes trained and worked as a nurse before obtaining a first degree and Ph.D. in Human Biology at the University of Surrey. Her research has included infant care and paediatrics prior to 1800. She is author of *Breasts, Bottles and Babies: A History of Infant Feeding* (1986) and *Wet Nursing: A History from Antiquity to the Present* (1988), and is editor of *Women as Mothers in Pre-Industrial England* (1990), also published in the Wellcome Series in the History of Medicine. She is currently researching infant feeding practices in the nineteenth and early twentieth centuries. Valerie Fildes is a member of the International Union of Nutritional Sciences Committee on the 'Nutritional Significance of Colostrum'.

Debby Gaitskell teaches history for London University's Centre for Extra-Mural Studies and at the Institute of Commonwealth Studies, where she also runs a seminar series entitled 'Women, colonialism and commonwealth'. She has previously lectured at the University of Witwatersrand, Birkbeck and Morley Colleges, and for the Workers' Educational Association. An editor of the

Journal of Southern African Studies from 1984 to 1988, she has published on African women and Christianity, domesticity and domestic service, and girls' education in South Africa.

Molly Ladd-Taylor is assistant professor of United States history at Carleton College in Northfield, Minnesota. She is editor of *Raising a Baby the Government Way: Mothers' Letters to the Children's Bureau, 1915–1932* (1986) and author of *Mother-Work: Women, Child Welfare and the State 1890–1930* (forthcoming from the University of Illinois Press).

Milton Lewis is a graduate of the University of New South Wales and the Australian National University. He is currently Australian Research Council Senior Research Fellow in the Department of Public Health at the University of Sydney. He was chairman of the organizing committee of the first national conference of the Australian Society of the History of Medicine, 1989, and is a member of the National Council of the Society.

Irvine Loudon qualified in medicine from Oxford University in 1951 and worked as a general practitioner until 1970, when he started to research the history of medicine. From 1980 to 1989 he was attached to the Wellcome Unit for the History of Medicine in Oxford, first as a Wellcome Research Fellow and later as a Research Associate. His publications include *Medical Care and the General Practitioner 1750-1850* (1986) and papers on the history of the medical profession, historical epidemiology and the history of childbirth. He has just completed a book entitled *Death in Childbirth: an International Study of Maternity Care and Maternal Mortality 1800-1950* to be published by Oxford University Press.

Lenore Manderson is a medical anthropologist and is professor of tropical health in the Tropical Health Program, University of Queensland, Australia. Her major fieldwork has been undertaken in Peninsular Malaysia, Japan and Australia, and her research interests include subjects relating to pregnancy and birth, infant feeding and weaning practices both in Malaysia and Australia. She is the author of *Women, Politics and Change* (1980) and editor of *Women's Work and Women's Roles* (1983) and *Shared Wealth and Symbol* (1985).

Contributors

Lara Marks completed a D.Phil. at Oxford University in 1990, 'Irish and Jewish women's experience of childbirth and infant care in East London 1870–1939: the response of host society and immigrant communities to medical welfare needs', which is to be published by Oxford University Press. She has written on Jewish prostitution, the Jewish Maternity Home, Irish and Jewish married women's work, Irish and Jewish unmarried mothers, ethnicity, religion and health care, and Poor Law maternity services 1870–1929. Employed as a research fellow at Queen Mary and Westfield College, University of London, she is presently working on 'The historical geography of the welfare state: maternal and infant welfare services in London 1902–1939'.

Hilary Marland obtained a Ph.D. from the University of Warwick in 1984 with her thesis 'Medicine and Society in Wakefield and Huddersfield, 1780–1870', published by Cambridge University Press in 1987. She has also published on the history of dispensaries, the nineteenth-century medical profession, chemists and druggists, and Dutch midwives. Now employed as research officer in the Institute for Medical History at Erasmus University, Rotterdam, her research interests include the history of public health and preventive medicine in the Netherlands, women medical practitioners, and the history of Dutch midwives, 1700–1900.

Elizabeth Peretz works for Oxfordshire Social Services as a Senior Training and Development Officer, and is researching and working towards a thesis on British maternal and child welfare in the interwar period. Prior to her present post, Elizabeth Peretz had a research position at the Wellcome Unit for the History of Medicine in Oxford.

Judith Richell took a humanities degree at Hatfield Polytechnic, and between 1984 and 1987 carried out research at the School of Oriental and African Studies on demography in colonial Burma. She is employed as a lecturer in history at the North Hertfordshire College of Further Education, and is completing her thesis 'Determinants of demographic change in colonial Burma'.

Philippa Mein Smith has lectured in economic history at the Flinders University of South Australia, and took up an

xiv

appointment as lecturer in history at the University of Canterbury, New Zealand, in 1992. She completed a Ph.D. at the Australian National University in 1990. Her research is concerned with maternal and infant health and welfare in Australia and New Zealand, and her publications include *Maternity in Dispute. New Zealand 1920–1939* (1986).

Marijke du Toit is a doctoral student at the Department of Economic History at the University of Cape Town. Her research concerns Afrikaan's women's participation in the construction and dissemination of Afrikaner nationalism.

Preface and acknowledgements

Many edited volumes have a difficult history before they finally arrive on the publisher's desk, and this volume has had a more troubled history than most. This book was conceived by Valerie Fildes in 1989, but, unfortunately, when the project was already well under way Valerie became seriously ill, and for a time it seemed that the volume would have to be abandoned. In May 1991 Lara Marks and Hilary Marland offered to assist with the editing, and to see the book through the production process. By this time, several articles were in, others were still being written, and a few new pieces were commissioned. Sadly, Valerie was unable to complete her planned piece on Truby King in New Zealand. Although Valerie was responsible for the book's conception and planning, this volume is the result of joint enterprise and co-operation between Hilary, Lara and Valerie.

Largely because of the volume's complicated history and the speed with which it was finally made ready for production, we owe many debts to people and institutions who supported us on the way. Thanks go to Gill Davies and Brad Scott of Routledge, and Bill Bynum and Roy Porter, editors of the Wellcome series, for their encouragement in seeing the book to completion. We are particularly appreciative of the support given by Elizabeth Peretz who urged us to continue with the project. The book could not have been finished without the help and financial support of the Department of Geography at Queen Mary and Westfield College, University of London and the Medical Faculty of Erasmus University, Rotterdam. The Nestlé Company Ltd funded Valerie Fildes' research. Thanks also go to Murray Gray, Roger Lee, Edward Oliver, Mart van Lieburg, Peter Verhoef, Tini and Tineke, the staff of the Medical Faculty

Library in Rotterdam, and the telephonists at Queen Mary and Westfield College.

We would also like to thank Dr J. T. H. Connor, editor of the *Canadian Bulletin of Medical History*, for permitting us to reproduce Cynthia Comacchio's article '"The infant soldier": the Great War and the medical campaign for child welfare', *Can. Bull. Med. Hist.*, 5 (1988), 99–119, the editors of the *Social History of Medicine* for allowing us to use sections of Irvine Loudon's article 'Maternal mortality: 1880–1950. Some regional and international comparisons', *Soc. Hist. Med.*, 1 (1988), 183–228, and the editors of the *New Zealand Journal of History* for enabling us to use extracts from P. Mein Smith, 'Truby King in Australia: a revisionist view of reduced infant mortality', *NZ J. Hist.*, 22 (1988), 23–43.

All our families were important supports throughout. Valerie's husband, Brian, and her sons, Andrew and Simon, provided crucial help and care at a time when it was most needed. Sebastian and Daniel van Strien, Shula, Yitz and Rafi Marks were all vital sustainers of our energy and enthusiasm throughout. Sebastian's practical assistance was especially important in getting the book ready to go to press. The remarkable co-operation of all the contributors, several of whom rescheduled work commitments in order to meet the deadline, made the task of completion quicker and easier.

Valerie Fildes, Lara Marks and Hilary Marland

Abbreviations

ABC	Archives of the American Board of Commissioners for Foreign Missions, Houghton Library, Harvard University
ABM	American Board Mission
ACVV	*Afrikaanse Christelike Vroue Vereniging*
Am. Anthropol.	*American Anthropologist*
Am. Hist. Rev.	*American Historical Review*
Am. J. Epidemiol.	*American Journal of Epidemiology*
Am. J. Obstet. & Gynecol.	*American Journal of Obstetrics and Gynecology*
Am. J. Publ. Health	*American Journal of Public Health*
AMS	Australian Mothercraft Society
Ann. Démog. Hist.	*Annales de Démographie Historique*
Ann. Trop. Med. Parasitol.	*Annals of Tropical Medicine and Parasitology*
A/R	*Annual Report*
Archs Ped.	*Archives of Pediatrics*
Asian Med. J.	*Asian Medical Journal*
Aust. Econ. Rev.	*Australian Economic Review*
Aust. & NZ J. Obstet. & Gynaecol.	*Australian and New Zealand Journal of Obstetrics and Gynaecology*
Aust. & NZ J. Sociol.	*Australian and New Zealand Journal of Sociology*
Aust. Paediat. J.	*Australian Paediatric Journal*
Australas. Med. Gaz.	*Australasian Medical Gazette*
Aust. Slav. E. Eur. Stud.	*Austrian and Slavonic Eastern European Studies*
BC Stud.	*British Columbia Studies*

BH	Board of Health
Biol. Neonate	*Biology of Neonate*
BL	British Library
BLPES	British Library of Political and Economic Sciences
BMA	British Medical Association
Br. J. Obstet. & Gynaecol.	*British Journal of Obstetrics and Gynaecology*
Br. J. Prev. Soc. Med.	*British Journal of Preventive and Social Medicine*
Br. Med. J.	*British Medical Journal*
Bull. Hist. Med.	*Bulletin of the History of Medicine*
Bull. NY Acad. Med.	*Bulletin of the New York Academy of Medicine*
Bull. WHO	*Bulletin of the World Health Organization*
Burma Med. J.	*Burma Medical Journal*
CA	Cape Archives (South Africa)
Can. Bull. Med. Hist.	*Canadian Bulletin of Medical History*
Can. Med. Ass. J.	*Canadian Medical Association Journal*
Can. Publ. Health J.	*Canadian Public Health Journal*
C & R, CB	Correspondence & Reports, Children's Bureau Records, National Archives, Washington, DC
CBS	*Central Bureau voor de Statistiek*
CMA	Canadian Medical Association
CO	Colonial Office (Malaya)
Coll. Anthropol.	*Collegium Anthropologicum*
CR	*Journal of the Community of the Resurrection* (Johannesburg)
Dan. Med. Bull.	*Danish Medical Bulletin*
Ecol. Food Nutr.	*Ecology of Food and Nutrition*
Econ. Hist. Rev.	*Economic History Review*
EEMH	East End Maternity Home
Eug. Rev.	*Eugenics Review*
Eur. J. Popul.	*European Journal of Population*
Fem. Stud.	*Feminist Studies*
FMSAR	Annual Report for the Federated Malay States
French Hist. Stud.	*French Historical Studies*
Guy's Hosp. Rep.	*Guy's Hospital Reports*

Hist.	*History*
Hist. Meth.	*Historical Methodology*
Hist. Philos. Life Sci.	*History of Philosophy and Life Sciences*
Hist. Stud.	*Historical Studies*
Hist. Workshop J.	*History Workshop Journal*
IMR	Infant Mortality Rate
Indian Med. Gaz.	*Indian Medical Gazette*
Indian Practit.	*Indian Practitioner*
Internat. J. Afr. Hist. Stud.	*International Journal of African Historical Studies*
Internat. J. Gynaecol. & Obstet.	*International Journal of Gynaecology and Obstetrics*
Internat. J. Health Serv.	*International Journal of Health Services*
Internat. Nurs. Rev.	*International Nursing Review*
Irish Hist. Stud.	*Irish Historical Studies*
J. Afr. Hist.	*Journal of African History*
J. Am. Hist.	*Journal of American History*
J. Am. Med. Ass.	*Journal of the American Medical Association*
J. Am. Med. Women's Ass.	*Journal of the American Medical Women's Association*
J. Aust. Stud.	*Journal of Australian Studies*
J. Biosoc. Sci.	*Journal of Biosocial Science*
J. Econ. Hist.	*Journal of Economic History*
J. Eur. Econ. Hist.	*Journal of European Economic History*
J. Fam. Hist.	*Journal of Family History*
J. Hist. Med.	*Journal of the History of Medicine and Allied Sciences*
J. Hyg.	*Journal of Hygiene*
J. Interdisc. Hist.	*Journal of Interdisciplinary History*
J. Malays. Branch Roy. Asiat. Soc.	*Journal of the Malaysian Branch of the Royal Asiatic Society*
J. Med. Ass. S. Afr.	*Journal of the Medical Association of South Africa*
J. Med. Ass. Thailand	*Journal of the Medical Association of Thailand*
J. Obstet. & Gynaecol. Br. Emp.	*Journal of Obstetrics and Gynaecology of the British Empire*
JORALS	*Journal of Regional and Local Studies*
J. Roy. Aust. Hist. Soc.	*Journal of the Royal Australian History Society*
J. Soc. Hist.	*Journal of Social History*

J. Soc. Pol.	*Journal of Social Policy*
J. South. Afr. Stud.	*Journal of Southern African Studies*
J. Trop. Med. Hyg.	*Journal of Tropical Medicine and Hygiene*
J. Trop. Pediat.	*Journal of Tropical Pediatrics*
J. Trop. Pediat. &	*Journal of Tropical Pediatrics and*
Environ. Child Health	*Environmental Child Health*
LGB	Local Government Board
Loc. Popul. Stud.	*Local Population Studies*
Lond. Hosp. Illust.	*London Hospital Illustrated*
Maandschr. Kindergeneesk.	*Maandschrift voor Kindergeneeskunde*
MCW	Maternity and child welfare
Med. Esp.	*Medicina España*
Med. Hist.	*Medical History*
Med. J. Aust.	*Medical Journal of Australia*
Med. J. Malaysia	*Medical Journal of Malaysia*
Med. Offr.	*Medical Officer*
MH	Ministry of Health
MMR	Maternity Mortality Rate
MOH	Medical Officer of Health
N. Am. Rev.	*North American Review*
Ned. Tijdschr. Geneesk.	*Nederlands Tijdschrift voor Geneeskunde*
Neth. J. Sociol.	*Netherlands Journal of Sociology*
New South Wales Med. Gaz.	*New South Wales Medical Gazette*
NSPCC	National Society for the Prevention of Cruelty to Children
NY State J. Med.	*New York State Journal of Medicine*
NZ J. Hist.	*New Zealand Journal of History*
NZ Med. J.	*New Zealand Medical Journal*
Oral Hist.	*Oral History*
PAC	Public Archives of Canada
Popul. Index	*Population Index*
Popul. Stud.	*Population Studies*
P & P	*Past and Present*
PRO	Public Record Office
PS	Plunket Society
Publ. Health	*Public Health*
RCH	Royal Commission on Health
RNZSHWC	Royal New Zealand Society for the Health of Women and Children

RPHAB	*Report on the Public Health Administration of Burma* (1921–36)
RSAB	*Report on the Sanitary Administration of Burma* (1890–1920)
RSABB	*Report on the Sanitary Administration of British Burma* (1870–89)
RSPHB	*Report on the State of Public Health in Burma* (1937–39)
RSWBM	Royal Society for the Welfare of Mothers and Babies
S. Afr. Med. J.	*South African Medical Journal*
S. Afr. Med. Rec.	*South African Medical Record*
S. Afr. Outlook	*South African Outlook*
Sel. Sec.	Selangor Secretariat
Soc. Hist. Med.	*Social History of Medicine*
Soc. Med. Maandschr.	*Sociale Medische Maandschrift*
Soc. Sci. Hist.	*Social Science and History*
Soc. Sci. Med.	*Social Science and Medicine*
Soc. Serv. Rev.	*Social Services Review*
Soc. Soc. Hist. Med. Bull.	*Society for the Social History of Medicine Bulletin*
Soc. Welf.	*Social Welfare*
Sociol. Health & Illn.	*Sociology of Health and Illness*
SSAR	Government of the Straits Settlements, *Annual Departmental Reports*
Stud. West. Aust. Hist.	*Studies in Western Australian History*
THL	Tower Hamlets Local History Library
Tijdschr. Gesch.	*Tijdschrift voor Geschiedenis*
Tijdschr. Soc. Geneesk.	*Tijdschrift voor Sociale Geneeskunde*
Tijdschr. Soc. Gesch.	*Tijdschrift voor Sociale Geschiedenis*
Trans. Australas. Med. Cong.	*Transactions of the Australasian Medical Congress*
Trans. Epidemiol. Soc. Lond.	*Transactions of the Epidemiological Society of London*
Trans. Intercol. Med. Cong.	*Transactions of Intercolonial Medical Congress*
Trop. Geog. Med.	*Tropical Geography and Medicine*
TSR	*Quarterly magazine of the Transvaal and Southern Rhodesia Missionary Association*
Twentieth Cent. Br. Hist.	*Twentieth Century British History*

Abbreviations

USDC, MER	University of Stellenbosch Document Centre, M. E. Rothmann Collection
USPG	Archives of the United Society for the Propagation of the Gospel
VBHCA	Victorian Baby Health Centres Association
Vict. Stud.	*Victorian Studies*
VON	Victorian Order of Nurses (Canada)
Women's Internat. Forum	*Women's International Forum*
WUL	Witwatersrand University Library
Z. Bevölkerungswiss.	*Zeitschrift für Bevölkerungs-wissenschaft*

Introduction

The international maternal and infant welfare movement of the last decades of the nineteenth century and first decades of the twentieth was a direct response to high maternal and infant mortality rates and falling marital fertility in most countries of the world. In some countries, it was given impetus by major conflicts, particularly the Boer War and the First World War, which decimated populations, robbed nations of their young men, and concentrated attention on ensuring the survival of future generations to people lands and empires, in a fit state to fight battles. Imperialist concerns were bolstered by a range of economic, social, and humanitarian motivations, and the desire to save the lives of mothers and young children.

This volume examines efforts to reduce maternal and infant deaths in a variety of countries, spread across the five continents, between the late nineteenth century and the Second World War. The articles show the great diversity in the timing of maternal and infant welfare campaigns and in the approaches used by governments, institutions and individuals: the problems they met, how these were overcome, and to what extent they were successful in reducing mortality and achieving the long-term health and well-being of women and children. Health and welfare provisions – obstetric services, maternity nursing, hospital facilities, infant welfare services, and accompanying financial assistance – differed widely from country to country, and within individual countries the variation in the coverage and the amount of help given could also be great. The responses of the mothers are central to the book, and the articles also focus on the many actors who were involved in conceiving and implementing programmes: women's organizations, local voluntary associations, doctors, midwives, health visitors and public health administrators, local and national governments.

The book opens with Irvine Loudon's analysis of international trends in maternal deaths between 1880 and 1950. While levels of mortality often differed widely, certain patterns were broadly similar. A closer understanding of deaths in childbirth is offered through an examination of national and regional trends and their relationship to geographical, socioeconomic and clinical factors. Between 1880 and 1935 evidence suggests that it was usually safest to be delivered at home by a well-trained midwife, than in hospital by a doctor. Although high maternal mortality was often associated with poverty, the link was indirect.

Milton Lewis's study of persistent maternal mortality in Sydney, Australia between 1870 and 1939 demonstrates that, while midwives were not without blame, high maternal mortality was partly attributable to the structure of maternity services and the reluctance of doctors to adopt recognized preventive measures when carrying out deliveries, especially when they were an obstacle to professional interests. Only in the 1930s did maternal mortality decline, coinciding with the introduction of sulphonamides, and a new co-operation between doctors, midwives and the state. Some Sydney hospitals achieved remarkably low rates of maternal mortality, and this theme is continued by Lara Marks in her study of The London Hospital between 1870 and 1939 which shows that the standard of care hospitals offered was not only dependent on medical expertise, but also on a hospital's location and interaction with the community, economy and local government. This East London hospital was based in an area with a surprisingly low rate of maternal mortality, given the terrible social and economic deprivation experienced by many of its patients. East London's charitable midwifery services, while not relieving poverty, offered a vital support to mothers who otherwise could not afford good midwifery care.

Moving outside the institutional setting to schemes developed by interested groups of medical professionals, Hilary Marland and Cynthia Comacchio discuss the setting up of infant welfare services and the specific role of paediatricians in this work in the Netherlands and Canada. Infant welfare services in the Netherlands between 1901 and 1930 arose from private, largely doctor-directed, initiatives. Professional interest, Marland argues, was not only motivated by infant mortality, as this had already been falling for two decades before the experts moved in; career consolidation also played a vital part. In early twentieth-century Ontario paediatricians were also significant in shaping services; using the motif of war, Comacchio argues, they put themselves forward as saviours of the nation, and defenders of future generations of healthy citizens.

Switching from professional interest to policy-making, Molly Ladd-Taylor explores the short-lived experiment in publicly funded infant and maternal health care in the United States. The Sheppard–Towner Act, passed in 1921 as the first US social welfare measure, was enthusiastically endorsed by women's organizations, who helped the female-run Children's Bureau with its administration. Although infant mortality rates dropped during the years it was in effect, funds were withdrawn in 1929 because of the opposition from physicians and conservatives who saw the Act as a threat to the home and motherhood. The defeat of the Act was a major setback for advocates of publicly funded entitlement programmes for women's and children's health.

While infant mortality was declining in the United States, in colonial Burma it remained unremittingly high in the period between 1891 and 1941. Judith Richell assesses the reasons for this trend by focusing on three aspects: the importance of cultural determinants on maternal and infant diet, the incidence of infectious diseases, and the influence of colonial administration. The conflict between colonization and cultural traditions is continued in Lenore Manderson's study of maternal and infant welfare in British Malaya between 1900 and 1940. During this period, the Medical Department became increasingly interested in women's health, and in the potential of women, native Malay, immigrant women and European female health professionals, as providers of maternal services.

Religious and missionary endeavours could also be critical in the provision and reception of services for mothers and infants. This key theme is developed by Debby Gaitskell in her investigation of missionary maternity and infant health schemes in interwar Johannesburg. While western missionaries had their own objectives, those using their facilities adapted and combined them with traditional practices to suit their own purposes. Marijke du Toit's exploration of Afrikaner identity and the idealization of motherhood between 1904 and 1939 demonstrates that nationalism was another important factor in moulding maternity care. Rather than tracing the transformation of childbirth from a female-dominated affair to a medical event controlled by men, du Toit emphasizes the ways in which women, motivated by the threat to the Afrikaner future imposed by poverty and infant and maternal mortality, campaigned for a better maternity service in the cause of Afrikaner nationalism.

The zeal demonstrated by missionaries and nationalists could be matched by individuals involved in infant welfare work. This is illustrated by Philippa Mein Smith's account of Frederic Truby King's struggle for the acceptance of his system in Australia between 1918 and 1939. This chapter highlights the importance of individuals and the role of sectarian conflict in shaping infant welfare, and the difficulties of transposing a system which worked in one country to another where climatic, economic and social circumstances were very different. The importance of regional differences is shown in Elizabeth Peretz's study of maternity services in four areas of England and Wales during the interwar period. Because of the permissive nature of legislation and the varied inputs of voluntary and public bodies, each locality shaped it own form and level of service in maternal and child welfare. The response to maternity services was determined to a large extent by the ability to pay, a burden which usually fell on poor mothers. Peretz's concluding remarks serve to remind us that, even when highly developed and expertly staffed, the effectiveness of maternal and child welfare services is still at the mercy of government policy and funding.

1

Some international features of maternal mortality, 1880–1950

Irvine Loudon

Maternal mortality was the great exception in what has been called the great mortality decline. From the end of the nineteenth century until the mid-1930s, when death rates in general and infant mortality in particular were steadily declining, maternal mortality scarcely altered. In England and Wales the maternal mortality rate (henceforth MMR) was 44.4 in 1867, 44.1 in 1898 and 44.2 in 1934.[1] When babies were born in Britain in or before the mid-1930s, the risk of their mothers dying in childbirth, regardless of social class, was essentially as high as it would have been had they been born in a mansion, a middle-class house or a working-class tenement when Queen Victoria was still a young woman.[2] Maternal mortality had remained on a high plateau for the best part of a century until, in the mid-1930s, it started to decline steeply and continuously. By 1980 the MMR was only one fiftieth of the rate in 1934. This is an extraordinary demographic story which raises many questions.

First, why did maternal mortality fail to decline until the mid-1930s? Second, what factors led to the sudden and profound fall just before the Second World War? (I will postpone the answer to this question until the end of this chapter.) Third, was the trend I have described confined to Britain or was it seen in other countries? Fourth, during the period of high maternal mortality, was the average MMR much the same in all western countries or were there wide differences?

Let us take the last two questions first. Figure 1.1 is a schematic representation of the trend in maternal mortality in western countries from 1880 to 1950 which also shows the MMR in 1920 in various countries. One can see that between 1900 and the mid-1930s the safest countries to have a baby were, by a very large margin, the Netherlands and Scandinavia; the most dangerous was the USA followed by France, New Zealand and Scotland. England and Wales came in the middle. The risk of dying in childbirth for American mothers in the 1920s was about three times as high as the risk for Dutch or Danish mothers, and for non-white mothers in the USA it was at least five times as high.

Figures 1.2 to 1.5 show the trend in the annual rates of maternal mortality in various countries. While they show that broadly speaking the plateau of maternal mortality and the post-1935 decline were common throughout the western world, they also show that the plateau was not completely flat. Between 1880 and 1910 there was a decline in maternal mortality which was steep in some countries such as Scandinavia and the Netherlands (and also as it happens Massachusetts) but slight in others such as England and Wales. From 1910 to 1935, however, this was reversed, and we find a rising trend in maternal mortality, the gradient being gentle in England and Wales, but quite steep in Scotland, Sweden and Denmark.[3]

Figure 1.1 Schematic representation of the pattern of maternal mortality seen in most developed countries, 1880–1950, together with the maternal mortality rates of certain countries in 1920

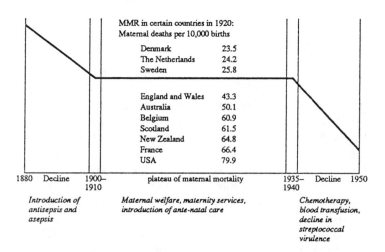

MMR in certain countries in 1920:
Maternal deaths per 10,000 births

Denmark	23.5
The Netherlands	24.2
Sweden	25.8
England and Wales	43.3
Australia	50.1
Belgium	60.9
Scotland	61.5
New Zealand	64.8
France	66.4
USA	79.9

1880   Decline   1900–1910   plateau of maternal mortality   1935–1940   Decline   1950

Introduction of antisepsis and asepsis   *Maternal welfare, maternity services, introduction of ante-natal care*   *Chemotherapy, blood transfusion, decline in streptococcal virulence*

Source: R.M. Woodbury, *Maternal Mortality. The Risk of Death in Childbirth and from all the Diseases caused by Pregnancy and Confinement* (Washington, DC, 1926), supplemented by published vital statistics of various countries.

Figure 1.2 Maternal mortality, 1870–1950, England and Wales, Scotland and Sweden

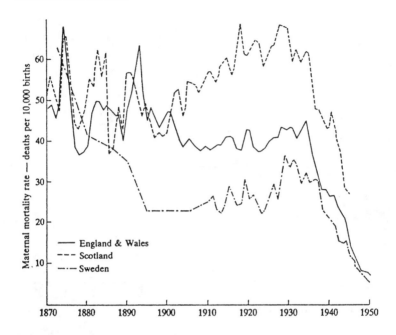

Sources: See Table 1.1.

Figure 1.3 Maternal mortality, 1900–1950, the Netherlands, Norway, and Denmark

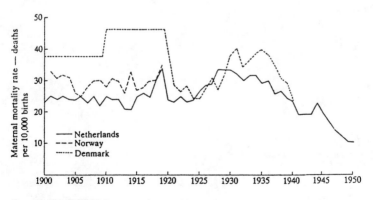

Sources: See Table 1.1.
Note: Denmark, 1900–9 (towns only), 1910–19 (whole country); annual statistics available from 1922 (whole country).

7

Figure 1.4 Maternal mortality, 1915–1950, USA and England and Wales

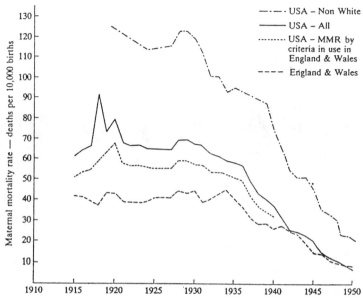

Sources: See Table 1.1.

Figure 1.5 Maternal mortality, 1905–1950, Australia and New Zealand

Sources: See Table 1.1.

We can now return to the first question: why did maternal mortality remain on a high plateau until the mid-1930s? Were the reasons primarily clinical, or were they social and economic, or a combination of both? If anyone or anything was to blame for the sustained high level of mortality was it the health of mothers and their living conditions, the indolence or indifference of government, or was it the standard and availability of obstetric care provided by midwives (trained and untrained), general practitioners, specialist obstetricians and maternity hospitals? And if we find (as we will) that it was a combination of many factors, how much weight do we give to each in different countries at different periods? Before we attempt to answer these questions we must appreciate the impact of maternal mortality on the public, the medical profession and health authorities.

Maternal mortality as a major problem

The decline in maternal mortality between 1880 and 1910, which was associated with the introduction of antisepsis and asepsis into midwifery, was accompanied by a transformation of hospital mortality. Before 1880 maternal mortality in lying-in hospitals all over the world had been horrific, sometimes reaching levels of 400 per 10,000 births or about ten times the rate in home deliveries. The cause of the terrible mortality before the 1880s was puerperal fever and there was even talk of closing down all lying-in hospitals. By 1910, however, hospital mortality had often fallen so steeply that the MMR was usually lower than it was for home deliveries, even though hospitals had an excess of complicated cases and emergency admissions.

Thus, at the Rotunda Hospital in Dublin, 2,060 women were delivered in 1907–8 and only three died from sepsis. At the York Road Lying-in Hospital in London over a period of 16 years in the early part of this century, 8,373 deliveries were carried out without a single death from infection. In Basle, Professor 0. von Herff reported in 1907 that 6,000 deliveries had taken place without a single death from sepsis.[4] In Australia the Sydney Women's Hospital reported ten years' work in 1904 with 4,000 cases and not a single death from puerperal sepsis, and the Australian Committee on Maternal Mortality stated boldly in 1917 that

9

Puerperal septicaemia is probably the gravest reproach which any civilised nation can by its own negligence offer to itself. It can be prevented by a degree of care which is not excessive or meticulous, requiring only ordinary intelligence and some careful training. It has been abolished in hospitals and it should cease to exist in the community. It should be as rare as sepsis after a surgical operation'.[5]

This transformation of maternity hospital mortality was so encouraging that people concerned with maternal care in the first decade of this century were confident maternal mortality would soon be conquered. It was only a question of bringing home deliveries into line with hospitals. One can appreciate their horror when, year after year, they saw what they never expected to see: a relentless rise in maternal deaths. To make matters worse, it was soon recognized that a large proportion of maternal deaths was preventable but not prevented. Hundreds, if not thousands of women were dying unnecessarily, leaving devastated families: husbands without wives, babies and young children without mothers and a continuous stream of miserable recruits for the orphanages. Maternal mortality was a scandal.

So it was that during the second and third decades of this century action was demanded. Maternal mortality committees and associations were established, some medical and some lay, and numerous investigations of maternal care were carried out. Governments passed Acts and funds were obtained from states or charities to establish clinics, increase the number of maternity beds, and provide additional medical personnel.[6] No one doubted the need for reform, and few doubted reforms would be successful. But different policies were adopted. Britain supported a broad portfolio of policies with better obstetric education heading the list. The Midwives Act of 1902 was followed by other Acts to regulate midwives and make trained care more widely available, notably the Midwives Act of 1936. The Royal College of Obstetricians was founded in 1929 and stimulated an increase in the number of consultant obstetricians whose job it would be to deal with complicated cases, to teach and to advise. But the backbone of British obstetrics remained for the time being the midwife and general practitioner delivering patients in their homes.[7]

In the USA it was believed that maternal mortality would only be defeated when hospital delivery by specialist obstetricians was the rule and delivery by the midwife and general practitioner obstetrician was abolished. After the First World War obstetricians and government were united in moving towards that goal as rapidly as possible. The Netherlands took the opposite view. The great bulk of deliveries took place at home attended by highly trained midwives, backed up by hospital care for complicated cases. New Zealand moved more rapidly towards hospital delivery than even the United States, but it believed in the midwife and retained her for hospital deliveries.[8] Everyone talked about obstetrics as a branch of preventive medicine and expressed their faith in antenatal (prenatal) clinics and health education. Yet, by the harsh evidence of the statistics, none of these measures was effective. This brings us back to the puzzle of the plateau and thus to the immediate causes of maternal mortality.

The causes of maternal mortality: sepsis and abortion

From the mid-nineteenth century to the mid-1930s, the three most common causes of maternal deaths were puerperal sepsis, toxaemia and haemorrhage, which usually contributed about 40 per cent, just over 20 per cent and just under 20 per cent to the total death rate respectively. The distribution of maternal deaths by cause was remarkably similar in all western countries, regardless of the rate of mortality from all causes.

The two causes of death which caused most concern during the interwar period were puerperal fever – the old name for post-partum sepsis – and septic abortion (see Tables 1.1 and 1.4).[9]

Puerperal sepsis before the 1930s is a very difficult field. In virtually all western countries induced abortion was a crime unless carried out by a doctor for a medical reason, so it was inevitable that some deaths from abortion were concealed and the true extent of abortion is extremely difficult to determine. To make matters worse, until 1930 most countries placed deaths from post-abortive sepsis together with deaths from post-partum sepsis in the single category 'puerperal sepsis', and the two quite different categories cannot be separated. We can be sure of one thing however: the official figures for the number of deaths from sepsis were never exaggerated. No doctor certified a death as being due to puerperal fever if he could avoid doing so,

11

Table 1.1 Maternal mortality rate per 10,000 births, and puerperal fever deaths expressed as a percentage of total maternal mortality, for certain countries, 1900–1934 (annual averages for five-year periods)

		1900–4	1905–9	1910–14	1915–19	1920–4	1925–9	1930–4
Sweden	MMR	22.0	23.0	24.6	27.3	24.6	29.9	33.0
	Puerperal fever %			41	46	46	51	51
Netherlands	MMR	25.2	23.8	23.0	28.1	24.0		31.5
	Puerperal fever %	32	31	28	34	33		20
Denmark	MMR	(1900–09) 37.9		(1910–19) 46.2		27.1	28.3	37.4
	Puerperal fever %	39		25		37	36	33
Belgium	MMR	58.0	57.0	59.1	79.8	57.6	57.2	51.2
	Puerperal fever %			42	46	46	55	37
England and Wales	MMR	42.7	37.4	40.3	41.2	39.0	42.7	43.0
	Puerperal fever %	45	41	35	37	36	41	41
Australia	MMR		53.5	48.7	49.1	49.6	55.4	54.5
	Puerperal fever %		32	35	33	34	33	40
New Zealand	MMR			40.6	53.4	53.4	46.8	46.2
	Puerperal fever %			26	33	35	32	39
USA (expanding death registration area)	MMR	77.6	72.0	68.6	72.8	68.9	66.9	63.6
	Puerperal fever %	48	45	43	39	37	37	38

Sources: England and Wales: 44th A/R of the LGB, 1914–15, Supplement on 'Maternal Mortality', PP 1914–16, XXV, Cd. 8085; MH, Report of an investigation into maternal mortality (London, HMSO, 1937), PP 1936–37, XI, Cmd. 5422, appendices; A. Macfarlane and M. Mugford, Birth counts: statistics of pregnancy and childbirth (London, HMSO, 1984).
Sweden: Sveriges Officiella Statistik (Stockholm, 1911–50); U. Hogberg, Maternal mortality in Sweden, Umeå University, medical diss, new series no. 156 (Umeå, 1985).
The Netherlands: Statistiek van de Sterfte naar den Leeftijd en de Oorzaken van den Dood (CBS, 1911–88).
Denmark: Summary of causes of death in the Kingdom of Denmark (National Health Services of Denmark, 1949).
Belgium: Annuaire Statistique de la Belgique et du Congo Belgique (Brussels, Office Central de Statistique, 1851–1951).
Australia: Official statistics, Commonwealth of Australia (Melbourne, Commonwealth Bureau of Censuses and Statistics: population and vital statistics, 1907–50).
New Zealand: Reports on vital statistics (Wellington, Census and Statistics Office various years).
USA: Miscellaneous Children's Bureau publications

because of the implication that such deaths were due to the birth attendant's negligence.

Thus deaths from post-partum sepsis and septic abortion both tended to be under-recorded. Nevertheless there is compelling evidence that the mortality from post-partum sepsis either stayed level or actually rose in most western countries between 1900 and 1934, and also that the incidence and the death rate arising from illegal abortion, which was already increasing at the beginning of this century, rose to often very alarming levels during the interwar period.[10] In Australia and New Zealand in particular, but also in some other countries, deaths from post-abortive sepsis had risen by the 1930s to a level which actually exceeded deaths from post-partum sepsis (Table 1.2). So, was the rising trend in maternal mortality simply due to abortion? The answer is 'no'. Even when abortion deaths are removed, the trend of maternal mortality was either rising slightly or remaining level.

This was an important point. During the interwar period when the major problem in maternal care was maternal mortality, enormous efforts were made to reduce the deaths of mothers. Few could believe these efforts were ineffective, so they tended to blame abortion, which lay outside their control. Unfortunately it became abundantly clear that maternal deaths from other causes – toxaemia, haemorrhage and above all post-partum sepsis – were not declining as expected.

In retrospect one can see that a major reason was that a large majority of deaths from post-partum sepsis was due to the haemolytic streptococcus, *Streptococcus pyogenes*, an organism whose virulence was probably increasing between 1914 and 1935. Moreover, the nature of puerperal infection was ill understood until, around 1930, it was at last realized that many healthy people were carriers of the streptococcus and that droplet infection from the birth attendant was the most common source of infection. Until this was known the antiseptic strategies most commonly employed were ineffective. Many of the antiseptics in common use were inadequate and the need for strict asepsis and wearing masks of the correct design was not appreciated or, if appreciated, not practised as it should have been.[11] The failure to prevent post-partum sepsis, especially in general practice, was in part due to carelessness, in part to lack of knowledge, and in part to an excessive tendency to interfere in normal labours, which increased the risk of infection.

Table 1.2 England and Wales, Australia and New Zealand: maternal mortality from post-partum sepsis and septic abortion per 10,000 births, 1931–1950

Year	England and Wales		Australia		New Zealand	
	post-partum sepsis	septic abortion	*post-partum sepsis*	septic abortion	*post-partum sepsis*	septic abortion
1931			8.6	12.4	6.8	10.9
1932			7.6	14.3	5.2	10.4
1933			8.2	12.5	5.2	10.4
1934			8.9	14.5	7.0	17.3
1935	10.4	4.2	8.6	14.0	3.3	9.6
1936	8.9	3.8	10.7	18.3	3.6	5.6
1937	5.5	2.8	5.2	10.0	5.4	9.2
1938	4.3	2.7	5.2	11.9	7.7	11.0
1939	3.9	2.6	3.9	9.3	5.5	6.9
1940	3.2	1.9	4.2	11.2	4.0	4.3
1941	2.4	2.4	3.1	7.8	4.8	6.8
1942	2.2	2.6	3.9	7.2	4.4	8.0
1943	1.9	2.4	3.6	7.6	2.6	5.0
1944	1.4	2.2	1.7	5.2	2.4	5.7
1945	1.2	1.6	1.0	3.2	1.1	3.0
1946	0.6	0.8	1.5	2.3	1.2	2.9
1947	0.4	0.6	0.4	3.0	0.7	2.2
1948	0.4	0.7	0.5	1.2		2.0
1949	0.4	0.8	0.2	1.4		0.7
1950	0.4	0.5	0.1	1.2		

Source: See Table 1.1.

But it was more than that. In all aspects of maternal care, especially in Britain and the USA, the general standard of obstetric care was low because of the low standard of obstetric education. Poor training lay at the root of it, and of course it was also a period when blood transfusion was not generally available for haemorrhage and there was no effective treatment for toxaemia. For all these reasons maternal mortality remained at a high and undiminishing level throughout the western world during the interwar period. But what about regional and international differences? How can these be explained?

Regional and international comparisons

England and Wales

In his classic study of maternal mortality, Dr Williams (Medical Officer of Health (hereafter MOH) for Glamorgan County Council) showed that if you drew a line from the Severn estuary to the Wash almost every county north of that line showed a higher than average maternal mortality, and almost every county to the south a lower than average (Figure 1.6).[12] The maps he produced suggest that high maternal mortality was correlated mainly with urban areas of heavy industry and to a lesser extent with remote rural areas (North Wales and Cumberland). Given that standards of obstetric care were also often low in industrial and remote areas, how can one tell whether high mortality was causally related to urban and rural poverty on the one hand, or to low standards of clinical care on the other? There are several approaches to this difficult question.[13]

The history of outpatient lying-in charities showed that very low rates of maternal mortality could be achieved by introducing high quality obstetric care (by the standards of the time) into areas conspicuous for the poverty of the inhabitants. The well-known Rochdale experiment in the 1930s illustrated this even more compellingly, suggesting rather surprisingly that ill health associated with poverty was not an important factor in maternal mortality, compared with the standard of obstetric care.[14] This was confirmed by the finding that maternal mortality (unlike infant mortality) was actually higher amongst middle-class women than working-class: an unexpected finding shown by a series of independent investigations from the 1880s to the 1930s.[15] Certainly an anaemic ill-nourished mother was, other things being equal, more likely to die in childbirth than a healthy well-nourished one. But the evidence that the availability and quality of clinical care was a more important determinant of the level of maternal mortality than social and economic factors is compelling.

In 1912 Geddes suggested an additional factor, which has not received the attention it deserves.[16] In areas of heavy industry there were numerous accidents causing wounds which became infected with the streptococcus, and erysipelas was common. Doctors dressed wounds as part of their daily practice and transmitted the infection to their obstetric patients. Most mid-

Figure 1.6 Maternal mortality in the administrative counties of England and Wales for the decade 1924–1933

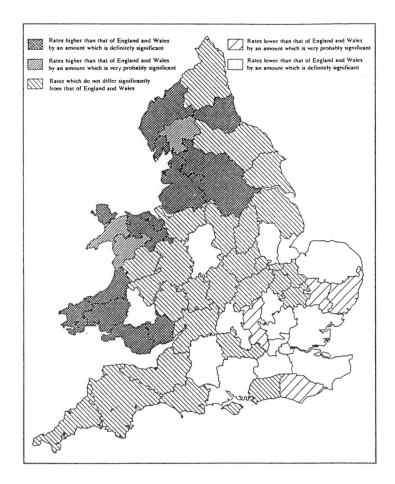

Source: MH, *Report of an Investigation into Maternal Mortality* (London, HMSO, 1937), Cmd. 5422.

wives, on the other hand, undertook no general nursing and did not come into frequent contact with septic conditions.[17] Indeed, one usually finds a low rate of maternal mortality wherever a high proportion of deliveries was undertaken by well-trained midwives rather than doctors or untrained midwives (Table 1.3). The trained midwife was less prone to

Table 1.3 Deaths per 10,000 births from puerperal sepsis, 1921–1927

Countries in which midwife deliveries predominated		Countries in which delivery by doctors predominated	
Britain*	3.3	New Zealand	18.2
The Netherlands	7.7	England and Wales	14.6
Denmark	9.5	Scotland	18.2
Norway	7.1	Ireland	17.9
		Australia	17.0

* The figures shown here for British midwives are those for 317,758 domiciliary deliveries by the Queen's Institute of District Midwives.

Source: H. Jellett, *The Causes and Prevention of Maternal Mortality* (London, 1929), n.p.

interfere in labour, less likely to be a carrier of the streptococcus, was often better educated in the basic techniques of obstetric care than the general practitioner and was certainly in many cases more skilled in normal deliveries.

In Britain, areas of high maternal mortality were generally those in which the quality of maternal care – whether by midwives or doctors – was low by the standards of the time, and industrial areas in which the risk of infection was high: the two were often the same. There may have been other factors but it is likely that these were the most important.

The United States

'The United States', wrote Josephine Baker in 1927, 'comes perilously near to being the most unsafe country in the world for the pregnant woman, as far as her chance of living through childbirth is concerned', and it occupied that unenviable position for the first 35 years of this century, leading to a flood of investigations and reports, many of very high quality.[18] During the decade of the 1920s about a quarter of a million women in the USA died in childbirth. There are no records of maternal morbidity, which is in any case impossible to define, but it was believed that five or even ten times as many mothers suffered from long-term disability resulting from childbirth.

17

Table 1.4 Hospital and home deliveries in the USA in 1945–1946

This table shows, for the USA and for certain selected states, the percentage of hospital and home deliveries by physicians, and the percentage of home deliveries by midwives.*

The maternal mortality rate (deaths per 10,000 births) is shown in the last column for the combined white and non-white population, the states with the lowest rate first.

Population	White			Non-white			MMR
Delivered by:	Physician		Midwife	Physician		Midwife	
Delivered in:	Hospital %	Home %	Home %	Hospital %	Home %	Home %	
USA	87.1	11.2	1.7	45.2	20.0	34.8	15.7
Connecticut	99.0	1.0	0.0	96.2	3.6	0.2	9.2
Oregon	98.0	1.5	0.5	92.1	2.6	5.3	10.3
Maryland	86.6	11.9	1.5	54.5	28.0	17.5	11.1
New York	97.1	2.7	0.2	94.4	4.6	1.0	12.0
Indiana	88.2	11.7	0.1	64.5	35.1	0.4	13.1
Pennsylvania	88.3	11.6	0.1	84.0	15.7	0.3	15.2
Texas	75.8	14.7	9.5	45.5	22.6	31.9	16.2
South Carolina	76.2	21.3	2.5	13.8	20.2	66.0	27.4
Florida	87.8	9.9	2.3	30.8	15.1	54.1	30.0
Mississippi	69.3	27.7	3.0	9.6	21.4	69.0	31.4

Source: *Further Progress in Reducing Maternal and Infant Mortality*, Children's Bureau Statistical Series, no. 4, Washington, Federal Security Agency, Social Security Administration, Children's Bureau, 1948.

* In the original table the terms used for those undertaking deliveries who were not physicians was 'non-medical personnel'. Since 'non-medical personnel' consisted in practice of the few trained midwives and the more numerous untrained neighbourhood midwives, 'midwife' has been substituted in this table.

Although it is only possible to outline a few of the factors which influenced maternal mortality and discuss a few conclusions, certain features stand out. The range of mortality between states (from 9.2 per 10,000 births in Connecticut to 31.4 in Mississippi, for example, in 1945–46) was much wider than the range seen in western Europe. The highest rates were always found in the south, where there was a large proportion of non-white births and home deliveries by coloured midwives who were untrained in any formal sense (see Figure 1.7). The lowest rates occurred in New England, and the Mid-west and

18

Figure 1.7 USA 1940: regional variations in maternal mortality, showing the values for each state in terms of four categories of maternal mortality

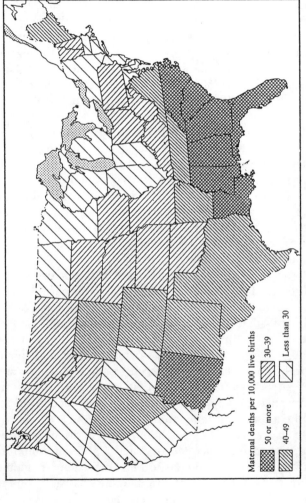

Maternal deaths per 10,000 live births

50 or more

40–49

30–39

Less than 30

Source: Births, Infant Mortality and Maternal Mortality, Children's Bureau pub. no. 288 (Washington, DC, 1945).

western states, where non-white births were few and where a majority took place in hospital (Table 1.4). Maternal mortality was generally about twice as high in non-white compared with white mothers.

In the period with which we are concerned, the causes of high maternal mortality tended to be rather different in rural and urban areas, and it is important to remember how large the rural population was. In the population move from rural to urban areas, which has been a constant feature throughout the western world, the halfway mark was reached in England and Wales as early as 1850 but in the USA not until 1930. In remote rural areas the difficulty of providing maternal care was a major factor in maternal mortality.

In a rural county in Georgia in 1923, where 'mountain spurs deploy in every direction, skirted and cut up by countless valleys, ravines and gaps which form a labyrinth of intricate passageways', a visit by a doctor to a patient only five miles away could mean a hazardous all-day journey on horseback. Births were often unattended, or attended long after the baby was born, and 'one mother, suffering from childbed fever, endured with Spartan fortitude a wagon ride over 15 miles of rough road to the nearest physician'.[19]

In a vast rural area of Montana in 1919 doctors were so few that over a fifth of mothers left the area to have their babies. 'Bad weather, swollen rivers and creeks and impassable roads frequently defeated plans to employ a physician or travel elsewhere for the confinement.' Of those remaining at home, 359 in all, 129 were attended by doctors, 3 delivered themselves entirely alone, 46 were delivered by their husbands and 181 were attended by other women, 'in a very few instances trained nurses, in a considerable number of cases practical nurses, but for the most part women quite untrained in obstetrics'.[20]

In many areas the 'neighbourhood midwife' was the only birth attendant. Grace Meigs visited a Midwest community in 1916 where the country was so wild and remote that almost all deliveries were by such local women. Few had any training, but one who had attended all her neighbours as well as her numerous grandchildren, had received training abroad. She had delivered all her own twelve children and lost little time from work on the farm. 'A massive weather-beaten woman, she still, though old, works in the field with the men, and can lift a huge kettle full of potatoes to the stove as though it were a feather.'[21]

In the USA the term 'midwife' embraced a much wider variety of women than in any other country, ranging from the untrained non-white midwives of the Deep South and the 'neighbourhood midwives' of the Midwest to a few groups of highly trained women.[22] An outstanding example of the latter were the nurse-midwives of the Kentucky Frontier Nursing Service, established by Mary Breckinridge in 1924 in a mountainous county in Kentucky.[23] It served a scattered population marked by poverty, malnutrition, poor housing and rural squalor. Strategically placed nurse-midwives, working in pairs, travelling on horseback and always available, provided a comprehensive maternal and child health service. The result was the astonishingly low rate of maternal mortality of just under 7 per 10,000 births when, in the nearby city of Lexington, Kentucky, where all deliveries were attended by doctors and most took place in hospital, the MMR stood between 80 and 90. (In the USA as a whole during this period the MMR varied between 56 and 68.[24]) There could hardly be a more vivid demonstration of what could be achieved by a high standard of midwifery under the most adverse conditions.

In urban America, on the other hand, the striking feature was the rapid acceleration towards hospital delivery after the First World War. The percentage of urban deliveries which took place in hospital was 60 per cent in 1925, 70 per cent in 1935 and 98 per cent in 1950. In Britain the corresponding figures were 25 per cent (1935) and 50 per cent (1950). Obstetricians were convinced that hospital delivery was the only way to meet the public demand for pain relief and a safe delivery in a 'germ-free' environment.[25] Safe it was not. The expectation that hospital delivery would produce a profound fall in maternal mortality was not realized. And the commonly stated reason, that in many hospitals a high maternal mortality was due to poor antisepsis and unnecessary intervention in normal labours, often to a gross extent, seems to be well founded. One investigation in 1934 led to the conclusion that 'Sepsis, toxaemias and haemorrhage play the major tragic roles [in puerperal mortality], and these are associated largely with hurried, operative and bizarre obstetrics',[26] a finding confirmed and roundly condemned in a wide range of surveys.[27] There was also, as elsewhere, the usual problem of abortion. By the 1930s septic abortion accounted for 45 per cent of deaths from sepsis and was as serious a problem in the USA as it was in Australia and New Zealand.[28]

The USA, enormous and highly varied, is one of the most complicated but most rewarding countries for the historical study of obstetric care and maternal mortality. I have only touched on a few of the factors that confirmed Josephine Baker's conclusion that it was the most unsafe country in the (developed) world to have a baby. Perhaps the most important general conclusion is that the safest and thus the 'best' form of maternal care in the interwar period was the highly trained midwife. This was shown by the achievements of the Kentucky Frontier Nursing Service in the USA, by the record of high quality care in the Netherlands, and by the splendid results obtained by the Queen's Institute rural nurse-midwives in England and Wales. It is ironic that well-to-do mothers who opted for private care in nursing homes and hospitals, paying a high fee for a normal delivery in the belief they were buying the best available care, were actually subjecting themselves to a higher risk of dying than if they had stayed at home and employed a midwife.

The fall in maternal mortality, 1937–50

What emerges from this brief review is the complexity of the factors which determined the level of maternal mortality. My main conclusion, that clinical factors were of paramount importance in determining the level of maternal mortality, echoes the conclusion of the Local Government Board in 1916: 'On general grounds there can be no reasonable doubt that the quality and availability of skilled assistance before, during and after childbirth are probably the most important factors in determining the remarkable and serious differences in respect of mortality from childbearing'.[29]

Between 1880 and the mid-1930s it was safer to be delivered at home by a trained midwife, provided she could call on competent medical assistance if complications arose. The stronger the tradition of home deliveries by well-trained midwives, the more likely that the maternal deaths in a country would be kept to a low level, as in the Netherlands and Scandinavia. Bad standards of practice by midwives, however, could be as dangerous as bad practice by doctors. There were real Mrs Gamps.

Why then did maternal mortality change direction so decisively after 1935? Initially, there is little doubt the downturn was due to the introduction of the sulphonamides. In Britain the first year in which maternal mortality fell to a level significantly lower than ever before, was 1937: the year in which sulphonamides became generally available. Between 1935 and 1940, 80 per cent of the reduction in total maternal mortality (from 39.4 to 26.1) was due to a reduction in deaths due to post-partum sepsis.[30] The sulphonamides were highly effective against *Streptococcus pyogenes* but not so effective against the organisms implicated in septic abortion. Deaths from the latter only fell steeply after the introduction of penicillin in 1944 (see Table 1.2). But there was much more to it than the sulphonamides.

A whole series of factors acted in succession after the beginning of the Second World War. Paradoxically, working-class mothers were better fed (through special allocation of rations) and better cared for during the Second World War than in the previous decade. Not that it is in fact a paradox, since both British and American governments were stimulated by the stress of war to make funds available to an extent which had been politically unacceptable in peacetime.[31] Significantly, the trend in maternal mortality levelled out or rose in occupied Europe, while continuing to fall in the unoccupied or non-combatant countries. In Britain, blood transfusion and obstetric flying-squads, combined with the introduction of ergometrine in 1942, led to a profound fall in deaths from haemorrhage. From 1944 penicillin stole the limelight, somewhat unfairly, from the sulphonamides. In addition, as a result of the

Table 1.5 Maternal mortality rates in the USA, England and Wales, and the Netherlands, 1920–1960

Rates expressed as maternal deaths per 10,000 live births

Year	USA	England and Wales	The Netherlands
1920	68.9	43.3	24.0
1930	63.6	44.0	33.3
1940	37.6	26.1	23.5
1950	8.3	8.7	10.5
1960	3.7	3.9	3.7

Source: The published vital statistics of the three countries. See Table 1.1.

devastating reports on maternal mortality (especially the 1937 report)[32] obstetric education and the standard of obstetric care steadily improved.

All these factors came into operation throughout the western world. In the 1940s, cautious obstetricians were far from sure the decline in maternal mortality could continue, and they guessed that if it did it would level out at the irreducible minimum of unavoidable maternal deaths of about 10 per 10,000 births. They were wrong to an extent which would have been inconceivable in 1935. Table 1.5 shows that maternal mortality rates in various countries which had been wide apart in the 1930s had converged by 1960 to rates which lay within a hair's breadth of each other and well below the estimate of 10 per 10,000 births. All this happened in a mere twenty-five years, with an immensely beneficial effect on the status and morale of obstetrics as a speciality. There were of course specific diseases which showed a dramatic fall as a result of a vaccine or a drug – poliomyelitis, for example. But there was no other mortality due to multiple causes and numerous factors which took the unique and fascinating pathway of maternal mortality. In the mortality decline maternal mortality continued to be the great exception; but after about 1940, it was exceptional for its success, not for its failure to decline.

Acknowledgements

This article is based in part on I. Loudon, 'Maternal mortality: 1880–1950. Some regional and international comparisons', *Soc. Hist. Med.*, 1 (1988), 183–228.

Notes

1. The MMR is defined as the number of maternal deaths occurring in pregnancy, labour or the postnatal period (conventionally defined as the 6 weeks following delivery), per 1,000, 10,000 or 100,000 births. The choice of the denominator is arbitrary; today when maternal deaths are rare, it is usually 100,000; for historical reasons I shall use 10,000 throughout this chapter unless otherwise indicated. Before stillbirths were registered, 'births' were defined as live births until the late 1920s. Thereafter most countries defined births as 'total births', that is, live births and stillbirths. Maternal deaths were divided

into 'true' or 'direct' maternal deaths due to complications of child-birth, and 'associated' or 'indirect' deaths when a woman happened to die during pregnancy, labour, or the postnatal period, of an incidental disease such as heart disease, pneumonia or tuberculosis. Some countries included both direct and indirect deaths in their published figures of maternal mortality. Others kept them separate. This is a point to remember in international comparisons, but such differences in statistical methodology did not produce much distortion and did not affect materially the rank order of countries according to their rates of maternal mortality shown in Figure 1.1.

2. From the limited data available before vital registration, it is likely that maternal mortality was particularly high around 1700 in England and Wales. Thereafter it fell steadily until it flattened out along what I have described as the plateau of maternal mortality, possibly as early as the late eighteenth century. I. Loudon, 'Deaths in childbed from the eighteenth century to 1935', *Med. Hist.*, 30 (1986), 1–41.

3. A minor but significant detail is that before the post-1935 decline, the MMR in almost every country climbed to reach the highest level in the twentieth century in 1934–35. In the USA and New Zealand alone a modest decline occurred between 1930 and 1935 before the steep post-1935 decline.

4. US Dept. of Labor, Children's Bureau Publications, report no. 152, R. M. Woodbury, *Maternal Mortality. The Risk of Death in Childbirth and from all the Diseases caused by Pregnancy and Confinement* (Washington, DC, 1926).

5. *Report on Maternal Mortality in Childbirth*: Committee concerning causes of deaths and invalidity in the Commonwealth, Commonwealth of Australia, Department of Trades and Customs (Melbourne, 1917), C.7867. It was this transformation of hospital mortality which began the long if slow process by which normal as well as abnormal childbirth was moved out of the family bedroom and into the hospital ward. However much this move has been criticized or deplored, one can understand the historical reason. In Britain between 1900 and the 1930s hospital deliveries were seen as becoming increasingly safe and successful; home deliveries, at least in the hands of general practitioners, were not. This is explored in the Context of East London in ch. 3 by Lara Marks. For maternal mortality in Sydney, see ch. 2 by Milton Lewis.

6. J. Antler and D. M. Fox, 'The movement toward a safe mater-nity: physician accountability in New York City, 1915–1940', *Bull. Hist. Med.*, 50 (1976), 569–95. For a discussion of political involvement in maternal welfare in Britain during this period, see the classic account by J. Lewis, *The Politics of Motherhood* (London, 1980).

7. J. S. Fairbairn (obstetric physician to St Thomas's Hospital, and the second President of the Royal College of Obstetricians and Gynae-cologists) in a chapter on maternal mortality in his textbook *Obstetrics* (London, 1926), 208–9, concluded that, 'a well-trained corps of midwives under medical supervision with provision for difficult cases is the one most likely to give the best results, because it both fulfils the

ideals of preventive medicine in midwifery and is supported by the experience of those countries in which the maternity service has developed on these lines and of associations and institutions in this country working on similar lines'.

8. P. Mein Smith, *Maternity in Dispute. New Zealand 1920–1939* (Wellington, 1986).

9. The use of 'instruments' to procure an abortion, whether it was done by the patient herself or by an abortionist, was very dangerous. In one study of 1,000 analysed cases of abortion in New Zealand, out of 374 cases in which instrumentation was admitted by the patient, 3.7 per cent (or 370 per 10,000) died. Many more were seriously ill. In 246 cases of spontaneous abortion, however, none died. W. H. B. Bull, 'Abortion and contraception', *NZ Med. J.*, 35 (1936), special section, 39–44.

10. P. V. Prichard, Maternal mortality: a critical review of the statistical references in the interim report of the departmental committee on maternal mortality and morbidity, DM thesis, University of Edinburgh, 1931. Prichard, Assistant MOH to the Borough of St Pancras, estimated deaths from criminal abortion, which were concealed in the statistics as entries under the headings 'peritonitis' and 'septicaemia'. He concluded there had been a substantial and continuous rise in criminal abortion in England and Wales between 1919 and 1929. See also J. M. Munro Kerr, *Maternal Mortality and Morbidity* (Edinburgh, 1933); J. Young, 'Maternal mortality and maternal mortality rates', *Am. J. Obstet. & Gynecol.*, 31 (1936), 198–212; U. Högberg, Maternal mortality in Sweden, Umeå University medical diss., new series no. 156 (Umeå, 1985); Mein Smith, *Maternity in Dispute*. Smith's account of septic abortion in New Zealand shows how often induced abortion was used as a form of contraception by married women and the devastating results on families. Between 1931 and 1935, 109 deaths from septic abortion left 338 motherless children.

11. See J. Campbell, 'Maternal mortality', *Reports of Public Health and Medical Subjects*, no. 25 (London, MH, 1924); G. F. Gibberd, 'Streptococcal puerperal sepsis', *Guy's Hosp. Rep.*, 81 (1931), 29–44; and esp. L. Colebrook, 'The prevention of puerperal sepsis', *J. Obstet. & Gynaecol. Br. Emp.*, 43 (1936), 691–714.

12. W. Williams, 'Puerperal mortality', *Trans. Epidemiol. Soc. Lond.*, (1895–96), 100–33; *idem, Deaths in Childbed* (London, 1904), being the Milroy Lectures delivered at the Royal College of Physicians of London, 1904. W. Williams was MOH at Cardiff. This north-west/south-east division was a constant feature, confirmed by the *44th A/R of the LGB, 1914–15*, PP 1914–16, XXV, Cd. 8085. Supplement on 'Maternal mortality in connection with childbearing and its relation to infant mortality' (the most complete source of data on regional differences in maternal mortality in England and Wales) and by the MH's report, *Report of an investigation into maternal mortality in England* (London, HMSO, 1937), PP 1936–37, XI, Cmd. 5422.

13. Loudon, 'Deaths in childbed'; *idem,* 'Obstetric care, social class and maternal mortality', *Br. Med. J.*, ii (1986), 606–8.

14. A. Topping, 'Maternal mortality and public opinion', *Publ.*

Health, 49 (1936), 342–9; *idem*, 'Prevention of maternal mortality: the Rochdale experiment', *Lancet*, i (1936), 545–7. Dr Andrew Topping was appointed MOH to Rochdale in 1930 when it had 'the unenviable distinction of having the highest maternal mortality of anywhere in the country over a period of years . . . Various theories were advanced to account for the appalling death rate: some thought it was due to occult rickets; some to the fact of so many women working in mills; some to malnutrition. Careful examination of the individual case reports for the preceding years showed that none of these suggestions could hold water.' By instituting large improvements in the quality of obstetric care in Rochdale, but without any alterations to the social or economic conditions of the population, Topping succeeded in lowering the MMR from 90 deaths per 10,000 births to less than 20 per 10,000 – one of the lowest levels in the country. This became known as the 'Rochdale experiment'.

15. Loudon, 'Obstetric care, social class and maternal mortality'; *idem*, 'On maternal and infant mortality 1900–1960', *Soc. Hist. Med.*, 4 (1991), 29–73.

16. G. Geddes, *Statistics of Puerperal Sepsis and Allied Infectious Diseases* (Bristol, 1912), and *idem*, *Puerperal Septicaemia: Its Causation, Symptoms, Prevention and Treatment* (Bristol, 1926).

17. I. Loudon, 'Puerperal fever, the streptococcus and the sulphonamides 1911–1945', *Br. Med. J.*, ii (1987), 485–90. The close similarity between the death rates from erysipelas and puerperal fever was first noted by G.B. Longstaff, 'On some statistical indications of a relationship between scarlatina, puerperal fever and certain other conditions', *Trans. Epidemiol. Soc. Lond.*, 4 (1875–81), 421–32.

18. S. J. Baker, 'Maternal mortality in the United States', *J. Am. Med. Ass.*, 89 (1927), 2016–17.

19. US Dept. of Labor, Children's Bureau, pub. no. 120, G. Steele, *Maternity and Infant Care in a Mountain County in Georgia* (Washington, DC, 1923).

20. US Dept. of Labor, Children's Bureau, pub. no. 34, V. Paradise, *Maternity Care and the Welfare of Young Children in a Homestead County in Montana* (Washington, DC, 1919).

21. G. L. Meigs, 'Rural obstetrics', *Transactions of the American Association for the Study and Prevention of Infant Mortality*, 7 (1916), 46–61, an outstanding account of maternal and infant care in rural USA in the early years of this century.

22. For data on the numbers of licensed and unlicensed midwives in each state in the 1920s, and the laws regarding midwives, see Woodbury, *Maternal Mortality*. For recent work on the history of the midwife in the USA, see F. E. Kobrin, 'The American midwife controversy: a crisis of professionalization', in J. W. Leavitt and R. L. Numbers (eds), *Sickness and Health in America* (Madison, Wis., 1985), 217–28; J. B. Litoff, *American Midwives: 1860 to the Present* (Westport, Conn., 1978); J. W. Leavitt (ed.), *Women and Health in America* (Madison, Wis., 1984); *idem*, *Brought to Bed: Childbearing in America, 1750 to 1950 (New York and Oxford, 1986); R. W. Wertz and D. C. Wertz, Lying-In: A History of Childbirth in America* (New York and Oxford, 1977).

23. M. Breckinridge, *Wide Neighborhoods. A Story of the Frontier Nursing Service* (New York, 1952); N. S. Dye, 'Mary Breckinridge, the Frontier Nursing Service and the introduction of nurse midwifery in the United States', *Bull. Hist. Med.*, 57 (1983), 485–507.

24. Dye, 'Mary Breckinridge'.

25. M. Sandelowski, *Pain, Pleasure and American Childbirth* (Westport, Conn., 1984).

26. R. A. Bolt, 'Maternal mortality study for Cleveland, Ohio', *Am. J. Obstet. & Gynecol.*, 27 (1934), 309–13. See also A. Flint, 'Responsibility of the medical profession in further reducing maternal mortality', *Am. J. Obstet. & Gynecol.*, 9 (1925), 864–6 and the discussion, pp. 704–8; I. Galdston, *Maternal Deaths – the Way to Prevention* (New York and Oxford, 1937); J. Whitridge Williams, 'Medical education and the midwife problem in the United States', *J. Am. Med. Ass.*, 58 (1912), 1–76 and *idem*, 'Criticism of certain tendencies in American obste- trics', *NY State J. Med.*, 22 (1922), 493–9.

27. Philadelphia County Medical Society, Committee on maternal welfare, *Maternal Mortality in Philadelphia* (Philadelphia, 1934); J. V. DePorte, *Maternal Mortality and Stillbirths in New York State: 1921–1925* (New York State Dept. of Health, 1928) ('Experts agree that one of the causes of excessive mortality is *excessive obstetrical interference*'); New York City Public Health Committee and New York Academy of Medicine, *Maternal Mortality in New York, 1930, 1931, 1932, 1933*: abstract in *J. Am. Med. Ass.*, 101 (1933), 1826–8. See also US Dept. of Labor, Children's Bureau, pub. no. 223, *Maternal Deaths in Fifteen States* (Washington, DC, 1934).

28. US Dept. of Labor, Children's Bureau, pub. no. 223, *Maternal Deaths in Fifteen States* (Washington, DC, 1934).

29. *44th A/R LGB, 1914–15*, Supplement on 'Maternal Mortality', PP 1914–16, XXV, Cd. 8085.

30. Loudon, 'Deaths in childbed'; *idem*, 'Puerperal fever'.

31. The classic instance was the Emergency Care Program introduced in the USA during the Second World War, which provided care for a quarter of a million mothers by the time it was disbanded in 1948. W. M. Schmidt, 'The development of health services for mothers and children in the United States', *Am. J. Publ. Health*, 63 (1973), 419–27.

32. MH, *Report of an Investigation into Maternal Mortality* (London, HMSO, 1937), Cmd. 5422.

2

Maternity care and the threat of puerperal fever in Sydney, 1870–1939

Milton Lewis

Mortality from puerperal infection in Sydney, as in other parts of the western world, remained high from the 1870s to the late 1930s.[1] The problem of puerperal fever and the difficulties associated with reducing it played a vital role in shaping the development of obstetric care in Sydney in these years. Puerperal fever constituted as high a proportion of total maternal deaths as diarrhoeal mortality did of infant deaths. Just as infant mortality declined substantially when mortality from diarrhoeal and associated conditions fell markedly, so the greatest reduction in maternal mortality occurred when the mortality from infection dramatically diminished.[2] A notable difference in the histories of infant and maternal mortality in Sydney is that while diarrhoeal and associated mortality first fell significantly in the early 1900s, mortality from puerperal infection showed little downward movement until the late 1930s. This change in the 1930s largely resulted from two developments: adequate understanding of the modes of transmission of puerperal infection and the introduction of chemotherapeutic means of controlling the infections. The availability of new 'sulpha' drugs from the late 1930s played a major role in reducing mortality from puerperal sepsis. One historian, seeking to explain the sudden decline in maternal mortality after 1935 in all developed countries, dismisses improvement in socio-economic conditions and in obstetrics as too long-term in effect to apply to the immediate situation; he concludes that explanations narrow down to 'a sudden world-wide decline in streptococcal virulence . . . (for which there is no evidence) or therapy' and that 'the most important factors were, in chronological order, the sulphonamides, blood transfusion and, after 1944–45, penicillin'.[3]

The great turning point in maternal mortality, therefore, depended heavily on the advent of new medical knowledge and new drug therapy. This contrasted with infant mortality, which declined sharply at a time when medical understanding of the causes of diarrhoeal and associated conditions was still incomplete. The wide dissemination of comparatively simple principles of infant care through the infant welfare movement and by other routes, together with improvement in the sanitation of Sydney, largely accounts for the great decline in infant mortality early in this century. This involved very little medical expertise. Maternity care, however, was highly dependent on the knowledge and skill of the attendant. The quality of attendance available may be considered as the most important determinant of maternal mortality, as was pointed out by the Royal College of Obstetricians and Gynaecologists in its 1944 report.[4] In the late nineteenth and early twentieth centuries, doctors blamed the untrained midwife for excessive mortality. By the interwar period, reformers within the medical profession were pointing to the contribution made by doctors themselves and were demanding better obstetric education. The structure of the established maternity services, however, was virtually ignored in relation to this question.

During the years 1870 to 1939 the organization of medical care in Sydney meant that access to skilled attendance depended upon individual capacity to pay for it; only the poor qualified for the charity of public hospitals. At no time was the idea of a public midwifery service seriously entertained by the state or the profession.[5] There was unequal access to skilled attendance within a system of maternity care monopolized by the private sector. By the late 1930s, when the sulphonamides dramatically reduced deaths from sepsis, the system did not have the capacity significantly to lower the maternal death rate. It may be that a dramatically lower rate of mortality could only have been achieved through a major therapeutic advance and that the level of scientific knowledge of puerperal infections set an upper limit to progress in this area. Yet health authorities in New Zealand engineered a decline in the puerperal sepsis death rate from 1927 (responsible in that year for more than 40 per cent of maternal deaths) well before the arrival of specific drug therapy: the rate declined from 2.01 per 1,000 births in 1927 to

0.33 per 1,000 in 1935. While the rate increased somewhat to 0.77 in 1938 (perhaps because of a natural growth in virulence or a certain complacency about asepsis following the introduction of the sulphonamides), the downward trend began again in 1944–5, aided no doubt by the introduction of antibiotics.[6]

The New Zealand campaign for safer childbirth was initiated in 1924 and was directed by T. L. Paget, Inspector of Hospitals, who was advised by the Health Department's Consulting Obstetrician, Henry Jellett, a former Master of the Rotunda Hospital, Dublin. Paget developed a standardized aseptic technique for adoption in maternity hospitals and by midwives in private practice. He also brought about a great improvement in maternity hospital equipment and staffing. Some remarkably low levels of maternal mortality (and puerperal sepsis mortality) were also achieved by public hospitals in Sydney and other western cities round the turn of the century. In the period 1893–1903 the Women's Hospital, Crown Street, Sydney had a maternal mortality rate of 3.34 per 1,000 births, and there had been no deaths from puerperal fever. More pertinently, since district work by hospitals is more relevant in a comparison with private domiciliary care, the Women's Hospital reported in 1911 that out of 3,281 cases in 7 years of district work there had been only six deaths, including one from sepsis. This was a mortality rate of only 1.8 per 1,000 births.[7] The women served in hospital district work were of the poorest classes, and would otherwise not have had access to skilled care. The organization of maternity care in a system which, to a large extent, made the quality of attendance dependent upon the individual's capacity to pay, and which promoted undue interference because doctors were under pressure to hasten delivery, contributed to the failure to achieve a really significant reduction of mortality before the late 1930s. Along with commonly identified factors like the low level of medical knowledge and the inadequacy of obstetric education, it much aggravated the problem of maternal mortality.

The threat of puerperal fever

Between 1893 and 1936 the death rate from puerperal infection in Sydney, while fluctuating, generally remained in the range of

1 to 3 per 1,000 births. It did not fall below 1 per 1,000 until 1937, after which it fell progressively. There was a downward trend before the late 1930s, but the gradient was slight. Maternal mortality rates computed for the years before 1893 are not really reliable because only in that year was a careful check on the registration of puerperal deaths instituted.[8]

Just as nineteenth-century doctors felt virtually helpless in the face of the scourge of infant diarrhoea, so puerperal fever evoked much anxiety, especially when it occurred in an 'epidemic' form. The mid-1870s saw very high puerperal fever death rates in the two leading Australian cities, Melbourne and Sydney. The Melbourne correspondent to the *British Medical Journal* reported in 1873 that there was 'a widespread feeling of alarm' when five puerperal fever deaths in the Melbourne lying-in hospital were followed by twenty deaths in other localities.[9] In 1875–6, scarlatina reached epidemic levels in both cities and puerperal fever mortality rocketed. Many of Sydney's leading doctors ceased to attend midwifery cases after they had had one or two deaths among their patients.

The question of how to respond responsibly to such situations was extensively debated at the 1889 Intercolonial Medical Congress. It was generally agreed that when two or more cases of puerperal fever occurred among a doctor's patients he should temporarily abandon the practice of obstetrics. But reliance on antisepsis soon led many to query the need to desist in the face of infection, as long as all antiseptic precautions were taken. In the 1890s, Dr Ralph Worrall, President of the New South Wales Branch of the British Medical Association (hereafter BMA), said that having taken precautions – ablution, complete change of clothing and disinfection of the hands – he continued to attend normal lying-in cases while treating puerperal fever patients.[10]

Knowledge of aetiology

There were three periods in the development of aetiological understanding of puerperal fever: before 1875, when essentially the causes remained a mystery; 1876–1925, when, following the rise of medical bacteriology, the pathogens were progressively identified; and after 1925, when much more was learned about the haemolytic streptococci and the anaerobic cocci, the most lethal of the pathogens. In 1843 the American, Oliver Wendell Holmes, drew attention to the role of the accoucheur in the transmission of the disease. Holmes suggested 'miasms' were the means by which the disease was transferred to the patient. The transmission of the disease by the accoucheur was further indicated by the work of Ignaz Semmelweis at the Allgemeines Krankenhaus, Vienna. Semmelweis postulated the existence of 'cadaveric particles' which carried the condition to the parturient woman.[11] But the identity of the infecting agent, its source and its mode of transfer had to be elucidated.

The first step in this long process was made by Coze and Feltz, two Alsatian doctors, who reported in 1869 the presence of *microbes en chainettes*, streptococcal bacteria, in the lochia of patients with puerperal fever. Ten years later, Pasteur found the same chains of streptococci in the blood of women with the condition. By the mid-1920s, the prime importance of haemolytic streptococci in puerperal fever was well established. In the meantime it was becoming clear that anaerobic cocci played an important role, and a third group of pathogens of various types was recognized. Staphylococci, enterococci, coliform bacilli and others were held responsible for what were often less severe infections. The work of a variety of researchers in the 1920s and the 1930s permitted the construction of an aetiology of the disease. The establishment of this deeper understanding meant that an effective preventive programme became more feasible.

The methods of prevention suggested by pioneers like Holmes and Semmelweis included temporary abstention from the practice of obstetrics and disinfection of the hands. Out of the work of the pioneers of germ theory there developed a policy of 'indiscriminate antisepsis'. Lister's approach in surgery was adopted in obstetrics. A series of different popular chemical agents were used in turn as recommended antiseptics. In the course of the 1920s, as greater understanding of the role of haemolytic streptococci emerged, a more informed policy of asepsis was adopted as part of a wider preventive programme.[12] The wearing of masks and adherence to procedures for the identification of carriers reduced the possibilities of infection being transmitted from those attending the mother. The use of rubber gloves reduced the chance of transfer via the hands of the obstetrician.

There were few therapeutic possibilities before the 1930s. Quinine and salicylic acid were early used as anti-pyretics. With the coming of Listerian antisepsis, antiseptic douches were employed. Some medical men advocated the curette, but others condemned it as dangerous. Late in the nineteenth century the usefulness of anti-diphtheria serum inspired development of anti-streptococcal sera. Overall, the results were indifferent because one serum could not safeguard the patient against the variety of streptococcal bacteria. For a time organic arsenical compounds such as Salvarsan were tried because their effectiveness against syphilis had been well established. In 1935 Domagk reported from Germany remarkable success with a red dye, later called Prontosil, against streptococci injected into laboratory mice. Workers at the Pasteur Institute found that the dye was broken down in the body to the substance para-aminobenzenesulphonamide. Soon to be known as sulphanilamide, this was the agent which cured the infection. A simpler compound became the drug used in human therapy. The dramatic change wrought by the new 'sulpha' drug is illustrated by the following comments of the New South Wales health authorities. As late as 1936 the state Director of Maternal and Baby Welfare, E. S. Morgan, wrote:

> The maternal death-rate in New South Wales shows very little tendency to fall, in spite of the efforts of public health authorities, the medical and nursing professions, and the various associations of public-spirited citizens who co-operate with them.[13]

Yet the following year the new Director, Grace Cuthbert, reported that the state had experienced the lowest level of maternal mortality ever; the happy situation was the result of early treatment with sulphanilamides, recognition of modes of infection, and a decline in the virulence of the bacteria.[14] The availability of penicillin from 1945 improved the therapeutic outlook still further.

Regulation of midwives

Doctors exercised self-regulation in response to the dangers of puerperal fever in the late nineteenth century. But some urged government control of unqualified midwives, who were held responsible for the excessive mortality from sepsis and other causes. The profession was quite justified in seeking regulation of the incompetent midwife, who caused a great deal of harm.[15] Because her services were cheap she was very often the only attendant a lower-class woman would have during labour. However, many doctors saw a conflict between regulation and economic self-interest because a corps of competent licensed midwives would compete for patients in a sphere of medicine recognized as the cornerstone of general practice, especially for practitioners at the beginning of their careers.

Writing in 1874, one Sydney doctor claimed that about two-thirds of labours were attended by midwives, the majority of whom had not been trained. He called for training facilities and for legislation to outlaw practice by the unqualified.[16] He cited instances of quite disturbing incompetence known to him. Such cases continued to be reported in Sydney and elsewhere in the Australian colonies over the next two decades. Yet fears of competition from a licensed body of competent midwives made many members of the medical profession wary of legislation.

The proportion of births attended by midwives only declined significantly in the years immediately following the First World War, while the number attended by doctors increased markedly: 58 per cent of births in New South Wales were attended by doctors in 1914; 73 per cent in 1923; and 80 per cent in 1935–6. The founding Director of Maternal Welfare in New South Wales, E. S. Morris, observed,

> This fact alone will exonerate the midwife from any sweeping charge that she is wholly responsible for the maternal mortality of the Commonwealth, unless one has the temerity to argue that such deaths occur for the most part in the progressively decreasing total which she attends.[17]

The mortality rate stubbornly refused to fall and Morris concluded that 'a considerable amount of responsibility' had to be shouldered by the medical profession. Similar conclusions were being reached overseas. The author of an extensive study of maternal mortality in New York City in the early 1930s argued that two-thirds of deaths might have been avoided had proper care been available and listed the many ways in which doctors contributed to the 'large number of avoidable deaths'.[18]

Legislation

The first attempt to establish regulatory legislation was made in 1895. James Graham, a well-known medical reformer, introduced in the New South Wales Parliament a bill providing for registration of midwives. This attempt failed and he introduced bills again in 1896 and 1898. A supporter, the eminent doctor and political figure, Sir Arthur Renwick, stated, 'Having perhaps the largest experience of any man in this colony in connection with this particular department of medical practice, I know that innumerable women have been injured through the carelessness and ignorance of those who have attended on them'.[19] H. N. (later Sir Henry) MacLaurin, successful physician and man of affairs, opposed the legislation on the grounds that it would bring into being a class of inferior medical practitioners.

When opponents multiplied, the New South Wales branch of the BMA requested that Graham withdraw his 1895 bill. Some objected to the bill in principle, arguing that midwives could not be allowed to supervise all labours because they lacked the necessary medical knowledge. Others were critical only of specific provisions, such as those relating to administration. In 1898 the profession's journal in New South Wales, the *Australasian Medical Gazette*, claimed that regulation would create an under-class of poorly educated practitioners which would prove disastrous for mothers of the colony. At meetings of the profession, the now familiar medical arguments were paraded but concern about economic interests was also expressed; registered midwives would steal patients and cut back obstetric practice, the established means to fuller family practice. Graham replied that legislation would in fact reduce competition because few midwives would qualify for registration.[20] But the profession was not persuaded and Graham's efforts came to nothing.

The matter of legislation was raised again in 1909 by C. K. (later Sir Charles) Mackellar, physician, philanthropist, and politician, who had already obtained legislation regulating private hospitals in the interests of stopping the procurement of abortions. Mackellar, strongly pronatalist and socially conservative, made it clear that he wished to prohibit practice by the unqualified midwife. But this, he had to concede, was impracticable, given the small number of qualified women; so his objective was limited to registration of qualified practitioners. The measure was welcomed across party lines. The Labor leader, J. S. T. McGovern, hoped that it would put an end to 'race murder' and would promote population growth.[21] During this era, concern about the nation's population regularly surfaced when maternal and infant health questions were discussed. The progress of the bill was halted on this occasion when Parliament was prorogued, and a similar fate befell other bills over the next few years. The coming of war in 1914 delayed this as it did other 'less essential' legislation. But in 1923 the Nurses Registration Bill, providing for general and psychiatric as well as obstetric nurses, was introduced. It passed through all stages. Thus 30 years after legislation had been introduced, and 50 years after the issue of registration had been publicly discussed for the first time, New South Wales made provision for the registration of qualified midwives.[22]

The medical profession and the defence of private medicine

The organized profession's opposition to registration was a significant factor in the failure to obtain early state regulation of midwives. The political power of the profession began to be consolidated around this time, and the basis for the twentieth-century predominance of the private market in health care was being established. The profession was determined to be independent of government on the one hand and the friendly societies or lodges on the other. Indeed when in the changed social and economic circumstances of the 1940s doctors were required to participate in a national health service, they fought hard, and successfully, to ensure that they entered a closer relationship with the state on their own terms: the fee-for-service method of payment to prevail; doctors to control areas defined as medical; and the preservation of the privacy of the doctor–patient relationship.[23]

Friendly society membership had grown markedly in the late nineteenth century and many less well-to-do (and, to the annoyance of doctors, some more well-to-do) Australians joined mutual aid, contributory schemes. About one quarter of Sydney's citizens was covered by the early 1870s, and by 1913, 42 per cent of the people of New South Wales were seen by 'lodge' doctors. Doctors disliked the power of these lay self-help bodies to dictate terms to them. They bitterly resented a situation where, aspiring to high professional status, they were required to tender for friendly society custom like common tradesmen.[24]

The fee-for-service system functioned tolerably well in rural localities and in more prosperous urban areas because the well-to-do, by paying more, subsidized services for the poorer patients. But in the inner city and industrial localities, this balance of classes was unknown, and very few could afford private fees. The 'respectable' working class and elements of the middle classes received treatment under lodge contract practice. However, with increasing specialization, contract practice, which only provided for a very limited range of therapy, failed to meet health care needs. Further, by the early 1900s doctors were even more vociferous in their protests against the 'friendlies'' capacity to impose unilateral contract terms. In 1908, the Australasian Medical Congress set low income limits for new and existing lodge members. The BMA in New South Wales implemented the resolution and then waged a strong campaign – doctors faced expulsion if they broke ranks – against friendly societies opposed to the model agreement drawn up by the Federal Committee of the BMA in 1912. By the end of 1914, 85 per cent of 3,000 society medical posts were held under the model agreement.[25]

Just as the profession largely defined the terms on which it worked with the friendly societies so it laid down the conditions under which it would work with the state. From the beginning, the BMA ensured that government baby health clinics in New South Wales did not compete with private practitioners. In 1916, the Clinics Board agreed that clinics would not offer treatment, and this agreement was reaffirmed in 1919 and 1930. School medical services were introduced in various states in the early 1900s. The profession co-operated only when it was agreed that children would be advised to seek treatment from private practitioners; those from poor families were to obtain care at outpatient departments of public hospitals.

The reforming Labor Government of New South Wales, in office between 1910 and 1916, aimed to replace voluntary with direct state control of public hospitals. Doctors strenuously opposed the government's plans, reaffirming the desirability of the traditional charitable orientation of public hospitals at the Australasian Medical Congress of 1911. The *Australasian Medical*

Gazette stated that the proposals of the Labor Minister for Health, the Honourable Fred Flowers, were advanced 'with the distinct object of uprooting all our cherished ideals . . . [they would destroy] that spirit of benevolence . . . which has always been the glory of the profession, and reduce Medicine to the level of a Trade'.[26] To relieve pressure on outpatient departments, Flowers proposed to the friendly societies that the government use their dispensaries – themselves not well regarded by private practitioners – for the free treatment of those who could not afford membership of a contributory society. The BMA rejected the scheme and confidently claimed that the tripartite system of charitable public hospital care for the poor, lodge cover for the provident working and lower middle classes, and fee-for-service treatment for those able to pay, was quite adequate. Like Flowers's 'nationalization' of hospitals, the free dispensary treatment scheme was not implemented.

Defects in the maternity care system

Many of the problems associated with the contract system stemmed from doctors' excessive work-loads. The large number of lodge cases, in addition to private patients, reduced the standard of service provided for women seen in contract practice. In the 1890s, a Sydney expert described in some detail the evils of the 'sweating' of doctors employed under friendly society agreements. Lodge midwifery cases were attended for a reduced fee, and general practitioners might deal with 150 to 180 midwifery cases a year under contract practice, besides private cases.[27] In the mid-1940s, an expert national committee said of contract medicine, which was still significant in capital cities and in industrial areas, that it often entailed 'fatigue and hurried work . . . to the detriment of the public welfare', and that in such areas doctors were forced, in order to obtain a reasonable income, to work 'at the expense of their professional efficiency'.[28] The organization of existing maternity care itself diminished the possibility of a major reduction in the maternal mortality rate.

There were other ways in which the maternity care system worked against improvement in the maternal death rate. At the Australasian Medical Congress in 1929, Henry Jellett cited as first among the main preventable causes of maternal mortality

39

the fact that the average labour was conducted by the busy general practitioner, the pressures of whose practice too often forced him to hasten labour by interference. Jellett also observed that the requests of relatives and friends to hasten labour were hard to ignore. Hubert Jacobs, obstetric surgeon to the Women's Hospital, Melbourne, also denounced 'meddlesome midwifery' and deplored the all too common situation where the doctor terminated a labour quickly to fulfil another engagement. Even conscientious asepsis could not protect the patient against the infection resulting from injuries caused by interference. Jacobs asserted that the improper use of forceps represented the greatest obstacle to improvement in morbidity and mortality statistics.[29] The *Medical Journal of Australia* regretted the pressure placed on the general practitioner by relatives and friends (and by nurse or midwife) to apply forceps and expedite delivery: 'If the general practitioner refuses . . . a less scrupulous practitioner will be called in'. In 1921, a distinguished Melbourne obstetrician and gynaecologist, Felix Meyer, claimed that the bulk of the unacceptably high morbidity relating to childbirth was caused by poor obstetrics. He strongly urged restraint in the use of Caesarean section. The *Medical Journal of Australia* stated, 'At times it would seem that general practitioners have recourse to this operation merely to expedite delivery or to avoid preventible trauma . . . It is frankly fraudulent to subject a woman to a major operation unnecessarily in order to enhance a doubtful reputation'.[30]

In 1927, E. S. Morris, New South Wales Director of Maternal Welfare, claimed that a private practitioner gained a competitive edge from being known to be willing to resort to forceps. 'A practitioner is liable to enhance his reputation by the almost universal use of forceps . . . So long as one competitor adopts this practice, all others must show an equal competence.' Moreover, said Morris, the private practitioner's control of puerperal infection, had not been 'commensurate with that effected in public hospitals'. His investigations of maternal deaths led him to conclude that the comparatively high maternal mortality rate in some populous urban areas was linked to confinements commonly being managed in a hurried manner.[31] The precise effects of excessive interference on the mortality rate, let alone the puerperal sepsis death rate, cannot be demonstrated. None the less, the criticism from expert sources is too frequent and too sustained to ignore. There seems to be little doubt that unacceptable practices like the speeding up of labour resulted in part from the bias of the maternity care system towards private practice.

The influence of other factors on mortality

As we have seen, the preventive campaign instituted by the New Zealand Health Department appears to have produced a notable reduction in the puerperal sepsis rate from 1927, well before the introduction of the sulphonamides or penicillin. However, in New South Wales neither the measures adopted by the health authorities nor the development of antenatal care and hospitalization for childbirth seem to have had much effect up to 1936–7, the great turning point in the history of puerperal sepsis mortality (and maternal mortality) in Sydney. Legislation providing for the registration of midwives was passed in 1923, but it was not until 1929 that effective administrative action concerning midwives was taken, when they were required to notify all cases of puerperal pyrexia. A midwife could also be suspended from practice if a febrile condition was connected with infection. In addition to this, in 1929 three nurse-inspectors from the Health Department's Division of Maternal Welfare began to supervise the work of all metropolitan midwives. They educated as well as policed, communicating new obstetric knowledge and techniques, especially to the older, uncertified midwife, and supervised private hospitals caring for obstetric patients. By 1930, about 90 per cent of registered midwives in New South Wales had certificates from one of the recognized schools. The problem of lack of training among the remainder could be alleviated but not solved by inspection and supervision. Moreover, for some years after the introduction of notification, the health authorities complained of poor co-operation in the reporting of deaths by private practitioners and by public hospitals.[32] The existence of untrained midwives and the lack of co-operation by medical practitioners and public hospitals reduced the effectiveness of administrative attempts to bring down the puerperal sepsis mortality rate.

Experts regarded antenatal supervision as the longer-term key to success in preventive obstetrics. Antenatal care can reduce the death rate from infection by ensuring that a woman enters labour in good health and by allowing the detection of conditions which could lead to difficulties in labour and so increase the risk of infection. It can also reduce the risk from other important causes of mortality such as the toxaemias. The ignorance and indifference (and in some cases, lack of means) of mothers was a great obstacle to the development of antenatal care, as was the resistance of some midwives and doctors. Only about 20 per cent of parturient women received antenatal care in the early 1930s. Younger women able to pay private fees appear to have been well covered, but the less well-to-do who presented at public maternity clinics seem often to have avoided prolonged supervision.[33]

One of the notable changes in obstetrics in the interwar period was the growing number of births which took place in public hospitals. As they ceased to be seen as charitable refuges for the disadvantaged woman and as appreciation of the benefits of hospitalization spread, the large Sydney maternity hospitals were increasingly used by all classes.[34] The proportion of metropolitan births occurring in such institutions increased from 26 per cent in 1929 to 48 per cent in 1939. Yet up to 1937, when the maternal death rate fell significantly, hospitalization appears to have had little impact. After 1937 the introduction of the 'sulpha' drugs and the proliferation of medical and other innovations make the task of disentangling the influences at work on the mortality rate very difficult. The 1940s saw the introduction of penicillin, a metropolitan blood transfusion service, and a departmental scheme for specialist care of patients who lacked the personal means to secure such services. These factors all reduced the threat of puerperal infection for women confined in Sydney. But penicillin particularly shifted the balance in favour of the doctor: 'For the first time the clinician, face to face, with desperate infection, held that power which is infinity in the palm of the hand'.[35]

Conclusion

The maternal mortality rate in Sydney fell dramatically from 7.4 per 1,000 births in 1936 to 5.5 per 1,000 in 1937. If deaths from illegal abortions are excluded, the fall was from 5.8 to 4.6, and a decline in sepsis deaths accounts for most of the fall. In the longer term, administrative controls, education, and other public health measures may have significantly reduced mortality.

But sulphonamides cut the Gordian knot and sepsis mortality fell suddenly and substantially. In the 1920s, medical critics showed that doctors could no longer simply blame the ignorant midwife, as they had since the 1870s. They had to assume some of the responsibility for the excessive mortality. Reasonably enough, the medical reformers proposed better obstetric education for medical students and an end to unnecessary interference in labour by established practitioners. The in-built limitations of a predominantly private practice maternity system which rationed good quality care were not discussed. Yet contract practice was the only channel through which the respectable working and lower middle classes could purchase care in a health care system where individual responsibility for health matters predominated over collective responsibility. Too often, contract practice led to overwork and poor quality care, and by its nature it did not encourage the provision of 'costly extras' such as antenatal supervision. Even those able to afford private fees faced the possibility of unnecessary interference in labour, behaviour generated by competition among private practitioners and by the time constraints imposed by busy general practices. The threat of puerperal fever was removed dramatically by the 'magic' of modern drug therapy, so such system-structural and social obstacles never had to be faced. Technological advance overrode the negative effects produced by a maternity care system which relied too heavily for quality service on the individual's capacity to pay and which sacrificed collective provision to the ethic of individual responsibility.

Acknowledgement

The author wishes to thank Professor Charles Kerr for his comments on this chapter.

Notes

1. For much of its history Sydney, the capital of New South Wales, has been the largest city in Australia. In 1871, it had a population of 137,586; in 1891, 383,333; in 1911, 629,503; in 1931, 1,200,830; and in 1941, 1,337,050.
2. Every Australian state experienced a sharp decline in infant mortality in the early 1900s. The new cities of Australia returned the

same high level of infant diarrhoeal mortality as European and North American cities. Lewis (for Sydney) and Durey (for Perth) have identified the substantial mortality attributable to 'weanling diarrhoea' in the late nineteenth and early twentieth centuries. M. J. Lewis, 'Sanitation, intestinal infections and infant mortality in late Victorian Sydney', *Med. Hist.*, 23 (1979), 325–38; M. Durey, 'Infant mortality in Perth, Western Australia, 1870–1914: a preliminary analysis', *Stud. West. Aust. Hist.*, 5 (1982), 62–71. In 1875–1900, Sydney returned a diarrhoeal mortality of 32 (or more) per 1,000 births. However, to deaths attributed to diarrhoea must be added those returned under 'dentition', 'atrophy' and 'marasmus', and many of those under convulsions. See W. G. Armstrong, 'Some lessons from the statistics of infantile mortality in Sydney', *Trans. Australas. Med. Cong.* (1905), 387–95. The problem of diarrhoeal disease gave rise to the infant welfare movement and to organized efforts to promote infant health in Sydney and in other cities of the western world. For Sydney, see M. J. Lewis, '"Populate or perish": aspects of infant and maternal health in Sydney, 1870–1939', unpub. Ph.D. thesis, Australian National University, 1976.

3. I. Loudon, 'Maternal mortality: 1880–1950. Some regional and international comparisons', *Soc. Hist. Med.*, 1 (1988), 223 and ch. 1 by Irvine Loudon. See also J. M. Munro Kerr, R. W. Johnstone and M. H. Phillips (eds) *Historical Review of British Obstetrics and Gynaecology, 1800–1950* (Edinburgh, 1954), 202.

4. Royal College of Obstetricians and Gynaecologists, *Report on a National Maternity Service* (London, 1944), 6. Thirty years earlier the Local Government Board had said the same thing: 'there can be no reasonable doubt that the quality and availability of skilled assistance before, during and after childbirth are probably the most important factors in determining the remarkable . . . differences in respect of mortality from childbearing'. Quoted in Loudon, 'Maternal mortality', 222. In the 1920s women's organizations pressed governments in New South Wales to support the establishment of a chair of obstetrics at the University of Sydney Medical School. A chair, the first in Australia, was created in 1925.

5. In 1912, the New South Wales Labor Government announced that it would ensure skilled attendance for all mothers; the scheme would be universal and publicly funded. War and lack of funds stood in the way, and while a policy of encouraging provision of small maternity wards in new country hospitals was implemented, no immediate increase in Sydney's public maternity accommodation occurred. In 1920, another Labor Government opened two small maternity institutions in the western suburbs, but these hardly amounted to a universal public midwifery service for Sydney.

6. F. S. Maclean, *Challenge for Health: A History of Public Health in New Zealand* (Wellington, 1964), ch. 12. See also P. Mein Smith, *Maternity in Dispute. New Zealand 1920–1939* (Wellington, 1986).

7. *Women's Hospital, Crown Street. Report for 1903*, 13–14. *Trans. Australas. Med. Cong.* (1911), 391–5. The London Royal Maternity Charity reported some remarkable maternal mortality figures from

district work in the period before antisepsis: Eastern District, 1828–50, 4.5 deaths per 1,000 births; Western District, 1842–64, 2.2 deaths per 1,000 births. Munro Kerr *et al.*, *Historical Review of British Obstetrics*, 262–3.

8. The New South Wales Statistician, Coghlan, stated that before 1893 'various ill-defined descriptions of the cause of death have been returned . . . where a defined cause has been given, the important qualification "puerperal" has been omitted in a large number of cases, especially of septicaemia and peritonitis'. T. A. Coghlan, *The Decline in the Birth-Rate of New South Wales and Other Phenomena of Childbirth* (Sydney, 1903), 66. Mortality from metria (inflammatory diseases of the puerperium in the vital statistics of the 1870s and 1880s) in Sydney was 2.68 per 1,000 births in 1871, 2.94 in 1873, 5.27 in 1875, 0.45 in 1877, 0.76 in 1879, and 1.57 in 1881.

9. *Br. Med. J.*, ii (1873), 354.

10. *Trans. Intercol. Med. Cong.* (1889), 695–6; R. Worrall, 'Analysis of thirteen cases of puerperal septicaemia, including one case treated by abdominal section', *Australas. Med. Gaz*, 12 (1893), 408.

11. Munro Kerr *et al.*, *Historical Review of British Obstetrics*, 202–3; L. Colebrook, 'The story of puerperal fever – 1800 to 1950', *Br. Med. J.*, i (1956), 247–8.

12. Colebrook, 'The story of puerperal fever', 248–9.

13. *New South Wales Director General of Public Health Report*, 1936, 37.

14. *New South Wales Director General of Public Health Report*, 1937, 40. More recent expert opinion does not give much weight to the idea that there was a decline in the virulence of streptococcal bacteria. Colebrook, 'The story of puerperal fever', 250.

15. In 1849, a doctor gave as one of the reasons for the frequency of uterine prolapse in New South Wales the fact that midwives used main force on the afterbirth if it did not immediately separate. F. J. Beardmore, 'Desultory observations on the diseases of New South Wales', *Lancet*, ii (1849), 144. In 1874, another doctor reported that when called into a case, he was puzzled by the presentation until the midwife handed him the mutilated arm of a premature baby; the arm had been torn from the socket. S. Knaggs, 'Report of 240 cases of midwifery', *New South Wales Med. Gaz.*, 5 (1874), 7–8. In 1890, a third doctor reported the case of a single woman, delivered by a midwife, who bled intermittently for 2 weeks after delivery; the doctor found a degenerated placenta still attached to the almost completely inverted uterus. R. Worrall, 'Case of transfusion', *Australas. Med. Gaz*, 9 (1890), 117.

16. J. Faithful, Letter to editor, *New South Wales Med. Gaz.*, 4 (1874), 290.

17. E. S. Morris, 'An essay on the causes and prevention of maternal morbidity and mortality', *Med. J. Aust.*, 2 (1925), 308.

18. R. S. Hooker, *Maternal Mortality in New York City: a Study of All Puerperal Deaths* (New York, 1933), 213.

19. *New South Wales Parliamentary Debates*, vol. 95, 24 Nov. 1898, 2503.

20. 'A meeting of the medical profession', *Australas. Med. Gaz.*, 17 (1898), 480–2.

21. *New South Wales Parliamentary Debates*, vol. 33, 5 Aug. 1909, 1041 and vol. 35, 5 Oct. 1909, 2513.

22. *New South Wales Parliamentary Debates*, vol. 94, 5 Dec. 1923, 3048 and vol. 97, 17 Sept. 1924, 2088. Similar legislation was passed in Tasmania and Western Australia in 1911, in Queensland in 1912, in Victoria in 1915, and in South Australia in 1920. For a historical account of obstetric nurse education, see M. J. Lewis, 'Obstetrics: education and practice in Sydney, 1870–1939', *Aust. & NZ J. Obstet. & Gynaecol.*, 18 (1978), 161–8.

23. See editor's introduction to J. H. L. Cumpston, *Health and Disease in Australia: A History* (edited and introduced by M. J. Lewis) (Canberra, 1989). See also T. Hunter, 'The politics of national health', unpub. Ph.D. thesis, Australian National University, 1969.

24. For an account of professionalization in New South Wales, see M. J. Lewis and R. MacLeod, 'Medical politics and professionalisation of medicine in New South Wales, 1850–1901', *J. Aust. Stud.*, 22 (1988), 69–82. For the Victorian profession, see T. S. Pensabene, *The Rise of the Medical Practitioner in Victoria* (Canberra, 1980).

25. Branches of the BMA were established in South Australia and Victoria in 1879. Branches appeared in New South Wales in 1880, Queensland, 1894, Western Australia, 1899, and Tasmania, 1911. The profession also expressed its unity in regular intercolonial medical congresses from 1887. After Federation, this body became the Australasian Medical Congress. In 1912, the Federal Committee of the BMA was created to oversee political and other developments affecting the profession's interests.

26. Quoted in B. Dickey, 'The Labor Government and medical services in New South Wales, 1910–1914', *Hist. Stud.*, 12 (1967), 550. Flowers's hospital policy is outlined in *A Pamphlet on the Hospital System in New South Wales* (Sydney, 1912).

27. L. Bruck, *The Sweating of the Medical Profession by the Friendly Societies in Australasia* (Sydney, n.d. [1899]).

28. Commonwealth Joint Committee on Social Security, 1943: social security medical survey sub-committee, 6th Interim Report, Appendix F; Commonwealth Joint Committee on Social Security, 1945: medical planning committee, 8th Interim Report, Appendix A.

29. H. Jellett, 'The future of obstetrical practice', *Trans. Australas. Med. Cong.* (1929), 306–12; H. Jacobs, 'The causes and prevention of maternal morbidity and mortality', *Med. J. Aust.*, 1 (1926), 593–611 and 627–44.

30. F. Meyer, 'Modern obstetrics: the case for nature', *Med. J. Aust.*, 1 (1921), 419–21; *idem*, 'The after-effects of Caesarean section', *Med. J. Aust.*, 1 (1922), 642–3.

31. *New South Wales Director General of Public Health Report*, 1927, 38; Morris, 'An essay', 338.

32. See *New South Wales Director General of Public Health Report*, 1930, 29–30; 1931–2, 34–6; and 1933, 31–2.

33. *New South Wales Director General of Public Health Report*, 1931–32, 36. C. D'Arcy, 'The problem of maternal welfare', *Med. J. Aust.*, 1 (1935), 389.

34. The Royal Hospital for Women (formerly the lying-in department of the Benevolent Asylum); the Women's Hospital, Crown Street; the South Sydney Women's Hospital; and St Margaret's Hospital. By the 1930s, two general hospitals, Royal North Shore and St George, were providing for a substantial number of maternity cases.

35. A. M. Hill, 'Why be morbid? Paths of progress in the control of obstetric infection, 1931 to 1960', *Med. J. Aust.*, 1 (1964), 109.

3

Mothers, babies and hospitals: 'The London' and the provision of maternity care in East London, 1870–1939

Lara Marks

'Haggard and worn'; these were the words often used to describe East London mothers. Reports from medical practitioners and social workers working in the area between 1870 and 1939 often cited malnutrition and ill health as being common among the women they visited. The fight for social and economic resources in East London was strained by the presence of a large pool of casual workers and unemployed men and women together with numerous poor Irish and East European Jewish newcomers. Bad accommodation and poor nutrition were the lot for many East Londoners.[1] Frequently highlighted by social commentators and politicians as the most impoverished part of London, the East End was not only a source of concern for many social reformers and politicians worried about urban degeneracy and the threat of social disorder, but also posed special problems in the sphere of maternal health.[2]

Directories for the years 1870 to 1930 indicate that despite, or because of, the appalling social and economic conditions of the area, the East End was characterized by a high level of maternity care dating back to the 1850s. In his study of poverty in East London, Charles Booth revealed a complex network of district nursing organizations, dispensaries, clinics, medical missions and voluntary hospitals providing medical care in the 1880s and 1890s.[3] Such services persisted through to the 1930s. In 1930, when members of the Carnegie Trust visited Stepney with the intention of establishing a large centre for maternity and child welfare, they declared the area so well equipped through the efforts of voluntary and municipal bodies that such a centre was not needed.[4]

Together with these services the maternity department at

The London (hospital) provided a crucial support for many mothers facing the continual strain of bearing infants on a low income. The first district maternity department established by the hospital in 1853, known as the 'Green Charity', was run by medical students who wished to acquire practical experience in midwifery. As a 'district' service this department provided midwifery care in patients' own homes. In 1885 a 'White Charity' was also set up, which provided district maternity care through the hospital's student midwives. Initially the hospital only accepted patients within a one mile radius of Whitechapel Road where the hospital was based, but later patients were taken from further afield. The maternity department grew rapidly over the following decades. Extending its outpatient service to become one of the largest in East London by the 1880s, the hospital also soon developed well-equipped maternity wards for inpatients and these came to dominate its maternity provision by the 1920s. Like other maternity associations in the area, the hospital provided a host of social welfare schemes beyond medical care.

These services were established during a period of increasing concern over the strength of the nation and declining health standards. A diminishing birth rate and persistent high infant mortality added to these fears. During the nineteenth century attempts had been made to curb infectious and diarrhoeal diseases among infants, but the issue became a national preoccupation when many recruits failed to pass the fitness tests needed to join the army during the South African War (1899–1902). In the drive to reduce infant mortality, voluntary and municipally funded schemes were set up around the turn of the century, providing a host of services, many of which had their roots in nineteenth-century philanthropic activities, mother's meetings and visiting.[5] Included in the various schemes set up to cover maternal and infant welfare were the provision of health visitors to visit and advise mothers in their own homes, the establishment of milk depots to provide subsidized or cheap milk to poor necessitous mothers unable to breastfeed their own babies, and schools for mothers. Emphasis was on teaching mothers the importance of proper feeding and rearing of babies. Alongside the creation of various maternal and infant welfare schemes, legislative efforts were made to raise the standards of midwifery and nursing through the Midwives Act of 1902. The Notification of Births Act (1907), made compulsory in 1915, made provision for visiting, ensuring that mothers would be advised on infant care within days of giving birth.[6]

The First World War revived anxieties about the nation's future generations and led to the Maternity and Child Welfare Act of 1918, which supported local authorities in establishing grant-aided infant welfare clinics. The Act also made provision for government grants to local councils and voluntary institutions wishing to provide paid midwives, health visitors, infant welfare centres, day nurseries, and milk and food for necessitous infants.[7] Implementation of the 1918 Act varied greatly between councils and regions, being dependent on a host of factors including social and economic conditions, the politics of individual councils, and the action of voluntary agencies and local personalities.[8]

In provisioning for antenatal care, the Act reflected a shift in emphasis from the infant to the mother. Concern about high levels of maternal mortality had appeared in a number of reports dating from 1875, but it did not achieve national priority in the same way as infant mortality until the early 1920s.[9] While little was done to ease the economic burdens of motherhood, persisting maternal mortality during the 1920s and 1930s caused a public outcry over the standards of midwifery care for mothers.[10] Services offered by hospitals reflected these national concerns; mothercraft courses and midwifery care had begun at the turn of the century, and immediately after the First World War antenatal and postnatal facilities were opened.

The level of care mothers and their infants received from hospitals was not only dependent on medical expertise, but also on a hospital's location and interaction with the local community, economy and municipal council. An outstanding feature of East London was its low rate of maternal mortality despite its high level of poverty. Figure 3.1 shows that in the years 1880–1939 East London had a consistently lower rate of maternal mortality than either England and Wales or London as a whole. This is partly explained by the large number of teaching hospitals. While they could do little to alleviate the social and economic stress in the area, their charitable midwifery services were a vital force in keeping maternal mortality rates down.

An examination of The London Hospital provides not only an important insight into how maternal and infant welfare services were adopted on a local level, but also into the role a

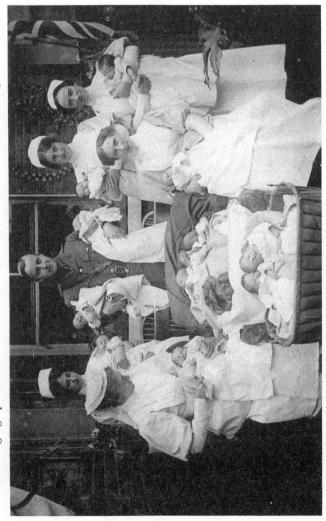

Plate 3.1 'Bringing up the reinforcements', Marie Celeste Ward, The London Hospital, c. 1916

Source: The Royal London Hospital Archives.

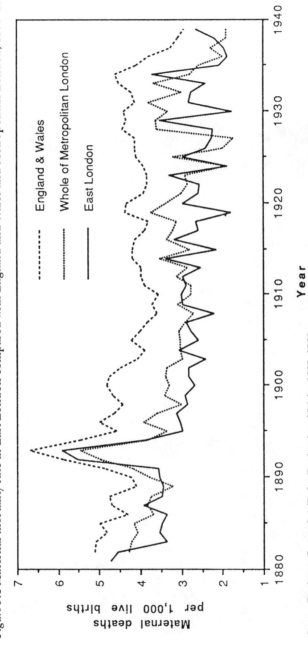

Figure 3.1 Maternal mortality rate in East London compared with England and Wales and Metropolitan London, 1880–1939

Source: Registrar General *A/Rs* for England and Wales 1889–1939.
Note: Statistics for East London cover Bethnal Green, Poplar and Stepney. All calculations are based on the number of deaths reported for accidental childbirth and puerperal fever per 1,000 live births.

hospital could play within an impoverished community. Known affectionately as 'The London', this hospital was a much cherished communal institution in the heart of the East End and its midwives and doctors were well-known figures, commanding great respect wherever they went. The London was one of the first voluntary general hospitals to accept maternity patients.[11] It was unusual in the types of care it provided and in its attitude towards the community it served. This chapter focuses on the ways in which the special conditions of East London fostered a sense of communal responsibility within the hospital and shaped the services it provided. It compares the maternity services of The London with other services in the area and examines the experiences of local women and immigrants using the hospital's facilities.

The availability of maternity care and the constraints attached to hospital provision

By the late nineteenth century, midwifery care was primarily provided for those who could pay, or dispensed by the local parish's funds – the latter being given only to those who were in desperate circumstances. While the stigma attached to parish maternity care noticeably diminished between 1870 and the 1920s, and medical treatment provided by the parish improved, this varied from parish to parish and many women still preferred to seek their aid elsewhere.[12] Some women obtained maternity services through the medical schemes of friendly societies, but this was limited to those whose husbands had regular employment, and wives were not always covered.

For many women, therefore, the expense of attendance in childbirth caused tremendous problems. Around 1910 the average midwife fee was 10s. which was a large sum given that most women had to pay for the family's food, rent and clothing on an income of 25s. a week.[13] There might be the additional expenses of hiring a nurse or someone to do the housework during the first few days after the birth, and the provision of necessities for the baby. Such expenses were harder to bear when mothers lost work because of their confinements.[14] Before the First World War the total cost of a confinement could be as much as £5.[15]

The introduction of National Health Insurance in 1911 enabled husbands who were in full employment to receive 30s.

on behalf of their wives, but women did not receive this directly until 1912.[16] The creation of Maternity Benefit in 1913, met, for the first time, some of the costs women were expected to pay for their confinements, but this was limited to those whose husbands were in regular employment. Given the preva- lence of casual work and unemployment in the East End, many women could not hope to claim the benefit. In 1913 one East London maternity hospital reported that many of their mothers, whose husbands were involved in dock work and casual labour, could not 'even get work to keep their insurance cards up to date' and were 'therefore ineligible even for Maternity Benefit'. Even those who could claim maternity benefit found that it was insufficient.[17]

In East London women perhaps had easier access to charit- able maternity services than elsewhere because of the presence of a high number of teaching hospitals which needed cases for their medical and midwifery students. None the less while these services were run on a charitable basis for poor women, patients had to satisfy certain requirements. Keen to demonstrate its respectability, and in common with other voluntary hospitals during the nineteenth and early twentieth centuries, The London Hospital insisted that their patients produce letters of recommendation from a governor or subscriber to the hospital and certificates of marriage. Frequently this meant much walking and waiting and made women think twice before applying.[18]

Increasing concern for the plight of the unmarried mother and her child at the end of the nineteenth century meant that voluntary hospitals began to aid single mothers for the first time.[19] Only those who could prove it was their first confine- ment, or were considered exceptional cases, were admitted. In 1905, when The London opened the Marie Celeste Ward, women no longer had to prove their marital status.[20] Although illegitimacy was clearly still a taboo issue during the period, hospital policy towards unmarried mothers softened over the years, and the hospital thought nothing of helping a woman in 1922 who was clearly cohabiting.[21] Some unmarried mothers were picked up through the venereal department. Many single mothers applied to the hospital for assistance from all over London and other parts of the country. A few single mothers were confined in the hospital, but many were referred to other agencies, such as the Salvation Army, who were specially organized to relieve the plight of the single mother.[22] The hospital kept in touch with the girls 'as far as possible'.[23] When compared with the overall numbers of mothers cared for by The London, the percentage of single mothers remained relatively small. The highest percentage of single mothers treated by the hospital was 2 per cent of total admissions in 1921, but in most years little more than 1 per cent were unmarried.[24] This reflected the small number of unmarried mothers in East London and also hospital restrictions.

Whatever their marital status, the number of women admitted to the hospital was restricted by the number of staff who could attend outpatients and the number of beds for indoor patients. In order to secure care from the hospital mothers had to book early and had to obtain references, even in the 1930s.[25] Those undergoing first confinements or those who had had more than five previous pregnancies were more assured of a hospital bed. With the introduction of effective antenatal care in the 1920s, abnormal cases also achieved higher priority amongst inpatient admissions.

As hospital confinement became safer and increasingly popular the demand for beds grew more urgent. During the 1920s The London continually lamented that it had to turn women away because it could not give them the inpatient care they were seeking. The number of women who applied to the hospital and were referred elsewhere varied from 44 per cent in 1922 to 22 per cent in 1927 when the hospital had acquired more beds. By 1930, however, the number turned away had again increased to 31 per cent, reflecting the rising demand for inpatient care.[26] Those ordered by doctors to go into hospital were taken without question, but others had to be judged according to their housing conditions and how suitable these would be for a home confinement. Given the prevalence of bad housing conditions in the area this meant that difficult choices often had to be made.

Standards of hospital care and inpatient treatment

The quality of maternity care offered by The London varied over time. Improvements in medical training and the introduction of antisepsis in the 1880s greatly diminished the risk of infection, but puerperal sepsis was still far higher in hospitals than in the home. Even in the home the safety of a birth was dependent upon the training and skill of the medical attendants. Those who secured district midwifery care from voluntary hospitals were, from the 1880s onwards, probably assured of better treatment.[27]

None the less a high standard of treatment was not always guaranteed. One medical student in 1905 remembered the exhaustion he suffered when, with very little previous clinical experience, he was expected to deliver fifty-four mothers in a fortnight.

> I lost all sense of time, I did not know whether it was yesterday, today or tomorrow. It sounds absurd but it is true. The month we spent on maternity was itself enough to undermine the stoutest constitution.[28]

The gruelling hours they worked must have had some impact on the standard of care even the best trained students could give.

By 1919 the situation had changed very little. Both medical students and midwifery pupils were expected to undertake district deliveries with very little previous training and minimal supervision. Medical students had sole responsibility for conducting the labours and the after-care of the mother and infant for the ten days following birth. Such students were in their fourth year and had taken a course of lectures on midwifery, but their clinical experience was minimal. A junior resident accoucheur supervised the first three labours students conducted on the district and the first two labours in the lying-in ward, but after that they were left to their own devices. Any abnormal labours were reported to the junior resident accoucheur.

In 1919 the authors of an official hospital report were amazed that there had been no public outcry against the negligent midwifery training and standards of midwifery care offered by The London. Calling for a reform of these conditions, they argued that medical students and pupil midwives could only gain adequate practical knowledge of the clinical conduct of labour in the environment of an inpatient maternity department.[29] The hospital subsequently increased its inpatient intake in the 1920s.

The preference for hospital confinements stated in the 1919 report was part of a more general public debate concerning the

Plate 3.2 Patients on the balcony of the Marie Celeste Maternity Ward, The London Hospital, 1914

Source: The Royal London Hospital Archives.

dangers of childbirth. Until the 1920s childbirth was predominantly an event which occurred at home and not in hospital. As early as 1920, however, the Ministry of Health was arguing for an increase in the number of maternity hospitals and homes to compensate for bad housing conditions.[30] Similar attitudes were voiced by many East London hospitals, including The London, which argued for the extension of inpatient care on the grounds of bad housing in the area. It called for the creation of 'sufficient lying-in accommodation for every woman who requires it', which, it claimed, would be for 'the good of the community'.[31]

This view, which became orthodox after the Second World War, was extreme in 1930. The College (later Royal College) of Obstetricians and Gynaecologists, founded in 1929, with its emphasis on building up the speciality of obstetrics and gynaecology, endorsed the government policy for a national maternity service in the 1930s; it was to be based on home deliveries by midwives and general practitioners as the backbone of the service, while hospital deliveries would be reserved for 'social' admissions, high risk cases and emergencies.[32]

This trend towards hospitalization took place slightly later in The London than other East London hospitals (see Table 3.1). This might have been because The London did not cater solely for maternity patients, and could not necessarily provide as many maternity wards as it wished, owing to the financial restraints caused by its status as a general hospital. None the less in the 1920s, when compared to other hospitals in London, such as the Queen Charlotte's Hospital in Marylebone and the General Lying-in Hospital in Lambeth, The London was taking in a much higher percentage of inpatients (see Figures 3.2 to 3.5). This reflected the strong emphasis on inpatient care in East London as a whole. From the 1920s the area had much higher rates of hospital births than the rest of London or nationally (see Table 3.2). The presence of numerous teaching hospitals in East London partly accounts for its high proportion of inpatients.33 Throughout the period maternal mortality rates were better in home confinements, but the medical staff faced many difficulties when delivering cases at home. Students also had certain advantages in treating women in hospital rather than at home, where help during an emergency was less forthcoming. By the late 1920s hospitals could deal more effectively with emergencies and abnormal cases from the antenatal clinics.

Table 3.1 Total number of maternity patients at The London Hospital and other hospitals in East London and London, 1922–1938

Year	Total inpatients						Total outpatients					
	4 East London hospitals*		4 non East London hospitals**		The London Hospital		4 East London hospitals*		4 non East London hospitals**		The London Hospital	
	no.	%	no.	%	no.	%	no.	%	no.	%	no.	%
1922	4,163	55	3,900	20	1,252	10	3,401	45	15,555	80	2,188	90
1923	4,121	57	4,163	21	1,314	13	3,131	43	15,897	79	2,081	87
1924	4,057	59	4,102	23	1,344	16	2,853	41	13,756	77	1,863	84
1925	4,321	61	4,203	22	1,347	15	2,732	39	15,325	78	1,898	85
1926	4,473	66	4,177	23	1,387	17	2,275	34	14,292	77	1,867	83
1927	4,645	68	4,540	23	1,569	29	2,139	32	15,003	77	1,405	71
1929	5,225	73	4,784	28	1,692	41	1,931	27	12,012	72	1,977	59
1930	5,370	74	5,088	29	1,677	43	1,883	26	12,670	71	1,887	57
1931	5,335	75	4,519	27	737	50	1,759	25	12,184	73	1,751	50
1932	5,442	76	3,958 ~	25	600	45	1,700	24	11,695 ~	72	678	53
1933	–	–	4,561 ~	28	646	51	–	–	11,628	72	1,612	49
1934	–	–	5,023 ~	27	790	60	–	–	13,866	73	1,521	40
1935	5,466	80	5,023 ~	28	1,888	65	1,326	20	12,906 ~	72	485	35
1936	5,403	81	5,017 ~	29	–	–	1,291	19	12,828	71	–	–
1938	–	–	–	–	1,075	74	–	–	–	–	384	26

Deliveries are divided into those undertaken in hospital as inpatients and those cared for in their own homes as outpatients by the hospital staff. This table does not show the overall trend of hospital confinements. It is limited to showing the pattern for voluntary hospitals and does not take into account what was occurring in poor law institutions or amongst district midwifery agencies.

* City of London Maternity Home, East End Maternity Home, Jewish Maternity Home and Salvation Army Mothers' Hospital.

** British Hospital for Mothers and Babies (Woolwich), Clapham Maternity Hospital, General Lying-in Hospital in Lambeth and Queen Charlotte's Hospital (Marylebone) 1922–31.

~ There are no figures for Clapham Hospital after 1930.

Sources: A/Rs of the City of London Maternity Home, East End Maternity Home, Jewish Maternity Home, The London and Salvation Army Mothers' Hospital; London County Council, 'Statistics of hospitals in Greater London not under public management', in *London Statistics*, 1922–36.

Table 3.2 The percentage of home and institutional confinements in East London and other areas, 1915–1946

Place		Date	% home confinements	% hospital confinements
London:	Bethnal Green*	1931	56.3	43.7
		1932	53.39	46.6
		1933	54.2	45.8
		1935	41.2	58.8
		1936	43	55.3
		1937	44.6	55.4
	Poplar**	1915	88.7	12.3
		1920	87.8	10.2
		1925	75	23
		1930	62	38
		1932	50.1	49.9
		1935	39	58
	Stepney**	1920	79	21
		1927	56	44
		1935†	26.6	73.4
	St Pancras	1915	87.5	12.5
		1935	44	56
Birmingham		1915	> 97	< 3
		1935	67	33
Hull		1915	> 97	< 3
		1935	88	22
Liverpool		1915	> 97	< 3
		1935	59	41
National		1927	85	15
		1933	76	24
		1937	75	25
		1946	46	54

* The figures are taken from hospital sources only, which might account for the stress on hospital care. The figures cited are for home and hospital deliveries undertaken by the major hospitals in Bethnal Green.
** These percentages are calculated from the number of births notified by doctors, midwives and parents that were home confinements, and from the births notified by hospitals. The percentages are approximate and do not add up to 100.
† The figures for this year are calculated according to an investigation undertaken by Stepney MOH in 1935 on the level of skilled midwifery in the area and are therefore more accurate than most statistics for the time.
Sources: Poplar MOH *Reports*; statistics relate to those births notified by doctors, midwives and institutions in 1915, 1921, 1931, 1932, 1936; Bethnal Green MOH *Reports* (1930–9); national figures and other areas taken from J. Lewis, *The Politics of Motherhood* (London, 1980), p.120.

Figure 3.2 Outpatient births as a percentage of total births in
London hospitals, 1922-1936

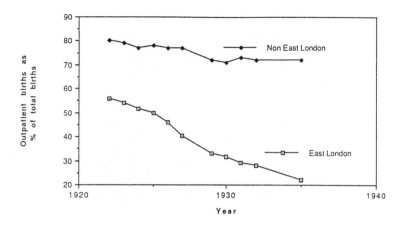

Sources: *A/Rs* of the City of London Maternity Home, East End Maternity
Home, Jewish Maternity Home, The London and Salvation Army Mothers'
Hospital; London County Council, 'Statistics of hospitals in Greater London
not under public management', in *London Statistics*, 1922–36.

Figure 3.3 Inpatient births as a percentage of total births in London
hospitals, 1922–1936

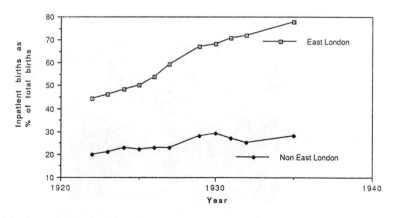

Sources: See Figure 3.2.

Figure 3.4 Annual inpatient and outpatient births in non East London hospitals, 1922–1936

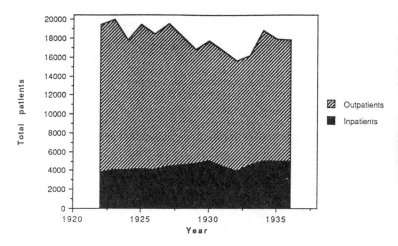

Sources: A/Rs of the City of London Maternity Home, East End Maternity Home, Jewish Maternity Home, The London and Salvation Army Mothers' Hospital; London County Council, 'Statistics of hospitals in Greater London not under public management', in *London Statistics*, 1922–1936.

Figure 3.5 Annual inpatient and outpatient births in five East London hospitals, 1922–1936

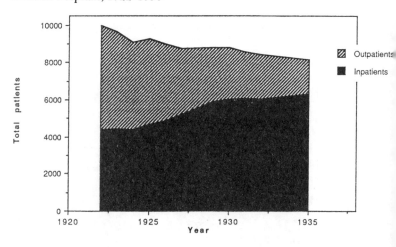

Sources: See Figure 3.4.

However, one of the most important causes of the high rate of hospital confinement in East London was undoubtedly the awful housing conditions in the area, which made domiciliary midwifery very difficult. Situated in the one of the poorest areas, The London had more than its fair share of housing problems to deal with. One medical student, reflecting on his medical training in 1905, recalled undertaking home deliveries in homes which were

> the poorest imaginable and often totally unprepared for the event. Once I attended a woman in a naked garret, reached by a ladder. There was a broken down bed and a single bed with a single blanket, a chair without a back, a tin basin without a towel, and the poor mother herself was practically naked. Of food and drink there was none.[34]

Cramped housing also meant there was no escape from the noise and arguments of families in the background. Salaman remembered on one occasion using the excuse of needing some boiled water to get some respite from a fight between a father and daughter in the next room.[35]

Similar descriptions appeared in a hospital report for 1922.[36] By the 1920s new blocks of flats were appearing in East London, with bathrooms and electric lighting, but the rent charged for such accommodation was 'quite prohibitive' to those who used the services of The London. Many were forced to continue living in over-crowded insanitary tenement houses.[37] One pupil midwife, Miss B, who worked for the hospital in the 1920s and 1930s, remembered the terrible inconvenience caused by the need to carry water from a tap outside the houses up flights of stairs. Lavatories were also outside and often shared by several families. The only source of heat, and very often the only facility for cooking, was an open fire.[38]

Bugs were also a problem. In the house where Miss B carried out her first delivery the walls had just been whitewashed. She waited most of the night for the baby,

> and once the gas was lit the bugs crawled through the new whitewash and came out through the walls, and before I'd got the baby I'd used up all the swabs killing bugs so I had to send father across to hospital to get another packet of swabs. Of course I'd used them all up . . . And I was told

that I shouldn't . . . have used them . . . of course, you weren't dirty because you'd bugs, the bugs were in the walls, they didn't belong to the person . . . I can remember bathing another baby, and you know I'd dressed it up and there it was lovely and clean and I picked it up to kiss it and there was a bug crawling up its gown . . . [39]

According to the medical reports, by the late 1920s women themselves were demanding hospital rather than home confinements.[40] In 1927 the hospital claimed that there was 'an even greater desire for inpatient treatment than in former years, owing no doubt to the abominable home conditions which prevail in many quarters'.[41] Some women saw their stay in hospital as a holiday and a chance to get away from the pressure of housework and family. Adequate provision for home confinements was also impossible in such conditions and most women could not afford to hire handywomen or home helps who could aid them in the house and with child-care during their confinement. Before the war most handywomen were paid 10s. for 10 days with food, which increased to a minimum of 15s. per week after the war.[42] This was a large sum compared with the average working-class wage of 25s.[43]

The borough council of Stepney, where The London was based, like some other East London councils such as Bethnal Green, provided the services of home helps to aid mothers in their own homes during their confinements. Some women could get a grant from the Stepney council to employ someone to help look after the house during the lying-in period, but this facility was limited.[44] By 1932 the council had dropped the scheme because it was difficult to engage suitable women for the work, and because neighbours were always on hand for emergencies.[45] In 1935 the Medical Officer of Health for Stepney argued against the indiscriminate provision of home helps, because he believed that it would 'encourage the poorest mothers to have their confinements in their own homes instead of in hospital'.[46]

Not all women, however, wanted to be confined in hospital. A number of women who were told by their doctor to go into hospital refused because they 'didn't trust their husbands, and wouldn't leave them'.[47] Many women could not rely on family or neighbours to look after the children in their absence and financial restraints also limited the possibility of employing

someone to undertake such work. Arrangements could be made
by the Stepney council to board out children in a large family
where there was no alternative, but this was not utilized on a
large scale.[48] At times The London recognized these difficulties
and realized that it faced 'no alternative' but to send its doctors
and nurses to undertake home confinements.[49]

Services provided

Although the hospital primarily relied on outside organizations
such as district nursing associations and borough councils for
the provision of home helps, it did make some attempt to give
help within the home. By 1922 The London, in collaboration
with Bethnal Green council from 1925, was supplying specially
trained maternity nurses and labour nurses to accompany their
district medical students and pupil midwives.[50] Labour nurses
assisted the students during the deliveries, and maternity nurses
took care of the patient for the following ten days.[51] Often
maternity nurses also provided extra nourishment, groceries
and baby garments for the women they cared for, at the expense
of the hospital and council. These nurses were reported to be in
high demand.[52] In later years over half of The London's outpatients were attended by maternity nurses, but this was due to
the significant drop in the number of outpatients rather than
because of an increase in the number of maternity nurses. The
number of maternity nurses increased from 286 in 1925 to 383
in 1931, attending between 15 per cent of the outpatients in
1925 and 58 per cent in 1934.[53]

Apart from the immediate task of nursing women during
their confinements, the maternity department, in common with
other hospitals in East London, undertook preventive health
care. Lessons on hygiene and infant care were provided at
sessions when the women booked into the hospital and at a later
date through antenatal and postnatal clinics. Guidance was
given on breastfeeding and extra nutriments were provided for
pregnant and nursing mothers along with milk for their infants.
Such work, which had its roots in activities operating since the
nineteenth century, such as health visiting and the establishment of babies' welcome clubs and schools for mothers, was
during the 1920s continued by postnatal clinics at the hospital
and other infant welfare centres.

After the Maternity and Child Welfare Act passed into law in 1918 antenatal provision formed a crucial part of hospital care. The persistence of high maternal mortality during the 1920s increased public awareness of the need to institute proper antenatal services.[54] Effective antenatal attendance relied on co-operation between midwives, general practitioners and hospital consultants, which was rare in the interwar period. Often antenatal services were split between many different institutions, clinics and general practitioners' surgeries with minimal communication between all parties. In addition antenatal practice during this period consisted only of testing urine and measuring blood pressure. This was useful for identifying toxaemia cases, for which treatment was limited.[55]

Antenatal provision at The London Hospital, however, probably came closer than elsewhere to the attainable ideal.[56] By 1927 the hospital was providing two antenatal clinics a week, one for abnormal cases and another for normal cases. Most women who sought help from The London could only book when attending the antenatal sessions. The hospital's policy of deliberately identifying high-risk mothers and of providing special attention before, during and after labour was perhaps the greatest service antenatal care could offer during this period. Young women about to undergo their first confinement were expected to attend the antenatal clinics more often than those who had already had children. The department kept 'strict watch' on 'possible defaulters'.[57] According to the hospital reports, most women returned to the clinics and they took full advantage of the facilities on offer.[58] The London also worked in close conjunction with voluntary and municipal infant welfare centres in the area. These centres undertook to visit the hospital's mothers regularly before their confinement and ensure that mothers attended antenatal clinics. They also reported any cases of unusual poverty or illness to the hospital.[59]

By the late 1920s maternity services extended into postnatal care, which was carried out by the infant welfare centres, including the one established by The London in 1926. Considerable emphasis was placed by this department on the vaccination of infants. Much of the postnatal work only constituted 'an examination of the new-born infant and the giving of advice to the mother, rather than a physical examination of the latter'.[60] Most of the advice given was on breastfeeding, a continuation of old policy.

How effective such education was is debatable. According to one medical officer ignorance remained.

> What is most annoying is the mother who comes once, with a breast-fed baby satisfactory in every way and then never again [until] about 18 months or two years later, when she brings a miserable, pasty, undersized child with bow legs. When reproached she *invariably* says that, as to the bow legs, the lady next door, or her mother, or her grandmother (and sometimes the doctor) says 'He will grow out of it as he gets older'.[61]

Nevertheless, by 1929 The London Hospital claimed that since it had opened its antenatal department, their mothers had become 'more solicitous, not only for advice for their infants but for themselves in matters of health during pregnancy'.[62]

The London's social welfare schemes

A recurrent theme in The London's reports was of the unemployment and poverty faced by the overwhelming majority of its patients. Such deprivation meant that many of its mothers could not 'provide themselves adequately with what they need for their infants'.[63] One way in which the hospital tried to ease this problem was in the provision of baby garments through its Samaritan Fund. Established originally as the Marie Celeste Society in 1791, the Samaritan Fund had a long tradition of supplying food and other comforts to the hospital's patients. Services provided by these funds for mothers included the provision of 5s. worth of groceries or milk for a fortnight. Garments for confinement as well as babies' clothes were also supplied by a needlework guild.[64]

The Samaritan Fund also helped send a small number of mothers to convalescent homes immediately after their confinements. In 1925 the hospital argued that

> though a confinement is not necessarily an illness, a fortnight's rest and change from the continual routine of home life is a great boon to the mothers of large families and indeed if they are to maintain a good standard of health, it is almost imperative that they should have this short rest after confinement.[65]

Most of the women from The London Hospital were sent to the St Mary's Convalescent Home in Birchington-on-Sea. Yet this service was very limited and the number of patients helped in this way never exceeded more than 2 per cent of maternity cases in the years 1922 to 1934.[66]

Such help was not unique to The London. Other maternity hospitals in East London, such as the East End Maternity Home and Salvation Army Mothers' Hospital ran similar schemes, some of which were more liberal than those of The London Hospital. Both these hospitals recognized the problems caused by poverty and often allowed their mothers to come in ahead of their confinements to rest in hospital and gain some of the nourishment they could not obtain outside.[67] Such assistance both from The London Hospital and others demonstrated that medical care alone would not suffice in an area of great deprivation. Yet, while these services were important, they were not enough to eliminate the greater part of the deprivation in the area. They could only help in a limited way, and were reserved for 'deserving' cases.

Fees charged and the response of patients to The London's services

Although The London was established with the explicit aim of providing medical care on a charitable basis, it is a mistake to presume that such services were entirely free. Viewing itself as an agent of social reform, The London Hospital aimed to make its patients self-supporting citizens. Like many voluntary hospitals, by the beginning of the twentieth century The London had its own lady almoner. It was her job to prevent any abuse of the charity provided by the hospital. She was to assess the degree to which patients could be expected to pay for the services offered by the hospital. Any tendency on the part of the patient towards thriftlessness and dependence was frowned upon in the almoner's reports.[68] In line with this tradition, rather than offering material support, the lady almoner put families in touch with other charitable agencies already organizing for this purpose. This even included various apprenticeship and skilled employment associations, intended to help the children of maternity cases obtain suitable trades.[69]

Such attitudes underlay the questioning mothers had to

undergo in order to gain the benefits of the maternity care offered by the hospital. Although women were always expected to pay some contribution towards the care they received, with the introduction of the maternity benefit in 1913 many women who previously were unable to pay were now expected to cover some of the expense of their confinement. The amount was dependent on their husband's income. One woman remembered how humiliated her mother felt by the personal questions she was always asked by the lady almoner, often after a long wait. As a Jewish patient she felt even more resentful of the ignorance shown by the staff in spelling her name incorrectly.[70]

This woman's feelings about the hospital contrasted with the claims of hospital reports, which stressed the glowing affection and gratitude of its patients. According to the house governor, everyone loved the hospital 'passionately. You heard it everywhere. And the hospital was "hard up" as they were. "Poor old hospital! God bless it! We *must* help it". That's why starving folk offer their 5/- and 7/6d to the hospital'.[71] Despite the patronizing attitudes of the hospital's governor, there was an element of warmth and sympathy for the poverty-stricken patients they were serving. Although the lady almoner was not necessarily a popular person, the midwives and maternity nurses of The London Hospital were looked upon as friends or 'angels' to the poor. Described as never receiving anything but 'gratitude', the nurses always left a 'trail of smiling and friendly faces' behind them.[72] Often the nurse's care extended beyond that of a nurse to becoming a confidante and a social worker. By the 1930s The London was serving a third generation of women, having previously helped their mothers and grandmothers in childbirth. If daughters were being persuaded by their mothers to go to the same hospital this suggests that patients felt some kind of satisfaction. A number of the women interviewed held The London in high esteem, but some also commented on how big and impersonal it was.[73]

Conclusion

Whatever the attitudes of the patients, The London Hospital seemed to offer a service which reflected the demands of the community around it. Based in an area of great poverty, the hospital to some extent understood the need for a service which stretched beyond medical care to offer a large number of social services. To what extent such provision compensated for the appalling living conditions facing most mothers in the area is hard to estimate, but it would seem that these services could account for the remarkably low rate of maternal mortality in East London in the years 1870 to 1939, which was lower than the rest of London and England and Wales (see Figure 3.1).

The medical and social services set up by The London and other agencies provided a vital network of communal aid in an area where the burdens of motherhood were worsened by terrible poverty. By the standards of the time, The London did remarkably well in terms of maternity care. The London, with one of the largest maternity departments in East London, was a leading force in providing facilities which poor mothers could not otherwise purchase for themselves. While The London, like all voluntary hospitals, suffered increasingly from a lack of funds as the twentieth century progressed and was forced to impose rigid economies, at the same time it provided a service which reached out into the homes of the patients it served.

Acknowledgements

Research for this paper was carried out with financial support from the Wellcome Trust, Leverhulme Trust and with the help of the Geography Department, Queen Mary and Westfield College, which are hereby gratefully acknowledged. I would also like to thank Irvine Loudon, Anne Summers, Elizabeth Peretz, Hilary Marland and Valerie Fildes for their useful comments. Gratitude also goes to Claire Daunton and John Evans, and to all those who recalled their personal experiences of the hospital for me.

Notes

1. The area referred to as East London in this chapter includes the metropolitan boroughs of Bethnal Green, Stepney and Poplar. Although based in Whitechapel in the borough of Stepney, The London Hospital served all three areas.
2. For more information on the special role East London played in contemporary debates on poverty and social order, see G. Stedman Jones, *Outcast London* (London, 1971, repr. 1984), 12, 14, 241, 244–5, 283–4.

3. C. Booth, *Labour and Life: East London* (London, 1889), vol. 1, 127–9; Booth Collection (BLPES) file A38, p. 4; file A32, p. 17; file 33, p. 43; file B181, pp. 105–7, 109.

4. Stepney MOH *A/R* (1930), 85.

5. A. Summers, 'A home from home – women's philanthropic work in the nineteenth century', in S. Burman (ed.), *Fit Work for Women* (London, 1979), 33; F. K. Prochaska, 'A mother's country: mothers' meetings and family welfare in Britain, 1850–1950', *Hist.*, 74 (1989), 379–99, pp. 393–4. The links between nineteenth-century philanthropic women's work and the development of the health visiting profession in the early twentieth century is explored in C. Davies, 'The health visitor as mother's friend: a woman's place in public health, 1900–14', *Soc. Hist. Med.*, 1 (1988), 39–59.

6. For the national development of maternal and child welfare, see A. Davin, 'Imperialism and motherhood', *Hist. Workshop J.*, 5 (1978), 9–66; J. Lewis, *The Politics of Motherhood* (London, 1980); J. Lewis, 'The working-class wife and mother and state intervention, 1870–1918' in J. Lewis (ed.), *Labour and Love* (Oxford, 1986); A. S. Wohl, *Endangered Lives* (London, 1983); I. Loudon, 'Deaths in childbed from the eighteenth century to 1935', *Med. Hist.*, 30 (1986), 1–41; D. Dwork, *War is Good for Babies and Other Young Children* (London and New York, 1987).

7. Lewis, *Politics of Motherhood*, 34.

8. See E. Peretz, 'A maternity service for England and Wales: local authority maternity care in the inter-war period in Oxfordshire and Tottenham', in J. Garcia, R. Kilpatrick and M. Richards (eds), *The Politics of Maternity Care* (Oxford, 1990), 30–46; E. Peretz, 'Regional variation in maternal and child welfare between the wars: Merthyr Tydfil, Oxfordshire and Tottenham', in D. Foster and P. Swan (eds), *Essays in Regional and Local History* (Hull, 1992); and ch. 12, by Elizabeth Peretz; L. Marks, 'Irish and Jewish women's experience of childbirth and infant care in East London, 1870–1939: the responses of host society and immigrant communities to medical welfare needs', unpub. D.Phil. thesis, University of Oxford, 1990, ch. 8; and H. Marland, 'A pioneer in infant welfare: "The Huddersfield Scheme", 1903–1920', *Soc. Hist. Med.* (forthcoming).

9. Loudon, 'Deaths in childbed', 2.

10. Lewis, *Politics of Motherhood*, 35–6.

11. F. B. Smith, *The People's Health, 1830–1910* (London, 1979), 29–30; J. H. Woodward, *To Do The Sick No Harm: A Study of the British Voluntary Hospital System to 1875* (London, 1974), 45.

12. M. W. Flinn, 'Medical services under the Poor Law', in D. Fraser (ed.), *The New Poor Law in the Nineteenth Century* (London, 1976); L. Marks, 'Medical care for pauper mothers and their infants: Poor Law provision and local demand in East London 1870–1929', *Econ. Hist. Rev.* (forthcoming).

13. M. L. Davies (ed.) *Maternity. Letters from Working Women* (London, 1915, repr. 1978), 5. See also M. Pember Reeves, *Round About a Pound a Week* (London, 1913, repr. 1979), 75–93.

14. E. Ross, 'Labour and love: rediscovering London's working-

71

class mothers, 1870–1918', in Lewis, *Labour and Love,* 78.

15. Davies, *Maternity,* 5.
16. Ross, 'Labour and love', 79.
17. East End Maternity Home (EEMH) *A/R* (1913), 19–20.
18. Smith, *People's Health,* 28–30; A. E. Clark Kennedy, *The London: A Study in the Voluntary Hospital System* (London, 1963), vol. ii, 33.
19. See A. Higginbotham, 'Respectable sinners: Salvation Army rescue work with unmarried mothers 1884–1914', in G. Malmgreen (ed.), *Religion in the Lives of English Women 1760–1930* (London, 1987).
20. Minutes of sub-committee appointed to consider the working of the new Marie Celeste Ward, n.d. but presumed 1905, in London Hospital Archive, Blue file LM/5/22.
21. E. W. Morris (House Governor), *Report of a Visit to the District Maternity Charity with Miss Nicholls, District Midwife,* 19 Dec. 1922. Morris repeated the same story in an article in *Lond. Hosp. Illust.* (1933), 10–11.
22. For more information on agencies helping the unmarried mother and her child, see A. Higginbotham, 'Respectable sinners', and L. Marks, '"The luckless waifs and strays of humanity": Irish and Jewish immigrant unwed mothers in London 1870–1939', *Twentieth Cent. Br. Hist.,* 3 (1992).
23. London Hospital *A/Rs* (1921), 187; (1926), 203.
24. London Hospital *A/Rs* (1922–29), see esp. (1921), 187; (1926), 203.
25. Mrs E. C., interviewed by L. Marks 23 Oct. 1988, transcript p. 3.
26. London Hospital *A/Rs* (1921–30).
27. This is dealt with in greater detail in ch. 1, by Irvine Loudon.
28. R. N. Salaman, *The Helmsman Takes Charge* (unpub. autobiography, n.d.) 27–8.
29. E. Holland, *Report on the extern maternity district and on the urgent need of reforming the work of students thereon,* April 1919, 5 (File LH/A/17/35).
30. Ministry of Health (hereafter MH) Memorandum: 'Maternity hospitals and homes', 1920, 1.
31. London Hospital *A/R* (1930), 210.
32. I am grateful to Dr Irvine Loudon for pointing this out to me. See also E. Peretz, 'A maternity service for England and Wales'.
33. St Pancras had a high rate of hospital births because of the large number of teaching hospitals and lying-in institutions in the area. Lewis, *Politics of Motherhood,* 120–1.
34. Salaman, *The Helmsman,* 27–8.
35. Salaman, *The Helmsman,* 30.
36. Morris, *Report of a Visit,* 19 Dec. 1922, 3–4.
37. London Hospital *A/R* (1925), 197.
38. Miss M. B., interviewed by L. Marks 7 July 1987, transcript p. 4. See also London Hospital *A/Rs* (1921), 187; (1924), 187.
39. Miss M. B. interview, transcript p. 6.
40. MH Memorandum: 'Maternity hospitals and homes', 1920, 1.
41. London Hospital *A/R* (1927), 201.
42. London Hospital *A/R* (1921), 186.

43. Davies, *Maternity*, 5.

44. MH 8 May 1920 (PRO file MH 52/202); Stepney MCW Committee *Minutes* (THL file 1083), 11 May 1920, 148.

45. MH: Stepney Public Health Survey and Stepney MCW Committee *Full Report*, 1932, 5 (PRO file MH 66/392).

46. Stepney MCW Committee *Minutes* (THL file 1088), 16 Jan. 1935, 207.

47. Miss M. B. interview, transcript p. 6.

48. MH 8 May 1920 (PRO file MH 52/202).

49. London Hospital *A/R* (1929), 209.

50. London Hospital *A/R* (1926), 202.

51. London Hospital *A/R* (1927), 201.

52. London Hospital *A/R* (1928), 215.

53. London Hospital *A/Rs* (1922–34).

54. London Hospital *A/R* (1927), 201.

55. See I. Loudon, 'Some historical aspects of toxaemia of pregnancy. A review', *Br. J. Obstet. & Gynaecol.*, 98 (1991), 853–8.

56. The London Hospital was not unique in this respect. The East End Maternity Hospital, which was based near The London Hospital, was often cited as having one of the lowest rates of maternal mortality as a result of its good antenatal department. See *Br. Med. J.*, i (Feb. 1930), 294–5 (I am grateful to Irvine Loudon for this reference) and also *Med. Offr.* (25 Aug. 1928), 79–80; (31 Jan. 1931), 45. See also Loudon, 'Some historical aspects of toxaemia of pregnancy'.

57. London Hospital *A/R* (1925), 197.

58. London Hospital *A/R* (1927), 201.

59. London Hospital *A/R* (1922), 181.

60. MH: Stepney Public Health Survey, 1932 (PRO file MH 66/392), xx and (PRO file MH 66/391), 44.

61. Bethnal Green MOH *A/R* (1924), 14 (his emphasis).

62. London Hospital *A/R* (1929), 201.

63. London Hospital *A/R* (1925), 198.

64. *Lond. Hosp. Illust.* (n.d. c. 1936), 5.

65. London Hospital *A/R* (1925), 197.

66. London Hospital *A/Rs* (1922–34).

67. EEMH *A/R* (1911), 14–15; Salvation Army Mothers' Hospital *A/R* (1933), 6–7.

68. First Report of the Lady Almoner, 1 Feb. 1910 to 31 Jan. 1911, cited in G. Black, 'Health and medical care of the Jewish poor in the East End of London 1880–1939', unpub. Ph.D. thesis, University of Leicester, 1987, 217–18.

69. Black, 'Health and medical care of the Jewish poor', 219.

70. Miss T. G., interviewed by L. Marks 22 Jan. 1988, transcript p. 8.

71. Morris, *Report of a Visit*, 10.

72. *Lond. Hosp. Illust.* (n.d. c. 1936), 5.

73. Miss T. G. interview, transcript p. 8; Mrs D. G., interviewed by L. Marks 27 Sept. 1987, transcript p. 13.

4

The medicalization of motherhood: doctors and infant welfare in the Netherlands, 1901–1930

Hilary Marland

In 1922, in an article describing the work of infant welfare centres in Holland, Dr J. H. G. Carstens declared that the proper direction of such work lay with children's doctors or general practitioners with special experience in the field.[1] Such specialized work, he argued, could not be left to the uncertain devices of midwives, district nurses, sick fund doctors, or family doctors. While Dr Carstens, a children's doctor in Utrecht and a leading light in the movement to reduce infant deaths, was unusual in stating his case so bluntly and precisely, he reflected a general sentiment felt amongst infant welfare workers in Holland. His statement also reflected the reality of the situation. In Holland infant welfare work was initiated and directed by doctors, with paediatricians and, to a lesser but still important extent, obstetricians playing a major part in building up services from 1901 onwards.

There is nothing remarkable about doctors being involved in work directed at infant life-saving. Throughout the western world at the turn of the twentieth century welfare programmes were introduced aimed at reducing high rates of infant mortality, and everywhere such work was embraced by medical professionals, paediatricians, public health doctors, general practitioners, nurses, and midwives. Yet the involvement of doctors in the actual drive to set up services was not automatic. In many countries this task was shared by medical and lay groups, including parliamentarians, local government officials, and middle-class voluntary workers, often women. Holland was no exception, but the task was less equally divided, and the management of infant welfare was dominated by doctors.[2] Medical dominance was also facilitated by late government

74

intervention; only in 1927, almost 30 years after the commencement of the campaign to reduce infant deaths, did the national government step in to play an important role in infant welfare work.

In the late nineteenth century the Netherlands had one of the highest levels of infant mortality in Europe. In 1871 227 out of every 1,000 live-born children died before their first birthday. By 1881, though subject to great annual variation, the rate had fallen to 182 per 1,000, but compared badly with other countries, such as France with a rate of 166 per 1,000, England and Wales 130, and Norway 97.[3] But with infant mortality declining continuously from the 1880s, the Netherlands quickly achieved a low rate; 155 in 1900, 108 in 1910, and by 1920 at 83 per 1,000 it had one of the lowest rates in Europe.[4] By the years 1931–5 one estimate put the rate for the Netherlands at 45 per 1,000, which was equal to or lower than all other European lands (Norway 45, England and Wales 62, and France 78) (see Figure 4.1).[5] Dutch infant mortality then had been falling for two decades before the setting up of the first infant welfare services at the turn of the century, but it was still high enough to provoke great anxiety and action to reduce the rates still further.

Compared with other countries, the Netherlands had a low rate of maternal mortality, indicating generally high standards of obstetric care, based on qualified midwives working in the home. Between 1865 and 1900 the maternal mortality rate fell from 87 to 50 per 10,000 births, due largely to a reduction in deaths from infection.[6] By the early twentieth century the Netherlands had one of the lowest maternal mortality rates in the western world: in 1920 it was 24.2 per 10,000 births, which compared with 25.8 in Sweden, 43.3 in England and Wales, 66.4 in France, and a massive 79.9 in the United States.[7] The fact that trained midwives attended a large proportion of births, which almost always took place in a domiciliary setting, is likely to have contributed towards this low maternal mortality. Institutional deliveries in Holland, though few, were, as in other countries, associated with high rates of maternal mortality.

However, there were local black spots, where both infant and maternal mortality remained high. These tended to be regions which lacked qualified midwives and supporting maternity services, usually the poor rural areas in the south of the country. For the years 1901–5 the national infant death rate was 136 per 1,000, but this hid great regional variations; 136 per 1,000 in the

Figure 4.1 The decline in infant mortality in the Netherlands, England and Wales, France and Norway, 1870–1930

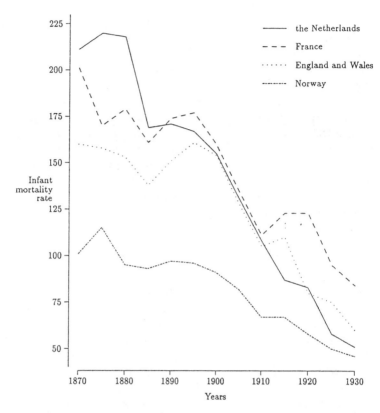

Source: B.R. Mitchell, *European Historical Statistics 1750–1970* (New York, 1975).
Note: Statistics taken at five-yearly intervals; infant mortality rates are in deaths per 1,000 live-born children.

urbanized province of South Holland, 92 and 109 in the northern rural provinces of Friesland and Groningen, and 173 and 183 in the southern rural and predominantly Catholic provinces of Limburg and North Brabant.[8] Infant death rates remained above the national average in Limburg and North Brabant well into the 1930s. These areas were specially targeted by infant welfare workers, but because of poverty, isolation, religious belief, and low levels of education, they were also the areas which reformers found most difficult to reach.[9]

Doctors involved in work to reduce infant deaths in the

Netherlands, especially at the point of direction and control, were often senior and well-established paediatricians and obstetricians. This contrasted markedly with the situation in England, for example, where local authority doctors, the Medical Officers of Health, played leading roles. Although up-and-coming as a separate professional group,[10] they were not particularly high-status figures, and they had to juggle infant welfare work with numerous other tasks, including disease notification, hospital administration, tuberculosis work, and school medical inspection. This factor perhaps helps explain the organizational structure of infant welfare work in the two countries. In England, up until, and even beyond the passing of the Maternity and Child Welfare Act in 1918, which laid down guidelines for the organization of maternity services and made grants available to local authorities, the emphasis was on local (either borough or county council) organization, and was subject to local economic conditions, the level of voluntary work in a given community, and local government support.[11] In Holland, though local organization was strong and local characteristics crucial in determining the form infant welfare work took and its effectiveness,[12] a central body, the *Nederlandsche Bond tot Bescherming van Zuigelingen* (hereafter *Bond*, the Dutch Confederation for the Protection of Infants), was set up in 1908 by a group of paediatricians and obstetricians to co-ordinate work in the field. Other co-ordinating structures were superimposed on infant welfare work in the 1920s.

As creators and members of the *Bond* at both the central and provincial level, through to the staffing of individual *consultatie-bureaus* (infant welfare centres or well-baby clinics), doctors were largely responsible for shaping Holland's programme to reduce infant deaths. By taking on this role, doctors were able to carve out a new specialism for themselves. It can be suggested that the form services took in Holland – and the propaganda message behind the services – was not, as has been argued, impelled primarily by the desire to impose middle-class ideals of motherhood on poor and ineffective mothers.[13] While this clearly played a role, it none the less had more to do with job creation, career consolidation and the carving out of a new specialist field of endeavour in the medical profession. Significantly, the dominance of doctors did not, however, result in services fundamentally different from those of other nations, in tone or in the kind of institutions created.

Trends shaping infant welfare services

A number of factors shaped the development of Dutch infant welfare services. The 'public health doctor' barely existed when the infant welfare movement commenced in 1901. It is only in the 1920s that we can begin to talk about the existence of such a group, as local authorities began to take over the tasks and burdens of public health work, and the local authority doctor began to acquire the trappings of professionalism.[14] Prior to this, as in all areas of social and preventive medicine, few initiatives were taken by the municipal authorities in infant welfare work.[15] Rather, from the 1870s onwards, public health work became the province of private bodies and individuals, particularly the *Kruisvereenigingen* (Cross Societies), who, frustrated by local government lethargy and ineptitude, moved into disease prevention and epidemic control, district nursing, health education, tuberculosis work, and infant welfare. The first *Kruisvereeniging* was set up in North Holland in 1875 by Dr Jacobus Penn, a state health inspector, after the failure of the local authorities to respond to the Epidemic Diseases Act of 1872. In subsequent societies, set up largely along denominational lines and focusing increasingly on nursing and infant welfare services, doctors had a high profile as both organizers and suppliers of services.[16]

Private initiatives were not confined to public health work. Doctors played an important part in the creation of the many new and expanding health care facilities directed at women and children from the late nineteenth century onwards: hospital facilities, maternity clinics, maternity and district nursing services, gynaecological and birth control clinics. Women doctors, entering medical practice in increasing numbers after 1900,[17] took up work in these areas, bringing new skills and insights to the development of health care facilities directed at women and children.[18] The private actions of doctors, for example, were crucial in the setting up of the first children's hospitals, established with philanthropic support, but without the participation of the universities or local authorities. The first, Rotterdam's Sophia Kinderziekenhuis, was founded in 1863 by Dr Hendrik Willem de Monchy, a general practitioner with a special interest in paediatrics, who perceived the need for better nursing and specialized facilities for children.[19] At the close of the nineteenth century, hospital services for children diversified further, with the development of outpatient clinics and wards for the care of new-born babies and infants, especially those with feeding difficulties.[20] The outpatient departments of children's hospitals gave advice to the mothers of healthy children as part of their activities, and a few larger hospitals also had milk kitchens. The *consultatiebureau* doctor participated in a wide-ranging programme for improving maternity care and women's and children's health services, and in the earliest years of the infant welfare movement, the private initiatives of doctors, often offering their services gratis, were crucial. Infant welfare mirrored the significance of private efforts in other areas of health care, representing the meeting point of public health work and services directed at women and children.

The high level of participation of doctors in the infant welfare movement was also linked to internal professional developments, the confirmation of obstetrics, gynaecology and paediatrics as special fields. It was only during the last decades of the nineteenth century that these specialities acquired their own university chairs, learned societies and journals. The *Nederlandse Gynaecologische Vereeniging* (Dutch Gynaecological Society) was initiated in 1887 and the *Nederlandsche Vereeniging voor Paediatrie* (Dutch Society of Paediatrics) in 1892.[21] Recently established, yet confident and expansionist, specialists were ready to take up the banner of infant welfare work, to grasp the opportunities offered, not only to reduce infant deaths, but to create new openings and a new sub-speciality.[22] Much more was at stake than 'jobs for the boys', but this clearly played a role. Many careers were built up in parallel with the growth of the infant welfare movement, with some 202 paediatricians and 171 general practitioners working in *consultatiebureaus* by 1930.[23]

The organization of infant welfare work

From country to country, regardless of the groups or individuals behind the setting up of services and the issuing of propaganda, solutions to the problem of high infant mortality were similar, differing in degree and the quality of services, rather than in content. Although much investment and energy was put into the creation of services for mothers and their new-born babies, the solutions of the Dutch campaigners were 'maternal' rather than 'material', based on advice rather than economic aid. The reduction in infant deaths was expected to follow on from the re-education of the mother, who would be persuaded not to work outside the home, to improve her domestic hygiene, to bathe, clothe and tend her infants properly, and above all else to breastfeed. The mother was to be taught by means of supervision at the *consultatiebureaus*, and through propaganda, courses, books and pamphlets. Material help was limited to the small-scale provision of free or subsidized milk.

The most important single initiative was taken in 1901, with the creation of the first *consultatiebureau* in The Hague.[24] Set up by a general practitioner, Dr B. P. B. Plantenga, its purpose was to provide close medical supervision of the healthy child, with enormous stress being placed on monitoring growth and feeding practices, and to give advice on general hygiene and care.[25] Strongly influenced by the French example, the *bureau* combined the *consultation des nourrissons* with the *goutte de lait*. Plantenga emphasized that the *consultatiebureau* was intended for rich and poor, and breastfed and bottle-fed infants, and he was a strong advocate of milk distribution. A milk depot was attached to the *bureau*, and the distribution of free and low cost milk was declared a priority; in 1902 Plantenga had seventy-four babies registered with his *bureau*, and, out of these, sixty-one had obtained milk or other infant food, half without charge.[26] The question of milk distribution was soon to become a source of fierce debate, many doctors arguing that mothers only came to the *consultatiebureau* to collect their free milk, abandoning breastfeeding because of the ease of obtaining bottled milk supplies. As one *bureau* doctor, expressing the most extreme view, claimed, 'It is mostly children of families where the mother is too stupid or too sloppy to prepare the food with enough care' who became dependent on milk kitchens.[27]

Plantenga's example was quickly followed, with or without the milk kitchen option. In 1903 a second *bureau* was established by Dr Vos, under the direction of the Public Health Department of Amsterdam's town council, followed by *bureaus* in Haarlem, Leiden, Rotterdam, Arnhem, Deventer, and Utrecht, all private initiatives. In Rotterdam the first *consultatiebureau*, complete with a milk kitchen, was opened by the local branch of the *Bond* in 1910, having grown out of the *Hygiënische melkstal 'De Vaan* (Hygienic milking parlour 'The Banner'), established by a group of local doctors in 1908. A second *bureau* opened its doors in Rotterdam in 1913.[28] By 1916 there was a total of fourteen *bureaus* concentrated in the major towns, in 1925 forty-seven. Following the introduction of government subsidies in 1927, the total had by 1929 risen sharply to 246, set up by the *Kruisvereenigingen*, the *Bond* and related organizations, and by a few local councils.[29] By 1930 the province of North Holland had a total of fifty *bureaus*. Some seventeen of these were in Amsterdam, all of which, by the 1930s, were run by the town council, but this was exceptional. Twenty-seven were organized by the *Kruisvereenigingen*, one by a district nursing society, and the remaining five by the *Bond* and associated organizations. North Brabant had forty-eight *bureaus*, run mainly by Catholic *Kruisvereenigingen*.[30]

Established paediatricians and obstetricians, with university chairs and senior hospital appointments, constituted the leadership of the infant welfare movement. The interest of obstetricians did not stop at the delivery of a healthy baby, but embraced the welfare of infants, their continued growth and well-being. Influential obstetric textbooks published around the turn of the century, including Hector Treub's *Leerboek der Verloskunde*, contained short chapters on infant care and feeding.[31] Pre-dating the emergence of neonatal sub-specialities, paediatricians were also much involved with research and services connected with infants. The volume produced to celebrate the fiftieth anniversary of the *Nederlandsche Vereeniging voor Kindergeneeskunde* in 1942 devoted a surprisingly large number of pages to infant welfare, which its membership had actively promoted, and which they clearly regarded as having been an important stepping stone in the development of their field.[32]

Bond activitists included B. P. B. Plantenga, J. H. G. Carstens, Israël Graanboom, honorary lecturer in paediatrics at the University of Amsterdam and founder of Amsterdam's second children's hospital in 1895, B. J. Kouwer, professor of obstetrics in Utrecht, G. Scheltema, professor of paediatrics in Groningen, Hector Treub, professor of obstetrics and gynaecology at the University of Amsterdam, and Cornelia de Lange, head of the infant ward at the Emma Kinderziekenhuis in Amsterdam. In 1927 De Lange was appointed to the chair of paediatrics in Amsterdam, becoming the first woman professor of medicine in Holland. The *Bond* was set up with the sole purpose of leading and guiding the infant welfare movement.[33] Largely self-supporting, but receiving government subsidies from 1927 onwards, it proved crucial in the spreading of propaganda, largely through its own publications, and in the co-ordination of activities, the setting up of *bureaus* and milk kitchens, the organization of mothercraft courses and training for *bakers* (maternity nurses), and home visiting. By 1931 there was a total of sixty-six branches of the *Bond* spread throughout the country, organized chiefly by local doctors.[34]

The day-to-day running of the *consultatiebureaus* became the responsibility of paediatricians and general practitioners, many of whom, largely on their own initiative, had previously held special consulting hours for infants. In 1912 Nicolaas Knapper Czn., an Amsterdam general practitioner, began to set aside special consulting hours for the infants of his sick fund patients. In 1917 the *Bond* published the text of a lecture by Knapper promoting the uptake of such work by general practitioners as an effective means of reducing infant mortality.[35] And while the *Bond* was important in directing infant welfare work, it also encouraged the efforts of general practitioners to reduce infant deaths. Individual doctors responded to the high infant death rate in a variety of ways, especially in the early years of the century, before a wide network of services had been established. In 1907 Dr Th. H. van de Velde, who worked as an obstetrician in Haarlem, set up a fund to help poor lying-in women, and organized courses for maternity nurses, who were to nurse women for two to three weeks following birth. His work combined the aims of helping poor women to recover from delivery and of reducing infant deaths in Haarlem.[36]

From the 1920s onwards, infant welfare work was increasingly controlled and standardized, under the provincial networks set up by the *Bond* and *Kruisvereenigingen*, and as a result of the appointment of state inspectors of children's health under the Third Health Act of 1919. The *Kruisvereenigingen* appointed their own district supervisors, some of whom became very influential. After his appointment in 1919 as provincial children's doctor to the *Groene Kruis* (Green Cross Society), the 'great enthusiasm' and 'high ideals' of the paediatrician Dr H. P. J. Koenen was said to have greatly strengthened the infant welfare movement in the predominantly Catholic province of Limburg. Heading the three local *consultatiebureaus*, Koenen successfully propagated his ideas among general practitioners and specialists, and the local population.[37]

Depending upon the size and location of the *bureau*, doctors were assisted by specialized infant nurses or district nurses, and sometimes voluntary workers. The eventual aim of many, including the *Bond* leadership, was to turn the direction of the *bureaus* over to paediatricians with a special interest in infants, but in many rural areas this was impossible to implement. Overall, however, paediatricians outnumbered general practitioners as *bureau* workers. By 1930 forty-nine paediatricians and twenty-one general practitioners headed the *consultatiebureaus* in urbanized South Holland, thirty-seven and thirteen in North Holland, but general practitioners took on a larger proportion of the work in rural areas.[38]

The propaganda message and the development of maternity services

Bureau work was supplemented by mothercraft courses, taught by paediatricians and general practitioners in towns, and nurses trained in infant care in the countryside. Reams of literature appeared on infant care and hygiene. Knapper listed thirty-four small works and twenty-eight large volumes published between 1919 and 1935, the majority written by paediatricians, obstetricians, and general practitioners, and a few by midwives and lay people, plus some fourteen journals aimed at the general public.[39] The books ranged from small pamphlets costing a few cents to detailed technical works on every aspect of the child in sickness and in health, such as Cornelia de Lange's volume, which, covering the years from birth to puberty, dealt with a broad range of topics from sickness to the selection of educational toys.[40] Interesting departures included tips to parents in the form of rhymes and pictures, and a volume published in 1934 aimed specifically at sailors' children. Many of these books went through numerous editions, indicating popularity. A travelling museum, the *Nationaal reizend Museum voor Ouders en Opvoeders*, was created to take the message around the country. In 1926 the *Bond* produced a film, running for some two hours, with the rather predictable theme of 'before and after the *consultatiebureau* visit', starring Plantenga as the *bureau* doctor.[41]

The overriding message of infant welfare propaganda was that responsibility for infant health lay with the mother; babies did not need to be protected from their environment or from poverty, but from inept and inadequate mothers, especially those shirking their duty by refusing to breastfeed. Infant deaths were largely attributed to improper feeding practices, poor hygiene and neglect. As the *Bond* literature declared, 'The sicknesses and deaths of healthy born children result mostly from mistakes made in their care and feeding. The mistakes are in general not made on purpose, but because the mother, especially if she is young and inexperienced, does not know what she should do'.[42] Above all else the mother was encouraged, compelled even, to breastfeed.[43] In the words of De Snoo, a leading obstetrician and head of the state school for midwives in Rotterdam, 'Concerning the feeding of the child we can be very brief, *she must, whenever it is possible, exist on mother's milk*'.[44] An impressive series of surveys, which dated back to the mid-nineteenth century, justified this emphasis. Reports covering the years 1908 to 1912, for example, showed the death rate of bottle-fed children in The Hague to be five times higher than that of breastfed children. Over 300 bottle fed babies out of every thousand born to the lower classes of The Hague died before reaching their first birthday, compared with sixty-three breastfed infants. Similar discrepancies were noted amongst higher social groups, emphasizing, for the infant welfare worker, the importance of maternal care above material and environmental factors.[45] Lower infant death rates amongst agricultural and Jewish populations and women who did not work outside the home were all attributed to higher rates of breastfeeding.[46]

Propaganda is not always paralleled by a development of supporting services.[47] Yet, although the maternal solution was stressed over material help in Dutch propaganda, work to reduce infant mortality was largely based on institutions, and considerable investment was made in setting up the *consultatiebureaus* and related services. Despite the opposition of those doctors who believed that milk provision encouraged lazy mothers to switch to bottle-feeding, many *consultatiebureaus* opted to provide milk, though recognizing this as a poor second to breastfeeding; by 1916, all but two of the fourteen *bureaus* had attached milk kitchens.[48] Milk and other infant foods were also provided on a small and varying scale to mothers by a few town councils, outpatient clinics and charitable institutions. The Rotterdam *consultatiebureau* staff saw milk provision as an important, though never large, aspect of their work. In 1910 forty-five children received milk, sixteen gratis, in situations where the mother was either considered incapable of feeding without help, or where the infant was failing to thrive. In 1914 the town's two *bureaus* had some 1,305 infants registered; 195 of these had received milk during the year. By 1933 the success of the eight Rotterdam *bureaus* was demonstrated in annual reports by the high attendance figures, with 4,850 infants being brought to the *bureaus* during the year, compared with the low demand for bottled milk, with only three to four containers being provided daily.[49]

By the 1920s many doctors participating in infant welfare work were recommending an expansion and unification of services to cover all aspects of motherhood and childhood. Dr Koenen, provincial children's doctor in Limburg, advocated the setting up of *consultatiebureaus* and milk kitchens, children's hospitals, mothercraft courses, improved obstetric and maternity services, factory crèches, and special help for large families.[50] In a paper presented to the general meeting of the *Bond* in 1924, Christine Bader, *bureau* doctor, school medical inspector, and state inspector for children's health in Limburg, stressed that work to reduce infant deaths should form just a small part of a more far-reaching programme, which would include prenatal care, access to trained midwives, an improved maternity nursing service, *consultatiebureaus* for pre-school children, and a school medical service.[51] Her concern about the lapse in the supervision of children between infancy and primary school age – 'healthy babies' becoming 'pale, nervous and feeble children' – inspired her to set up the first open-air nursery school in Holland in 1920.[52] Bader's proposals projected a future perfected service for mothers and children, but by 1925 much of what she was suggesting had been achieved, although levels of coverage varied from region to region. Three state midwife training schools had opened (Amsterdam 1861, Rotterdam 1882 and Heerlen 1913); hospital deliveries had slowly increased, catering especially for difficult pregnancies and births;[53] an organized maternity nursing service, staffed by trained and licensed nurses, was being extended; *consultatiebureaus* were expanding to include pre-school children; a school medical service established in 1904 was increasing its coverage; and in larger towns crèche facilities for the children of working mothers were being set up.

The message received

The creation of services is a two-way process, dependent on both the energy of those setting up and staffing facilities, and the response of those for whom the services are intended. The existence of the *consultatiebureaus* and a body of advice literature, even if backed up by high attendance figures (which was certainly not the case in early years) and a proliferation of services, does not indicate uncritical acceptance of the advice tendered. Attendances tell us little about attitudes. Many mothers may have visited the *consultatiebureau* to obtain free milk, to have their babies weighed, or to meet other mothers, without attending to the advice offered by the new experts; others may have been convinced by the new childrearing theories without ever attending a *bureau*.

The *bureau* staff placed great emphasis on attracting mothers, especially first-time ones, and on providing a suitable clinical environment. It is, however, questionable whether mothers shared the need doctors perceived, especially in the larger towns, of having carefully planned, orderly, spotless,

Plate 4.1 The examination room of an infant welfare clinic, Public Health Department, Amsterdam, *c.* 1930

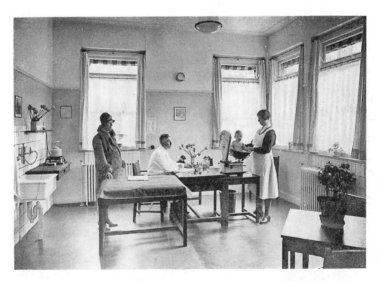

Source: R. N. M. Eykel, *Overzicht over het Sociaal Hygiënisch Werk in Nederland op het Gebeid van den Dienst der Volksgezondheid* ('s-Gravenhage, 1932), facing p. 44.

purpose-built institutions, rather than using church halls, cafés, neighbourhood buildings, and schools, where, as the Amsterdam *bureau* chief Van der Zande remarked, 'Now and then one of the infants was kind enough to ensure that the ink was substantially watered down'![54] The importance was recognized of offering frequent opening and short waiting times for hard-pressed working-class mothers, but photographs of packed waiting rooms show that this often failed to materialize.

Failing to attract large numbers or the very poor which they were especially aimed at, the *consultatiebureaus* often had a slow start. In 1903 only 160 mothers attended Amsterdam's four town council *bureaus*, a figure which increased to 294 in 1913.[55] Numbers rose steadily for individual *bureaus;* the number of mothers attending at the *bureau* set up by the *Amsterdamsche Vereeniging voor Zuigelingen* (Amsterdam Society for Infants) increased from 215 in 1910 to 911 in 1918,[56] and for the town as a whole, to 9 per cent of live births in 1920, 43 per cent in 1925, and 55 per cent in 1930.[57] In spite of the still low attendance figures, in 1921 Dr C. J. Brenkman, one of Amsterdam's *bureau* doctors, claimed that the problem was not only that of persuading mothers to attend, but also of correcting a shortage of facilities, which he believed would need to be doubled in Amsterdam.[58] Perhaps surprisingly, Brenkman's calculation proved to be an underestimate, with attendance not doubling but increasing five-fold between 1920 and 1930.

Not all towns and regions had such a high level of success, and the Amsterdam figures disguise low attendance rates in some parts of the city. Some small towns achieved good attendance figures, such as Emmen in the east of the country, where it was claimed that out of the 140 children born in 1933, two-thirds were registered at the *consultatiebureau;* over the year there were a total of 917 consultations, an average of ten per child.[59] Attendance was often poorer in isolated rural areas; although the percentage of infants registered was not necessarily lower than in the towns, attendance was more irregular.[60] National figures show that much remained to be done, for although the number of *consultatiebureaus*, greatly stimulated by state subsidies, had increased almost seven-fold between 1926 and 1930 to 383, and the number of infants registered almost five-fold to over 47,000, many infants were still not being reached. In 1925 only 77 out of every 1,000 live births recorded came to be registered at the *bureaus;* by 1930 this had increased to 259, but still three-quarters of babies born in the Netherlands never attended a *bureau*.[61]

Bureau doctors struggled to rid mothers of what they considered out-dated and wrong-headed notions, and from the influence of their mothers, neighbours and untrained maternity nurses. The problem of unregulated maternity nurses, '*wilde kraamhulp*', was still being referred to as late as 1946.[62] As well as tradition and religious beliefs, cost and housing conditions were important factors in influencing the take up of the new ideas. Adaptation to the new methods of rearing infants was expensive, and the achievement of the high standards of hygiene required by the experts was beyond many poor households.[63] The good advice proffered was often misguided, given that home circumstances and poverty made it impossible to implement. Moreover, the philosophy of *bureau* doctors and poor mothers failed to converge at many points. Letters sent to Amsterdam *bureau* doctors early in the century illustrate the despair of mothers who could not convince the new experts of the need for their babies to gain weight at maximum speed.[64] The *bureau* doctor was unable to appreciate the anxiety of mothers whose babies grew more slowly than those of their neighbours. For the mother, the shame of having a 'skinny' child was a sure indication of poverty and inability to provide. Meanwhile, the mother who stuffed her children full of cereals, producing an overweight *pap kind* (porridge child), remained the bane of the *bureau* staff. However, the popularity of the advice literature[65] and the rising numbers taking advantage of the mothercraft courses were positive signs for the *bureau* doctors. In 1926, 164 mothercraft courses were organized with 2,303 subscribers; by 1930, with the help of state subsidies, the number had increased to 294, with 7,176 mothers attending.[66]

The question of whether medicalization is imposed from above or involves a converging of the opinions of experts and clients remains an open one. The campaigns of women seeking hospital deliveries and pain relief in childbirth in England and the United States[67] and the demands of the English Women's Co-operative Guild for maternity benefits[68] – examples of consumer pressure leading to a stepping up of institutionalization and medicalization[69] – had few parallels in Holland.[70] None the less, a number of Dutch women's organizations were working to improve maternity services, and the spread of knowledge on childbirth and infant care. This included the small Dutch Women's Co-operative Guild and other larger organizations campaigning for better working and social conditions for women. In both aims and timing these women's organizations had much in common with the doctor-led infant welfare movement, and co-operation was achieved at several points. A number of female-run voluntary organizations, set up around 1900 to provide maternity nursing, mothercraft courses and crèche facilities, enjoyed the support of doctors, many of whom offered their services gratis.[71] Within the *Bond* itself, lay women, usually wealthy and educated with time on their hands, played an increasingly important role, in fund-raising efforts, committee work, and as voluntary workers in the *bureaus*.

Conclusion

The solutions offered by Dutch infant welfare workers were far from unique. Yet, with a predominantly medical leadership and specialized work-force, services were quickly built up, especially in the late 1920s, following the introduction of state funding. The *consultatiebureaus* soon formed an impressive network, although concern was expressed, justly, about the unevenness of coverage. The countryside remained a special problem; well into the 1930s many areas, especially in the south, were untouched by the impact of *consultatiebureaus*, trained maternity nurses, or even qualified midwives. By 1930 there had been a great increase in *bureau* attendances, reflecting not only increased funding, but also their growing popularity. However, a great many babies were still not being reached.

The drive of medical practitioners involved in the movement was of great significance. For many the *consultatiebureaus* offered not simply one solution, but the *only* solution to the problem of infant deaths. They concentrated expertise and facilities in one building, saw large numbers of babies, and looked at all aspects of infancy, in sickness and in health, and as Carstens affirmed in 1922, they could not, and should not, be replaced by any other form of service.[72] As to their effectiveness, doctors involved in infant welfare were often hard pressed to claim positive results for their work. For while infant mortality fell in regions well served by *bureaus*, it also fell where they had made less impact.

Plate 4.2 Mothercraft course in Drenthe, the Netherlands, organized by the Green Cross Society, *c.* 1930

Source: R. N. M. Eykel, *Overzicht over het Sociaal Hygiënisch Werk in Nederland op het Gebeid van den Dienst der Volksgezondheid* ('s-Gravenhage, 1932), facing p. 52.

Infant deaths remained highest in the rural Catholic areas of the south, where they had always been high, despite the efforts of local *bureau* workers.

Those involved in infant welfare, individuals whose careers were built up or strengthened in parallel with the expansion of the movement, confirmed Carsten's conclusions. In the early years, however, those who were left out of such work, in particular the general practitioner and sick fund doctor, who believed that the *consultatiebureaus* robbed them of patients, were less easy to convince. But, by the 1920s, the *Bond* leadership had successfully involved general practitioners in work to reduce infant mortality. The emphasis of the work was also changing by the 1920s, from combating infant deaths to keeping babies healthy. What had started as a professional lobby was evolving into a health lobby. *Consultatiebureau* work was being absorbed into preventive medicine, becoming the province of the '*sociale kinderarts*' (social paediatrician), a separate sub-speciality. Infant welfare work, in its pioneering years, no doubt intensified the expert knowledge of paediatricians, and helped consolidate the specialists, but by the 1920s this group was spreading this knowledge effectively to family doctors, midwives, and the lay public.

Acknowledgements

I would like to thank Lara Marks, Valerie Fildes, Frank Huisman, Mart van Lieburg, and Elizabeth Peretz for commenting on earlier versions of this paper.

Notes

1. J. H. G. Carstens, 'Consultatiebureaus voor zuigelingen en melkkeukens', *Ned. Tijdschr. Geneesk.*, 66 IIB (1922), 1859–67.

2. For the role of doctors, in particular paediatricians, in infant welfare work in the USA and Canada, see K. W. Jones, 'Sentiment and science: the late nineteenth century pediatrician as mother's advisor', *J. Soc. Hist.*, 17 (1983), 79–96; R. A. Meckel, *Save the Babies: American Public Health Reform and the Prevention of Infant Mortality 1850–1929* (Baltimore and London, 1990), esp. ch. 2; and ch. 5 by Cynthia Comacchio.

3. B. R. Mitchell, *European Historical Statistics 1750–1970* (New York, 1975), 40–1.

4. Mitchell, *European Historical Statistics*, 43.

5. J. H. de Haas, *Kindersterfte in Nederland. Child Mortality in the Netherlands*, pub. in Dutch and English in one vol. (Assen, 1956), 80–3. See also R. I. Woods, P. A. Watterson, and J. H. Woodward, 'The causes of rapid infant mortality decline in England and Wales, 1861–1921', pt I, *Popul. Stud.*, 42 (1988), 348–50. For the relationship between Dutch infant mortality decline and social and economic factors, see C. Vandenbroeke, F. van Poppel, and A.M. van der Woude, 'Le développement séculaire de la mortalité aux jeunes âges dans le territoire du Bénélux', *Ann. Démog. Hist.* (1983), 257–89; F. van Poppel, 'The relationship between socioeconomic position and infant and childhood mortality in the Netherlands in the period 1850–1940', in *International Population Conference Manila 1981* (Liège, 1983), vol. 5, 649–89.

6. C. van Tussenbroek, *De ontwikkeling der aseptische verloskunde in Nederland* (Haarlem, 1911), 212.

7. I. Loudon, 'Maternal mortality: 1880–1950. Some regional and international comparisons', *Soc. Hist. Med.*, 1 (1988), 186. See also ch. 1 by Irvine Loudon.

8. C. Vandenbroeke, F. van Poppel, and A. M. van der Woude, 'De zuigelingen en kindersterfte in België en Nederland in seculair perspectief', *Tijdschr. Gesch.*, 94 (1981), 481. Religious practices seem to have influenced regional mortality variations, including infant deaths. In the Catholic regions of the south, shorter periods of maternal breastfeeding, the tradition of binding the breasts of young girls, and low levels of schooling were all potential influences on infant survival. See F. van Poppel, 'Religion and health: Catholicism and regional mortality differences in 19th-century Netherlands', *Soc. Hist. Med.* (forthcoming).

9. P. A. Barentsen, 'Over de kindersterfte ten plattenlande van Oost-Noordbrabant', *Ned. Tijdschr. Geneesk.*, 66 IIA (1922), 610–22; J. van Galen and A. Mevis, 'Zuigelingenzorg in Oost-Brabant, 1918–1940', in N.Bakker *et al.* (eds), *Een tipje van de sluier. Vrouwengeschiedenis in Nederland* (Amsterdam, 1980), vol. 2, 73–83; M. Pruijt, 'Roeien, baren en in de arbeid zijn. Vroedvrouwen in Noord-Brabant, 1880–1960', in M. Grever and A. van der Veen (eds), *Bij ons moeder en ons Jet. Brabantse vrouwen in de 19de en 20ste eeuw* ('s-Hertogenbosch, 1989), 122–42.

10. D.E. Watkins, 'The English revolution in social medicine, 1889–1911', unpub. Ph.D. thesis, University of London, 1984.

11. For the organization of infant and maternity care on a local basis, see H. Marland, 'A pioneer in infant welfare: "The Huddersfield Scheme", 1903–1920', *Soc. Hist. Med.* (forthcoming); L. Marks, 'Irish and Jewish women's experience of childbirth and infant care in East London 1870–1939: the responses of host society and immigrant communities to medical welfare needs', unpub. D.Phil. thesis, University of Oxford, 1990, esp. ch. 8; E. Peretz, 'A maternity service for England and Wales: local authority maternity care in the inter-war period in Oxfordshire and Tottenham', in J. Garcia, R. Kilpatrick and M. Richards (eds) *The Politics of Maternity Care* (Oxford, 1990), 30–46;

idem, 'Regional variation in maternal and child welfare between the wars: Merthyr Tydfil, Oxfordshire and Tottenham', in D. Foster and P. Swan (eds), *Essays in Regional and Local History* (Hull, 1992).

12. For infant welfare work at the regional level, see A. C. Drogendijk, *De verloskundige voorziening in Dordrecht van 1500 tot heden* (Amsterdam, 1935); J. H. Hagenbeek, *Het moederschap in Overijssel. Een onderzoek naar de verloskundige en de zuigelingenzorg in de provincie Overijssel* (Zwolle, 1936); P. E. G. van der Heijden, 'De zorg voor moeder en kind in Noord-Brabant', doctoral thesis, University of Amsterdam, 1934; J. H. Starmans, *Verloskunde en kindersterfte in Limburg. Folklore: geschiedenis: heden* (Maastricht, 1930), and the works cited in note 9.

13. See, for example, J. Spoorenberg, 'De opvoeding van arbeidersvrouwen. Zuigelingenzorg in Amsterdam 1903–40', unpub. diss., University of Amsterdam, 1981.

14. For the background to this development, see E. S. Houwaart, *De hygiënisten. Artsen, staat & volksgezondheid in Nederland 1840–1890* (Groningen, 1991).

15. With the exception of Amsterdam's municipal health department. See Spoorenberg, 'De opvoeding van arbeidersvrouwen'. For an overview of preventive medicine, see A. Querido, *The Development of Socio-Medical Care in the Netherlands* (London and New York, 1968), and H. Marland, 'Public health in the Netherlands 1780–1945: from medical police to state collectivism', unpublished paper, 1991.

16. The full history of the *Kruisvereenigingen* remains to be written, but see A. Querido, *De Wit-Gele Vlam. Gedenkboek ter gelegenheid van het 50-jarig bestaan van de Nationale Federatie het Wit-Gele Kruis 1923–1973* (Tilburg, 1973).

17. M. Bosch, 'Blauwkousen en hobbezakken in een witte jas. De eerste vrouwelijke artsen in Nederland, 1872–1913', in J. Blok *et al.*, *Derde Jaarboek voor Vrouwengeschiedenis* (Nijmegen, 1982), 63–97; H. Marland, 'The half open door: the education and careers of early women doctors in the Netherlands, 1878–1930', in M. J. van Lieburg and H. Marland (eds), *Medical Practitioners in the Netherlands 1700–1930* (Rotterdam, forthcoming).

18. H. Marland, '"A woman's touch": women doctors and the development of health services for women and children in the Netherlands 1879–c.1925', in H. Binneveld and R. Dekker (eds), *Sickness and History in the Netherlands* (Hilversum, forthcoming).

19. M. J. van Lieburg, *Het Sophia Kinderziekenhuis 1863–1975* (Rotterdam, 1975).

20. J. Gewin, 'Ziekenhuis-verpleging van zuigelingen', *Ned. Tijdschr. Geneesk.*, 53 IA (1909), 625–39.

21. For the consolidation of obstetrics and gynaecology, see F. J. J. van Assen (ed.) *Een Eeuw Vrouwenarts* (Amsterdam, 1987), and for paediatrics, Nederlandsche Vereeniging voor Kindergeneeskunde, *De Ontwikkeling van de Kindergeneeskunde in de Afgeloopen 50 Jaar* (Leiden, 1942); S. van Creveld, 'De ontwikkeling van de kindergeneeskunde in de laatste 75 jaren', *Maandschr. Kindergeneesk.*, 35 (1967), 109–24; and A. de Knecht-van Eekelen, *Naar een Rationele Zuigelingenvoeding*.

The medicalization of motherhood

Voedingsleer en Kindergeneeskunde in Nederland 1840–1914 (Nijmegen, 1984), ch. 3.

22. For the utilization of specialist hospitals in career building, see L. Granshaw, '"Fame and fortune by means of bricks and mortar": the medical profession and specialist hospitals in Britain, 1800–1948', in L. Granshaw and R. Porter (eds), *The Hospital in History* (London and New York, 1989), 199–220.

23. R. N. M. Eykel, *Overzicht over het Sociaal Hygiënisch Werk in Nederland op het Gebeid van den Dienst der Volksgezondheid* ('s-Gravenhage, 1932), 46–51.

24. For the organization of the *consultatiebureaus*, see Eykel, *Overzicht* and N. Knapper, *Een Kwart Eeuw Zuigelingenzorg in Nederland* (Amsterdam, 1935).

25. B. P. B. Plantenga, 'Kindersterfte en zuigelingenklinieken', *Ned. Tijdschr. Geneesk.*, 38 II (1902), 922–8.

26. Plantenga, 'Kindersterfte en zuigelingenklinieken', 926.

27. F. van der Zande, *Ervaringen van een consultatiebureau-leider in Amsterdam* (Amsterdam, n.d.), 17.

28. *Jubileum Verslag over 25 Jaar van de Rotterdamsche Vereeniging tot Bescherming van Zuigelingen* (n.p., 1935).

29. Eykel, *Overzicht*, 45.

30. Eykel, *Overzicht*, 46–7.

31. H. Treub, *Leerboek der Verloskunde*, 3rd edn (Haarlem, 1905).

32. *De Ontwikkeling van de Kindergeneeskunde.*

33. *Gids voor de Zuigelingenbescherming tevens Tweede Jaarboekje uitgegeven door den Nederlandschen Bond tot Bescherming van Zuigelingen, 1917.*

34. Eykel, *Overzicht*, 26.

35. *Een raadplegingsdienst voor zuigelingen in de algemeene praktijk.* Cited in De Knecht-van Eekelen, *Naar een Rationele Zuigelingenvoeding,* 78, 316. Knapper later wrote one of the standard works on Dutch infant welfare work, *Een Kwart Eeuw Zuigelingenzorg.*

36. Th. H. van de Velde, *Verbeterde Verzorging van Minvermogende Kraamvrouwen* (Haarlem, 1907).

37. R. Philips, *Gezondheidszorg in Limburg. Groei en acceptatie van de gezondheidsvoorzieningen 1850–1940* (Assen, 1980), 213–14. See also Starmans, *Verloskunde en Kindersterfte in Limburg*, 286–350.

38. Eykel, *Overzicht*, 46–51.

39. Knapper, *Een Kwart Eeuw Zuigelingenzorg*, 140–7.

40. C. de Lange, *De Geestelijke en Lichamelijke Opvoeding van Het Kind*, 4th edn (Amsterdam, 1914).

41. *Tijdschr. Soc. Geneesk.*, 4 (1926), 6–8.

42. *Handleiding bij de Verzorging van den Zuigeling* (Utrecht, n.d.) (pub. jointly by the *Bond* and Dutch Society of Children's Doctors), 3.

43. For infant feeding, see De Knecht-van Eekelen, *Naar een Rationele Zuigelingenvoeding,* and, for a summary in English, 'Towards a rational infant-feeding: the science of nutrition and paediatrics in the Netherlands 1840–1914', in J. Cule and T. Turner (eds), *Child Care through the Centuries* (Cardiff, 1986), 153–64.

44. K. de Snoo, *Beknopt Leerboek der Verloskunde* (Groningen and

Den Haag, 1922), 304 (his emphasis).

45. *Sterfte in Verband met Voedingswijze en Sociale Omstandigheden onder de kinderen beneden het jaar in 1908 geboren te 's-Gravenhage en Scheveningen,* 3 vols ('s-Gravenhage, 1911, 1912, 1913); H. W. A. Voorhoeve (ed.) *75 jaar Kinderhygiëne in Nederland* (Assen and Amsterdam, 1977), 4–5.

46. De Knecht-van Eekelen, *Naar een Rationele Zuigelingenvoeding,* 213–38; J. A. Verdoorn, *Het Gezondheidswezen te Amsterdam in de 19e Eeuw* (Nijmegen, 1981), 189–207.

47. As is well evidenced by English infant welfare work. See, for example, J. Lewis, *The Politics of Motherhood* (London, 1980), and the works cited in note 11.

48. Eykel, *Overzicht,* 45.

49. *Jubileum Verslag,* 8, 12.

50. Philips, *Gezondheidszorg in Limburg,* 214.

51. C. Bader, 'Wat kunnen wij doen om onze gezond geboren kinderen tot gezonde menschen te doen opgroeien?', *Tijdschr. Soc. Geneesk.,* 3 (1925), 2–4, 20–3.

52. W. H. Posthumus-van der Goot and Anna de Waal (eds) *Van Moeder op Dochter. De Maatschappelijke Positie van de Vrouw in Nederland vanaf de Franse Tijd* (Utrecht and Antwerp, 1968, repr. Nijmegen, 1977), 175–6.

53. See M. J. van Lieburg and H. Marland, 'Midwife regulation, education, and practice in the Netherlands during the nineteenth century', *Med. Hist.,* 33 (1989), 296–317, esp. pp. 306–9, 313–14.

54. F. van der Zande, 'Over de inrichting van een consultatie-bureau voor zuigelingen', *Tijdschr. Soc. Geneesk.,* 2 (1924), 40.

55. Jaarverslagen van de G. G. D., 1904, 1913. Cited Spoorenberg, 'De opvoeding van arbeidersvrouwen', 49.

56. Jaarverslagen van de Amsterdamsche Vereeniging voor Zuigelingenzorg, 1913, 1918. Cited in Spoorenberg, 'De opvoeding van arbeidersvrouwen'.

57. Spoorenberg, 'De opvoeding van arbeidersvrouwen', 50; *Tijdschr. Soc. Geneesk.,* 10 (1932), 221.

58. C. J. Brenkman, 'Zuigelingenzorg te Amsterdam', *Soc. Med. Maandschr.,* 1 (1921), 140–2.

59. Knapper, *Een Kwart Eeuw Zuigelingenzorg,* 84.

60. H. P. J. Koenen, 'Zuigelingenbescherming op het platteland', *Tijdschr. Soc. Geneesk.,* 2 (1924), 219.

61. Eykel, *Overzicht,* 51–2.

62. *Tijdschr. Soc. Geneesk.,* 24 (1946), 140–3.

63. See ch. 12 by Elizabeth Peretz.

64. J. Spoorenberg, 'Bakerpraat of doktersadvies? Arbeidersvrouwen en zuigelingenzorg in Amsterdam tussen 1900 en 1914', in A. Angerman *et al.* (eds), *Een tipje van de sluier. Vrouwengeschiedenis in Nederland* (Amsterdam, 1984), vol. 3, 78–95.

65. This coincided with rising levels of literacy amongst women. In 1908 primary education became compulsory for women, and by 1928 it was claimed that all women under 25 years of age had attended school. Around 1900 there was also an enormous increase in women's

journals, aimed at all levels of Dutch society. Posthumus-van der Goot and de Waal, *Van Moeder op Dochter*, 161; I. Polak (ed.), *Geloof mij vrij, Mevrouw. Een bloemlezing uit vrouwentijdschriften tussen 1870 en 1920* (Amsterdam, 1984).

66. Eykel, *Overzicht*, 60.

67. See J. W. Leavitt, 'Birthing and anaesthesia: the debate over Twilight Sleep', *Signs*, 6 (1980), 147–64; *idem, Brought to Bed: Childbearing in America, 1750 to 1950* (New York and Oxford, 1986), and J. Beinart, 'Obstetric analgesia and the control of childbirth in twentieth-century Britain', in Garcia *et al., Politics of Maternity Care*, 119–21.

68. M. L. Davies (ed.), *Maternity. Letters from Working Women* (London, 1915, repr. 1978).

69. See J. Lewis, 'Mothers and maternity policies in the twentieth century', in Garcia *et al., Politics of Maternity Care*, 15–29, for an account of the changing demands of English women with regard to maternity services.

70. But in the area of birth control, the coinciding aims of expert and consumer is well illustrated by Aletta Jacobs's work amongst the poor of Amsterdam. Both the need she perceived, and the demands of her patients, led her to set up courses in hygiene and child care and free consultation hours for poor mothers and their babies. Contact with these women later inspired her birth control work. A. Jacobs, *Herinneringen* (Amsterdam, 1924, 5th edn, Nijmegen, 1985), and A. Jacobs, 'The first birth control clinic', in E. S. Riemer and J. C. Fout (eds) *European Women. A Documentary History, 1789–1945* (Brighton, 1980), 214–16.

71. *Nationale Vrouwenraad van Nederland* (opgericht 29 Oct. 1898).

72. Carstens, 'Consultatiebureaux voor zuigelingen en melkkeukens'. See also the studies in note 12, for confirmation of the importance accredited by doctors to *consultatiebureaus* in the different regions of the Netherlands.

5

'The infant soldier': early child welfare efforts in Ontario

Cynthia R. Comacchio

Internationally, the turn of the century brought a new appreciation of childhood, a cultural awakening which manifested itself in a new awareness of the importance of childrearing methods in shaping healthy, well-rounded and productive adults.[1] The medical speciality of paediatrics also progressed with the general growth of scientific medicine in the later nineteenth century. At the same time, Canadian social reformers were opening their eyes to what they perceived as an acute need to protect and reinforce the home and family against the evils unleashed by increasing industrialization and urbanization. Children became the focus of their efforts. The opening decades of the twentieth century saw the evolution of a complex institutional structure designed to serve child welfare concerns and to socialize the results of medical advances. It would take the impact of the First World War, however, to enlarge the campaign's scope and organize its efforts behind the expressly-qualified leadership of the medical profession.

The pace and nature of change – social, economic, cultural and political – were intensified by Canada's experience during the First World War. Both historians and contemporary observers agree that this war represents a watershed in Canadian history, the true beginning of modern Canada.[2] Various reformist groups, foremost among them the Social Gospel movement, were infused with new hope for the Canadian society that would rise from the ashes of war.[3] The Great War also had a profound effect on the medical profession in Canada. Canadian medicine expanded its contours with achievements in research, teaching and internal organization.[4] By the close of the Great War, physicians had risen to the forefront of a

97

burgeoning movement to save and improve the lives of Canadian children. As they saw it, modernization had complicated the parenting process. Traditional childrearing methods were outmoded, ineffective, and even dangerous. Science, they believed, held the key to salvation for the nation's children.

With the increased specialization taking place in medicine, information about such basic matters as health and child-care escaped the grasp of the interested lay person. At the same time, societal complexity had induced permanent changes in the old relationships of family and neighbourhood. The new child-rearing experts were only too happy to fill the void created by these developments. The means would be the education of Canadian parents in modern scientific methods by those best qualified to teach them: the physicians. Physicians believed, with some justification, that if they could guide mothers and influence their behaviour towards their children, they would be faced with fewer cases of the preventable yet frequently fatal diseases of childhood. Using the imagery of wartime, they depicted the mother as the 'first line of defence' for the helpless 'infant soldier' whose preservation depended on her 'training, education and preparation'.[5] Early attempts to advise mothers on infant feeding and hygiene evolved into an authoritative system for habit training and socialization during the interwar period. In the 1920s and 1930s, the art of motherhood was transformed into the science of 'mothercraft'.[6] The medical profession dominated the child welfare campaign throughout the interwar period, until the exigencies of another global emergency saw its gradual demise.

While the child welfare campaign was national in scope, this examination concentrates on its manifestations in Ontario. Ontario deserves to be considered the leader in the campaign. It was the first province to establish a child welfare division as part of its Board of Health. Toronto's Hospital for Sick Children was the first of its kind in Canada. The pre-eminent Canadian paediatrician of this period and the campaign's unofficial 'grand master' was the hospital's Dr Alan Brown. Both the city and the province provided national leadership in the health and welfare fields. Finally, in the socio-economic sphere, Ontario was the first province to experience the full impact of modernizing forces: it was both the industrial and cultural prototype for a modern Canada.

'The infant soldier'
Early child welfare efforts in Canada

Medical management of childhood developed gradually out of
the ideological shift of the late nineteenth century. In its initial,
prewar phase, it was expressed mainly through an increasing
interest in childhood ailments and greater medical participation in local drives to reduce infant mortality.[7] It was not until
the immediate postwar years that Canadian paediatrics itself
began to acquire a more distinct professional form. As paediatric specialization gathered strength and prestige internationally, leading to the creation of the Canadian Society for
the Study of the Diseases of Children in 1922, physicians carved
out a much larger role for themselves in the care and training
of the nation's children.[8] Although Canadian paediatricians
were few in number throughout the entire period, their express
interest in the conservation and improvement of child life and
their precise knowledge of the child's emotional and physical
make-up made natural leaders of the reform-minded within
their restricted circle.

The medical profession acknowledged and encouraged the
new cultural attitudes towards childhood.[9] At the turn of the
century, however, their social consciousness remained largely
within the bounds of their own field. Consequently, physicians
focused their attention on the progress that had been made in
treating the diseases of children in the late nineteenth
century.[10] Until the first decade of the twentieth century, infant
mortality was not considered a matter for public concern. The
prevailing attitude was one of resignation, at times even a
Darwinistic view grounded in the notion of the 'survival of the
fittest'.[11] The medical profession began in earnest to raise the
cry to save the children just as social reformers in Canada were
becoming aware of the gravity of the problem.[12] Medical
specialization was hailed as a positive force in encouraging both
general and professional acceptance of the value of preventive
medicine. In 1913, Dr A. H. Wright, Chairman of the Ontario
Board of Health, asserted that

> We believe . . . that the general practitioner and the
> specialist will work together and thus accomplish the
> greatest possible good in the interests of suffering
> humanity . . . We believe that even now a large portion of
> the public would prefer to pay the doctors for keeping

99

their children well instead of waiting until they get sick before asking for professional treatment.[13]

Prevention was important for pragmatic as well as purely altruistic reasons. In the early twentieth century, paediatric medicine was far more effective in preventing than in actually treating childhood diseases.

From the late nineteenth century until 1920 attempts to deal in an organized fashion with infant morbidity and mortality were largely in the hands of private philanthropy. In particular, middle-class female reformers took up the cause as an appropriate component of the 'social mothering' platform of women's organizations.[14] Various turn-of-the-century campaigns aiming to reduce infant mortality were conducted by social reformers, public health advocates, and concerned medical practitioners. In 1897, for example, the Victorian Order of Nurses was founded under the auspices of the National Council of Women of Canada, with the special purpose of nursing mothers and infants, and demonstrating techniques of household sanitation in the interests of disease prevention. The Victorian Order of Nurses, along with the nurses of the Red Cross Society, and most importantly those of the municipal and provincial Departments of Health, were the essential foot-soldiers in the campaign to save the 'infant soldier'.[15]

The quality of milk was also a social reform cause in this period. In 1903 the New York paediatricians W. L. Park and L. Emmett Holt published a report conclusively establishing the link between feeding and infant illness during hot weather, the so-called 'summer complaint' or *cholera infantum.* Their efforts contributed significantly to an international movement to regulate milk production and distribution, which was seen as the key to vanquishing this widespread, but eminently preventable, disease.[16] The Canadian Medical Association (CMA) appointed a Milk Commission in 1908 and devised standards for milk collection, inspection, storage and delivery.[17] Ontario was the first province to legislate in the interests of carrying out the commission's programme. Although milk regulation was initially a municipal concern, the CMA continued to pressure the provincial government for compulsory pasteurization legislation, which was finally attained in 1938.[18]

In the early twentieth century there was no lack of private child welfare initiatives in the province's urban centres. But on the whole these were sporadic, localized attempts to deal with specific aspects of the larger problem of illness and death in childhood.[19] Although the medical profession and the general public alike appeared to be awakening to the issue of infant mortality, until 1910 it remained primarily the concern of women's organizations.[20] The campaign lacked a scientific assessment of the extent of infant mortality in Ontario, as well as a professional analysis of its nature and causes.

In 1910 Dr Helen MacMurchy was commissioned by the provincial government to produce three reports on the situation. According to her findings, of 52,629 births in Ontario in 1909, death had claimed 6,932 children before their first birthday. In Toronto alone, the rate was 230 deaths per 1,000 live births. 'National action, government action, collective action, not individual action, can save the baby', was MacMurchy's ultimate conclusion. MacMurchy urged Canadians to shake off their complacency in the name of social welfare and national pride. The real enemy, she pointed out, was not *cholera infantum* in itself but an infant mortality attributable to a wide range of causes, most important among them being ignorance, poverty and inadequate medical attention.[21] Private philanthropy alone was insufficient to deal with the enormity of the problem.

MacMurchy's series of reports finally made Ontarians aware of the tragic wastage of human life that was occurring around them. Reform-minded individuals regarded these statistics as impediments to the march of national progress. The medical profession stressed anew the potential for prevention of infant disease and death. While recognizing their professional responsibility for saving these infants, they cited public apathy as the major obstacle to their efforts: 'At times it would seem, from the apparent indifference shown in the matter, as if the public yet believed that this high rate of mortality among children at or soon after birth was a wise dispensation of nature to eliminate the unfit.'[22]

The medical profession contended that both public and state involvement were essential for the reduction of infant mortality rates. Gradually, governments at the municipal, provincial and federal levels would expand their participation in the child welfare campaign. In the immediate postwar years, their newly-created health departments provided official sanction for the medical reformers' principal efforts. However, from the campaign's initial stirrings, state involvement was restricted to the administration and direction of largely educational child welfare measures. The major share of the duty of bringing up children did not belong to the state but to the mothers, and, as one spokesman argued, 'whatever we do we must not be too ready to relieve them of their responsibility'.[23] It was in the educational sphere that the state could best do its work 'to see that the rights of the children are not ignored and that the mothers have the opportunity given them of learning how best to rear their children'.[24]

From its earliest days, the campaign's leaders were obsessed with education. Education would upgrade parenting skills while bringing both mother and child under the watchful eye of the new childrearing experts. The real economic basis of infant mortality may have been acknowledged, but it was frequently played down in favour of locating the source in a failure of motherhood. Infant illness and death could then be interpreted as problems separate and distinct from those of inadequate housing, sanitation, or even poverty. The most efficacious prescription for the physical and social ailment of high infant mortality, consequently, lay in the improvement of mothering techniques. An editorial in the *Canadian Public Health Journal* in 1915 urged that

> The problem will be solved only when the value of intelligent motherhood is placed above that of philanthropy, of hospitals, of the medical profession and of the state. Neglect and ignorance are, therefore, more important than poverty as causative factors in the cause of infant illness and death . . . Intelligent motherhood alone can give to the infant that which neither wealth nor state nor yet science can offer with equal benefit to mother or child.[25]

The survival of infants and the health of children depended not on improved economic conditions, not on state involvement and assuredly not on the universal provision of medical care. Mothers, and by implication particularly those of the working class, simply had to improve. This diagnosis of the problem not only obscured the environmental and economic factors affecting health, but ultimately shaped the remedial programme devised by the medical reformers. Even before the child welfare movement was launched in earnest, physicians began to see the education of mothers as their principal task in this field of activity.[26] This early commitment to motherhood training would dictate the direction taken by the campaign and the nature of its measures throughout its course.

In the aftermath of the MacMurchy report, the medical practitioners who were developing a deeper interest in child welfare decided that ignorance and irresponsibility on the part of parents – especially mothers – were the primary causes of disease and death in early childhood. They established moral sanctions on the grounds of health and the national interest and denigrated traditional methods of childrearing as dangerous, negligent and rooted in superstition:

> Lack of the proper knowledge accounts for possibly the largest number of [infant] deaths – lack of hygienic and eugenic knowledge; ignorance of the penalties of immorality; of the trouble enacted by defiance of sanitation and tolerance of filth; of the fatal results of carelessness and malnutrition; and of the realization of the social and economic value of the child's life . . . The needless death of the child is the death knell of the race.[27]

The traditional sources of child-care information were considered pernicious, particularly where 'neighbourly advice' was concerned. Physicians decried the fact that the woman who had 'buried six' was regarded as an authority on the upbringing of children: 'and the results are four white coffins taken in procession through the streets of the city every day'.[28]

The Great War and child welfare

The profession's greater interest in saving infant lives and treating childhood illness reflected the wider social change in perceptions of children. More important, this period, from the turn of the century through the years of the Great War, witnessed a gradual broadening of the medical profession's sphere of influence with respect to children. Slowly, but ever more forcefully, physicians began to dispense child-care advice in ways that were not purely clinical. They argued that this responsibility to educate parents was an integral part of the function that they served in the community. In order to attain the aims of their movement and to justify their increasing influence and social status, the medical experts needed parents who wanted to be informed. They participated in the creation of a need and then strove to become the predominant source of its attenuation. In so doing, they played a major role in transforming the parent–child relationship while the nation itself was undergoing socio-economic transformation.[29]

In the process of educating mothers, paediatricians validated the usefulness of their expertise and attained wider social appreciation for their commitment to childhood health and welfare.[30] 'Is the paediatrician only a practising physician, only a teacher of his specialty?', asked one medical writer. In response, he asserted, 'Most assuredly he is first and foremost a member of the body politic, a citizen of the country and as such it is his duty to exert all the influence that is at his command in the interest of the welfare of his community and in a larger sense of his country.'[31] By the end of the Great War the setting was especially conducive to the physician's acceptance of this duty. For the postwar generation of parents, the medical experts in child-care would be looked upon as the rightful commanders in the battle to save the 'infant soldier'.

In 1919, Dr Alan Brown, the acknowledged 'father of Canadian paediatrics', stressed that paediatricians must maintain leadership in 'all matters pertaining to problems of child life'.[32] The vast majority of Canadian children would continue to be seen by general practitioners whenever they required medical attention, 'but there is a growing tendency for them to refer the more difficult cases, especially of feeding, to men trained in paediatrics'.[33] The paediatricians wielded an influence within the child welfare movement and its official agencies in a proportion much greater than their numbers would suggest.

The nation's experience at war helped crystallize this new interest in the child and set into place the foundations of a modern Canadian childhood. In diverse ways, the Great War served as a catalyst to the movement for the medical management of childhood. The dire effect of the heavy casualties of war on so sparsely populated a nation as Canada was one theme that was constantly reiterated in contemporary medical and reform journals. It became a patriotic obligation to save infants and keep them healthy in order to replace those young men who had left empty places in Canadian society:

The Great War has impressed upon us as never before the grave necessity not only of conserving the children, but of affording them every opportunity to develop normally. It has become a patriotic duty as well as a professional one for the physicians who come into close touch with the family life of the nation to thoroughly inform themselves of the best method of preventing infant mortality and of conserving child life . . . The whole trend of modern child welfare work demands closer cooperation of the physicians with all organizations working for the welfare of children.[34]

The phrase 'as never before' resounded throughout medical commentaries on child welfare in the decade following the Great War.[35] Along with the new awareness of national duty, these few words underscored a pervasive sense of urgency with respect to the conservation of child life. The opportunity to work for the children and to ensure the nation's future had clearly presented itself. It was essential that physicians grasp that opportunity to play a decisive role in guiding national destiny.[36]

For the medical profession, the war's impact was double-edged. On the one hand, there was apprehension and urgency; on the other, optimism and a sense of rising to the challenge.[37] Canada had suffered tremendous losses but was on the verge of gaining victory none the less, both in national and health terms. The child welfare problem was only just emerging into 'proper significance' in the minds of Canadians. The intensive study and growing sense of responsibility towards children which were coming into being were judged 'a not unnatural side product' of the war. Canada had lost some 60,000 of the finest of her developing citizens – 'finest physically and finest in the spirit of selfless idealism from which national greatness springs'. In order for Canadians to retain 'the position in the ranks of greatness which their blood has bought', it was necessary to ensure that those who would take the place of the fallen be given every chance to realize the full range of their 'physical, mental and spiritual possibilities'.[38]

Among the most serious losses of war were those entailed by the slaughter of millions of combatants 'of a class drawn from what must be considered the most valuable, so far as productivity is concerned, of the population'.[39] At a time of rapid technological advance, and especially in view of the existence of an industrial giant to the south, it was essential for a fledgling industrial nation like Canada to man its factories with hardy, efficient workers. The class which produced the majority of workers and soldiers alike was also the most vulnerable in terms of health. With so many of its adult males destroyed, both present and future husbands and fathers, it became a matter of national economic and military survival to replenish the supply by providing for the welfare of Canadian children.[40] Dr Alan Brown declared that 'the future of our country depends on its poor children. If they are eventually to justify their place in the world they must be saved from ill-health, ignorance and vice'.[41]

As in the United States and Great Britain, the war also reaffirmed fears of racial degeneration.[42] In Canada, it was observed that 'the veto of the medical examiner has prevented many a splendid spirit from obeying the call to duty which today is sweeping our country'.[43] During the period of the Military Service Act, only 83,355 of the applicants for enlistment were accepted; 181,000, or 68 per cent, were rejected as unfit.[44] The ill health of these young men could only be the result of 'our life before the war' and had to be remedied in the present generation of infants in order to prevent a foreseeable slide into national degeneration.

The nation had been deprived of many men in their prime: that their places would be filled by immigrants of 'inferior' origins appeared a very real threat to the Canadian middle class.[45] In the immediate aftermath of the war, government support of immigration seemed particularly misguided. The 'Red Scare' which swept North America during the 1920s and fearsome indications of intensifying class conflict fuelled chauvinist fires.[46] The call was sent out to the government to focus its efforts and invest its dollars more effectively in a medically-supervised crusade for child conservation.[47]

These nationalist tremors were strengthened by anxieties about 'race suicide'. Although such worries predated the war, statisticians had recently confirmed the long-held suspicions of the medical profession that the birth rate was indeed dropping within the 'better stock'. Dr J. J. Heagerty of the federal Department of Health believed that the chief factor behind this falling birth rate was voluntary restriction, 'the cowardly offspring of Higher Civilization'. The practice of birth control which had begun with the 'educated classes' was 'spreading continually' throughout the entire community.[48] From 1881 to 1911, Ontario had the lowest birth rate of any province; in 1921, only that of British Columbia was lower.[49] At the same time, infant mortality rates remained elevated despite the efforts of the prewar reformers. Not surprisingly, the war magnified fears about race suicide and national degeneration which had been developing since the turn of the century.[50]

The war also effected a widening of the child health objectives of medical and lay reformers. From the strict focus on infant mortality that had shaped early efforts, it was recognized that children needed medical supervision beyond the first birthday until they could be delivered safely to the school medical inspectors. Childhood disease posed a menace both to individual health in adulthood and to the long-term health of race and nation. Physicians argued that indifference to the ailments of early childhood

> [sowed] the seeds of weakness, deformity and impaired vitality in those who survive to take their share in the duties of citizenship; and it contributes in no small degree to the physical degeneracy of the race, which we can see only too plainly taking place around us in the large cities. Thus we see that these damaged and weakly infants, if not cared for, are liable to grow up into men and women crippled in body and deficient in mind who fill the hospitals, prisons and homes.[51]

Failure to heed the medical gospel would exact a high social price.

The physicians repeatedly stressed the concept of the child as a 'national asset'. As such, children were easily the most deserving of all citizens in so far as attempts to improve national health and welfare were concerned. The imagery of war permeated this revitalized campaign with explicitly racial and nationalistic tones. 'A sound mind in a sound body' was the prerequisite for survival, and in the degree that a nation's people possessed these qualities, the nation itself would rise or fall:

> These two things we must give our Infant Soldier . . . That first year of life is the worst year in all life's battle. Terrible is the carnage for thousands of our Infant Soldiers perish there . . . His father had ten times his chance in Flanders.

And of all this sorrow, the very crown is that it is needless
... Fully 40 percent of these deaths can be prevented.[52]

Medical science would provide the means and methods for
ensuring that, for every life sacrificed on the battlefields of
Europe, 'a thousand children shall have stronger, straighter,
freer bodies and stronger, straighter, freer spirits'.[53] The process of modernization, intensified by the experience of wartime,
had taught Canadians to question traditional methods and to
strive for greater efficiency and 'scientific organization and
cooperation'. The reason for deficiencies in the health and
welfare of Canadians lay in the fact that there existed 'no
programme for the scientific organization of mankind, no
agency to study such a programme, no teaching given on the
matter'.[54] In the years following the outbreak of the First World
War, the Canadian medical profession attempted to devise and
implement such a programme in the area where their efforts
seemed to hold most promise: childhood.

The creation of child welfare services

The starting point for this scientific approach to child welfare
was the well baby clinic. The earliest clinics in Ontario, established in Toronto and Hamilton in the immediate prewar years,
began service as pure milk depots organized and staffed by local
reform groups. By 1915, as this function became obsolete, due
to government regulation of the milk supply, they had evolved
into all-round clinics for the supervision and maintenance of
the health of infants and young children.[55] However, the obso-
lescence of their role as suppliers of certified milk was not the
sole reason for the broadening of their function. It was discovered that merely providing milk to the city's poor mothers
was futile unless they were also instructed in its handling and
preparation and, most important, in the proper feeding of their
infants. The child welfare clinics and the home nursing visits
which together served as the campaign's hallmark services came
into being 'to fill a want created by the great numbers among
the poor who, because of overcrowding and ignorance, require
advice relating to health, hygiene and manner of living'.[56]
Above all, the clinics were to be centres of maternal education
and supervision in scientific childrearing.

In Toronto, the original clinics were established in 1912 at Evangelia and University Settlement Houses in the heart of the city's immigrant district. In accordance with the aims of the child welfare crusaders, these clinics did not offer treatment but instructed the mother as to the care of her child, especially with respect to diet. It was considered that 'the mothers of the poor need to learn a lot of things to bring children up safely through the perils that surround them through the conditions in which they are forced to live'.[57]

By 1915, Toronto had organized a separate Department of Child Hygiene under the aegis of its municipal Department of Public Health. The Department's work commenced with the registration of births at City Hall, whereupon a booklet on infant care and feeding was immediately posted to the mother. The next step was a visit by the public health nurse as soon as possible after birth registration. With the permission of the family physician, the nurse then arranged for the mother to attend the nearest clinic. Infants were weighed at each visit (monthly for the first year) and a card recording the weight was given to the mother, along with information and advice as required.[58]

By the early 1920s, Toronto's two original clinics had grown into a network of twenty-eight. In the year 1917, 1,033 clinic sessions were held, attended by 16,849 babies.[59] In order to emphasize that the clinics were to be solely for the education of mothers and the supervision of general infant health and to secure the co-operation of the 'neighbouring physicians', notification of each new case was sent to the attending physician. These notice cards explained that the clinic would supervise the child only with the family doctor's approval, and that the child would be referred back to the doctor, along with all pertinent records, if medical attention should be required.[60]

From the very beginning, the child welfare crusaders were adamant that their major practical measures – the clinics and nurse visits – would remain entirely in the realm of education. The clinics which gradually spread across Ontario from these initial efforts were meant to complement and never to replace regular attendance by the family physician. The clinics were generally staffed by a rotating body of physicians who volunteered a few hours out of their general practice. In some locations, they were paid a nominal fee for their attendance. Only the administering physicians and the nurses were employed directly by the various municipal health departments.

While the physicians were careful to maintain their directory and supervisory capacities, mothers were reached largely through the public health and visiting nurse organizations. From the perspective of the campaign's medical leaders, the nurse was a vital liaison between the mother and the profession. Most of all, however, nurses were expected to carry out doctors' orders and see that these orders were obeyed by mothers. Although the nurses' work was crucial to the campaign's progress, their position from the beginning was one of deference to the physicians-in-command. The medical profession feared a loss of status and earning power if the nurses were allowed to perform services in the line of prescription and treatment. Many physicians felt that there was a very fine distinction between advice and the kind of service only they were entitled to give.[61] Visiting nurses were conscious of the physicians' fears and generally carefully avoided antagonizing them. Yet they often resented this enforced submissiveness because they believed that they were offering mothers a valuable service. 'The amount of good done by the doctor at the clinic can be done by the nurse in her visit to the home', argued one provincial nurse, but she added cautiously, 'where needed the nurse can advise seeing the family physician'.[62]

The Hamilton Babies' Dispensary followed a pattern of development similar to that of Toronto. Opening its doors in June 1911 as a milk dispensary, the clinic later provided a physician to examine babies and prescribe individual feeding formulae. Weekly prenatal clinics were also held. Again, the clinic's medical purpose was purely diagnostic. Through home visits, the nurse was able to 'establish herself in the confidence of the mother', and thereby win a convert to the cause.[63] They were also an effective means of keeping the family under surveillance. The nurse was authorized to take notes regarding the financial standing of the family and the general condition of the home; these records were preserved along with the medical history of the infant patient. The child welfare reformers generally did not hesitate to advocate such obvious intrusion into the family's private affairs. They believed that their cause amply justified scrutiny of this nature.

The Hamilton child welfare crusaders were especially adept at publicizing their cause and attracting the interest and co-operation of the city's mothers. In June 1915, the clinic organizers held a week-long exhibition to bring the city's mothers to the clinic. They also recruited in a more direct fashion. While some cases were referred by Hamilton physicians, as in Toronto, the majority were reached by a 'Mother's Letter' posted as births were registered. It was discovered that 'not infrequently' mothers were being referred by those who had already attended and had 'appreciated the benefits to their children'. Physicians were urged to co-operate fully by registering births promptly in order to prevent the problem of getting to the babies too late to be of benefit. They were also encouraged to recommend the dispensary to their poor patients who 'on account of the expense will hesitate to call in a medical man until it is too late'. In this way, the medical staff of the Hamilton clinics attempted to create a network of co-operation with private physicians.[64]

Child welfare clinics were also organized in London in 1915. Three clinics were held weekly in public schools. However, the London Child Welfare Association broke with the pattern established in Hamilton and Toronto. The association extended its services beyond the supervisory and educational and conducted a separate weekly clinic for sick children at Victoria Hospital.[65] So successful was London's programme from the point of view of its organizers, that they confidently attributed the decline in the city's infant deaths directly to the efforts of the clinic. Before the clinics were opened, over 160 children between the ages of 1 month and 5 years died in London each year. By the early 1920s this number had been reduced to 59. The greatest cause of death, intestinal infections, had been practically eliminated 'by preaching mother's milk as the only safe food for infants and where this food was not possible by teaching how to safeguard against infection of the cow's milk and feeding utensils'.[66]

Significance and results of the child welfare movement

By the mid-1920s, most urban centres in Ontario had some system of clinics and home visits in operation. For the medical profession, the greater involvement in local child welfare drives represented an expansion of their parameters of concern and self-imposed responsibility. From the early, intermittent and purely individualistic participation, medical involvement eventually became better organized, more tightly directed and profession-wide. The physicians' involvement mirrored the evolution of the campaign itself. The Great War drew these periodic and generally voluntarist local drives into a concerted, physician-led and government-sponsored movement. Child welfare concerns had previously derived from 'the natural impulses of human sympathy'. In the aftermath of the Great War, these concerns came to be seen as 'part of the defensive foresight of citizens who would protect the future of the state'.[67]

This shift from philanthropic motivation to state interests was reflected in the activities of the child welfare reformers. While their early efforts concentrated on well baby care from birth to the first birthday, the combined effects of the wartime resurgence in concern for child welfare and increasing government involvement translated into a broadening of the medical platform. The child from birth to the age of 5 became the object of child welfare services. It was recognized that large numbers of children, although healthy at birth, quickly became 'the physically defective entrants whom the education authority is required at no small cost to restore as far as possible to their original state of health'.[68] Yet most of these problems were preventable, or could be remedied more quickly and cheaply if detected early through clinics or nurse visits.

Although the clinics were established to supervise the children of the working class, physicians believed that their success record served as an effective promotion of the benefits of regular medical oversight for children of all classes. For those middle-class children who would not receive the attention of the clinic staff, the family physician was encouraged to accept the duty of 'doing for his patient what the child welfare clinic aims to do for the children of the poor'. On the occasion of each examination of the child, he was to take the opportunity to 'give directions as to the hygiene, diet, clothing and every detail pertaining to the life and welfare of his small patient'.[69]

Moreover, it was believed that the clinic system had a 'marked influence'; it was said that the more fortunate members of society now understood 'not only the necessity of consulting their physicians regarding the feeding of their babies in difficult cases', but would 'bring their children regularly for inspection and advice when they [knew] they [were] well'.[70] The clinics and visiting nurse services were established by middle-class child welfare advocates in order to educate and elevate the working-class family to middle-class standards of health and hygiene. However, their emphasis on education and disease prevention penetrated class barriers, providing their medical directors with a larger audience and a more significant role to play within the Canadian family. In effect, the clinics and nurse visits functioned in a 'watchdog' capacity. The enhanced status and community position this gave physicians corresponded neatly with their professional aspirations. More than mere practitioners of medicine, they could now stake a claim for themselves as tutors of the masses, purveyors of scientific enlightenment, guides and overseers of the beleaguered family, rescuers of children and ultimately saviours of Canadian society.

These early child welfare services were undoubtedly instrumental in winning victory in the first round against infant mortality due to intestinal diseases. Encouragement of breastfeeding, improvement in the quality of milk available for artificial feeding, medically prescribed infant formula for individual cases and instruction on general child care gradually translated into infant lives saved by preventive measures. From the initial private efforts and the focus on pure milk, it was a short step to the realization that the overall quality of childrearing could be improved.

It was also quickly recognized that the enormity of this task made it better suited to government work than to philanthropy. Before the war's end, the municipal health authorities had generally taken over the operation of existing clinics and the employment of public health nurses.[71] These municipal clinics came under the supervision of the provincial Department of Health when it was reorganized in 1920. By providing well baby care free of charge, medically backed information and early diagnosis of potential health problems to those who could not otherwise afford such services, the clinics filled a definite need in these Ontario communities. Furthermore, as testimony to the benefits of preventive medicine in the field of child health, they served as an example to those middle-class parents whom they did not serve directly. The development of these clinic and visiting nurse programmes in the urban centres of Ontario during the early years of the Great War laid the foundations for the more centralized and widespread services of the interwar period. The expansion of these services under municipal auspices and their supervision by the new provincial Division of Maternal and Child Hygiene did not, however, bring about a significant change in their strategy, structure or function.

The period of Canadian history bounded by the two World Wars witnessed a clear redefinition of the value of the child and a concomitant attempt to reformulate the childhood experience. By the turn of the century, the forces of industrialization and urbanization were already changing the day-to-day lives of Canadians. The process of modernization exacerbated existing socio-economic problems on the one hand, and opened up the possibility of new, more effective 'progressive' solutions on the other. The Great War accelerated modernizing trends at the level of structures, but it also spurred the modernization of perceptions and attitudes. As a result, children were perceived 'as never before' to be the nation's most valuable assets, by virtue of their prospects as worthy citizens in a vigorous and internationally respected future nation.

Too precious to be relegated solely to its parents, the health and welfare of the modern Canadian child were to be guarded by the community for its own ultimate benefit. The reins of this social guardianship were taken up by those best equipped by knowledge, skill and increasing professional specialization to effect the desired results. Armed with an improved scientific appreciation of childhood health, bolstered by the cultural ideal of childhood which had been evolving since the turn of the century, and infused with a sharpened sense of social obligation brought on by the combined forces of societal complexity and global cataclysm, the physicians intervened in the parent–child relationship for the sake of the nation's future.[72] They maintained that the repercussions of unfavourable modern conditions would be felt in the later phases of life, when too often 'under the strain of difficulties' the adult shaped by such an experience would 'make a failure of life and its duties, entailing misery upon the family and not infrequently, expense upon the country generally'.[73]

The child welfare campaign began to accelerate noticeably in the immediate postwar years. Incremental gains in the battle against infant mortality were interpreted as heartening signs of the possibilities of medically-designed child welfare programmes. As the opening decades of a 'modern Canada' drew to a close, the physicians proclaimed confidently that interest in child welfare had become so widespread and adoption of their 'constructive programme' so general, that the most accurate measurement of progress in any community was the death rate of its infants and young children.[74] Their initial confidence would be borne out through the course of the interwar years. Although there were occasional, frightening increases in infant and maternal mortality rates during the Great Depression, there is no doubt that overall progress was being made. Between 1926 and 1940 there was a reduction in infant mortality of 45.1 per cent.[75]

It cannot be established conclusively that these improvements were due primarily to the campaigners' efforts. The ability of education to influence morbidity and mortality was undoubtedly limited. By the Second World War, it seemed to have reached the outer bounds of its efficacy. The campaigners were eventually forced to concede that, although their movement had made some contribution, progress in child welfare work was due largely to factors over which it had exercised little influence: the advent of antibiotic drugs, advances in the practice of obstetrics and paediatrics, the improved economic situation, and better public health services in the cities and towns of Ontario. Yet it would be inaccurate as well as ahistorical to accuse the child welfare campaigners of having suffered from a naive and misplaced faith in science and in their own medical leadership. They believed wholeheartedly that if Canadian parents would accept their expert assistance and rally around 'the infant soldier', then the nation would rise to glory in the modern world order ushered in by the Great War.

Acknowledgements

This article first appeared as C. R. Abeele, '"The infant soldier"': the Great War and the medical campaign for child welfare', *Can. Bull. Med. Hist.*, 5 (1988), 99–119, and is reproduced with permission.

Notes

1. For contemporary views, see, for example, E. Key, *The Century of the Child* (New York, 1909); A. W. Calhoun, *The Social History of the American Family*, vol. III, *Since the Civil War* (Cleveland,1919), 131. For the Canadian 'reawakening', see N. Sutherland, *Children in English Canadian Society* (Toronto, 1976).

2. G. Richardson, Preface, in D. Read (ed.) *The Great War and Canadian Society* (Toronto, 1978), 7; R. Cook and C. Brown, *Canada, 1896–1921: A Nation Transformed* (Toronto, 1974), 337; B. Wilson, 'Introduction', in B. Wilson (ed.) *Ontario and the First World War*

(Toronto, 1977), cxvii. For a contemporary view, see W. B. Hurd, 'Is there a Canadian race?', *Queen's Quarterly*, 20 (1928), 615.

3. The Philosopher, 'The new era', *National Home Monthly*, 14 (1917), 31. For the war's effects on the Social Gospel, see R. Allen, *The Social Passion* (Toronto, 1971), 41.

4. H. E. MacDermot, *One Hundred Years of Medicine in Canada* (Toronto, 1967), 12; C. M. Godfrey, *Medicine for Ontario* (Belleville, 1979), 230.

5. W. W. Chipman, 'The infant soldier', *Soc. Welf.*, 4 (1921), 48–9.

6. L. M. Lindsay, 'Secretary's Report, 1919', *Can. Publ. Health J.*, 11 (1920), 80. For historical analyses of scientific childrearing in the USA, see B. Ehrenreich and D. English, *For Her Own Good* (New York, 1978). For England, see J. Lewis, *The Politics of Motherhood* (London, 1980); A. Dally, *Inventing Motherhood* (London, 1982); A. Davin, 'Imperialism and motherhood', *Hist. Workshop J.*, 5 (1978), 9–66; C. Hardyment, *Dream Babies* (New York, 1983). On Canadian aspects of the campaign, see V. Strong-Boag, 'Intruders in the nursery', in J. Parr (ed.) *Childhood and Family in Canadian History* (Toronto, 1982), 160–78; N. Lewis, 'Creating the little machine', *BC Stud.*, 56 (1982–3), 44–60.

7. These local drives were based largely in the towns and cities of Ontario, although such groups as the Women's Institutes and Imperial Order of Daughters of the Empire worked to establish clinics and promote vaccination and pure milk distribution in some rural areas. T. Crowley, 'Educating for home and community: the genesis of the Women's Institutes in Ontario', unpub. paper, University of Guelph, July 1988.

8. J. H. Ebbs, 'The Canadian Paediatric Society: its early years', *Can. Med. Ass. J.*, 109 (1980), 1235. The Society for the Study of the Diseases of Children was the immediate forerunner of the Canadian Paediatric Society. For the role of paediatricians in Dutch infant welfare work, see ch. 4 by Hilary Marland.

9. B. K. F. Rashford, 'The child is not a little man', *Canada Lancet*, 16 (1896), 208. See also R. A. Bolt, 'The education of the medical student in his relation to child welfare', *Can. Publ. Health J.*, 9 (1918), 304; Editorial, 'The gift of a child', *Soc. Welf.*, 7 (1924), 1.

10. Editorial, 'Progress in paediatrics during the Victorian age', *Canada Lancet*, 16 (1898), 575.

11. Sutherland, *Children*, 57.

12. Sutherland, *Children*; Editorial, 'Save the children', *Canada Lancet*, 22 (1907), 934.

13. A. H. Wright, Chairman, Provincial Board of Health, Ontario, 'Preventive medicine and the family doctor', *Can. Publ. Health J.*, 4 (1913), 648.

14. T. Morrison, 'Their proper sphere', *Ontario History*, 68 (1976), 45–72; V. Strong-Boag, *The Parliament of Women* (Ottawa, 1976); S. Buckley, 'Ladies or midwives?', W. Robertson, 'Rocking the cradle for the world', and L. Kealey, Introduction, in L. Kealey (ed.) *A Not Unreasonable Claim* (Toronto, 1979); and C. Bacchi, *Liberation Deferred* (Toronto, 1983).

15. Buckley, 'Ladies or midwives?', 136; Strong-Boag, *Parliament*, 112–13.

16. K. W. Jones, 'Sentiment and science: the late nineteenth century pediatrician as mother's advisor', *J. Soc. Hist.*, 17 (1983), 80; Sutherland, *Children*, 59. See also Editorial, 'The Milk Commission', *Can. Publ. Health J.*, 1 (1910), 459–60; J. H. Elliott, 'Shall we have pure milk in Canada?', *Can. Publ. Health J.*, 2 (1911), 353; Editorial, 'Hygiene and the Ontario legislature', *Can. Publ. Health J.*, 2 (1911), 170. On the pure milk campaign in Great Britain, see D. Dwork, *War is Good for Babies and Other Young Children* (London, 1987).

17. Editorial, 'The Milk Commission'; Elliot, 'Shall we have pure milk?', 353–7.

18. Ontario Board of Health, *A/R* (1910), 137–71; Editorial, 'Hygiene and the Ontario legislature', 170.

19. Public Archives of Canada (PAC), MG 29, vol. 1318, file 495-1-2, Victorian Order of Nurses (VON), typescript, 'Historical development of services on behalf of women and children', Sept. 1952, 1.

20. The following were listed as the most important of the organizations in terms of their involvement in maternal and child welfare efforts: the Women's Institutes of Ontario (1903) concentrated on improved sanitation in small municipalities and rural schools, school medical services, and health education through the distribution of literature and conferences; the National Council of Women (1893) through its various Local Councils, set up well baby clinics and milk depots, held baby contests, campaigned for tuberculosis control, improved housing, and Mothers' Allowances. See Strong-Boag, *Parliament*, for detailed coverage of their activities. The Imperial Order of the Daughters of the Empire (1900) also established and maintained well baby clinics and collected funds for nursing services in rural areas. Ottowa, PAC, MG 29, vol. 1318, file 495-1-2, VON, 'Work of voluntary agencies', 1.

21. H. MacMurchy, *Infant Mortality: First Special Report* (Toronto, 1910); *Infant Mortality: Second Special Report* (1911); *Infant Mortality: Third Special Report* (1912).

22. Editorial, 'Infant mortality', *Can. Publ. Health J.*, 6 (1915), 510; W. A. L. Styles, 'Infant mortality: its causes and prevention', *Soc. Welf.*, 2 (1920), 164; H. MacMurchy, 'The baby's father', *Can. Publ. Health J.*, 9 (1918), 317.

23. C. A. Hodgetts, Chief, Division of Statistics and Publicity, Dominion Department of Health, 'Statistics and publicity in child welfare work', *Can. Publ. Health J.*, 3 (1921), 111.

24. Hodgetts, 'Statistics and publicity', 111.

25. Editorial, 'Infant mortality', 510.

26. A. Brown, 'The relation of the paediatrician to the community', *Can. Publ. Health J.*, 10 (1919), 54; C. S. Walters, Mayor of Hamilton, 'The duty of the city to the child', *Can. Publ. Health J.*, 6 (1915), 540.

27. Editorial, 'These little ones', *Soc. Welf.*, 1 (1918), 53; Editorial, 'Child welfare', *Can. Publ. Health J.*, 6 (1915), 162.

28. Editorial, 'Human sacrifice', *Can. Publ. Health J.*, 4 (1913), 95.

29. B. F. Royer, 'Child welfare', *Can. Publ. Health J.*, 12 (1921), 293.

For discussions of medical professionalization and child welfare concerns, see Jones, 'Sentiment and science', and H. Levenstein, '"Best for babies" or "preventable infanticide"? The controversy over artificial feeding of infants in America, 1880–1920', *J. Am. Hist.*, 70 (1983), 75–94.

30. Jones, 'Sentiment and science', 82.
31. Bolt, 'Education of the medical student', 304.
32. Brown, 'Relation of the paediatrician', 54–5.
33. Bolt, 'Education of the medical student', 305.
34. Bolt, 'Education of the medical student', 309.
35. See, for example, M. Sherwood, 'Some problems of child hygiene', *Soc. Welf.*, 6 (1921), 54; M. Power, Ontario Child Welfare Division, 'Child welfare', *Soc. Welf.*, 6 (1919), 100; Editorial, 'A Children's Bureau for Canada', *Soc. Welf.*, 1 (1919), 84; MacMurchy, 'The baby's father', 318; A. C. Jost, 'The conservation of child life', *Can. Publ. Health J.*, 11 (1920), 503; M. H. Malcolmson, Convener, Child Welfare Committee, 'How we reduced infant mortality in St. Catharines', *Soc. Welf.*, 7 (1922), 215; A. D. Blackader, 'Fundamental facts in organization', *Can. Publ. Health J.*, 3 (1921), 97–8; Editorial, 'The gift of a child', 1; Walters, 'The duty of the city', 540.
36. Royer, 'Child welfare', 290–1.
37. Editorial, 'The Canadian mother', *Soc. Welf.*, 5 (1923), 158; Bolt, 'Education of the medical student', 309; P. Bryce, 'Two problems in child welfare', *Soc. Welf.*, 3 (1921), 187–8.
38. 'Things Editorial', *Soc. Welf.*, 2 (1919), 2.
39. Jost, 'Conservation of child life', 503.
40. A. W. Coone, 'The child as an asset', *Soc. Welf.*, 11 (1918), 38. See also P. H. Bryce, 'Infant mortality and disease', *Soc. Welf.*, 3 (1919), 133. Davin, 'Imperialism and motherhood', and Dwork, *War is Good for Babies* discuss the war's effect on child conservation in Britain from the military and economic point of view.
41. A. Brown, 'Infant and child welfare work', *Can. Pub. Health J.*, 7 (1918), 147.
42. Davin, 'Imperialism and motherhood', 12; Dwork, *War is Good for Babies*, 208. Reports that 40 per cent of the youth examined for the American army had been found unfit had similar effects in the United States. Sherwood, 'Some problems of child hygiene', 54.
43. Walters, 'The duty of the city', 540. One Canadian estimate declared that 36 per cent of those examined for service were found to be physically fit, 23 per cent were pronounced 'fairly good', 31 per cent 'unsound' and 10 per cent 'absolutely no good'. A. H. Sovereign, 'Report of the Child Welfare Association of British Columbia', cited in Strong-Boag, *Parliament*, 345; Editorial, 'Social hygiene', *Soc. Welf.*, 12 (1924), 48.
44. H. E. Spencer, 'For a healthy Canada', *Chatelaine*, 3 (1930), 50.
45. Coone, 'The child as an asset', 38.
46. D. Avery, *Dangerous Foreigners* (Toronto, 1979), 12. See also G. S. Kealey, '1919: the Canadian labour revolt', *Labour/Le Travail*, 13 (1984), 11–44. For Canadian labour in the twentieth century, see B. D. Palmer, *The Working Class Experience* (Toronto, 1984).

47. A. G. Fleming, 'Study of infant deaths in Toronto during the summer of 1921', *Can. Publ. Health J.*, 5 (1922), 199. The women's organizations felt the same anxiety about immigrants. 'Report of the Provincial Vice-President for Ontario', *National Council of Women of Canada Yearbook*, 1913, 35.

48. J. J. Heagerty, 'Birth control', *Soc. Welf.*, 7 (1924), 57; Editorial, 'Birth control', *Soc. Welf.*, 6 (1923), 243–4. The most thorough account of birth control and abortion in Canada is A. McLaren and A. T. McLaren, *The Bedroom and the State* (Toronto, 1986).

49. J. Henripin, *Trends and Factors of Fertility in Canada* (Ottawa, 1977), 21. In the opening decade of the twentieth century, population increase due to births alone had been 21 per cent. Between 1921 and 1931, this rate dropped to 17 per cent and to 11 per cent during the tumultuous Depression decade. *Trends in Vital Statistics, 1921–1954* (Ottawa, 1956), 8.

50. For a contemporary description of fears of racial degeneration in Canada, see Editorial, 'Social hygiene', 48; London Social Service Council, 'Report of the Public Health Committee on Infant Mortality', *Can. Publ. Health J.*, 12 (1921), 402. See also Bacchi, *Liberation Deferred*, 104–16, for the views of the women's movement on this issue. On the eugenics movement in Canada, see A. McLaren, *Our Own Master Race* (Toronto, 1990).

51. Brown, 'Infant and child welfare work', 147; D. Forsyth, 'The care of children under school age', *Can. Publ. Health J.*, 7 (1916), 381.

52. Chipman, 'Infant soldier', 48.

53. A. Brown, 'Child health', *Can. Publ. Health J.*, 11 (1920), 49.

54. A. Sand, 'Social medicine', *Soc. Welf.*, 2 (1919), 526.

55. W. L. Cody, 'The scope and function of the medical staff of the Babies' Dispensary, Hamilton', *Can. Publ. Health J.*, 6 (1915), 545; J. H. Mullen, 'Child welfare in a democracy', *Can. Publ. Health J.*, 9 (1918), 448; E. M. Forsythe, 'Child welfare clinics', *Can. Publ. Health J.*, 9 (1918), 170.

56. Brown, 'Relation of the paediatrician', 51.

57. Editorial, 'Baby clinics', *Can. Publ. Health J.*, 4 (1913), 94.

58. G. Smith, 'The result of three years' work in the Department of Child Hygiene, Toronto', *Can. Publ. Health J.*, 9 (1918), 310–1.

59. Smith, 'Result of three years' work', 313; Forsythe, 'Child welfare clinics', 170.

60. Smith, 'Result of three years' work', 313.

61. Toronto, Archives of Ontario, RG 10, 30-a-1, box 6, file 6.4, Ontario Department of Health, Public Health Nursing Division, Historical Literature, typescript outlining the scope and function of baby clinics in Ontario, 1920, 2. See also M. Power, Division of Maternal and Child Hygiene and Public Health Nursing, *Bulletin* (Sept.–Oct. 1924), 20.

62. Toronto, Archives of Ontario, RG 62, 1-f-1-b, box 473, letter of M. R. Heeley to Nursing Director Mary Power from Barrie, 9 July 1921, Ontario Department of Health, Public Health Nurses' Correspondence. For the status of nurses in Ontario in the early twentieth century, see J. Coburn, 'I see and am silent: a short history of nursing

in Ontario', in J. Acton, P. Goldsmith and B. Shepard (eds.) *Women at Work: Ontario 1850–1930* (Toronto, 1974).

63. Mullen, 'Child welfare in a democracy', 449.

64. Cody, 'Scope and function', 546–7.

65. Report of the London Child Welfare Association, 'The well-baby clinics in London, Canada', *Can. Publ. Health J.*, 16 (1925), 207. This treatment clinic was maintained by the Association until the early 1930s, when Depression finances necessitated that the Association's clinic and nurse visiting efforts be taken over by City Hall. From the point of view of the campaign's administrators in the provincial department of health, the treatment clinic had handicapped the movement's broader educational aims by antagonizing local physicians.

66. 'The well-baby clinics in London, Canada', *Can. Publ. Health J.*, 16 (1925), 202.

67. P. Bryce, 'Recent constructive developments in child welfare' (Child Welfare Report of the Ontario Social Service Council), *Soc. Welf.*, 2 (1920), 19.

68. Brown, 'Relation of the paediatrician', 51; Forsythe, 'Child welfare clinics', 169. See also Forsyth, 'Care of children under school age', 384; Blackader, 'Fundamental facts in organization', 97–8.

69. Brown, 'Relation of the paediatrician', 52.

70. Mullen, 'Child welfare in a democracy', 450–1; Sutherland, *Children*, 68.

71. Brown, 'Infant and child welfare work', 158–9.

72. A. Blackader, 'The problem of the nervous child', *Can. Publ. Health J.*, 15 (1924), 97–8.

73. J. T. Phair, 'Child hygiene', radio talk prepared for the Canadian Social Hygiene Council, 8 March 1927, pub. in *Can. Publ. Health J.*, 18 (1927), 132.

74. Phair, 'Child hygiene'.

75. E. Couture, *A Study of Maternal, Infant and Neonatal Mortality* (Ottawa, 1942).

6

'Why does Congress wish women and children to die?': the rise and fall of public maternal and infant health care in the United States, 1921–1929

Molly Ladd-Taylor

The United States, unlike most other industrialized nations, has no national health insurance, maternity benefit, or family allowance. It guarantees no maternal or child health services to its citizens. Racial and ethnic diversity, strongly held ideas about self-help and states' rights, and the American Medical Association's hostility to 'state medicine' historically limited the development of federal health entitlement programmes and the American 'semi-welfare' state. As a result, the USA now has a two-tiered health care system, which provides high-quality care to middle-class families with private health insurance and inferior services or nothing at all to the poor. African-American infants die at twice the rate of whites, and non-white mothers die nearly four times more often than white.[1] Fortunately, the soaring cost of medical care has renewed discussion of public responsibility for health care, prompting some policy makers and activists to look back to a largely forgotten experiment in federally supported maternal and child health care, the Sheppard–Towner Maternity and Infancy Protection Act of 1921.

The first 'women's' bill to pass into law after women won the vote in 1920, the Sheppard–Towner Act distributed federal matching funds to the states to disseminate information and instruction on nutrition and hygiene, for prenatal and child health conferences, and maternity nurses for pregnant women and new mothers.[2] Sponsored by Texas Senator Morris Sheppard and Congressman Horace Towner of Iowa, the maternity bill was the first federal social welfare measure. However, like other American welfare programmes, Sheppard–Towner was a weak bill with a pitifully small appropriation. It allocated only $1,480,000 for the fiscal year 1921–2 and $1,240,000 for the next

5 years. Of this sum, $50,000 was given to the US Children's Bureau for administrative expenses, $5,000 went to each state outright, and an additional $5,000 went to states which provided matching funds. Moreover, the aim of Sheppard–Towner was purely educational; the bill expressly forbade outright financial aid and medical care, and gave states and individuals the right to refuse aid. States had wide discretion in the development of maternity and infancy programmes. Each state had to pass special enabling legislation and provide a plan for implementing the programme before it could receive funds. Nevertheless, only Massachusetts, Connecticut, and Illinois eventually refused aid.[3]

Despite the modesty of its provisions, the Sheppard–Towner Act did not survive the 1920s. It was vigorously opposed by a coalition of medical societies and right-wing organizations, who believed it was a Communist-inspired step toward state medicine which threatened the home and violated the principle of states' rights. The anti-Sheppard–Towner coalition gained strength over the course of the 1920s, and in 1927 it forced the bill's mostly female supporters to accept a compromise which allocated funds for two more years, but repealed the law itself in 1929. Although federal funds for maternal and child health were restored under Title V of the 1935 Social Security Act, the programme established during the New Deal was fundamentally different from the Sheppard–Towner Act. Social Security health services were not conceived as an entitlement for all women and children, as Sheppard–Towner had been, but were a charity for those who could not afford a private physician.[4]

Maternal and child health was a major women's issue in the 1910s and 1920s, largely because the United States had one of the highest infant and maternal mortality rates in the western world. In 1915, approximately six women, and one hundred infants in the US birth registration area (where statistics were collected) died for every 1,000 live births. Deaths were even greater outside the registration area, and mortality was twice as high among people of colour. Nationally, at least 11 black women and 181 black infants died for every 1,000 live births. In some areas one-quarter of all babies failed to reach their fifth birthday.[5]

Although poor women and children were especially vulnerable, such appalling conditions touched all classes. Women activists and health reformers thus made 'baby-saving' a top priority. Members of women's clubs, parent–teacher associations, and settlement houses ran prenatal and well baby clinics, disseminated information on child hygiene to the poor, and lobbied the government for public health services. The Sheppard–Towner Act was the culmination of their efforts. Written by Children's Bureau chief Julia Lathrop and introduced into Congress in 1918 by Jeannette Rankin, the first woman in the House of Representatives, it was supported by virtually every women's organization and prominent woman reformer. 'Of all the activities in which I have shared during more than forty years of striving', declared social welfare activist Florence Kelley, 'none is, I am convinced, of such fundamental importance as the Sheppard–Towner Act'.[6]

The principal organization behind the Sheppard–Towner Act was the US Children's Bureau, established in 1912 as a division of the Department of Commerce and Labor. The Bureau was the first federal agency to be headed and staffed primarily by women – eight years before they won the vote – and it operated as the women's branch of the federal government in the 1910s and 1920s. Directed by Julia Lathrop (from 1912 to 1921) and Grace Abbott (from 1921 to 1934), both long-time residents of Hull House, the famous Chicago settlement, the Bureau was originally designed as a research and education agency. However, Lathrop, a brilliant political strategist, who had close ties to women's clubs and social settlements all over the country, designed a research and educational programme – which included childrearing publications, studies of infant mortality, and a birth registration drive – that she hoped would lead to further child welfare reform.[7]

The Children's Bureau baby-saving campaign was two-pronged, aimed simultaneously at the individual and the community. Lathrop wanted both to raise the childrearing 'standards' of individual mothers, and to eliminate the social and economic conditions leading to infant deaths. And she saw an integral connection between the two. She believed that educating women about the new scientific thinking on child-care would convince them that infant deaths were preventable and lead them to demand health and welfare services for their families. Also, Lathrop lived at a time when women were not taught vital information about childbirth and reproduction – and in a society that held science as the solution to social ills – and she believed that health education would remove the mystique surrounding prenatal care and childbirth and give women more control over their lives.

Education did not only flow one way. Mothers wrote the Children's Bureau as many as 125,000 letters a year, and they educated the mostly middle-class Bureau staff about their poverty, ill health, and concerns. For example, Lathrop was struck by the courage of an Idaho mother of four, with another on the way, who was burdened by overwork and poverty and feared she would die. 'Talk about better babys', the woman wrote bitterly, 'when a mother must be like some cow or mare when a babys come. If she lives, all wright [sic], and if not, Just the same'. The Children's Bureau chief also had a lengthy correspondence with a Wyoming mother expecting her third child, who lived 65 miles from a doctor and was 'filled with perfect horror at the prospects ahead [because] so many of my neighbors die at giving birth to their children'. Lathrop and her staff sent this woman money for hospital expenses and a layette, and designed a bill that they hoped would provide other expectant mothers with medical and nursing care. The Bureau staff's helpful and encouraging letters, and their willingness to send money for food, clothing and health care out of their own pockets to the mothers who wrote to them, led to strong grass-roots support amongst women for the federal Children's Bureau and its baby-saving campaign. In turn, the letters from poor mothers taught the Bureau staff how 'very urgent [was] the great question of protecting motherhood' and persuaded them to make maternal and infant health care a legislative priority.[8]

The federal government's interest in maternal and child health helped undermine traditional fatalism about infant mortality, raise women's expectations for their own health, and inspire some women into activism. Although the Wyoming woman had often assisted neighbours during childbirth, she wrote that it was not until the Children's Bureau campaign that she realized that those deaths were not inevitable. 'It seems strange that conditions . . . year after year . . . have been perfectly needless. It is only necessary to make the people realize that their conditions are not normal.' She, like thousands of others, volunteered to help the Children's Bureau 'in any way'. By 1918, more than 11 million women participated in the federal baby-saving campaign.[9]

Despite the popularity of the federal baby-saving campaign,

medical and right-wing groups vigorously opposed the Sheppard–Towner Act. They described it as an 'invasion of the castle of the American citizen', which would promote birth control, Bolshevism, and government control of children, and accused the Children's Bureau staff of being spinsters and Communists. Asserting that mother love was all women needed to raise healthy children, Sheppard–Towner opponents called the bill's emphasis on scientific childrearing information an insult to American motherhood. One conservative senator, noting that most members of the Children's Bureau staff were unmarried women, sarcastically proposed a bill that would teach them 'how to acquire a husband and have babies of their own'. However, in 1921 most congressmen were so bound up by the sentimental ideal of motherhood – and so afraid of the unknown female vote – that they passed the Sheppard–Towner Act by a wide margin. President Warren G. Harding signed it into law on 23 November 1921.[10]

An assessment of the Sheppard–Towner Act, as of all social welfare programmes, requires an analysis of its actual operation in local areas. Like other US welfare schemes, Sheppard–Towner was marked by local variation in funding and support. Its decentralized administration allowed communities to devise programmes that suited their needs, but it also made maternity work vulnerable to political opposition, racial discrimination, and incompetent administration. Thus, while Sheppard–Towner had a tremendous impact – and popular support – in states where the Children's Bureau worked effectively with local physicians and women's groups, it never got off the ground in others.

The most successful states used Sheppard–Towner funds both to provide services and to build a grass-roots campaign for maternal and child welfare. Literature distribution is a case in point. When women shared bulletins on childrearing and pre-natal care with friends and relatives, they both passed on much-needed information and created a wider demand for health care. Similarly, child health clinics also functioned both as a useful service and an effective tool for building community support for public maternal and infant health care. In rural areas clinics had a social as well as educative function; families came for refreshments, prizes, to watch films and the carnival atmosphere of the clinics, as well as for physical examinations and childrearing advice. A meeting in a remote county in

125

Mississippi was attended by over 200 women, some of whom rode horseback or walked several miles carrying small children. However, in places where difficult terrain, inclement weather, lack of roads, or a busy harvest season made it difficult to get a crowd to clinics, nurses spent most of their time on home visits. They helped with childbirth, treated sick children, and showed mothers how to prepare formula or get the house ready for childbirth using materials available in their homes. In New Mexico, a 14-month old baby weighing less than 9 pounds gained weight after the nurse taught his mother how to prepare milk formula and keep it cool, clean, and free from flies.[11]

Despite the good intentions of most Sheppard–Towner nurses, their faith in modern science and medicine frequently conflicted with traditional healing practices and sometimes put a wedge between them and prospective patients. In Florida, six white women left a meeting after the nurse began to talk about prenatal care, thereby challenging their religious beliefs about feminine modesty and maternal suffering. 'The Lord gives and the Lord takes and we have no business talking of such things', the women explained. Even women who sought Sheppard–Towner services rarely abandoned traditional practices, such as employing midwives and having female friends and relatives present during childbirth. Many mothers combined old and new methods of child-care and delivery, but rejected the efforts of Sheppard–Towner agents to replace traditional healing with modern medicine. For example, the family of a New Mexico woman who had been in labour for six days would not relinquish the midwife's services, even though the doctor refused to help if the midwife were there. Similarly, a Sheppard–Towner nurse in Montana reported with annoyance that a Native American family refused to allow whites to intervene in a case they considered the domain of the traditional healer.[12]

The clash between modern medicine and traditional healing is particularly evident in Sheppard–Towner work among midwives. Thirty-one states used Sheppard–Towner funds to establish midwife training programmes, despite opposition from medical societies who wanted to eliminate midwives entirely. The Children's Bureau defended licensed midwives, but shared physicians' faith in modern medicine and objected to what they considered some midwives' 'very ignorant and superstitious ways'. In some states, Sheppard–Towner nurses lacking sensitivity to local customs exercised their power to withhold licenses and to threaten the livelihood of midwives. Many mid-wives, understandably distrustful of these nurses, resisted the government's intrusion into their practices. In New Mexico, for example, the Sheppard–Towner nurse reported difficulty finding Mexican midwives, who were apparently hiding out in the hills until she left the county.[13]

Many midwives resisted government efforts at instruction, but there is evidence that some enjoyed the classes. Like expectant mothers, they turned government programmes to their advantage and incorporated modern innovations into traditional practices. Birth attendants readily adopted suggestions they found useful, such as substituting newspaper for old quilts during childbirth, but held on to other traditional practices. For example, an African-American midwife from Virginia carefully followed Sheppard–Towner instructions on hygiene, but refused to give up the practice of placing a pocket knife under the mattress to 'cut' the after-pains.[14]

Despite the cultural bias of its staff, the Children's Bureau made a serious effort to reduce mortality among all racial ethnic groups. Although most Sheppard–Towner nurses were white, the Bureau employed some black nurses to work in African-American communities, Spanish-speaking women to work among Mexicans, and American Indians to work on reservations. Still, the Sheppard–Towner Act's decentralized administration permitted states to provide inferior services to people of colour. Thus, although American Indian infants in Montana were 2.7 times more likely to die than whites, the state did not have a full-time nurse on the reservations, ostensibly because it did not want to challenge the authority of the federal Indian Medical Service.[15] Similarly, despite significantly higher death rates among blacks, the Georgia State Board of Health hired an inexperienced nurse to work with black midwives be- cause it considered the salary demanded by an experienced nurse 'too much for any negro'. The Children's Bureau staff, perhaps unwilling to jeopardize support for the Sheppard–Towner Act among white politicians and voters, did not comment.[16]

Despite its shortcomings and eventual repeal, Sheppard–Towner convinced many mothers that infant deaths were not inevitable, helped them find better ways to care for their babies given the constraints of poverty and isolation, and raised their expectations for health care. In seven years, Sheppard–Towner workers held 183,252 prenatal and child health conferences, made 3,131,996 home visits, distributed 22,030,489 pieces of literature, and established 2,978 permanent health clinics. According to the Children's Bureau, approximately 700,000 expectant mothers and more than 4,000,000 babies were served by Sheppard–Towner programmes. By 1929, the last year of the Act's operation, the Children's Bureau estimated that almost half of all babies born in that year had been touched by its advice.[17]

Infant mortality also declined during the Sheppard–Towner years. Nationally, the infant death rate fell from 76 to 69 per 1,000 live births between 1921 and 1928. Deaths due to gastro-intestinal disease, most easily prevented by educational programmes, declined by 47 per cent. Yet mortality remained high among babies of colour. When Sheppard–Towner began in 1921, 108 babies of colour died for every 1,000 live births; by 1928, the infant death rate was 106 (compared to 64 for whites). The 1921 rates were probably artificially low because several states with high African-American death rates had not yet joined the birth registration area. However, Sheppard–Towner's decentralized administration and the Bureau staff's hostility to traditional healing probably contributed to its failure to reduce significantly deaths among people of colour.[18]

The Sheppard–Towner Act was popular among the women who used its services, and the federal and state Children's Bureaus received hundreds of letters showing women's support. 'I trust you'll find by many letters that your work is doing much and will continue it', wrote a West Virginia mother of twins. 'There are many who do not Pay attention But It Is a great Benefit to those that do.' A Georgia woman agreed: 'I don't see how we poor mothers could do without them [prenatal clinics] . . . I am the mother of 14 children, and I never was cared for till I begin going to the good will center clinic . . . We are so glad the day has come when we have someone to care for our babies when they get sick.'[19]

Despite its popularity among women and apparent success at reducing mortality, at least among white infants, the Sheppard–Towner Act fell victim to the increasingly conservative political climate of the 1920s. Three additional factors played a part in the Act's defeat. First, politicians' support had always been soft; most congressmen initially backed Sheppard–Towner more out of fear of women voters than out of commitment to the programme. By 1926, when Sheppard–Towner appropriations were to be renewed, congressmen knew that they had nothing to fear. The knowledge that women did not vote as a bloc significantly reduced the effectiveness of the pro-Sheppard–Towner lobby.[20]

Second, the powerful American Medical Association relentlessly opposed Sheppard–Towner as a step toward 'state medicine'. Throughout the 1920s, the Children's Bureau tried to appease physicians by distinguishing Sheppard–Towner preventive health education from private medical care. They argued that doctors treated sick children, while infant welfare clinics were educational and were geared toward the healthy child. In some places, Sheppard–Towner workers even refused to examine children who did not have permission from their doctors! Yet despite these measures, medical opposition to Sheppard–Towner increased. Moreover, Children's Bureau efforts to win medical support by defining their work as educational and including doctors in child health conferences undermined Children's Bureau authority in maternal and child health. During the 1920s, male physicians incorporated many Sheppard–Towner techniques into their private practices and replaced most of the women in top positions in the state bureaus of child hygiene.[21]

A third factor in the defeat of the Sheppard–Towner Act was the inability of its supporters to sustain a grass-roots women's health movement in the states. Although women continued to support Sheppard–Towner throughout the decade, its modest provisions and decentralized administration, combined with political problems in the states, limited the Children's Bureau's ability to use Sheppard–Towner services to strengthen the lobby for maternal and child welfare. Most of the Children's Bureau staff saw Sheppard–Towner as a step toward universally-available medical and nursing care, but they supported a bill which forbade outright financial aid and medical care in order to secure passage of some form of maternity aid. After the passage of the very moderate Sheppard–Towner Act, the Bureau's position changed from the leader of a political campaign for child welfare into the administrator and defender of an existing – and inadequate – programme. The tension between the Bureau's dual role as service-provider and leader of the child welfare reform movement made it difficult for staff

129

members to defend their own positions in government while protecting the welfare schemes for which they had fought so hard.[22]

Ironically, the success of the Sheppard–Towner Act contributed to its ultimate defeat. Sheppard–Towner raised women's expectations about their health and made them more knowledgeable about prenatal and well baby care. Their enthusiasm for Sheppard–Towner services led doctors to incorporate preventive examinations into their private practices and to improve obstetrical training in medical schools. These changes led to a decline in mortality among white infants and made federally-funded health care appear less urgent to white voters.

The repeal of the Sheppard–Towner Act reasserted the long-held principle that children's health was the responsibility of individual mothers, not society. Although some states continued maternity and infancy aid after 1929, the financial constraints of the Depression forced deep cuts, making health care once again unavailable to women who lived in remote areas or who could not afford private physicians – women to whom the Maternity and Infancy Act was geared. When federal funds for maternal and infant health care were restored in the 1935 Social Security Act, public health services were limited to the poor.[23] Today, with prenatal and infant care still considered private responsibilities, but an alarming increase in the number of babies needing special care, we would do well to look back to the brief US experiment in federally-funded maternal and infant health care.

Notes

1. Children's Defense Fund, 'A call for action to make our nation safe for children: a briefing book on the status of American children in 1988', 3–4; 26–7.

2. The 'visiting nurses' funded under the Sheppard–Towner Act were often, but not always, maternity nurses. This described what they did rather than their speciality. Children's Bureau reports often called them 'field nurses'. These nurses undertook many tasks, caring for children as well as birthing mothers. A project funded by Sheppard–Towner in several states was a training programme for 'maternity and infancy nurses'.

3. J. S. Lemons, *The Woman Citizen: Social Feminism in the 1920s* (Urbana, Ill., 1973); S. Rothman, *Woman's Proper Place: A History of Changing Ideals and Practices, 1870 to the Present* (New York, 1978),

136–53; R. L. Muncy, *Creating a Female Dominion in American Reform, 1890–1935* (New York and Oxford, 1990); R. A. Meckel, *Save the Babies: American Public Health Reform and the Prevention of Infant Mortality 1850– 1929* (Baltimore and London, 1990); M. Ladd-Taylor, *Mother-Work: Women, Child Welfare and the State 1890–1930* (Urbana., Ill., forthcoming).

4. See L. B. Costin, *Two Sisters for Social Justice: A Biography of Grace and Edith Abbott* (Urbana, Ill., 1983); S. Ware, *Beyond Suffrage: Women in the New Deal* (Cambridge, Mass., 1981).

5. US Bureau of the Census, *Historical Statistics of the United States Colonial Times to 1970*, pt 1 (Washington, DC, 1975), 57; US Children's Bureau, *Maternal Mortality*, Bureau pub. no. 158 (Washington, DC, 1926), 37.

6. Quoted in Lemons, *Woman Citizen*, 155.

7. On the Children's Bureau, see M. Ladd-Taylor, 'Hull House goes to Washington: women and the Children's Bureau', in N. S. Dye and N. Frankel (eds) *Gender, Class and Reform in the Progressive Era* (Lexington, Ky, 1991); J. Parker and E. M. Carpenter, 'Julia Lathrop and the Children's Bureau: the emergence of an institution', *Soc. Serv. Rev.*, 55 (1981), 60–76; N. Pottishman Weiss, 'Save the children: a history of the Children's Bureau, 1903–1918', unpub. Ph.D. diss., University of California, Los Angeles, 1974; and Muncy, *Creating a Female Dominion.*

8. Mrs M. R., Idaho, 4 Jan. 1916; Mrs A. P., Wyoming, 19 Oct. 1916, repr. in M. Ladd-Taylor, *Raising a Baby the Government Way: Mothers' Letters to the Children's Bureau, 1915–1932* (New Brunswick, NJ, 1986), 134, 49–51.

9. Ladd-Taylor, *Raising a Baby*, 18, 49; G. Abbott, 'Ten years' work for children', *N. Am. Rev.*, 218 (1923), 189–200.

10. *Congressional Record*, vol. 61, 67th Congress, 1st session, 21 July 1921, 8764; House Committee on Interstate and Foreign Commerce, *Public Protection of Maternity and Infancy: Hearings on H.R. 10925*, 66th Congress, 3rd Session, 23 Dec. 1920, 116. See Ladd-Taylor, *Mother-Work.*

11. See, for example [Mississippi], 'Narrative and Statistical Report', March 1924, File 11-26-1, Central Files, 1914–40, Children's Bureau Records, National Archives, Washington, DC (hereafter CB); 'Semi-Annual report of maternity and infancy work [Arizona]', 1 July 1924 to 13 Dec. 1924, File 11-4-8, Correspondence & Reports, Children's Bureau Records (hereafter C&R, CB); D. Anderson to G. S. Luckett, 6 Oct. 1926, File 11-33-8, CB.

12. D. Anderson to G. S. Luckett, 6 Oct. 1926, File 11-33-8, CB; Child Welfare Division, Montana State Board of Health, 'Narrative report of activities', 1 July to 31 Dec. 1924, File 11-28-8, C&R, CB.

13. 'Report of work done under the Maternity and Infancy Act in the state of New Mexico', 1 July 1925 to 30 June 1926, File 11-33-8, C&R, CB.

14. 'Midwife classes held in Halifax County, Virginia', 5, File 11-50-8, C&R, CB. For more detailed discussion, see M. Ladd-Taylor, '"Grannies" and "Spinsters": midwife training under the Sheppard–

Towner Act', *J. Soc. Hist.*, 22 (1988), 255–75.

15. 185.4 American Indians, compared to 69.1 whites, died for every 1,000 live births. 'Report of work done under federal Maternity and Infancy Act in the state of Montana', 1 July 1926 to 30 June 1927, File 11-28-8, C&R, CB.

16. 'Report of work done under federal Maternity and Infancy Act in the state of Montana', 1 July 1926 to 30 June 1927, File 11-28-8, C&R, CB; [Georgia] Division of Child Hygiene, *A/R*, 1925, File 11-12-8, C&R, CB; Clark Goreman, Georgia Committee on Interracial Cooperation, to B. Haines, 8 July 1926, File 11-12-2, CB.

17. US Children's Bureau, *Promotion of the Welfare and Hygiene of Maternity and Infancy for the Year Ending June 30, 1929* (Washington, DC, 1931), 27, 21.

18. The white infant mortality rate was 72 per 1,000 in 1921. US Children's Bureau, *Promotion of the Welfare and Hygiene*, 132.

19. West Virginia Division of Child Hygiene and Public Health Nursing, 'Extracts from statements of mothers who took motherhood correspondence course', enclosed in Katharine Lenroot to Julia Lathrop, 23 Sept. 1926, File 11-0, CB; 'Letters from Georgia women attending prenatal clinic', enclosed in J. Bowdoin to D. K. Brown, 30 April 1929, Dorothy Kirchwey Brown Papers, Arthur and Elizabeth Schlesinger Library, Radcliffe College, Cambridge, Mass.

20. See Lemons, *Woman Citizen*, 157.

21. 'Conference of Directors of State Divisions Administering the Federal Maternal and Infancy Act', 19–21 Sept. 1923, 24, File 11-0, C&R, CB; Rothman, *Woman's Proper Place*, 150–2.

22. See J. Sealander, *As Minority Becomes Majority: Federal Reaction to the Phenomenon of Women in the Work Force, 1920–1963* (Westport, Conn., 1983), 3–11, for a similar phenomenon in the Women's Bureau.

23. See Costin, *Two Sisters*, 221–6.

7

Ephemeral lives: the unremitting infant mortality of colonial Burma, 1891–1941

Judith Richell

Throughout the country's colonial period the average Burmese family had to come to terms, at least once, with that particularly cruel bereavement, the death of an infant child. Of every hundred children born alive, twenty-five to thirty-five died before their first birthday. Such a high rate of infant mortality was not unusual in the nineteenth century, but by the early twentieth century in many countries sanitarians, bacteriologists and the medical profession were at last saving infant lives. In Burma, however, the rate of infant deaths stayed obstinately high despite health innovations such as a midwifery service and a hospital programme. Why did this happen? Was it due to epidemic disease or poor hygiene or were there other factors at work?

Burma became a British colony in the nineteenth century. The annexation took place in three stages: in 1826 the coastal provinces of Arakan and Tenasserim were ceded, followed in 1852 by the second Anglo-Burmese war and the occupation of Pegu, and then in 1886 Upper Burma was formally annexed. The fighting in 1852 and 1885 was followed by long periods of unrest and guerrilla war, which (amongst other disruptions) had a damaging effect on the accuracy of the census, the taxation data and the establishment of vital registration records.

Vital registration of births and deaths was introduced into selected towns from the 1870s, and was gradually extended to most of lowland Burma by 1905. However, for a number of reasons, including the reluctance of the British to provide adequate funding, administrative changes and a rebellion in 1930, the vital registration records persistently omitted approximately 30 per cent of infant births and deaths.

The data on infant mortality discussed here was drawn from two statistical sources and also from comments in the records of the British colonial administration. The statistical sources used were the vital registration records and the decennial census records. Census records yielded indirect estimates of crude birth and death rates through use of survival analysis and model life tables.[1] The infant mortality rates obtained from the adjusted data are probably the most accurate that can be calculated at present, and a fair degree of confidence is felt in these rates because they are based on an analysis of female mortality which agrees with the contemporary estimates made by officials working in Burma. Owing to the wartime loss of most of the 1941 census records, it was not possible to produce rates for the period 1931 to 1941 by this method. But annual health reports and registration data, together with evidence from the experimental health centres set up by the administration and from reports, articles and commentaries, all indicate that the high rates persisted through the 1930s. The results of the census survival analysis and the rates taken from the vital registration records are both shown in Table 7.1, and illustrate clearly that a high infant mortality rate (hereafter IMR) was sustained during the British administration.

The figures suggest that during the forty-year period from 1891 to 1931, an average of only 68 per cent of infant mortality

Table 7.1 Infant mortality rates in Burma, 1891–1941

Estimated rates from West Model life tables			*Registered rates, ten year averages*	
	Female	*Male*		
1891–1901	250	295	1891–1900	178.0
1901–1911	250	295	1901–1910	200.5
1911–1921	295	335	1911–1920	220.0
1921–1931	295	335	1921–1930	196.6
			1931–1939	199.8

Sources: *Census of India, Burma, 1891 (London), 1901–31 (Rangoon); Report on the Sanitary Administration of Burma 1891–1939 (Rangoon)*; A. J. Coale, and P. Demeney, *Regional Model Life Tables and Stable Populations* (New York, 1983).

134

was officially registered. To put it another way, for every ten children born alive in British Burma, at least one was born and then died before its first birthday without entering the registration system.

The cost of infant mortality in human terms is enormous. Economic factors are also important; each infant death can be regarded as a lost investment and the loss of potential credit for the country. In addition to this, infant mortality is a very potent determinant of population change and therefore needs to be carefully explored in that context. But there is a more subtle reason why infant mortality is important, which has been accepted for more than a hundred years: the IMR is a measure of the health and prosperity of a community.[2] British health officials were well aware of this fact and records indicate their sensitivity to potential criticism in this area. In 1909, C. E. Williams, the Sanitary Commissioner, made a bald summary of the situation when he commented that the high infant mortality in Thayetmyo Town was 'intimately associated with the social and sanitary conditions under which the townspeople live'.[3]

A useful way to examine the significance of Burma's infant mortality rates is to compare the figures with those of neighbouring countries. In the Straits Settlements the IMR had declined from 255 per 1,000 in 1906 to 168 in 1936, while in the Federated Malay States it had been reduced from 203 in 1927 to 142 in 1936.[4] The average IMR in the city of Bangkok from 1932 to 1934 was 168,[5] and in India, the probability of dying in the first year of life declined after 1920 'from the highest values of 301 per 1,000 live births (1911–20) for males and 284 for females (1901–11), to 190 and 175, respectively, in 1941–50'.[6]

It makes little difference whether these rates for neighbouring countries are contrasted with the registered IMR for Burma or the estimated rates, as neither indicate a decline in infant mortality. The average official rate for 1931 to 1939 is almost identical with the rate for 1901 to 1910 as both are almost 200 per 1,000. An even grimmer picture is painted by the estimated IMR, which shows an increasing rate rather than a decline as seen in the neighbouring countries. The following discussions on infant nutrition and disease are an attempt to understand what happened to those infants in Burma.

Infant nutrition

The first public health report for British Burma, written in 1867, commented on the 'excessive mortality amongst Burmese children'[7] and chiefly attributed this to indigestible food. Criticisms of infant diet in Burma were a consistent theme in the health reports and constituted the most popular explanation of the high infant mortality, putting the blame on the mothers' deficiencies instead of those of the administrations. Despite some slight and healthy scepticism, the weight of comment suggests that nutrition was important and the only available statistics link between 20 and 40 per cent of infant deaths in Mandalay and Rangoon to prematurity and 'nutrition related' causes.[8]

Infant nutrition is not solely a matter of the child's diet, but is perhaps equally concerned with maternal diet. There are two obvious phases in the nutrition of an infant, the *in utero* and postnatal period (including supplementary feeding). At both these stages the child is dependent on the quantity and quality of its mother's diet ; chronic under-nutrition or malnutrition of the mother is a threat to the child's health.

It is difficult to find evidence of such a private and domestic matter as the diet of pregnant Burmese women. A few references exist to a poor state of health in pregnant and parturient women, but the most illuminating evidence appears in an extract from the report of a Lady Assistant District Health Officer published in the Health Report of 1939. In the course of her duty of investigating the high IMR of a Burmese town, this Health Officer visited mothers and infants in their homes and reported that,

> From the infants I inspected during my home visits, I have formed a very strong conviction that most of the deaths which occur within the first three months are primarily due to malnutrition. Most mothers even those of the middle class that can afford luxurious diet, try to starve themselves during pregnancy. This I may say is due to the Burmese custom and prejudices that they still follow even now. They believe that if during this period they live strictly on rice diet with some dried fish and other dried products, they are bound to be free from ailments that people who take plenty of fresh and rich foodstuff would suffer from. In some very poor cases pregnant mothers

would restrict themselves to such an extent that they would eat nothing but rice and a few grains of salt as they cannot afford to have dried fish. Is there any wonder then that a child born of such a mother is so poorly nourished? On examination some mothers were found to be devoid of subcutaneous fat, some have angular stomatitis and gastro-intestinal disturbance, etc. The infants are also devoid of subcutaneous fat, their bones are very soft, and on the whole they are very undersize.[9]

Several postwar sources support the suggestion that maternal diet was determined and restricted by custom in Burma. Surveys conducted from the 1950s onwards found that pregnant women omitted vegetables and fruit from their diet and many excluded all first class proteins such as meat, fish and eggs. These foods were believed to be harmful to the baby and prejudicial to the mother's health.[10] The desire of Burmese women to have small babies was another powerful reason for eating such a restricted diet, leading one researcher to comment that the low average birth weight (2.75 kg) of babies in Burma was 'not a genetic characteristic but is due in part to maternal malnutrition'.[11]

These postwar reports strengthen the prewar evidence that malnutrition during pregnancy affected the viability of the new-born child. Burmese infants were disadvantaged because their mothers' diet was restricted by custom, as well as by the vagaries of harvests and food shortages. A diet that reduced the protein, mineral and vitamin intake and was also designed, under-standably, to restrict the size of the baby at birth, placed the child at great risk especially in the first, most hazardous month, when the principal causes of death were low birth weight and infection.[12]

One of the problems in assessing these arguments for the earlier period is that infant mortality was not classified according to age at death until 1920. An additional difficulty is that approximately one-third of the deaths were omitted from the data, making an interpretation of the trends risky. The use of neonatal data is even more hazardous as the majority of these young lives were probably lost within a few days of birth, thus lessening the significance to the community of both their arrival and departure and making registration seem even more of an unnecessary bureaucratic chore.

Breastfeeding, the second stage of a Burmese infant's

nutrition, was universal and prolonged. Early commentators suggested a duration of up to three years[13] and postwar studies found an average duration of two years.[14] Although the British administrators took the necessity of breastfeeding for granted, some were offended by its duration. In the Annual Sanitary Report for 1894 the Officiating Sanitary Commissioner, G. T. Thomas, astonishingly described breastfeeding for two years as an 'insanitary habit which requires correction'![15] (Fortunately for Burmese infants, Thomas was 'officiating' only for a matter of weeks.)

Today breastfeeding is regarded as the most important weapon in the fight against infant malnutrition, but unfortunately in prewar Burma the diet of lactating women was so restricted by cultural beliefs that their milk may have been impoverished in both quality and quantity. This in turn meant that the infant was malnourished and vulnerable to attack by infectious disease. The strongest evidence for this suggestion appears in the Public Health Report for 1928. The Assistant District Health Officer for Bassein, Dr Saw Kyaw Zit wrote that

> It is very usual for women in Burma, in their anxiety to have healthy children, to restrict their diet to rice and salt only during lactation. I think this voluntary semi-starvation practised by the over-anxious mother contributes much to the unhealthy condition of the suckling mother and consequent high infant mortality.[16]

This statement by Dr Zit should be taken as strong evidence of a widespread practice. As a Burmese doctor, with intimate knowledge of his patients and their families, his assessment was of greater value than the more cursory understanding of a European doctor. Dr Zit's argument is also strongly supported by postwar reports on the diets of lactating women which stress the avoidance of vegetables, pulses and meats and the preference for a rice and salt diet.[17] It should be emphasized here that this very restricted diet probably evolved originally to protect the child from the diarrhoeal diseases which cause such heavy mortality in hot countries.

It is impossible to prove that a restricted diet impaired the quality or quantity of the lactation of Burmese women prior to 1940. The role of nutrition in lactation and birth weight is neither simple nor agreed. Modern studies, however, have shown that birth weights may be increased by providing pregnant women with dietary supplements,[18] and that birth weight probably also helps determine the quantity of the mother's breast milk; the production of a larger, stronger baby results in a larger lactation capacity.[19] Therefore, although the precise significance of maternal diet is still open to discussion, the consumption of adequate quantities of vitamins and minerals and their effect on birth weight, and the relationship between birth weight and lactation, are all factors relevant to the situation in Burma. Studies of postwar Burma suggest that the quantity of the lactating mother's breast milk is affected by poor nutritional status or multiparity, or both. It is not unreasonable, therefore, to suggest that similar conditions would have had the effect of reducing the supply of breast milk available to the infant in prewar Burma.

Does poor nutrition affect the quality of breast milk, measured in terms of vitamin presence? One of the most important vitamins for infants is thiamine, as a deficiency of this is associated with infantile beri beri. Two modern studies of Burma have related the low thiamine content of breast milk to the way in which cultural demands have restricted the diet of mothers.[20] The importance of this is discussed below.

The final aspect of infant nutrition to be considered is supplementary feeding. This was a more visible aspect of infant diet than those linked to maternal nutrition, and as such was widely commented on by British medical staff between 1867 and 1939. Their statements were almost uniformly hostile, derogatory and sometimes bigoted. Boiled rice was the supplementary food most commonly given to Burmese infants, to which plantain was gradually added, and then sometimes small amounts of proteins, such as fish. The Sanitary Report of 1870 states that fish curry was used in addition to plantain, plus a few whiffs of the cheroot for the infant. J. McNeale Donnelly, the author of the report, considered that under this treatment, 'natural selection soon winnows the weakly children from the robust'.[21] A slightly less derogatory description appeared in the *Indian Medical Gazette* in July 1920; it was written by N. K. Kunhikannan, a sub-assistant surgeon who spent fourteen years in Burma. He described the method of feeding as follows: 'the mother chews boiled rice, and, when it has been reduced to a semi solid mass, spits it into the mouth of her infant, who swallows the bolus without difficulty'.[22]

It was this preparatory chewing of boiled rice by the mother or other relative which offended many medical staff and aroused them to invective. In 1931 the District Health Officer for Sandoway wrote that

> The disgusting habit of chewing rice is undoubtably responsible for much of the infantile mortality. Granny gives a hand in keeping baby quiet. She takes a bolus of boiled rice in her grubby fingers, and pops it into a septic mouth. There the rice is intimately mixed with saliva, film from unbrushed teeth and possibly pus from pyorrhoea. This is then fed to the baby. Violent gastro-enteritis is the only possible result. Further septic feeding continues until the baby is killed.[23]

No precise information is available on the quantities of supplementary foods given to Burmese babies before 1939, so only tentative comment can be made. It is probable that the diet, as reported by the health officials, was deficient in protein, especially if the introduction of fish and other proteins was delayed until the infant was 1 year old. Postwar studies confirm that by tradition the Burmese infant was given rice and rice only as a supplementary food, sometimes until 2 years of age. Eggs, meat, fish, pulses and vegetables were withheld, as they were believed to be harmful, causing colic, indigestion, diarrhoea and intestinal worms.[24]

Before leaving the subject of feeding the infant with boiled, chewed rice, one other possible aspect of this diet should be considered. In South-east Asia there may well be a 'widespread belief in the strength-giving, nutritional and mystical qualities of rice'.[25] Certainly for the Burmese people rice has great importance and it could be that by chewing and offering rice to her infant, the mother is both bonding and offering her infant the best food that she can. In 1920, Kunhikannan noted the symbolic strength given to the infant with its first rice. There was a belief 'universal amongst Burmans that unless an infant soon after birth is given some boiled rice it will never have the strength to bear the pain of the bite of an ant'.[26]

So far the discussion in this chapter has concentrated on Burmese cultural influences which deprived the mother and her infant of essential proteins, vitamins and minerals. But in the twentieth century the Burmese diet was further damaged. The development of the Irrawaddy delta as an important rice growing area with a thriving export and milling industry, resulted in mass consumption of highly milled white rice instead of the brown or home pounded rice previously eaten. An approximate estimate, based on the only dietary survey carried out in Burma, published in 1948, suggested that 80 per cent of the population of Lower Burma and 50 per cent of the population of Upper Burma were eating machine milled, highly polished rice by 1939.[27] This rice contained less than half the quantity of thiamine retained by hand pounded rice and reduced the thiamine content of the Burmese diet to dangerously low levels.

The population most at risk from this change would have been pregnant or lactating women and infants, especially those attacked by an infection which commonly triggers frank beri beri or infantile beri beri, a cause of high mortality among babies between the ages of 1 and 6 months. A postwar study in Burma suggested that 'infantile beri beri is an extremely important cause of infant mortality', but admitted that little was known about the real incidence of the disease.[28] Studies in Burma and Thailand found that sudden death in a previously apparently healthy, breastfed baby was typical of infantile beri beri, and that in most cases, although the mother had a thiamine deficiency, it was not severe enough to give her clinical symptoms of beri beri.[29]

No precise or concrete historical data exists to confirm the importance of infantile beri beri in colonial Burma. But these postwar studies indicate that it probably became an important cause of infant death as the practice of eating highly milled white rice spread. This dietary change, when combined with the customary restrictions imposed on pregnant or lactating mothers' food, created a possibly lethal thiamine deficiency for many Burmese infants, and this may be the major reason why infant mortality remained persistently high despite the decline in major epidemic disease. The vulnerability of the Burmese infant to malnutrition would appear to have followed the child in its journey through the *in utero* stage up to its first birthday. This can therefore be considered as the most important, underlying cause of infant mortality.

Infant disease

In the nineteenth and early twentieth centuries, diseases were usually classified by their symptoms rather than by a specific pathogen. This makes records hard to interpret and is illustrated by the high numbers of infant deaths attributed to 'convulsions' appearing in Burmese records. In 1931 the Sanitary Commissioner of Burma said, in some exasperation no doubt, that 'convulsions' might mean anything 'from cerebrospinal meningitis or tetanus to simple diarrhoea, fever or unsuitable feeding'.[30]

The mention of tetanus is significant as this probably took a heavy toll of infant lives. Neonatal tetanus is commonly introduced through the open wound of the severed umbilical cord and the incubation period of the disease is six to fourteen days.[31] This means that accurate age of death figures can be diagnostic as tetanus deaths are most common in the second week of life. Such data, however, is unfortunately not available for colonial Burma.

By 1894 the link between tetanus incidence and the severing of the cord was recognized by the British medical staff. In that year the Sanitary Report mentioned that the practice of cutting the umbilical cord 'with a piece of dirty bamboo' still persisted in some places. At Akyab the civil surgeon ascribed 'the prevalence of infant lock-jaw to this relic of barbarism'.[32] (No mention was made as to how the rural Burmese were supposed to obtain access to aseptic conditions!) Authoritative statements on the number of neonatal tetanus deaths in colonial Burma cannot be made as the quantitative evidence is too sparse. However, there have been a number of postwar studies in Thailand and Bangladesh which attribute between 30 and 40 per cent of all neonatal deaths to infantile tetanus and these figures may well be comparable to the earlier incidence in Burma.[33]

This depressing scenario of low birth weights, malnutrition, infantile beri beri and neonatal tetanus is not the end of the story. Burmese infants also succumbed to dysentery, diarrhoea and respiratory diseases and lurking epidemics of smallpox and malaria. The only available statistics on infant deaths from bowel complaints or respiratory diseases are tabulated below. These figures are limited in that they are confined to urban areas only, and by the fact that the cause of death was often diagnosed after death. Even so, the data provide an interesting

guide to possible levels of infection, and suggest that the incidence of respiratory disease was higher in the dry zone of Upper
Burma than in the wetter delta.

Table 7.2 Registered infant deaths from bowel and respiratory
disease as a percentage of total infant deaths in Mandalay, Rangoon
and Bassein in selected years

Town	Year	Dysentery, diarrhoea, digestive diseases %	Respiratory diseases %
Mandalay	1913	5.95	23.0
Mandalay	1914	–	19.5
Mandalay	1915	4.4	25.7
Mandalay	1916	7.7	29.1
Rangoon	1915	8.33	21.16
Rangoon	1924	7.3	17.4
Bassein	1910, 1911, 1914	28.35 (av.)	11.14

Source: *Report on the Sanitary Administration of Burma 1910–24 (Rangoon).*

To say that an infant died of diarrhoea or respiratory disease
was a 'blanket' terminology which may be misleading. It probably conceals many of the deaths due to a combination of
malnutrition, viral infection and secondary bacterial infection.
For example, very little evidence exists on the prevalence of
measles in Burmese infants, a disease which is very likely to have
caused infant fatalities that were registered as diarrhoeal or
pneumonic deaths. Although adult mortality from measles was
recorded in Burma, sanitary authorities did not seem to connect
the disease with infant mortality.[34]

Some British health officials recognized the links between
malnutrition, sanitary conditions and infectious disease, but
others preferred explanations based on prejudice and racism.
Captain Kelsall, Civil Surgeon for Thayetmyo Town, attributed
the high IMR at Thayetmyo largely to syphilis, despite admitting
that the town hospital's statistics did not verify this theory.[35]
Then in 1910, Kelsall, although still citing 'congenital syphilis'
as 'largely the cause of deaths in Thayetmyo',[36] found a more

external and Darwinian cause to blame. He claimed, 'A further factor tending to increase the mortality [of infants] is the extraordinary amount of mixed breeding in Thayetmyo whereby the high vitality of the Burman is lowered by the large admixture of the physically weaker Madrass'.[37]

Although congenital syphilis must have contributed to the IMR in Burma, it is difficult to estimate its incidence because of the lack of statistical information and the chauvinistic nature of some of the comments. Syphilis may have been a factor in the IMR of some of the coastal and riverine towns in Burma, but smallpox was of far greater importance. Infant deaths from smallpox, when considered over a fifty-year period from 1880 to 1930, declined from approximately 20 per cent of the total smallpox mortality to 4.5 per cent. The adult smallpox mortality also showed a tendency to decline, but as the disease pattern took the form of three- to six-year waves of epidemics, the decline was not constant in either infants or adults. The highest figure recorded for infant smallpox deaths was 1,088 in the epidemic of 1884 in Lower Burma, but by 1930 the number of deaths had dwindled to a mere 41 for the whole of Burma. Infant smallpox deaths (and other notifiable diseases) were probably considerably under-registered, but nevertheless the decline of the disease was real and largely due to a vaccination programme.

The discussion on infant disease has, so far, been confined to factors which were not unique to Burma; they were common to many societies. But the incidence of these diseases does not explain why the IMR remained high in Burma while it declined in adjacent countries. In addition to the nutritional deficiencies discussed above, I would suggest that epidemic malaria was one of the causes of the differences between Burma and the other nations. The evidence to support this suggestion lies in the acknowledged high (although unquantified) levels of the disease in Burma, the reports (which are very limited) by the authorities on its impact on the IMR, and the known epidemiology of malaria.

There are no specific statistics on malaria which would confirm that infants were dying of the disease. Prior to 1910 the official Sanitary and Health Reports made few references implicating malaria as a cause of infant mortality. Such an omission from the reports, however, does not mean that malaria or related disease were not the cause of infant deaths. Rather, it implies that any infant deaths due to malaria were unobserved in the rural areas. By 1909, however, an increasing awareness of malaria among the medical profession all over the world coincided with an awakening interest in infant mortality, making more officials and medical practitioners alert to the possible connections between the two.[38]

In areas where malaria is endemic the infant's first encounter with the disease is during its foetal life; in pregnancy malarial immunity in the mother is attenuated, resulting in increased parasitaemia. For the mother this higher infestation can result in anaemia and possibly premature labour,[39] and for the baby it can mean a premature birth and a lowered birth weight, owing to malarial infection of the placenta.[40] This factor, when combined with the mother's malnutrition due to the cultural factors already discussed, must have contributed greatly to neonatal mortality.

When a Burmese infant died of malaria and the death was reported (if it was registered!), the cause of death was probably attributed to the observed symptoms. In epidemic areas this was probably infantile convulsions, respiratory or diarrhoeal disease,[41] making it difficult to estimate the incidence of malaria. Many districts in Burma were acknowledged to be malarious, especially the littoral zones whether coastal, mountainous or riverine. High rates of malaria in the districts of Upper Burma also caught the attention of the health authorities. Coinciding with this, from 1907 to 1910 health officials also reported that the IMR for Upper Burma was higher than that for Lower Burma, the rates differing by 45 per 1,000 in 1907, 21 per 1,000 in 1908, 23 per 1,000 in 1909, and 39 per 1,000 in 1910.[42]

In the annual health reports, the commissioners discussed which urban and rural districts had particulary high or low IMRs. Three dry-zone districts of Upper Burma, Mandalay, Kyaukse and Shwebo, were identified in these reports as having IMRs which constantly exceeded the rural rate for the province. Between 1916 and 1939 the Kyaukse and Shwebo district rate was mentioned nineteen times and Mandalay district fourteen times. In ten of the reports one of the district rural rates was more than 100 per 1,000 above the province rural rate. No separate rural tables of infant deaths were published. This means that the only way of obtaining rural figures, as against district figures which included the towns, was when the rural rates of a district were so high that they warranted special mention in the health reports. The consistency with which these districts were named is, therefore, highly significant as are their consistently high IMRs compared to the average rates for the province as a whole.

Another of the issues discussed in the reports of 1916 and 1917 was the deficit of children under 10 years of age in Kyaukse, Mandalay and Shwebo; this must have been partly due to stillbirths and infant deaths. Table 7.3 shows the figures given in the 1916 report on the numbers of children per 100 married females of childbearing age. The first column represents malarial districts and the second column other districts in Upper Burma considered by the health authorities to be affected less by the disease. The high IMRs and the abnormally small number of children per married female in the former districts suggest a disease pattern fatally affecting infants and small children.

Further evidence appears in the health records of the epidemic malaria that existed in these dry-zone districts. In 1916 and 1917 surveys in Mandalay and Kyaukse revealed hyperendemic and holoendemic malaria in both districts, with spleen indexes (measurable splenic enlargement in children under 10 years), of up to 100 per cent.[43] Despite this, no attempt was made to identify the anopheline mosquito responsible for disease transmission or to prevent it from breeding.

In 1917 the health report admitted, for the first time, that the prevalence of malaria in Mandalay and Kyaukse districts may have been aggravated to epidemic proportions by the British extension of the irrigation canals.[44] (Although not discussed in this report, this factor also applied to Shwebo and other dry-zone districts, where new canals had been built and existing ones

Table 7.3 Numbers of children per 100 married females of childbearing age in selected districts of Upper Burma

Malarial districts		*Less malarial districts*	
Kyaukse	183	Magwe	245
Mandalay	188	Sagaing	244
Shwebo	218	Meiktila	244

Source: *Report on the Sanitary Administration of Burma 1916* (Rangoon).

remodelled.) This is a fundamental point. Although malaria was not new to Burma, the alterations brought about by the British authorities were a vital force in destabilizing the disease pattern. Changes in transport, civil engineering works, an infected immigrant work-force and the provision of new anopheline breeding places all contributed to transforming the disease from being endemic to hyperendemic or holoendemic. Districts such as Kyaukse, Mandalay and Shwebo, which had ancient canal systems, suffered particularly badly. This was because, in addition to the civil engineering works, the remodelled canal systems had headworks and regulators which checked the previously rapid entry of flood waters into the canals. This supplied the most important malaria vector in Burma, *A. minimus*, with its ideal breeding ground: slowly moving water. The cost of this was reflected in the high IMRs and the smaller numbers of children in these districts. This grim situation was allowed to continue in the rural areas and, sadly, not until the late 1930s was there a belated recognition of the effect malaria had on infant mortality.[45] For thousands of families and their children it was too late.

The British response

What steps did the British authorities take in their effort to reduce infant deaths and were they successful? Quite often the British response was determined by the combination of charitable and official funding. Hospitals, hospital wards and maternity shelters were built from subscriptions raised from private sources, but they were often maintained largely by government or local authority funding. An example of this was the Dufferin Hospital in Rangoon which was opened in 1897 'under the aegis of the Countess of Dufferin Fund'.[46] Until 1923 the hospital was managed by the Dufferin Fund with government support, and from 1923 to 1934 by a newly formed trust and again government support. After 1934 it was taken over by the government. The hospital became the most important institution for the teaching of midwifery and gynaecology in Burma, although the Mandalay and Moulmein Hospitals also developed teaching facilities for midwives.

Most of the midwives, after their eighteen months' training, were employed by the municipal authorities.[47] They were usually recruited as 'Results System Midwives', an arrangement whereby they received a small basic salary from their employers. This was augmented by an additional payment for each confinement attended. The effect of this system was to limit the midwives to the towns only. A midwife living in a rural area would spend an enormous amount of time travelling between villages to confinements, even in dry weather. The result was that by 1934 there were unemployed trained midwives in Burma, who were waiting for vacancies to arise in municipal areas.

Voluntary societies, such as the one at Mandalay, also employed midwives within the urban areas. The first 'Society for the Prevention of Infant Mortality in Burma' was inaugurated on 15 September 1906 and was a Burmese initiative, not a British one. It was started by Burmese men of 'known influence' and Burmese ladies of 'recognized position' as a central committee from which, eventually, local organizations developed in most of the major towns in Burma.[48] The original objective of the society was to make trained midwifery assistance available to women in Burma and, as the need became apparent, attempts were also made to provide a health visiting service.

The local societies were of charitable origin but many, once formed, were grant-aided by local councils. The societies at Rangoon and Maymyo were among the most successful. By 1929 the Rangoon Society had 1,223 confinement cases under its care, all of which took place in maternity 'shelters'.[49] There were four shelters under the management of a Matron Superintendent in Rangoon and the society employed on average seven to nine midwives. Voluntary subscriptions, however, had long ceased to be adequate and by 1929 the society in Rangoon was largely funded by the government. The Maymyo Society, established in 1926, was from the beginning well organized and active. It established a system of home visits, distributed food, clothing, advisory pamphlets and medicines and arranged public health lectures. The society also set up a Maternity and Child Welfare Centre and employed a trained health visitor.[50]

The original central committee became the Child Welfare Endowment Fund in 1921 and its objective was the co-ordination of local societies. By 1923 this fund was being administered by the Burma branch of the Indian Red Cross Society, which had itself been revived in 1922. The Red Cross was to become important in infant welfare work as most of the local societies became affiliated to it. In addition, the Red Cross funded the training, in Delhi, of ten health visitors for Burma and in 1935 largely underwrote the initial financial costs of a training centre for health visitors in Burma.[51] Finance was often a problem; in 1931 a slump in local subscriptions was attributed to the economic depression.[52] That year, midwives were sacked as an economy measure by three local societies in Mandalay, Prome and Pegu.[53] The training centre for health visitors, originally planned for 1929, was also delayed owing to 'financial stringency' before being rescued by the Red Cross in 1935.[54]

How extensive was this network of voluntary societies and domiciliary midwives? By 1939 there were 270 midwives employed by local authorities who attended 29,351 confinements in that year. Fifty-two local societies employed a total of twenty-five health visitors and an additional thirty-four midwives, who attended 5,540 confinements. But to put the figures in some perspective, in 1939 trained midwives attended only 36 per cent of registered births in the urban areas and only 4 per cent in the rural areas.[55] This meant that out of the total of 427,738 births registered that year only 34,891 or 8 per cent of mothers received trained assistance. With the advantage of hindsight, it is easy to see that the only possible answer for the rural areas would have been the formal training of the traditional birth attendants, a practice which is now widely followed. This was attempted on an experimental basis at Maymyo in 1929, but the project was abandoned the following year.[56] Two years later, in 1930, traditional birth attendants were barred from practising in the town under the first application of sub-section (2) of section 8 of the Burma Nurses and Midwives Act, 1922.[57]

One highly popular initiative was the introduction of 'baby shows'. The first show was held in Rangoon in February 1916 and by 1927 sixteen towns in Burma were hosting baby shows.[58] Exhibitions or 'baby weeks' also became a feature of the programmes of enthusiastic voluntary societies. Both the shows and baby weeks were opportunities for the voluntary societies and the health officials to present hygiene exhibitions, advise on infant feeding and to distribute official publications on infant welfare.

These publications covered a wide range of issues connected

with hygiene and disease, and by 1929 a total of ninety-five booklets were available. They were published by the Hygiene Publicity Bureau, some in English, some in Burmese, and by 1929 ten dealt with aspects of infant and maternal care, such as *Hints on Sickness of Babies* and *Care of Infants.*[59] If the administration's priorities can be judged by the numbers of publications distributed, then infant welfare came well down the list. The only booklets which had a distribution of 30,000 or more were about plague or smallpox (more than 70,000 copies of one booklet about smallpox were distributed), but the widest distribution of booklets concerning infant welfare was 13,000.

Did these efforts by the administration and the voluntary societies have a measurable result? Did the efforts of the midwives, committees and the Publicity Bureau result in a decline in the IMR? In some of the few areas of urban Burma where trained midwives worked and records were kept, there was a measurable decline in infant mortality. Not many figures comparing the IMR in areas where there were trained midwives with those lacking this service are available, but a note on the situation in Mandalay in 1915 gives an IMR of 265 deaths per 1,000 amongst infants attended at birth by a trained midwife, against a registered IMR of 444.8 for the city as a whole.[60] In 1920, in Mandalay, 159 infants per 1,000 died before their first birthday after delivery by a trained midwife, as against a registered IMR of 360 for the whole city.[61]

But in the 1930s the registered IMR was still well over 200 per 1,000. As already stated, in 1939 only 8 per cent of registered births had been attended by trained personnel. If the estimated 25 to 30 per cent of unregistered births are included in this calculation, then the attendance figure drops to approximately 6 per cent. If it is surmised that a trained birth attendant approximately halved the probability of an infant dying before its first birthday – but that only 6 per cent of births were delivered in this way – then the total effect must have been negligible. No doubt the efforts of the administration and the voluntary sector were saving lives, but measured against the problem, such efforts were puny. Given more time, it seems probable that in the urban areas there would have been a measurable decline in infant mortality, but the Second World War ended any hopes of improvement.

Notes

1. For explanation and examples of this technique, see A. J. Coale and P. Demeney, *United Nations Manual*, IV (New York, 1967).
2. W. T. Gairdner, 'On infantile death rates in their bearing on sanitary and social science' (n.p., 1861), 15. In India Office Library, Pamphlets, PT. 2348-57, Secretary of State for India Library, and H. S. Shrycock and J. S. Siegal, *The Methods and Materials of Demography*, edited by E.G. Stockwell (London, 1976), 235.
3. *Report on the Sanitary Administration of Burma 1909* (Rangoon, 1910), 6. These reports are referred to in the text as health reports and were issued yearly. From 1870 to 1889 they were entitled *Report on the Sanitary Administration of British Burma* (*RSABB*), from 1890 to 1920 *Report on the Sanitary Administration of Burma* (*RSAB*), from 1921 to 1936 *Report on the Public Health Administration of Burma* (*RPHAB*), and from 1937 *Report on the State of Public Health in Burma* (*RSPHB*).
4. L. Manderson, 'Blame, responsibility and remedial action: death, disease and the infant in early twentieth century Malaya', in N. Owen (ed.) *Death and Disease in Southeast Asia* (Singapore, 1987), 276. See also ch. 8 by Lenore Manderson.
5. *League of Nations Epidemiological Reports*, 14–15 (1935–36), 32.
6. L. T. Ruzicka, 'Mortality in India: past trends and future prospects', in T. Dyson and N. Crook (eds) *India's Demography* (New Delhi, 1984), 18.
7. *Public Health and Births and Deaths* (Rangoon, 1868), 51.
8. *RSAB* (1913), 8; *RSAB* (1915), 6.
9. *RSPHB* (1939), 42.
10. C. V. Foll, 'An account of some of the beliefs and superstitions about pregnancy, parturition and infant health in Burma', *J. Trop. Pediat.*, 5 (1959), 53. Also Ma Ma Tin, 'Feeding patterns of infants and young children', undated paper (c. 1970s) (amongst a collection on nutrition in Burma in the Library, Department of Nutrition, London School of Hygiene and Tropical Medicine; other papers from this collection will be cited as 'undated paper'), and S. Postmus, 'Beri beri of mother and child in Burma', *Trop. Geog. Med.*, 10 (1958), 365.
11. Cho Nwe Oo, 'Nutrition in pregnant and lactating mothers', paper presented at second Orientation Course in Nutrition, 1974, Burma, 3.
12. F. Faulkner, 'Key issues in infant mortality', *J. Trop. Pediat. & Environ. Child Health*, 17 (1971), 3.
13. A. P. Phayre, *Memorandum on the Sparseness of Population in British Burma* (Rangoon, 1862), 6; K. N. MacDonald, *The Practice of Medicine among the Burmese* (n.p., 1879), 11.
14. Foll, 'Beliefs and superstitions about pregnancy', 56; C. V. Foll, 'The perils of childhood in Upper Burma', *J. Trop. Pediat.*, 4 (1958), 124; Ma Ma Tin, 'Feeding patterns of infants', 2; Ohn Kyi, 'Beliefs and practices about foods and feedings in Mon State (Moulmein)', undated paper.
15. *RSAB* (1894), 28.
16. *RPHAB* (1928), 11.

17. Foll, 'Beliefs and superstitions about pregnancy', 53; Sao Yan Naing, 'Beliefs and practices in nutrition', undated paper; Aung Kyin, 'Beliefs and practices in nutrition in Central Burma (Magwe)', undated paper.

18. J. Pryer and N. Crook, *Cities of Hunger: Urban Malnutrition in Developing Countries* (Oxford, 1988), 13.

19. Pryer and Crook, *Cities of Hunger*, 14.

20. Cho Nwe Oo, 'Nutrition in pregnant and lactating mothers', 5; Sein May Chit, 'Nutritional problems in Burma', undated paper, 6.

21. *RSABB* (1870), 115.

22. N. K. Kunhikannan, 'Infant feeding in Burma', *Indian Med. Gaz.* (Current topics), 55 (1920), 265–6.

23. *RPHAB* (1930), 13.

24. Ohn Kyi, 'Beliefs and practices about foods', and Ma Ma Tin, 'Feeding patterns of infants', 2.

25. R. O. Whyte, *Rural Nutrition in Monsoon Asia* (Kuala Lumpur and Oxford, 1974), 61.

26. Kunhikannan, 'Infant feeding in Burma', 266.

27. Maung Gale, *Reports on the Dietary and Nutritional Surveys Conducted in Certain Areas of Burma* (Rangoon, 1948).

28. Kywe-Thein, Thane-Toe, Tin-Tin and Khin-Khin Tway, 'A study of infantile beri beri in Rangoon', *Union of Burma Journal of Life Sciences*, 1 (1968), 2.

29. K. Vinijchaikul, 'Pathological studies of acute infantile cardiac beri beri', *J. Med. Ass. Thailand*, 47 (1964), 58, and Postmus, 'Beri beri', 368.

30. *RPHAB* (1931), 15.

31. R. L. Broadhead, 'Tetanus neonatorum. A review of epidemiology, management and prevention', *Postgraduate Doctor*, 8 (1985), 456.

32. *RSAB* (1894), 28.

33. M. S. Islam, M. M. Rahaman, K. M. S. Aziz, M. Rahman, M. H. Hunshi and Y. Patwari, 'Infant mortality in rural Bangladesh: an analysis of causes during neonatal and postneonatal periods', *J. Trop. Pediat.*, 28 (1982), 295; S. Rahman, 'The effect of traditional birth attendants and tetanus toxoid in reduction of neonatal mortality', *J. Trop. Pediat.*, 28 (1982), 163; T. D. Stahlie, 'The role of tetanus neonatorum in infant mortality in Thailand', *J. Trop. Pediat.*, 6 (1960), 17.

34. P. C. Banerjee, 'Report of a measles survey in Sagaing', *Burma Med. J.*, 16 (1968, 219–23).

35. *RSAB* (1909), 6.

36. *RSAB* (1910), 6.

37. *RSAB* (1910), 6.

38. See, for example, C. A. Bentley, *Malaria and Agriculture in Bengal* (Calcutta, 1925), Government of Bengal Public Health Department, Bengal Secretariat book depot; S.R. Christophers, J. A. Sinton and G. Covell, 'How to do a malaria survey', *Health Bulletin*, 14, Government of India Central Publications Branch, 1928; R. Ross, 'Researches on malaria. The Nobel medical prize lecture for 1902' (Stockholm, 1904).

39. G. J. Ebrahim, 'Malaria in childhood', Editorial, *J. Trop. Pediat.*, 30 (1984), 194.

40. Ebrahim, 'Malaria in childhood', 194.

41. J. A. Sinton, 'What malaria costs India', *Health Bulletin*, 26, Malaria Bureau, 13 (n.d.), 2.

42. *RSAB* (1909), 4; *RSAB* (1910), 5.

43. *RSAB* (1917), 11–12.

44. *RSAB* (1917), 10–11.

45. *RSPHB* (1938), 42. The Sanitary Commissioner wrote, 'A vast majority of deaths among infants in the malarious regions ought really to be attributed to malaria.'

46. League of Nations Health Organization. Intergovernmental Conference of Far Eastern Countries on Rural Hygiene, Preparatory Papers, 2: Note on medical organization in Burma, Geneva, 15 March 1937, 45.

47. League of Nations Health Organization: Note on medical organization in Burma, 43.

48. *RSAB* (1906), 4.

49. *RPHAB* (1929), 10.

50. *RPHAB* (1928), 14.

51. *RPHAB* (1935), 44.

52. *RPHAB* (1931), 16.

53. *RPHAB* (1931), 17, 19.

54. *RPHAB* (1929), 11.

55. *RSPHB* (1939), 43.

56. *RPHAB* (1929), 10; *RPHAB* (1930), 15.

57. *RPHAB* (1932), 50.

58. *RSAB* (1916), 4; *RPHAB* (1927), 17.

59. *RPHAB* (1929), 59-61.

60. *RSAB* (1915), 7.

61. *RSAB* (1920), 11.

8

Women and the state: maternal and child welfare in colonial Malaya, 1900–1940

Lenore Manderson

I hold firmly to the belief that the State has a definite duty towards every child which it has allowed to be born within its boundaries, and that, in the words of the Declaration of Geneva, 'The child must be given the means requisite for its normal development'.[1]

In 1936 Dr Mary Blacklock of the Liverpool School of Tropical Medicine published an article on aspects of the welfare of women and children in the colonies.[2] The article was based on a tour of the colonies of Hong Kong, Malaya, Ceylon, Palestine, China, Burma and India, undertaken by Dr Blacklock in 1935 and supplemented by her earlier experiences as a member of the Women's Medical Service for India and the Colonial Medical Service in Africa. The article is lengthy, and deserves more than the cursory attention it is afforded here. In summary, however, it made the following points. Colonial affairs were, historically, the affairs of men, and, as an artefact of this, education, health, and housing all also reflected the needs of men. Over time both health and education services were reformed, but even so, progress in the field of the welfare of women and children was poor: infant and maternal mortality rates remained high; exploitation of women and girls continued; few girls went to school; and medical care for women left much to be desired. Blacklock argued that inadequate funds were directed towards women and children; that there had not been sufficient commitment to train local nurses; and that, because of the lack of female staff in hospitals, women did not present themselves for care. She further claimed that medical services and the education of women were interrelated, and that schooling simultaneously served two objectives. Firstly, it trained some women to take up employment in clinics, hospitals and dispensaries. Secondly, it offered other girls a training in domestic science and mothercraft, including an understanding of the importance of sanitation, ventilation, control of mosquitos and other vectors, food and water storage, and dietetics, thereby providing the basis for better individual and family health.

Blacklock made a number of recommendations to improve maternal and child health: the expansion of maternity centres and wards; an increased number of women doctors; the training of native women as medical assistants and doctors; improved nursing education, including that of hospital nurses, health visitors (community nurses) and midwives;[3] and community participation. At the same time, she noted the broad economic and social context of prevalent patterns of morbidity and mortality:

> The health of women and, even more, the health of small children depends very much on economic conditions, and much of the sickness seen at welfare clinics, both among women and children, can be attributed solely to poverty. I have heard a health sister beg to be excused from visiting among a particularly poor section of a people, because she felt it was ironical to talk of a balanced diet to people who had practically nothing to eat but rice, or to advocate cleanliness when water and fuel were only obtainable with great difficulty.[4]

The social context of infant mortality in Malaya

For those in colonial Malaya – the Straits Settlements of Penang, Malacca and Singapore, and the nine Malay States[5] – Blacklock's comments on the inadequacy of maternal and infant health services, the social and cultural factors that inhibited women's use of medical services, and the education of girls, were familiar; such matters had received increasing attention from around the turn of the century. Building on my earlier publications,[6] this chapter documents government policies and programmes initiated to reduce infant mortality and improve the health of women and their children; it examines too the way that health and welfare were associated with education.

The infant mortality rate in early twentieth-century Malaya was around 250 per 1,000 births, at times rising to around 500 per 1,000.[7] In Singapore, for example, in 1908 the rate was 347.8, with 54 to 60 per cent of these deaths occurring during the first three months of life. The rate in Malacca in 1902 was 669.1; the peak for Penang of 306.5 was reached in 1907. In the Malay States, the situation was no better: in Kuala Lumpur it was 349 in 1906; 313 in 1907; and rose again to 350.5 in 1915.[8]

The rate varied according to season, area of residence and ethnic group, and according to changes in the precision of data. The exact causes of infant deaths remain unclear. We can speculate that then, as now, diarrhoeal disease and respiratory infections were major causes. Many deaths were not certified by medical practitioners, and were reported as resulting from *sawan* (convulsions): the majority of infant deaths were included in this category,[9] which subsumed a variety of ailments such as neonatal tetanus, malaria, and in older infants, 'dietetic errors'.

Concern over the high infant mortality rates accompanied more general government and public concern with morbidity and mortality rates associated with social and economic conditions. W. J. Simpson, for example, in his 1907 report of urban conditions in Singapore, drew attention to the dense settlement of the inner city, the overcrowded dwellings, and the lack of air and light, sewerage disposal and drainage. Often a family of five or six would live in a cubicle of around 10 feet by 12 feet, in 'regular rabbit warrens of living humanity'; cooking facilities and drinking water were beside a drain of excrement and other household waste.[10] Similar descriptions from elsewhere in Malaya indicate that overcrowding occurred in both town and country. In Kuala Lumpur in 1907, for example, there was an estimated average of 14.3 people per dwelling.[11] In rural areas, the extreme overcrowding that characterized the cubicles of the Chinese town was absent, but reports were equivocal of conditions in tin mines, on rubber estates, and in rural Malay *kampongs* (villages).[12] On the whole, however, poor infant health in rural areas was associated with lack of access to medical services and to 'maternal ignorance' rather than to the environmental and sanitary conditions held especially important in the cities.

Scrutiny of the infant mortality rate continued from 1900 to the suspension of British rule in 1941 during the Pacific War. Commentators inevitably attributed broader social factors rather than, simply, the proximate medical causes of death. These included environmental conditions, maternal and infant nutrition, inadequately trained midwives and the dependence of women on village *bidan* (midwives), the prevalence of syphilis and malaria, childrearing practices, and 'maternal ignorance' and indifference. The British Resident of Pahang, for example, argued that many children died from 'improper feeding during the first year' and that many were 'killed by their filthy dwellings', and from 'inherited disease from their parents'.[13] Most health officers shared this broad understanding of the social context of infant and maternal health. In practice, however, focus was placed on two factors regarded as contributing to the high infant mortality rate: native midwifery and infant feeding.

Midwifery and the state

Midwives were the first group targeted by the government in an attempt to reduce the infant mortality rate, both because of their role as health practitioners and because of their perceived role as conveyors of information to mothers. Because midwives, both *bidan* and western trained nurses, were a distinct group, they became an obvious focus for government intervention. From 1908, medical department officials claimed that the provision of registered and qualified midwives would bring down the infant and maternal mortality rates, and enable infants and small children to be monitored, particularly through the first year of life. Concentrated efforts to reduce perinatal mortality allowed for positive action and produced results without intervening in other economic and structural areas.

The maternal and child health programme, developed from 1905 in view of these considerations, consisted of three parts: the registration and in-service training of traditional midwives; the recruitment and training of other local women as biomedically trained birth attendants; and the establishment and expansion of biomedical services through infant welfare centres and home visiting by trained nurses. The first two strategies were seen to facilitate the last. Kempe, Acting British Resident for Perak, for example, noted that the appointment of trained midwives in villages was an 'excellent method of furthering acquaintance of the kampong Malay with Western medicine'.[14]

The training of local women to become midwives, and the in-service training of practising indigenous midwives, commenced in 1911, which was around the same time as European nurses and Lady Medical Officers were appointed to make postnatal home visits and to establish maternal and child health services. In-service training was aimed at minimizing risks associated with village midwifery practices: teaching midwives to use aseptic instruments to cut the umbilicus to reduce the incidence of neonatal tetanus, and to identify and refer problems of late pregnancy and complications of labour. According to Clarke, Health Officer for Kinta District (1914), these measures were badly needed, although, rather than educating the established practitioners, he advocated training a 'better class of native':

The native midwife in the F.M.S. is completely ignorant of her work, and in addition to being ignorant is usually dirty. She is undoubtedly responsible for many deaths. An effort should be made to get a trained woman to do this kind of work. Effort will not come from outside and must come from the Government, and I have no doubt that if the Government trained a few women they would be employed at first by the better class of native and that knowledge would gradually spread. There is no doubt that even a very short training which would teach these women the value of cleanliness, how to use antiseptics if only for their hands, the advantage of leaving things alone and of when to call in skilled help would save a lot of life. These partially trained women should be under the control and supervision of a thoroughly trained Midwifery Nurse. They might be of any nationality, but preferably European; the trained woman would have to be European.[15]

According to official documentation, child welfare began in Singapore (and hence colonial Malaya) in 1910, with the regularization of midwifery under the guidance of Dr Middleton, then Municipal Health Officer, although this step was anticipated by Dr Fowlie, Honorary Visiting Surgeon to the colony, some years earlier.[16] Under the first training scheme, the colonial government covered the cost of tuition and the Singapore Municipal Government the cost of uniforms and subsistence for the trainees. Accreditation was provided in line with qualifications graded according to the length of training (six months to three years). Six women began and two completed the course in 1911; by 1914 fifteen women had qualified. In Malacca, in-service training for practising traditional midwives began in 1912, with lectures offered in Malay on topics such as the antiseptic care of patients and umbilical dressing. All midwives, in whose practice infants had died from neonatal tetanus, were interviewed; and all were issued with a free supply of antiseptic, cotton wool and lint.[17] In addition, in Malacca from 1908, Lady Inspectors were appointed to Medical Departments and were responsible for instructing new mothers on cord care and general hygienic practices.

By 1914, plans to train local women in the Federated Malay States were also in place, and the British Resident of Selangor had approached the Sultan with a scheme, putting forward the advantages of training Malay women as nurses and midwives at a time when the establishment of the Medical Department had opened up a number of vacancies, owing to the non-availability of trained Eurasian women and the inadequacy of women recruited from India.[18] District officers were requested to find out the number of local women prepared to undertake a minimum of one year's training at Kuala Lumpur General Hospital, the time determined as necessary to ensure witness of a sufficient number of maternity cases.[19] The response from the districts was poor. Most *penghulu* (village heads) were not interested in the scheme and reports suggested its general lack of appeal.[20] In July 1915, however, the names of two women from Jeram were put forward: both women were about 40 years old; one, Fatimah binti Rapok (Rapah), was widowed; the other, Jaharah binti Lebai Salam, was divorced. Jaharah fell sick and she was replaced by another older widow, Mai binti Udin. Fatimah and Mai began training in Kuala Lumpur on 28 September 1915 but did not complete the course: Fatimah 'succumbed to the attractions of a Malay youth' and wished to marry; Mai found life 'unbearable' as a result of the courtship and her exclusion, and wished to return to her *kampong*.[21] The Matron of the Hospital, A. E. Fletcher, reported,

> The two Malay midwives sent here for instructions at the beginning of Sept. have had the opportunity of assisting at twelve deliveries. They have missed several through being absent from their quarters when sent for. Some others

they have been present at during part of the labour only
as they have found more important things to attend to –
prayers, food, etc. They have shown little interest in
methods here and I think they are too old and settled in
their ways to be taught.[22]

Despite this inauspicious early start, some training was offered
to practising midwives or to women desiring to become
midwives throughout the Federated Malay States by the 1920s,[23]
and later also in Penang and the Unfederated Malay States.
However recruitment was slow. In Perak as well as in Selangor,
early recruits often proved unsuitable, because of their age,
their apparent intellectual shortcomings, or because their
recruitment was through a relative in government service rather
than as a result of genuine interest in midwifery. Later recruits
were more successful: they were often women already working
as ward attendants in a hospital, or were young women whose
mothers were *bidan*, or who had otherwise expressed their
especial interest in midwifery. By 1931, six women in Perak had
received hospital training, and an additional four were being
trained that year.[24] In Penang, in January 1930, there were
fourteen trained midwives for a population of 190,000.[25] Whilst
unqualified midwives were replaced gradually by women who
had received training in a six-month residential course, in the
interim *bidan* were encouraged to attend one class a week over
a period of some months, at the end of which they received
certificates and were issued with obstetric supplies including an
enamel bowl, forceps and surgical scissors.[26] Contemporary reports suggest that midwives showed some resistance to training
and registration. This might have reflected a certain antipathy
towards these women who were continually characterized as
ignorant, dirty or stupid:

> The *bidans* were so ignorant that they had to be taught
> again and again the names of the contents of their baskets,
> such as lotions for baby's eyes, cord dressings, etc., and
> how to use them . . . even after several years of intensive
> training some of them still need the most careful watching
> – being prone to slip back into dirty habits and super-
> stitious habits.[27]

Additionally, *kampong* women were reported as refusing to use government trained midwives, but this was not necessarily the result of native conservatism. In Kuala Langat, for example, resistance was attributed to the fees charged for attendance at confinements, and the District Economic Board in Perak in 1937 approached the government to provide the district with a midwife for a six-month trial period to enable *kampong* women to engage her free of charge.[28]

Training schemes for local women occurred later in the Unfederated Malay States. Although the Kelantan Government opened its first maternal and child welfare centre at the women's hospital in Kota Bharu in 1930, it was reluctant to invest further in midwifery extension services since, it claimed, the 'Malays have very definite ideas concerning midwifery, and it is not expected that Malay women will seek advice concerning pregnancy or be willing to come to hospital for labour'.[29] In Perlis, midwifery training began modestly in 1937, with one student per annum.[30] In Kedah, too, few women had been trained by the late 1930s. A scheme aiming to provide limited training for women from Kedah and Perlis at maternity clinics attached to hospitals was introduced in 1936, with the intent of striking 'a direct blow at the very heavy infant mortality in *kampongs*, and to lay a sound foundation for the establishment of welfare work on lines suitable to the specific peculiarities of this state'.[31] Four *kampong* women were trained in the first intake, with four more recruited the following year, but local midwives and village women resisted the scheme. By 1937, there were 723 registered or trained midwives in Singapore, 566 in Penang, and 193 in Malacca, but far fewer in the Federated Malay States and fewer still in the Unfederated States.

Because the recruitment of local women to train as midwives was so slow, legislative control of *bidans* and their eventual displacement with western-trained women was delayed. In the Straits Settlements, legislation foreshadowed in 1905 was eventually introduced in 1917; it provided for the compulsory registration of midwives within the municipal limits of Singapore, Penang and Malacca. These provisions were extended in 1923 with a new ordinance which constituted the Central Midwives Board. Compulsory registration was not introduced for rural areas of the Settlements until 1 January 1930; in the Malay States, this was further delayed. The British Resident of Selangor recommended that qualified midwives be registered, with provision for suspension due to misconduct,[32] while the

Colonial Secretary, E. L. Brockman, argued against regulation to avoid perceived interference with *adat* (custom), and recommended instead a gradual educational process through the appointment of Lady Doctors that would render controls unnecessary.[33]

In the Malay States, legislation for the registration of midwives was not introduced until 1954. Until then, village midwives sometimes received brief instruction by government health workers in antisepsis and were taught to recognize complications of pregnancy and parturition; they were also subject to inspection by government officers.[34] Often, this was primarily symbolic, as one official stated, 'These inspections are of doubtful value, as many of the [obstetrics] bags have obviously never been used, and have probably been borrowed for the occasion'.[35]

The state enters the home

The registration, training and control of traditional midwives, and the recruitment and training of younger local women to replace them, was part of an aim to lower infant mortality and to extend state control over reproduction. Its success was tempered by what has been described as 'militant opposition' by the *bidan* to state control of midwifery.[36] The alternative strategy focused on the mother herself. Belief in the inappropriate mothering of indigenous and other immigrant women was central to this programme, which sent health visitors into the homes of newly-delivered women and encouraged women to attend infant welfare centres for continued advice on infant feeding and care, and to monitor the infant's health. These health visitors were ideally European as it was believed that Eurasian women were unreliable and would never equal European health visitors.[37]

Indeed, Malay, Indian and Chinese women were often represented in government documents as negligent, and this provided the ideological justification for the ethnic boundaries of maternal and child welfare. Some health workers were sympathetic to the social and economic circumstances of women, attributing poor infant and maternal health to these causes. A number of them argued that mothers of certain ethnic groups were better carers than others. None the less many health workers reinforced the negative attitudes and used them to justify surveillance. A submission to the Commission of Enquiry into estate labour, for example, stressed the importance of the midwife in supervising Tamil women during the puerperium, to see 'that the newborn infant is properly attended to, as there is a danger to the life of the baby unless it is properly looked after'; another recommended that midwives serving estate populations should be provided with rickshaws in order to attend to women unable to reach a hospital in time for delivery and 'to keep an eye on both mothers and infants after their discharge from hospital' to ensure that the infants were properly clothed and fed in order to prevent bronchial pneumonia and diarrhoea.[38] Others stressed the need for surveillance among women of all races, particularly to prevent improper infant feeding, regarded as a major cause of infant mortality.[39]

Reasons for the shift from breastfeeding to bottle-feeding are complex. One reason was the promotion of bottle-feeding through the distribution of powdered and condensed milk by infant welfare clinics as part of the early attempt to improve infant nutritional status. Some doctors believed that the breast milk of Malay women was 'deficient', owing to their restricted postpartum diet. Other reasons included the marketing of formula and other baby food and milk products by multinational corporations; an association between bottle-feeding and modernity, promoted especially by the infant feeding practices of expatriate and wealthy local women; and the incorporation of women into wage labour away from home, making the maintenance of breastfeeding difficult. Breastfeeding declined from the late nineteenth century both as a result of earlier weaning and of women opting to bottle-feed from birth. The Medical Report for Selangor for 1904, for instance, noted that many infants were brought to the hospital suffering from diarrhoea caused by 'improper feeding' with tinned milk. Similarly in 1907 the Health Officer of Kuala Lumpur attributed the infant mortality rate for that year of 313 per 1,000 to the use of sweetened condensed milk.[40] In Singapore in the same year, it was estimated that over 94 per cent of infant deaths were due to 'avoidable circumstances', 37 per cent the result of artificial feeding using adulterated and polluted fresh and imported cows' milk. The annual report of the Straits Settlements for 1910 suggested that a major cause of infant death was the 'faulty feeding of infants', and in 1913 J. T. Clarke, Health Officer for

Kinta District, Perak, suggested that, given the perceived irreversibility of the decline in breastfeeding, 'effort would be directed best towards guiding the hand feeding along correct lines' and seeing that suitable baby food was used.[41] Similar testimony of increased artificial feeding came from relatively remote areas, although in urban areas the incidence of bottle-feeding was especially high. By 1940, even the most isolated states with limited capitalist penetration had identified artificial feeding as a major problem of infant health:

> So far as breastfeeding is concerned, Europeans do not show a very good example to their Asiatic sisters, but the latter are more prone to wean their babies, and that [sic] on to sweetened condensed milk. An attempt has therefore been made to emphasise the importance of breastfeeding, and failing this, to advocate one of the dried milks with added vitamins, but expense is an objection to the general acceptance of this substitute. Babies fed on sweetened condensed milk only, without added vitamins, are invariably fat and flabby, and suffer from one of the common catarrhal disorders – diarrhoea, bronchitis, nasal catarrh, etc.[42]

As already indicated, courses which trained local women to become midwives and information talks conducted for practising *bidan* included instruction on child-care and infant feeding, since birth attendants were regarded as an effective means of getting information to new mothers. But newly-delivered women were also directly approached. In 1911 the Singapore Municipal Health Department appointed female Health Inspectors to visit postpartum women, using a list of births provided by the Office of the Registrar of Births and Deaths. Malacca and Penang also introduced limited programmes of home visiting by Lady Inspectors within urban areas. In Kuala Lumpur, provision was made for a trained nurse to visit new mothers in 1914.[43] In rural areas, home visiting was instituted later; in rural Malacca and Penang in 1927. Maternal and child health schemes were well behind in other states, where home visiting was introduced after the establishment of infant welfare clinics attached to general hospitals.

In areas with adequate staff, where transport was available and settlement relatively dense, home visiting became established practice, and was the first encounter between a new mother and infant welfare staff. A major purpose of home visiting was to encourage women to attend the infant welfare clinics in order to standardize the monitoring of infants, whilst increasing women's familiarity with the centre and staff and with the hospital service. It was hoped that this would increase their utilization of western medical services and their presentation for antenatal care during future pregnancies, as well as encourage them to go to hospital for treatment when they or their infants were sick.[44] Home visiting also fulfilled more immediate educational needs, since the home visitor could offer the new mother advice on the care and feeding of the infant. This fitted with other prevailing ideas on the most effective means of public health education; thus the government also recommended 'friendly talks' by District Sanitary Inspectors and discussions initiated by officers in charge of travelling dispensaries.[45]

Infant welfare centres had been established by Government Medical Departments throughout the Straits Settlements and the Federated Malay States by the late 1920s and in the Unfederated Malay States by the late 1930s. The Singapore and Malacca Municipalities also held infant welfare clinics, and the Singapore Children's Welfare Society ran two more clinics and conducted home visits.[46] By 1936, there were seventy centres and nine sub-centres in the Settlements and Federated Malay States, each staffed minimally by a health nurse, midwife and attendant. Attendance varied. At the Paya Lebar maternal and child health clinic,

> Children from all classes of society attend the centre, some arrive in private cars, taxicabs, omnibuses, others in rickshaws or even riding on their grannies' backs. Our experience is that many children of well-to-do parents are the victims of errors of diet, unsuitable clothing and wrong management just as much as the poorer neighbours.[47]

In Penang, however,

> Malay mothers are seldom at the clinic in time, as they are usually beautifying themselves at home. Time means little or nothing to them, in spite of the fact that most houses possess clocks of some sort, which however are usually

Plate 8.1 Chinese grandmother and toddler, Singapore, *c.* 1910. The child is sucking on a teat with a feeding tube of the type confiscated by health workers

Source: N. G. Owen (ed.) *Death and Disease in Southeast Asia* (Singapore, 1987), p. 270. Originally from Royal Commonwealth Society, London, Files of the British Association of Malaya, BAM/1 – Singapore.

abnormally wrong. Then again there may be a festival, and as everyone in the kampong wants to go to the party, clinic or no clinic, the only thing to be done is for the clinic to go also.[48]

The few centres operating in the Unfederated Malay States, and their home visiting programmes, faced greater difficulties. The health nurse in Kota Bharu in 1934, for example, made a total of 2,334 home visits, of which 626 were to newly-delivered women. The effectiveness of these visits, as reflected in attendance at the clinic attached to the General Hospital, was poor: less than 10 per cent of those visited (211 infants) presented over the year. Infant welfare work was difficult, for 'old customs and beliefs are deeply rooted and . . . the majority of the women folks are illiterate. Education, patients [*sic*] and time are required to bring about changes in out look'.[49]

Kedah faced similar problems. In the following extract, the Lady Medical Officer, Dr M. G. Brodie, described maternal and child health work in 1938, and the difficulties faced in this work:

Expectant mothers, who come in (to the maternity ward of the hospital) for a period beforehand, can be overhauled and given a certain amount of treatment before the child is due. The majority have intestinal parasites and some degree of anaemia. Many have dental cavities – but they have not yet been educated to part with their bad teeth while pregnant. All lying-in mothers, while in the ward, are urged to continue breastfeeding at home. They are given a card on which is the baby's weight and advised to return to the hospital or attend the Town Dispensary for further weighing and to take the card with them. A fair percentage do return, but it is not unusual to find that the babies have gained 4 or 5 pounds in the first month due to irregular and overfeeding. An attack of Colic or Diarrhoea then sends the mother to seek advice – and after a further homily on feeding, she seems to realise the mistake of giving the breast or the bottle to the child every time it cries . . . and that there is a limit to the capacity of a baby's stomach.[50]

Whilst Brodie is relatively optimistic here, she notes elsewhere that few Malay women attended the hospital or gave birth there, and that the clinic sessions for Malay infants had little support.[51] This partly reflected unstable staffing. The first Lady Doctor was appointed in 1927; from 1927 to 1929 there were three Lady Medical Officers and the final appointee went on sick leave soon after taking up the post.[52] This did little to encourage local women, who were believed to object to going to the hospital under any circumstances and who were nervous of seeing a doctor whom they did not know.[53]

At clinic sessions held at infant welfare centres or hospitals infants were weighed, their temperatures checked, medical attention given to minor ailments, and more serious cases referred to the hospital medical officer. The centres also supervised local midwives and distributed basic equipment to them. Additionally, a major function of the centres was health education, through exhibitions and advice. This was the 'proper preventative work of educating mothers': to teach women to feed, clothe and care for their infants, and to 'restrain them from some of their more objectionable and injurious practices'.[54] In Blacklock's mind it was, indeed, the primary function of the clinics.[55] Most education was undertaken at clinics rather than during home visits, although many women involved in running this programme doubted the effectiveness of this:

> Although as much as possible is done, there is so little time to teach in the outpatient department. It is utterly impossible to cope adequately with all the cases attending the clinics, who require such instruction . . . The majority of the diseases for which one has to advise treatment are preventable, and a campaign of education in personal hygiene is urgently required . . . One feels sure that one result of such instruction, would be the reduction of artificial feeding and in the incidence of convulsions and enteritis, with a corresponding drop in the death-rate of children under 4 weeks old. A very large number of children (far too many) die within the first month of life.[56]

Infant welfare centres resorted to various strategies to encourage women to bring in their infants, including the provision of transport to fetch them into the centres; the distribution of free milk formula (including milk donated by Nestlé); baby shows; and, in Kuala Lumpur, by direct appeal to government servants to take their wives to clinics for antenatal care and for their infants to be assessed and monitored. Education offered at the centres was supplemented by other displays relating to health, hygiene and infant welfare that were mounted at agri- cultural shows held annually in various towns in the colony; by poster displays; and by films such as *Mother's Milk is Best, Aminah,* and *Rescue of Swee Kim,* shown in schools and to voluntary associations (*Mother's Milk is Best* dealing with the danger of infected milk and the advantages of breastfeeding, *Aminah* with infant welfare, and *Rescue of Swee Kim* with tuberculosis).[57]

Educating mothers of the future: domestic education in schools

The inefficiency of these services caused much discontent. From the outset, there was continual debate regarding the willingness or otherwise of women to attend clinic sessions or to take note of advice given by clinic staff or home visitors. For many the great barrier to the utilization of biomedical health services and the adoption of 'hygienic practice' was cultural. According to personal biases, commentators argued that it was Malay, Chinese, Indian or the 'poorer class' of women who availed themselves least of the advice of the European medical and nursing staff, although most agreed that, whilst progress was slow, it was not 'altogether devoid of encouragement'.[58]

Increasingly, those assessing maternal and child health care services argued the prior need of educating young women. Mary Blacklock was one of these, and the publication of her article and the field trip on which it was based was a reflection of a wider general interest in the education of girls as a longer-term strategy to improve family health. The links between education and health were not new ones. In colonial Malaya arguments for the education of girls had surfaced in the nineteenth and early twentieth centuries and were used to justify the importance of women's role as the nurses, nurturers and first educators of their children. Domestic science skills (sewing, cooking, laundry, 'household management', etc.) were invariably incorporated into the curriculum of all-girl schools, and, where numbers were sufficiently large to warrant the appointment of a special teacher, in boys' schools where girls were also enrolled.[59]

Interest in domestic science education, and its emphasis on the preparation of young women for their roles as wives and mothers, paralleled a general interest in teaching hygiene and the enforcement of sanitary measures. Belief in the value of educating school children extended to include issues as specific as infant feeding. Thus the Health Officer of Kuala Lumpur wrote in 1907,

> In my last report I spoke about endeavouring to instruct the people as to the proper management of children, but when it was realized how impossible it is [to] get reliable fresh cows' milk the idea was temporarily abandoned. It seems that the only way to endeavour to prevent the waste of life is by means of educating the school children, and thus the prospective parents; I am afraid little good can be done by endeavouring to induce parents to give up their prejudices as to how their infants should be reared.[60]

Routine enquiry in 1912 on the teaching of hygiene in schools in the Federated Malay States indicated that in both girls' and boys' schools there was some elementary instruction in hygiene and cleanliness. A few schools also offered instruction on the prevention and treatment of malaria, the importance of vaccination, and first aid. The conduct and frequency of these classes, however, depended upon staff interest and knowledge, and timetabling.[61]

Whilst the teaching of hygiene was strengthened in the curricula, there were discussions within the Malayan Department of Education and within the Colonial Office in London regarding the importance of domestic science education. From the mid-1930s, government attention focused increasingly on this, making explicit its perceived links between girls' education and family health and welfare. In girls' schools, health and hygiene subjects were incorporated under the umbrella of domestic science.

At the time, domestic science teaching in colonial Malaya was undertaken in Malay schools primarily by graduates of the Malay Women Teachers Training College (WTTC) whose own training had included domestic science subjects: economic management of the home; selection of diets; cooking of local foods; laundry and ordinary housework; and the supervision of lavatories and drains. Few domestic science mistresses, however, were charged solely with teaching this subject in schools, and staff availability varied considerably from state to state. By late

1939 around fifty-four of the sixty-two girls' schools in the colony were teaching some domestic science, but with schools at times resorting to temporary appointments, including the use of retired trained teachers, to meet the need. [62] Despite the rhetoric, the teaching of domestic science was not given priority.

Domestic science education fulfilled two major functions. The first, which provided the rationale for the inclusion of the subject in the curriculum, was the importance of teaching young girls fundamental principles of hygiene, nutrition, and housekeeping because of their anticipated future role (and responsibility) as wives and mothers. At its simplest, domestic science gave girls a practical education that educators believed was most appropriate for them: 'A knowledge of cookery is much more useful than a knowledge of geometry.'[63] But others gave a more sophisticated rationale, which linked education, the role of women, family health and medical services. In terms of policy, the incorporation of domestic science into the school curriculum was intended to provide the link between child welfare and public health work.[64] Dr Esdaile, in a memorandum on domestic science, argued,

> The health and future of our country and her Colonies depends on the women and the way they are educated. The Colonies should attach greater importance to female education and should provide increased facilities for the teaching to them of domestic subjects. Mother-craft and home-making will become not only the fundamental, but also the most highly prized, subjects of the native schools.[65]

In support of these arguments, officials within the Colony of Malaya argued that the promotion of domestic science should take priority in funding and the appointment of new teaching and supervisory staff. It was also stressed that the introduction of domestic science teaching and the appointment of special teachers enabled the surveillance of children and other teachers. Domestic science mistresses or their assistant supervisors visited all schools whose curriculum included domestic science; in Perak these occurred on a weekly basis. The inspections that were carried out included the physical examination of children and their clothing, and especially the examination of heads and

the treatment of lice; and the inspection of the school itself:
furniture, the classrooms, the compound, the well, latrines,
arrangements for the disposal of rubbish, and so on. In addition, the mistress or assistant supervisor provided a teaching
resource.[66] Linehan, Adviser on Education, echoed others in his
emphasis on the policing role of the mistresses:

> Even with the picked students at the Malacca Training Col-
> lege there has to be a hard fight to get personal cleanliness.
> It is more important for the future mothers to learn to value
> personal cleanliness than to achieve scholastic success . . .
> Selangor should get a Domestic Science Supervisor because
> . . . [of the] difference [that] had been made in the personal
> habits of the teachers and the girls in the Malay schools as a
> result of the work of the Perak Supervisor.[67]

Government officers in states where domestic science mistresses
had already been appointed stressed resulting improvements in
'the standard of cleanliness' and 'general alertness' as a result.
Additionally, in some cases, education in health and hygiene
was expected to increase curative as well as preventive knowledge. The Kedah State Government, for instance, included the
care of the sick and the use of standard medicines in its school
curriculum in 1939.[68]

Conclusion: women and the state

The appearance of Blacklock's article was, therefore, timely
although not at all coincidental. In January 1937 it was distributed to the colonial governments, together with a resolution
of the Advisory Medical Education Committee recommending
increased training and employment of women in medical
services and a letter from the Secretary of State recommending
increased expenditure on and the expansion of female education.[69] In April 1937 a memorandum by Dr Philippa Esdaile
was sent to the colonies, requesting a survey of domestic science
teaching in schools and calling for its increased teaching, and
drawing attention to the lack of funds for the education of girls
and the need to increase the number of girls in schools in order
to train 'lady doctors', nurses, midwives and health visitors.[70] In
response, a sub-committee on the education and welfare of

women and girls was established; it spent much time debating the merits of female education and the ideal mix of practical and theoretical subjects in the curriculum against a continued call for the expansion of domestic science. It also considered the difficulty of providing staff for an expanded curriculum and the possibility of recruiting a local resident, 'with some knowledge' of domestic science, on a voluntary or semi-voluntary basis to do the teaching.[71] The debates captured the tension between the ideology of women as mothers and the pragmatic demands of social policy:

> In order that trained women may be available in the development of the social services, it is of highest importance to press ahead with the training of teachers, nurses, midwives, health visitors, etc, and this training must be based on an adequate measure of general education . . . The woman, as the maker of the home and the mother of children for whose upbringing she is responsible, is by nature much more the 'pillar of society' than the man.[72]

Not all people involved in the development of policy relating to the education of young girls accepted the value of the inclusion of domestic science into the curriculum:

> The idea that girls' education should be heavier weighted with domestic science *at the expense of* general education is likely to suggest that higher education of the kind which fits girls to become doctors and teachers . . . is somehow unwomanly and academic.[73]

The debate regarding the value and content of female education, infant welfare, and the employment of women as doctors, nurses and midwives continued throughout the war period and as the colonial administration was reinstated in former occupied territories. By the time the administration was in a position to revive its proposals regarding maternal and child welfare health, events had overtaken it: a new colonial administration was in place, independence was imminent, and the training of local professionals an urgent task. In the 1950s new systems for the registration of traditional birth attendants and the establishment and extension of infant welfare clinics were set in place.

Developments in colonial Malaya in the fields of education, health and medicine, and social welfare reflected ideological changes and practical developments in England. The incorporation of pregnancy and birth into hospital-based medicine, the establishment of home visiting, and the development of maternal and child clinics all closely followed developments in the United Kingdom. Yet discussions in the late 1930s within the Colonial Office concerned with the provision of maternal and child health services are remarkable for their lack of reflection on the prior four decades of these services both in colonial and home settings. A decade later, P. F. de Souza wrote to the Advisory Committee on Education within the Colonial Office that 'before the war, no local girl could aspire to become a nursing sister';[74] much later commentaries on maternal and child welfare had entirely rewritten history, claiming that midwifery and infant health services had only developed after independence and after ideas of primary health care had gained general currency and official support.[75]

Acknowledgements

This article is based on research undertaken at the National Library of Australia, Rhodes House (Oxford), the Public Records Office (Kew), and Arkib Negara Malaysia (Kuala Lumpur). Part of the research was undertaken in March–April 1984 when I was a Visitor to the Department of Biological Anthropology, Oxford University, and I am grateful to the department for its hospitality. Financial support for this research was provided by the Australian Research Grants Committee and the Australian National University.

Notes

1. M. G. Blacklock, 'Certain aspects of the welfare of women and children in the colonies', *Ann. Trop. Med. Parasitol.*, 30 (1936), 224.

2. Blacklock, 'Welfare of women and children', 221–64.

3. Blacklock, 'Welfare of women and children', 248–60.

4. Blacklock, 'Welfare of women and children', 261.

5. Four (Perak, Selangor, Negri Sembilan and Pahang) were known as the Federated Malay States; the remainder, brought under British control later and with less direct presence, were known

collectively as the Unfederated Malay States and included Kelantan, Trengganu, Johore, Kedah and Perak.

6. L. Manderson, 'Bottle feeding and ideology in colonial Malaya: the production of change', *Internat. J. Health Serv.*, 12 (1982), 597–616; L. Manderson, 'Blame, responsibility and remedial action: death, disease and the infant in early twentieth century Malaya', in N. Owen (ed.) *Death and Disease in Southeast Asia* (Singapore, 1987), 257–82; L. Manderson, 'Political economy and the politics of gender: primary health care in colonial Malaya', in P. Cohen and J. Purcall (eds) *The Political Economy of Primary Health Care in Southeast Asia* (Bangkok, 1989), 76–94. This chapter presents new data, supplementing that included in previous work.

7. A. S. Jelf, *Report of the Royal Commission appointed to enquire into certain matters affecting the Health of Estates in the Federated Malay States* (Singapore, 1924), B25.

8. Files of Selangor Secretariat (hereafter Sel. Sec.) 1307/1908; 3006/1915.

9. For example, 65 per cent of infant deaths in 1909 were so attributed. See Government of the Straits Settlements, *Annual Departmental Reports 1909* (hereafter SSAR) (Singapore, 1910), 469. Around 20 per cent of these were from neonatal tetanus.

10. Government of Singapore, Housing Commission (Commission appointed to inquire into the causes of the present housing difficulties in Singapore, and the steps which should be taken to remedy such difficulties), *Proceedings and Report: Vol. 1: Instruments of Appointment and Report* (Singapore, 1918), A63.

11. Sel. Sec. 1307/1908, 1.

12. R. M. MacGregor, *Annual Reports of the Medical Departments, Straits Settlements and Federated Malay States for the year 1937* (Singapore, 1938), 83.

13. Sel. Sec. 3006/1915, Memorandum, Sheet no. 4.

14. J. A. Kempe, *Perak Administration Report for the year 1932* (Kuala Lumpur, 1933), 6.

15. Sel. Sec. 3006/1915, 10, 12–13. See also Manderson, 'Blame, responsibility and remedial action', 264 ff.

16. SSAR, 1905 (Singapore, 1906), 232, 715.

17. SSAR, 1904 (Singapore, 1916), 482.

18. Government medical officers argued for the preferability of training Malay (as opposed to Chinese and Indian) women, not only because of the reluctance of Malay women to use non-Malay birth attendants, but also because of the popularity of Malay *bidan* amongst other women.

19. Sel. Sec. 3006/1915, Memorandum, Sheet no. 4, 6 June 1915.

20. Sel. Sec. 1754/1915, 5.

21. Sel. Sec. 1754/1915, 35.

22. Sel. Sec. 1754/1915, 20.

23. Files of the Institute of Medical Research, IMR 59/1923, 2.

24. Sel. Sec. G2142/1931.

25. In the Settlements, midwives were trained at the government maternity hospitals in Singapore, Penang and Malacca. In the

Federated Malay States, Chinese women trained at the Chinese Maternity Hospital in Kuala Lumpur; Malay women were trained at the Kuala Lumpur General Hospital, and in 1937 Tamil women had still not been trained as midwives. MacGregor, *A/Rs*, 81. Midwives were classed as follows: 1 year formal training at the hospital, then practical training in English, examined, diploma awarded (Class A); 6 to 9 months' practical training in Malay, examined (Class B); midwives who had been in regular practice for a year before the ordinance (Class C), who might subsequently receive some formal training to be rescheduled as Class B midwives. MacGregor, *A/Rs*, 44.

26. E. W. Darville, 'Maternity and child welfare work in Penang, 1927–35, 1935–41', Lectures given at the London School of Hygiene and Tropical Medicine, in *MSS Indian Ocean S134*, Rhodes House Library Colonial Records Project 17 (1935), 19.

27. Darville, 'Maternity and child welfare work'.

28. Sel. Sec. G118/1937.

29. L. W. Evans, *Kelantan. A/R Medical Department for 1930* (Penang, 1931), 16.

30. J. Portelly, *Kedah and Perlis. A/R Medical Department for 1937* (Alor Star, 1938), ii.

31. Portelly, *Kedah and Perlis. 1936* (Alor Star, 1937), 2.

32. Sel. Sec. 3006/1915, Memorandum, Sheet no. 4, 6 June 1915.

33. Sel. Sec. 3006/1915, Memorandum, Sheet no. 4, 6 June 1915.

34. Files of the Colonial Office (hereafter CO) 859/46/12101/4A, 943, 9.9

35. MacGregor, *A/Rs*, 82.

36. Portelly, *Kedah and Perlis. 1936* (Alor Star, 1938) i.

37. Sel. Sec. 3006/1915, 10, 13–14.

38. J. H. Ponnampalam, in Jelf, *Report of the Royal Commission*, B24; B. Day in Jelf, B16.

39. Sel. Sec. 3006/1915, 12, 2.

40. Sel. Sec. 1307/1908, 4. For details on changes in infant feeding, see Manderson, 'Bottle feeding and ideology', and L. Manderson, 'These are modern times: infant feeding practice in contemporary Malaysia', *Soc. Sci. Med.*, 18 (1984), 47–57. See also Manderson, 'Blame, responsibility and remedial action'.

41. *Straits Times*, 2 May 1907, 7; SSAR, 1910 (Singapore, 1911), 581; Sel. Sec. 3006/1915, 9.

42. J. C. Carson, *Kedah and Perlis. A/R Medical Department for 1938* (Alor Star, 1940), 6.

43. Sel. Sec. 3156/1915, 20.

44. C0859/46/12101/4A, 6.

45. SSAR, 1933 (Singapore, 1933), vol. II, 945.

46. The Singapore Children's Welfare Society was a voluntary organization of expatriate and local elite women, which ran two child health clinics and conducted home visiting from 1923 to 1933.

47. SSAR, 1927 (Singapore, 1929), 901.

48. MacGregor, *A/Rs*, 82.

49. T. F. Strang, *Kelantan. A/R Medical Department for 1936* (Kota Bharu, 1936), 15.

50. M. G. Brodie, in Carson, *Kedah and Perlis*, 7.

51. Brodie, in Carson, *Kedah and Perlis*, 6.

52. D. Bridges, *The A/R of the Medical and Health Departments, Kedah and Perlis, for the year 1347 A.H. (20th June, 1928 to 8th June, 1929 A.D.)* (Alor Star, 1930).

53. Bridges, *A/R of the Medical and Health Depts*, 7.

54. Federated Malay States, *A/Rs, 1930* (Kuala Lumpur, 1932), 56; Federated Malay States, *A/Rs, 1935* (Kuala Lumpur, 1937), 20.

55. Blacklock, 'Welfare of women and children', 224.

56. Brodie, in Carson, *Kedah and Perlis*, 7.

57. SSAR, 1930 (Singapore, 1932), 1015.

58. SSAR, 1936 (Singapore, 1938), 1010.

59. L. Manderson, 'The development and direction of female education in Peninsular Malaysia', *J. Malays. Branch Roy. Asiat. Soc.*, LI (1978), 100–22.

60. Sel. Sec. 1307/1908, 4.

61. Sel. Sec. 2056/1914.

62. Sel. Sec. G544/1937, 55.

63. Sel. Sec. G544/1937, 17.

64. SSAR, 1929 (Singapore, 1931), 681.

65. Dr P. Esdaile, in Sel. Sec. G544/1937, 1A, 2.

66. M. C. Taylor, in Sel. Sec. 359/1937, no folio no., 30 Dec. 1938, 1.

67. Sel. Sec. 359/1937, no folio no., 17 Jan. 1939.

68. CO859/4/1241/A, 1939, 3.

69. CO859/1/SCWE6/39, 1.

70. CO859/1/SCWE6/39, 1–7.

71. CO859/1/1201/19, 1939, 6.

72. CO859/1/1201/39, 1939, Education, Advisory Committee. Sub-committee on education and welfare of women and girls, 2.

73. CO859/4/1236, 1939, 4 (emphasis in the original), E. Oakden, 19 Sept. 1939.

74. CO953/2/51032, 1948, 7 (19 Dec. 1947).

75. P. C. Y. Chen, 'Providing maternal and child health care in rural Malaysia', *Trop. Geog. Med.*, 29 (1977), 444; Malaysian Medical Association, *The Future of Health Services in Malaysia* (Kuala Lumpur, 1980), 23–5.

9

'Getting close to the hearts of mothers': medical missionaries among African women and children in Johannesburg between the wars

Debby Gaitskell

Introduction

Healing has been central to the appeal and expansion of African Christianity in southern Africa in this century. Churches founded independently by Africans, as opposed to churches of European and American missionary origin, have particularly recruited members through faith-healing and diagnostic sessions grappling with spiritual causes of misfortune.[1] In explanations of independent church membership, the refrain recurs: 'I was ill. They prayed for me. Now I am well.' As one South African prophet told his congregation, 'This is not a church, it is a hospital.'[2] In Soweto in the 1970s, women healers helped church members with a wide variety of social and psychosomatic as well as medical problems. The clear resort to supernatural power; the prophets' understanding of the nature and cause of the complaints; the treatment offered, which seems both simpler and more spectacular than that offered by western doctors; and healing given in familiar, often domestic, surroundings, all account for the prophets' appeal.[3]

These developments have taken place against a background of increasing provision of western medicine, by both missions and government. One drawback of such expansion was that 'medical work became so specialized that the ordinary priest or minister ceased to take much share in service for the sick, and in most mission congregations, healing and worship became quite separate'.[4] None the less, as Ranger has pointed out, 'the multiplication of medical facilities and the increasing enthusiasm of African recourse to them has not been paralleled by a corresponding decline in African concepts of healing'. Rather,

178

in a situation of 'medical pluralism', European medical science has not 'monopolized the therapeutic field', in part because it has been 'too individual and too mechanical to be able to confront African idioms of healing in their totality'.[5] The persistence of African notions of health and disease provides an important undercurrent in the case study of Johannesburg women explored in this chapter.

Nevertheless, while confirming this general assertion, this research challenges the primary reason suggested by Ranger for the weakness of western medicine in effecting 'a cosmological transformation': it has been 'so often used in the interested service of colonial capitalism':

> Outside the state sector most Africans in Central and Southern Africa came into contact with doctors not so much in benevolent mission clinics but in the mining and railway compounds or in the municipal locations, once again very much as part of a coercive system.[6]

This observation overlooks crucial gender differences. Excluded from the single-sex gold-mining compounds with their rigorous use of medical expertise to keep black men working cheaply and efficiently, African women and children in Johannesburg in the 1920s and 1930s saw a different face of western medicine, through clinics, hospitals and various forms of health education run by the mission churches. Not only was this medical care dispensed outside a nakedly coercive system, but the personnel involved were female rather than male. In mission work, there was a well-entrenched separation of spheres by sex, so that women missionaries worked largely with African women and, increasingly in this period, with children. (The number of African children in the city soared fivefold between 1921 and 1936, as it did with females generally, providing powerful demographic prompting for mission priorities.[7]) Medical initiatives on behalf of Reef women and children were likewise almost exclusively in women's hands.

The female mission work preceded and proved more popular than municipal health provision for blacks along the whole string of mining towns east and west of Johannesburg that formed the Witwatersrand or 'Reef'; not only did it do this, but a strikingly large share of its medical endeavour also pioneered the promotion of maternal and infant welfare for Africans.

Models and staff came from Britain particularly, and this brief account describes one of no doubt many instances of the cultural export and reshaping of the western maternal and child welfare movement of the early twentieth century in a colonial, racially divided setting.[8]

Even more noteworthy is the special religious context in which these health efforts evolved. In sharp contrast to the African emphasis in their independent churches on spiritual battles with evil forces or on the power of the Holy Spirit to heal, the mission churches' white medical personnel seem to have seen their task as both a scientific onslaught and a spiritual assault on ignorance, insanitary conditions, superstition and ill health. This is particularly true of the single women doctors and trained nurses.

What may at first sight appear distinctive about this venture, however, is its wider context of assumptions about Christian families and maternal roles, particularly highlighted by married women advocates of improved maternal and infant care. Vaughan's work on colonial British East and Central Africa shows that

> whereas secular medicine saw modernity and the disintegration of 'traditional' societies as fundamental causes of disease, missionary medicine, throughout most of this period, took the view that disease would only be conquered through the advancement of Christian morality, a sanitized modernity and 'family life'.[9]

These concerns resonate very strongly with the urban South African material explored below: cleanliness and hygiene were vigorously promoted – as part of 'sanitized modernity' – but Christian sexual and family mores, and an elevated conception of devout and responsible motherhood, were also deemed central to improved maternal and child health, just as they underlay the whole range of ventures undertaken by Johannesburg women missionaries: women's prayer unions, hostels for domestic servants, girls' uniformed youth movements and an elite boarding school.[10] Nevertheless, British research demonstrates that British family welfare was initially strongly influenced by numerous church-founded mothers' meetings in which religion and needlework provided a context for encouraging respectable motherhood among the poor.[11] Thus these

South African mission precursors of municipal and state intervention in the arena of maternal and infant welfare work resonate with both the religious and the 'scientific' slant of the British model.

The interwar period was an important formative time for South African medicine generally. In 1919 the first Public Health Act was altered and reshaped in response to the shock of the 1918 influenza epidemic. The epidemic prompted 'a thorough, country-wide survey of health and living conditions at an early stage of South Africa's industrial revolution'.[12] Compulsory registration of births and deaths was instituted in urban areas, highlighting the relatively high white maternal mortality rate, a cause for increasing concern. After 1935 the Public Health Department's Maternal and Child Welfare Board developed a District Nursing Service for whites.[13]

As far as the African urban population was concerned, developments within missionary bodies on the Reef coincided with and fed off a new official awareness of the need for action. In 1927, the Hospital Survey Committee reported that public hospital provision was 'utterly inadequate', especially for 'Coloureds' and Africans, with no maternity beds for them in the Transvaal at all.[14] At the same time the high African infant mortality was reported in Johannesburg, with figures of at least 700 per thousand being cited in the mid-1920s, which was ten times that of whites.[15] Even though the figures are flawed, the trend is clear from Table 9.1, highlighting the racial disparities in infant mortality which so concerned 'the friends of the Natives' in mission and liberal circles in the interwar years. In 1928, a government committee investigating the medical training of Africans called for a thousand more doctors if the untreated African 'hordes' were not to become a 'menace to the rest of the community' and threaten the eventual failure of the labour supply. The committee also drew attention to the deplorable dearth of African nurses and midwives, and urged that ways of overcoming various obstacles to the development of the profession should be found so that more such women could be appointed to urban 'locations'[16] (as African suburbs were called).

Consequently, the triennial gathering of South African missionaries that same year, 1928, reflected the new prominence of African health needs on the public agenda. Participants evinced a greater awareness of the dire social and economic conditions

Table 9.1 Infant mortality rates, city of Johannesburg, 1918–1939

Year	Whites	Africans and Coloured (mixed race)	Asians
1918–19	89.79	225.7	212.7
1919–20	81.44	355.8	–
1920–21	110.03	448.9	219.2
1921–22	86.60	438.77	263.88
1922–23	88.26	414.31	198.11
1923–24	81.2	437.06	205.88
1924–25*	78.55	–	–
1925–26*	74.01	–	–
1926–27	83.29	240.06	146.87
1927–28	83.39	215.41	144.0
1928–29	72.77	175.12	116.96
1929–30	78.62	210	174.0
1930–31	79.08	206.34	121.21
1931–32	76.61	254.60	149.29
1932–33	80.04	188.32	141.05
1933–34	82.43	213.06	174.25
1934–35	69.21	179.69	155.70
1935–36	74.13	238.97	175.26
1936–37	64.63	182.56	180.36
1937–38	57.47	212.77	133.65
1938–39	49.83	223.48	135.10

* Statistics were not broken down in the MOH reports for these years. Had calculations been based on registered births, natives (blacks) would have had a rate of 922. The MOH noted that the non-registration problem was so great in these years as to make compilation of the infant mortality rate for this group an absurdity.

Source: Tables 6 and 7 from B. Unterhalter, 'Inequalities in health and disease: the case of mortality rates for the city of Johannesburg, South Africa, 1910–1979', *Internat. J. Health Serv.*, 12 (1982), 617–36, pp. 627–8.

of African life, while men like the Revd. J. D. Taylor of the American Board Mission (ABM) lamented that the gospel would fall on deaf ears if the church appeared indifferent to poverty or in league with 'an industrial system that blocks the road of the Native to economic security'. They learnt of the general and infant welfare clinics which had proliferated on the Reef in 1927–8 under 'eager, efficient young women' from the missions, and the planned opening of the Bridgman maternity hospital later that year. They passed resolutions encouraging further expansion of African medical training.[17]

Such debate – whether ignorance or poverty was the major problem – was also receiving attention elsewhere and was discernible in the professional literature of non-medical experts by the early 1930s.[18] The Medical Officer of Health in Peitermaritzburg brusquely asserted that more instruction was the answer: 'the greater proportion of the non-European mortality is born by disease out of ignorance, preventable if the children of the present generation can be taught how to live'.[19] However, the Medical Officer of Health for East London took a much more environmentalist view that 'it is native pauperism that is the predisposing cause of sickness'. While his views might have implied the need for economic redress, he also favoured extensive education:

> We know what should be done. What is needed is a steady onward movement originating in the schools, with facilities for the training of teachers in these subjects, extension of school medical inspection and establishment of training facilities, as doctors and sanitary inspectors and health assistants, for natives.[20]

Reef Africans and healing

On the whole, following the trajectory of medical professionalization in Britain and the primacy given by Protestants to words and the Word, South African mission hospitals were a much later development than mission schools. They also tended to be located in rather remote rural areas where there was no state provision. The hospitals in cities, such as McCord Zulu Hospital in Durban or the Bridgman in Johannesburg, were usually set up by American initiatives rather than British ones.

Although African mission hospitals were not built in Johannesburg until the late 1920s, the British churchwomen who began visiting and teaching among black Anglicans in the compounds and slum yards of the Reef's mining towns after 1907 soon found themselves applied to for medical help. One joked about building up a 'Harley Street reputation' for her elementary medical remedies, which amounted to 'Mustard without and ginger within'!²¹ They wished they had a dispensary or small hospital, if only for the protection of their own impoverished communicants:

> Our people are fleeced by all sorts of quacks calling themselves doctors – 15/- for a bottle of medicine is not at all unheard of, and those in the country places die without any treatment as £5 down is a common charge before a doctor will go out from the nearest town – perhaps 10 or 15 miles.[22]

They argued that a dispensary might be a tool of evangelism and Christian conversion 'the *one* thing needed to reach the vast mass of semi-heathen and indifferent natives round us'.[23]

The scanty references to indigenous African approaches to disease in the early Johannesburg missionary correspondence betray a failure to grasp the central importance of prayer in African conceptions of coping with illness. This comes through in Miss Williams's indulgent, but unwittingly revealing, comment on her regular hospital visiting of Africans: 'Some of the Christians are so dear and innocent, they even say grace devoutly over medicine!'.[24] Revd. Wilfrid Parker found men at the hospital touchingly grateful for visits and help: 'It is refreshing to find that the sick really want the ministrations of the church, and patients have actually complained if by chance they have not been prayed with.' This attitude contrasted markedly with the European reaction on the lines of 'I don't mind [if you pray for me]', coupled with obvious embarrassment at audible prayer on their behalf.[25] The openness of mission Africans to faith-healing (by prayer alone) was well demonstrated in their enthusiastic and expectant attendance in large numbers at the few services for Africans organized during the Healing Mission to South Africa of the Anglican J. M. Hickson in 1922.[26]

In the light of such receptivity, an unusually strong emphasis on faith-healing was not surprising in the fervent African women's prayer unions or *Manyanos* established in the Anglican and Methodist churches on the Rand in 1907–8, and in the Natal ABM in 1912 (which shaped ABM women's groups on the Rand after the First World War).[27] This was true of the 'great camp meetings attended by thousands of people' of the sister movement, *Rukwadzano*, in Southern Rhodesia, where 'there were public confessions, surrender of witchcraft implements, repentance, seizure by the Holy Spirit, healings'.[28] In my interviews with Reef African women who had been *Manyano* members since the 1930s, the practice of visiting sick prayer union members was recalled emphatically: '*that*, they enjoyed very much'. If you were sick, others from your branch might come singing your distinctive hymn, pray for you, help out sympathetically and practically, or after a death in the family, assist with food or money. In sharing their troubles in the weekly meetings' extempore prayer and preaching, women would naturally mention sickness or medical problems. They would pray (perhaps only privately) to conceive if there seemed to be undue delay in falling pregnant. Supernatural healing or renunciation of witchcraft did not surface in these urban recollections.[29] Triumphant accounts of successful *Manyano* confrontations with traditional diviners or spirit possession emerged rather from rural strongholds of 'tradition' such as Swaziland.[30]

Mission medicine for mothers and babies: Anglicans and 'Princess Alice'

The need for missionary medical services, alluded to by Anglican women missionaries before the First World War, was reiterated by Bishop Furse in 1918. Mine hospitals were fine for males, he commented, and the Johannesburg General Hospital took African patients, but they clearly had 'the greatest reluctance to go there'. As a start, he favoured dispensaries in town locations and a central hospital for women.[31] Both these aims were in fact achieved a decade later.

The Anglican medical work took off at the beginning of 1927 under Dr Mary Tugman, who was then in her late twenties, had trained at the London School of Medicine and at St Mary's Hospital, and came to Johannesburg at the behest of her uncle, the Anglican Archdeacon Skey. Described as 'a glorious blend of missionary, medico and mystic', she was 'gallant and gay and tempestuous in her attack on sickness and suffering and social evil'. Her venture had the encouragement of Wilfrid Parker, the energetic priest working among Africans in the city centre. Parker was extending Anglican influence into Sophiatown on the city's western fringe, a vibrant area of mixed-race settlement where Africans could own property and which was later made famous by (among others) another Anglican priest, Trevor Huddleston.[32] Dorothy Maud, daughter of the Bishop of Kensington, and her English women friends were also establishing their pioneering settlement-type 'House of Peace' *(Ekutuleni)* adjoining the Anglican church in Sophiatown simultaneously with the growth of the medical work. (Mary Tugman and Dorothy Maud, like Ruth Cowles who later worked in Alexandra, were very much the bold exception to white urban mission practice of the time.) Madeleine Tugman, Mary's mother, a trained midwife who had done a lot of 'rescue work' in England, also came to work in the area.[33]

Tugman described herself as contending with 'Ignorance, Dirt and Disease' in her work among the great variety of races for which the western areas of the city were well known: Chinese, Indian (including a rich store-keeping family prepared to pay £1 a day for her to attend to their ailing only son and heir), Malay, African, Coloured and poor whites. She described the case of one poor white family

> living in native hovels, the father out of work, the mother lying in bed with acute rheumatic fever and heart disease, and six children fed only on mealie meal, one of which lives on a mattress in the corner of the room covered with flies and prostrate with pneumonia.[34]

The eagerness and desperation of patients was highlighted by the great distances people would travel once they learnt of a doctor's services; a father rode 40 miles from Heidelberg to Boksburg with his 9-year-old son (with pneumonia and a temperature of 103) on the handlebars.[35]

Expansion was rapid and substantial – so much so, that colleagues 'at times grew a little alarmed'.[36] In March 1927 Dr Tugman started a daily clinic in Sophiatown, in the back room of the African priest's house, then a bi-weekly clinic at Nancefield, an African location to the south, and another at Germiston, a mining town east of Johannesburg (again using a room in the African priest's house). She was assisted for four years by Ethel Skinner, a nurse from Kwamagwaza Mission Hospital in Zululand. Dr Janet Robertson took charge of Germiston from December 1927, and later extended her work to further East Rand towns (Benoni, Boksburg and Springs), while Dr

Marjorie Store expanded Anglican medical provision to the West Rand in July 1929. By then the three women doctors were running ten clinics altogether, each doctor seeing 500 cases a month (mostly pneumonia, enteric fever, enteritis, dysentery and VD) and making a hundred calls each, monthly.[37] An estimated 15,000 patients were treated in 1930, by which time two European and three African nurses, helped by four interpreters and three European volunteers, were also employed.[38] The doctors were becoming exhausted as the work grew very fast, but they had, according to Dr Tugman, saved many babies from pneumonia and hoped they were teaching the mothers how to look after their children. Their facilities, however, were second-rate. She wanted to improve treatment by keeping patients under their care in a small ward, and also needed room to test specimens and store instruments, so a small nursing home was planned for Sophiatown.[39]

An initial misunderstanding arose when Dorothy Maud publicized the need for the nursing home by talking at a fund-raising drawing-room meeting arranged by the wife of the editor of the *Rand Daily Mail.* She cited a case found by Dr Tugman of 'a baby dangerously ill with pneumonia being nursed on the floor' because the washing which the mother was about to return to a lady in Parktown 'occupied every inch of the bed in the room'. Although this might have roused the privileged to their social obligations, black Sophiatown washerwomen feared the loss of custom that would occur if the rich whites of suburbs like Parktown became alarmed at the risk of infection from their laundrywomen. So they got the township superintendent to write asking her to desist from such talk. For two hours 'the women poured out their indignation' at a peace meeting arranged by Miss Maud.[40] A medical facility intended to increase the physical security of women and their children had threatened to jeopardize that security, through loss of vital earnings.[41]

In December 1931 the home was opened by the Countess of Clarendon, wife of the new Governor-General of South Africa, and was called the Princess Alice Nursing Home, in recognition of the patronage which the British women had mustered from the Countess of Athlone, wife of the previous Governor-General. It had room for five adults and six children, though as many as seventeen patients were sometimes accommodated in the first few months. There was a frequent interchange of personnel between Anglicans and the ABM within the small group of medical mission activists. In 1932 the personnel changed many times as a result of the deaths of Dr Tugman and her mother in a car accident when back in England, and 'the whole of the central work seemed to fall to pieces'.[42] In the financial depression, Africans could not afford the fees, and were slow to trust replacement staff, especially as daily home visiting had to be cut back. Dr Marjorie Store's work, however, now on the East Rand (since 1930), was growing 'by leaps and bounds', with three enormous clinics: Benoni daily, Springs bi-weekly and Nigel weekly:

> To see Dr Store cope with over 100 patients a day is an absolute education. Her patience and tact have endeared her to the natives all along the East Rand, and one always knows who is meant when a native says she has been to see the lady doctor with the glasses and the smile.[43]

In 1934, by which time it was felt that the African mothers' prejudice against allowing their babies into hospital (for fear that they would die there) had been overcome, a children's ward with room for thirty babies was added to the Princess Alice Nursing Home. Gynaecological diseases, broncho-pneumonia and VD remained prominent among general admissions.[44] By 1937, on the East Rand, Dr Lylie Chapman ran the Springs and Nigel clinics full time, while in Benoni work had developed so much that Dr Store worked there exclusively, seeing 500 to 600 patients a month at the daily clinic and a hundred a week at the VD clinic (built by the municipality in 1931 and run at their request). Her patients were mostly women and children since men, it was noted, preferred a male to a 'missis' doctor. Most of the babies had enteritis or nutritional diseases.[45]

All the Anglican medical work outlined thus far was done by women and particularly directed at women and children but, additionally, interesting pioneering urban maternal and infant welfare work for Africans occurred alongside the general health care provided. Somewhat predictably, British models were followed. The early mother and baby centres in Britain, which explicitly provided no medical treatment but rather short talks, tea and a bun, and advice on baby-clothing, foreshadowed the mother and baby clinics established in Johannesburg. By the

1930s, having grown fastest after 1915, there were some 2,343 such centres in Britain run through local authorities and 770 via voluntary associations. About 60 per cent of babies whose births were notified were brought to the centres in their first year.[46] The Johannesburg clinics particularly resembled the 'Schools for Mothers, Babies Welcomes and Infant Consultations', first pioneered in 1907 by the St Pancras School for Mothers. The British 'schools' combined classes and health talks for mothers, and individual consultations, during which the baby was weighed and advice on feeding and management was given. Their aim was to educate mothers in their responsibilities towards their homes and families and their activities included infant weighing, baby shows, sewing meetings, cookery demonstrations and provident clubs.[47]

Following the British example, by 1929 baby welfare clinics, run by volunteers, had been established at all four East Rand Anglican dispensaries and seemed to have a 'most encouraging' response from mothers. As for the Johannesburg area, Mrs Tugman, the doctor's mother, reported from Sophiatown that, after their long walk up the hill the mothers appreciated their cup of tea and bun – but tended to give the bun to the baby – while they loved jumble sales. At Nancefield, with over a hundred babies on the books, she noted that survival rates had markedly improved from the previous year. Attendance at the clinic was 'excellent' and the mothers all took part in a little service of prayer which included an address and hymn. (This underlines the ideological support which the Christian faith was meant to supply for model African motherhood.) A baby show had even been organized, with prizes distributed (to *all* the entrants) by the actress Sybil Thorndike who was then touring South Africa. The Anglican women's publicity skills were confirmed when a photograph of Miss Thorndike holding a black baby duly appeared in *The Times!*[48]

Even though the evangelical concerns of the clinic organizers were clear, regardless of race or religion, the women seemed to be united by an underlying desire for the children's well-being.[49] Another indication of a positive response appeared in a letter from an African mother published in a church periodical, who claimed that her baby was healthy as a result of the teaching she had received through Mrs Tugman and the baby clinic at Nancefield, where she had learnt to feed and clothe and care for her baby.[50] Dr Tugman likewise remarked on the 'sparkling improvement' after she talked seriously to an African mother about her dirty house and ill child.[51]

Clearly, though, it was not always easy to impart nutritional teaching or the religious devotion deemed essential to model motherhood. When Mrs Tugman attributed the high death rate among babies to improper feeding, she spoke of the hard battle they had with the prevalent ignorance: 'we can only go on patiently teaching and talking even if we are laughed at for our trouble'. Her account highlighted how mothers were drawn by the structure of the clinics, the availability of practical information (the baby's weight) and the chance to buy inexpensive baby clothes. Christian injunctions, however, had to be offered judiciously. As Mrs Tugman stated,

> It is not easy to have any very organized meeting, as the natives know little of *time*, but usually after weighing the babies we have a mothers' prayer, and a little serious talk and finish with a small jumble Sale which appeals to them greatly.[52]

Although Mrs Tugman was not seeing the problem of infant mortality in broad environmental terms, at about the same time a former Johannesburg missionary attempted to move beyond the familiar parameters of 'ignorance' and 'incorrect feeding'. The scientifically-minded Dora Earthy[53] sent a questionnaire to sixty informed sources in southern Africa. They identified four main reasons for the high infant mortality rate: the social diseases (the most cited), that is, VD, tuberculosis and alcoholism; poor living conditions and low wages forcing mothers to work, which precluded proper antenatal care; the ignorance of midwives and mothers, leading to irrational feeding and carelessness in child welfare; and superstitious practices (such as infanticide of twins). Miss Earthy thought it advisable to teach mothercraft and child welfare to young girls as well; this issue was explored in a mission-run girls' youth movement at that time. She praised the churchwomen's societies for 'raising the ideals of African mothers, and helping them to realize the high calling of motherhood'.[54] Her questionnaire reiterated the Christian emphasis, which was to provide religious back-up in the mission exhortation to self-improvement and the encouragement of high aspirations in the spiritual vocation of motherhood.

But it would be wrong to overlook the fact that, for some of the women doctors, medical care involved a clash between medicine and religion. Janet Robertson provides a rare and forthright glimpse of this conflict in her assertion that clinic work gave a chance to prove Christ mightier than the devil:

> It saddens one to see the number of Christian people who bring their children all tied up with heathen charms and native medicine. These charms all have to come off, and they go right into the fire in front of the patients, and so far we haven't lost any child who was thus adorned, and I believe that this in itself has taught some of these women many things.[55]

Although this had parallels with the cross-cultural tensions that emerged between unsympathetic British middle-class health visitors and their working-class clients, in South Africa religious dimensions, together with racial and class attitudes, also appeared. In South Africa 'heathenism' and 'superstition' were being confronted, not simply ignorance. The doctors were probably fighting a losing battle. In the 1930s the urban sociologist, Ellen Hellman, interviewed some Rooiyard women of central Johannesburg. Although most of these women were nominally Christians, they consulted diviners, used protective and preventive medicine against sorcery, and adhered to customary seclusion practices at the onset of menstruation and at childbirth. Seeking infant baptism was much less urgent or frequent than holding some kind of celebration or party for the child's 'coming out'.[56]

In that era, even the devout Methodist mother of theologian Gabriel Setiloane, herself a staunch member of the women's prayer union or *Manyano*, still doctored her babies traditionally and followed traditional African ritual after the death of a child.[57] This was despite the fact that no *Manyano* member was 'allowed to smoke or to take snuff or consult with witchdoctors', and was 'expected to abstain from all heathen customs and superstitions that are opposed to Christianity'.[58] Indeed, as late as 1970, Comaroff estimated that 95 per cent of Mafeking Christians still carried out traditional purification and prevention measures, together with ancestral veneration.[59]

The American Board: Alexandra and the Bridgman Memorial Hospital

In medical work, as in other mission ventures with broad social aims, the numerically insignificant American Board church in Johannesburg started earliest and continued longest. The Bridgman couple were central to its inception. In 1920 Revd Fred Bridgman was approached by a Swiss woman doctor, Dr Crinsoz de Cottens (whose husband was also a physician), wanting to start a clinic for Africans in the central Johannesburg slums. Though she was not a missionary – indeed, she lived in a 'beautiful home on the Houghton Ridge', an exclusive white suburb – Bridgman found her 'a little cottage opposite the notorious Gabriel Yard in Doornfontein where hundreds of families were herded, and [which] thronged with mothers and babies'. Soon she was running a clinic every weekday from premises at the nearby ABM African church in Doornfontein, and 'acquired an enviable reputation for bringing babies into childless homes' over the next five years.[60]

By 1923 Bridgman was arguing that the most promising line of approach in future mission work for women and children on the Reef lay in district nursing, kindergartens and day nurseries for children of working mothers.[61] He was probably partly influenced by the enthusiasm and availability of his niece, Ruth Cowles, for such work. Having long intended to follow her parents (based in Natal among the Zulu) into missionary service, Cowles had just recently completed her nurse training in New York, specializing in public health, followed by district nursing experience at the Henry Street Settlement on New York's lower East Side.[62] When on leave back in the USA in 1924, the Bridgmans made funding for urban medical work a priority; and in 1925, after Bridgman's unexpected death, plans for Cowles's mission employment and a memorial maternity hospital were put into action.

In 1925, the ABM sent Cowles to assist Dr Crinsoz de Cottens. After some language practice and familiarization in Zululand, she started work in Doornfontein in 1926. At the time 180 new and an equal number of old patients came each month. Additional help was provided by the American doctor who was the wife of Raymond Dart, head of the university's medical faculty, and two African interpreters. A dental clinic was also held twice a week. At this stage the weekly baby clinic attracted only about six women. Cowles explained that the lack of attendance was because preventive health care was such an entirely new idea, and so many slumyard mothers were too busy eking out their incomes via (illicit) beer-brewing to attend. One baby had been to prison with his mother four times already in 8 months of life. Through a contact, Cowles obtained a site in Alexandra, a 'private location' on the city's north-eastern fringe, where Africans could own land (as in Sophiatown). Her own clinic opened there in June 1927, by which time 160 new and 140 old patients had been treated. She wanted to stress both preventive health care and also to have a Christian aim in her work. By the beginning of 1928 the ABM, with the addition of Eastern Native Township, where the municipality had offered a room, had three medical and four baby clinics, with over 400 babies on the books.[63]

Attendance dropped at Alexandra when a baby became ill and its mother was sure it had been bewitched by someone with a grudge putting medicine in the scales (yet another reminder of traditional fears of sorcery). Excessive staff changes in 1929 caused a further loss of confidence and weakening of financial support. Two baby clinics closed because Johannesburg City Council undertook to establish location medical services, but these were unpopular because a quick-tempered European woman was in charge. The ABM medical venture picked up with the assistance of Dr Krogh, who replaced de Cottens in Doornfontein; the baby welfare work proved most rewarding, the clinic at Alexandra becoming 'quite a social event', and Christmas parties were held for both areas. The two African nurses in Alexandra made over 3,000 home visits in 1930, but when staffing problems recurred there in 1931–2, the clinic was given into temporary Anglican care.[64]

Some of the difficulties arose from the temporary absence of Cowles, who was undertaking a course in midwifery in Cape Town at the Ladies Branch of the Free Dispensary, in order to fit in with the British tradition which prevailed in South Africa. Her nurse training in America during the 1920s had not included midwifery, as was usual at that time. Furthermore, from 1930, the South African government linked district visiting with midwifery, by requiring that midwives also have training in public health.[65]

The numbers at the Doornfontein medical clinic were larger than ever before: 2,262 new and 1,987 old patient attendances in 1931, and 5,178 altogether in 1932.[66] However, the baby clinic numbers fell off in 1931–2. This would confirm Hellman's findings amongst the Rooiyard women she interviewed, who reported that they sometimes took their sick babies to the ABM, but rarely went to receive instructions on the hygiene of child welfare when their babies were healthy.[67] Besides, to Cowles's despair, preventive baby welfare precepts were not always guaranteed to work, as she remarked,

> Jacob and Esau, the dirtiest examples of babyhood I have ever seen, and their thoroughly bad and drunken mother are still going strong, while little Simon, carefully nurtured and brought up according to latest methods, quickly succombed [*sic*] to enteritis months ago.[68]

Reflecting more generally on African attitudes, she concluded, 'We have to deal with a child people, and it is very difficult for them to see in "large terms", or to take the "long view"'.[69]

In 1933 it was reported that the medical clinics had been practically self-supporting while attendance at well baby clinics had soared to 3,444 in 1 year, a spin-off, it was claimed, of the rise in the number of babies born at the ABM maternity hospital (discussed below). None the less there were still plenty of discouragements for a believer in preventive work like Cowles, when the babies of faithful mothers died while 'those whose mothers defy all rules of infant care live on'. The tremendous increase in baby welfare work, however, was 'opening up very great opportunities in getting close to the hearts of mothers'.[70] This terminology underlines how much the ABM health project (like that of the Anglicans) was about a new spiritual approach to motherhood. The description of their work reflected late Victorian convictions that female health visiting drew on a distinctive feminine gift for persuasive sympathy in personal relationships, essential to the reshaping of working-class family mores (and subtly complementing the more public, 'scientific', law-enforcement role of the male sanitary inspector).[71] Maternal and infant welfare work was seen as part of that 'work for women that only women could do', which was a view that frequently appeared in Victorian mission literature.

Despite 1934 being a record year, with over 5,000 attendances at the two ABM baby clinics, that year work was retrenched because of the mission's financial straits during the

Depression. With the break-up of the slumyards and removal of their African inhabitants to Orlando, the township nucleus of the later Soweto, the Doornfontein clinics, however, had come to a natural end. Within six months of the devastating loss of her mission post, Nurse Cowles was asked by leading Johannesburg citizens of the Alexandra Health Committee to develop intensive pioneering health work there.[72] As a result, she stayed on in the city for another twenty years, making a notable contribution by taking up residence in Alexandra itself and helping to develop the Alexandra Health Centre, subsequently linked with the University of the Witwatersrand. She also continued her important nurturing role among the members of the Bantu Trained Nurses' Association.[73]

As already shown, the gynaecological and maternity services of the Bridgman Memorial Hospital provided an important back-up to the mother and baby welfare project. After her husband's death in 1925, Mrs Clara Bridgman started raising funds – half in the USA, half in South Africa – towards a maternity hospital in his memory, with provincial and city council funds among the contributions to its annual upkeep. The hospital was opened in 1928, administered by an interdenominational mission committee and staffed at times by the women doctors who had either already worked for the Anglicans or subsequently went on to their medical projects. Christianity was promoted through daily prayers, a weekly service for staff, and visits and services for patients by African ministers and other Christian workers.

The Bridgman was seen as part of a wider programme which would develop a comprehensive scheme of public health work for Africans. Thus, for example, annual health weeks were begun on the Witwatersrand. In 1930 these annual health weeks were undertaken on a large scale and included Thursday afternoon mothers' meetings held in the twelve Reef locations with attendances of between 50 and 200, and with a thousand women at the united meeting. As injections against VD began to take effect and many mothers went home with their first living child out of six or eight, the Bridgman's prenatal clinic also became more popular. By 1931, over a thousand women had passed through the hospital, 700 leaving with babies.[74]

By 1934, reflecting on all the thousands of mothers passing through the missions' pioneer women's medical agencies, Mrs Bridgman took courage 'in the conviction that slowly but surely ideals are forming and principles of hygiene and order are being instilled. We catch glimpses of honest desires for a purer and happier home life.' Surely the women would in the near future 'be able to withstand the backward pull of ignorance and superstition'.[75] In her comments, we see the social, medical and religious purposes of the women missionaries' medical work summed up: the upholding of the ideals of good mothering and homemaking; the battling with infection, dirt and disorder; and the repudiating of traditional approaches to birth, imbued with non-Christian cosmology.

The Bridgman Hospital stayed open until 1965, far outlasting the other mission-initiated female medical efforts. By 1938 a second extension to the original twenty-bed wards had already been built; 12,468 inpatients and 45,659 outpatients had come to the hospital; fifty-two of the sixty-five nurses who completed the training school course had received the government medical certificate for midwives. Thousands of women had gone home, reported Mrs Bridgman, with new ideals of cleanliness, hygiene and proper feeding.[76] Within a decade, therefore, the Bridgman already appeared to have effected important changes in the African approach to maternity and birth both in terms of medical training and the type of clientele it attracted.

The longevity of the Bridgman was accounted for by the broad-based financial support which it secured, as well as the very urgent need that it so perfectly met. The costliness of medical endeavours meant that, in a time of financial crisis like the 1930s, shortage of funds made it impossible for hard-pressed missions to begin or even continue with health care projects. The Methodists, for instance, were metaphorically looking over their shoulders (as they had done earlier in the matter of hostels for women and girls) at their 'rivals' in social involvement, the Anglicans and the ABM. At the end of the 1920s, the Methodists were also feeling that they should try to tackle the conditions of African women by means of a lady doctor and a trained nurse for a Johannesburg clinic, but in the end this did not materialize.[77] Finance likewise proved a continual problem at the Princess Alice Nursing Home, so that in 1938 it was handed over to the Johannesburg Hospital Board. In 1934 Cowles's strictly missionary employment was forced to end because of an enforced retrenchment at mission headquarters. Perhaps once the municipalities started making more provision for medical services by the mid-1930s, the missions were glad to bow out of work which was difficult and expensive to maintain but to which they had by then made an important ideological and scientific contribution.

Conclusion

What was the overall significance of the urban female mission project with African mothers and infants? A 1937 South African Institute of Race Relations questionnaire on hospitals revealed that 255 African nurses were undergoing training nationally, 86 of them taking the full course (general or midwifery). In providing the only midwifery training for African women in the Transvaal in the 1930s, the Bridgman Memorial Hospital was making an important contribution to the growth of this key profession.[78]

African women could find much positive value in the mission clinics and mother and baby classes. Records showed the women doctors and nurses to be hard-working, humane, warm and devoted. Ruth Cowles's fondness and enthusiasm for the African babies is unmistakable. (She took many photographs and the mission magazine was not slow to capitalize on the appeal of small black infants.[79]) This affectionate account of the progress of a baby clinic client is typical of her reports:

> Little Bekitemba, instead of coming on his mother's back, now walks in on his own two sturdy feet and solemnly hands me his weight card. Then, like the model baby he is, he proceeds to strip himself – though he has a weakness for forgetting his shoes – and steps on to the *adult* scale with the greatest importance.[80]

It has been suggested that, in their stress on educating African women for motherhood, some Reef church personnel over-looked the importance of environmental factors, particularly poverty. Nevertheless, in the 1930s, there was a growing liberal and missionary awareness of the impact of low wages on family life generally, while Cowles's clinic experience was incorporated into the more thorough-going, community-related Alexandra Health Centre along 'preventive medicine' lines. Finally, by illustrating the centrality of the Christian context in which healthy motherhood and childbirth were pursued, this account serves to remind us of the often religious origins of the maternal and child welfare movement.

Acknowledgements

I gratefully acknowledge financial assistance towards my research from the Central Research Fund of London University and the International Federation of University Women.

Notes

1. See, among a large literature, M. L. Daneel, *Old and New in Southern Shona Independent Churches*, vol. 2, *Church Growth: Causative Factors and Recruitment Techniques* (Paris, 1974), 2, 260, 338.

2. B. G. M. Sundkler, *Bantu Prophets in South Africa*, 2nd edn (London, 1961, 1st pub. 1948), 222–37.

3. M. West, *Bishops and Prophets in a Black City* (Cape Town, 1974), ch. 6.

4. M. Wilson, *Religion and the Transformation of Society* (Cambridge, 1971), 114. Quoted in West, *Bishops and Prophets*, 91.

5. T. Ranger, 'Healing and society in Colonial Africa', unpub. paper, 1978, 1–2, 7.

6. Ranger, 'Healing and society', 7, 3.

7. African females in Johannesburg numbered 4,357 in 1911; 12,160 in 1921; 60,992 in 1936 (of whom 16,292 were under 15 years old). The number of African children under 15 on the Witwatersrand increased from 16,000 in 1921 to nearly 80,000 in 1936, with Johannesburg providing just under half of each total. See Union of South Africa, *Third Census of the Population of the Union of South Africa, enumerated 3rd May, 1921, Report* (Pretoria, 1924), Table CCCXXVII and pt B and pt VIII, Table 7; *Sixth Census of the Population of the Union of South Africa, enumerated 5th May, 1936*, vol. IX (Pretoria, 1942), xiii, and Table 10 and Supplement, Table 3.

8. This has similarities with maternity and child welfare provision in other British colonial settings. See, for instance, ch. 8 by Lenore Manderson.

9. M. Vaughan, *Curing Their Ills: Colonial Power and African Illness* (Oxford, 1991), 57.

10. See D. Gaitskell, 'Housewives, maids or mothers: some contradictions of domesticity for Christian women in Johannesburg, 1903–39', *J. Afr. Hist.*, 24 (1983), 241–56.

11. F. K. Prochaska, 'A mother's country: mothers' meetings and family welfare in Britain, 1850–1950', *Hist.* 74 (1989), 379–80, 392–6.

12. See H. Phillips, *'Black October': The Impact of the Spanish Influenza Epidemic of 1918 on South Africa*, Archives Year Book of South African History (Pretoria, 1990), 232. Although the official flu death-toll was

139,471, of whom 110,118 were African, Phillips suggests the figure was probably nearer a quarter of a million or 350,000, making South Africa one of the five worst-hit countries. See pp. 158–9, 176.

13. E. H. Cluver, *Public Health in South Africa*, 2nd edn (Johannesburg, 1939), 253, 267, 275, 302–3.

14. *Report of the Hospital Survey Committee* (Cape Town, 1927), pars. 6, 10.

15. Although Unterhalter tabulates infant mortality rates for three race groups for the interwar years (African and 'Coloured' were grouped together), she points out their severe limitations. African births were only partially registered, whereas the registration of infant death was essential to facilitate burial, and so 'the infant mortality rate cannot be accurately measured'. The MOH reported in 1926–7 that the supposed figure for that year of 922.74 'would amount to a calamity' – except that it was 'actually . . . absurd. Gross errors are involved in arriving at this figure . . . in some months more deaths are registered than births'. The estimate in the mid-1920s was a rate somewhere between 200 and 250, compared with white rates of 70 or 80 per 1,000. B. Unterhalter, 'Inequalities in health and disease: the case of mortality rates for the city of Johannesburg, South Africa, 1910–1979', *Internat. J. Health Serv.*, 12 (1982), 617–36, pp. 625–6.

16. *Report of the Committee Appointed to Enquire into the Training of Natives in Medicine and Public Health* (Pretoria, 1928), pars. 8–11, 68–75.

17. *Report of the Seventh General Missionary Conference of South Africa* (1928), 22–3, 85, 69. See also K. Shapiro, 'Doctors or medical aids? – the debate over the training of black medical personnel for the rural black population of South Africa in the 1920s and 1930s', *J. South. Afr. Stud.*, 13 (1987), 234–55, on the opposition to providing university medical training for Africans despite the heightened public concern about African ill-health.

18. For the centrality of the notions that infant mortality chiefly stemmed from 'the ignorance of the mother' and 'the remedy is the education of the mother' in the British debate, see J. Lewis, *The Politics of Motherhood* (London, 1980), 89. This approach skirted, even denied, the influence of the socio-economic environment: 'low incomes, poor housing conditions and sanitation, and contaminated milk'. See p. 81.

19. C. C. P. Anning, 'Municipal health problems of the non-European population', *S. Afr. Med. J.*, 7, 20 (1933), 679.

20. P. W. Laidler, 'The relationship of the native to South Africa's health', *S. Afr. Med. J.*, 6, 19 (1932), 626–7.

21. Archives of the United Society for the Propagation of the Gospel, Rhodes House, Oxford (USPG), Women's Work (WW) Letters Africa, Theodora Williams to Miss Trollope, 10 April 1911.

22. USPG, WW Letters Africa, Deaconess Julia to Miss Humphrey, 21 March 1909.

23. USPG, Series E, Report from T. Williams, 1913.

24. USPG, WW Letters Africa, T. Williams to Miss Saunders, 11 Sept. 1913.

25. *TSR* (*Quarterly magazine of the Transvaal and Southern Rhodesia Missionary Association*), IV, 4 (Oct. 1930), 141.

26. Accounts for Johannesburg may be found in *CR (Journal of the Community of the Resurrection)*, no. 80 (1922), 16, and *Transvaal Missions*, II, 3 (1922), 8; and for Bloemfontein, see USPG, E, 1923, Sister Margery Angela, C.S.M. & A.A., 'The Healing Mission' in *The Barolong*, 15 (June, 1923), 11, and Report, E. M. Stringer, St Patrick's, Bloemfontein. Apart from these items from the diocese of Bloemfontein, all USPG material in this chapter comes from the papers of the diocese of Johannesburg.

27. These missions were selected for special treatment as Anglicans and Methodists had the highest number of African members of all Reef mission churches up to the mid-1930s (when Catholics began catching up), while the ABM, despite its small size, repeatedly took the lead in key social initiatives.

28. T. Ranger, 'Women in the politics of Makoni district, Zimbabwe, 1890–1980', African Studies Association of the United Kingdom, Symposium on Women and Politics in Africa, September 1981, 18.

29. Interviews by D. Gaitskell, Mrs Mavimbela, 3 March 1978, and Mrs Nettie Mguli, 13 February 1978. On the origin and nature of Reef prayer unions, see D. Gaitskell, 'Female mission initiatives: black and white women in three Witwatersrand churches, 1903–1939', unpub. Ph.D. thesis, University of London, 1981, chs 5 and 6.

30. See, for example, *Transvaal Methodist* (April 1925), 5; Wesleyan Methodist Church, *Directory of the Transvaal and Swaziland District* (1930–1), 2.

31. USPG, Medical Mission Files, Folder 'Bishop of Pretoria', Bishop Furse to Lt. Col. J. Armstrong, 7 Nov. 1918.

32. See T. Huddleston, *Naught for Your Comfort* (London, 1956).

33. Biographical details and comments on the Tugmans in this paragraph are drawn from obituaries in Witwatersrand University Library (WUL), Church of the Province of South Africa records (CPSA), AB 838, Bishop Karney's circular letter, 26 April 1932; *Transvaal and Southern Rhodesia News Sheet* (May 1932); *The Watchman* (April 1932).

34. M. Tugman, 'The adventure of healing', *TSR*, IV, 2 (April 1930), 52.

35. USPG, D, St Cyprian's Native Mission Johannesburg. Report for the year ending 31 March 1929, 12.

36. *The Watchman* (April 1932).

37. WUL, fAB, CPSA, Diocese of Johannesburg, Ekutuleni Mission, *Medical Work Amongst the Native People Living on the Rand* (1929).

38. 'Letter from the Bishop of Johannesburg', *TSR*, IV, 2 (April 1930), 50.

39. M. Tugman, 'Sophiatown Clinic', *TSR*, III, 3 (July 1929), 92–3.

40. USPG, Ekutuleni Papers, 'Sister Dorothy Raphael. Notes', unheaded typescript.

41. For further details on the essential economic contribution of African women's laundry-work, beer-brewing and domestic service, see Gaitskell, 'Female mission initiatives', ch. 3.

42. J. Robertson, 'Report of the Princess Alice Nursing Home', *TSR*, VI, 4 (Nov. 1932), 69.

43. 'Medical mission work on the Rand', *TSR*, VII, 2 (June 1933), 46–7.

44. USPG, *Cape to Zambezi*, 1, 2 (1934), 38–40; 2, 1 (1935), 20–2.

45. *The Watchman* (June 1937).

46. J. E. Lane-Claypon, *The Child Welfare Movement* (London, 1920), 48–50; G. F. McCleary, *The Maternity and Child Welfare Movement* (London, 1935), 46.

47. Lewis, *Politics of Motherhood*, 13–14, 96–7.

48. USPG, D, St Cyprian's Report, 31 March, 1929. For the photograph, see *The Times*, 9 Oct. 1928, 20.

49. USPG Pamphlets, St Cyprian's Native Mission, Johannesburg. Report for the Year 1930, 14.

50. *The Watchman* (Sept. 1930).

51. M. Tugman, 'The adventure of healing', *TSR*, IV, 2 (April 1930), 52.

52. *SWM [Society of Women Missionaries] Journal*, 26 (June 1930), 9.

53. Author of the anthropological monograph, *Valenge Women* (London, 1933).

54. E. D. Earthy, 'Stillbirth and infantile mortality in South Africa from the social and economic point of view', *Internat. Nurs. Rev.*, VI, 4 (July 1931), 347, 354. The article was based on a paper read at the International Conference on African Children, held in Geneva in June 1931. Interestingly, while insisting that African babies were 'calling' for help, she also underlined European self-interest in the improvement of African birth rates: the inferior would cause the superior to degenerate if it did not work for their betterment. 'It would seem that a strong healthy African race is indispensable, not only for its own survival, but for the future of the British Empire in South Africa . . . The reckless squandering of [the native labour supply] by the steady drain of men from tribal areas to the mines is killing the goose which lays the golden eggs'. See pp. 345–6. This echoes the rationale for early British maternal and child welfare work, the value of a healthy and numerous population as a national resource for an imperial power. See A. Davin, 'Imperialism and Motherhood', *Hist. Workshop J.*, 5 (1978), 9, and the reinterpretations of D. Dwork, *War is Good for Babies and Other Young Children* (London, 1987).

55. *The Watchman* (Oct. 1932).

56. E. Hellmann, *Rooiyard: A Sociological Survey of an Urban Native Slum Yard* (Cape Town, 1948), 101, 54–61.

57. G. M. Setiloane, *The Image of God among the Sotho-Tswana* (Rotterdam, 1976), 174–82.

58. Manyano Rules, no. 8 (from 1920s copy, among papers in private possession of Ruth Allcock, London, daughter of the Methodist chairman of the Transvaal district 1922–34).

59. J. Comaroff, 'Barolong cosmology: religion in a Tswana Town', unpub. Ph.D. thesis, University of London, 1972, 197.

60. WUL, A1059/E, 'Mrs Bridgman's Reminiscences', in *Bridgman Memorial Hospital Johannesburg, South Africa. Silver Jubilee 1928–1953*.

61. Archives of the American Board of Commissioners for Foreign Missions (ABC), Houghton Library, Harvard University, Cambridge,

Mass., USA – ABC: 15.5 v. 5, Bridgman to Miss Lamson, 2 May 1923.

62. ABC: 6 v. 92, Application of Ruth Cowles.

63. ABC: 15.4 v. 39, Johannesburg Clinic Reports, July 1927 and June 1928.

64. ABC: 15.4 v. 43, Johannesburg Clinic Reports, 1930–2.

65. See M. Wright, 'Nurse Cowles and Alexandra', in Proceedings of workshop on health, science and activism: annual conference of the project on 'Poverty, health and the state in Southern Africa', Columbia University, Nov. 1985, 10.

66. ABC: 15.4 v. 43, Johannesburg Clinic Report, 1932.

67. Hellmann, *Rooiyard*, 65.

68. ABC: 15.4 v. 43, 'American Board Mission Clinics Johannesburg 1931'.

69. ABC: 15.4 v. 50, R. Cowles to Miss Emerson, 12 Feb. 1930.

70. ABC: 15.4 v. 43, Johannesburg Clinics Report, 1934.

71. See C. Davies, 'The health visitor as mother's friend: a woman's place in public health, 1900–14', *Soc. Hist. Med.*, 1 (1988), 39–59.

72. ABC: 15.4 v. 43, Johannesburg Clinics Report, 1934, and Annual Letter, by Mrs Bridgman, 1935.

73. See further, M. Wright, 'Nurse Cowles and Alexandra'.

74. ABC: 15.4 v. 39, 'The Bridgman Memorial Hospital Scheme'; ABC: 15.4 v. 43, *A/Rs*, Bridgman Hospital 1929–30, 1931.

75. ABC: 15.4 v. 43, Mrs Bridgman's *A/Rs*, 1934.

76. ABC: 15.4 v. 44, Mrs Bridgman's *A/R*, 1938. For more details of their work, for example, medical and patient statistics, staff changes, progress in midwifery training, see WUL, A1059/A1, Bridgman Memorial Hospital *A/Rs*. Catherine Burns at Northwestern University has turned this early statistical material into a series of graphs as part of an on-going exploration of the full history of the hospital for her doctoral research on the history of reproduction, sexuality and birthing practices in southern Africa.

77. School of Oriental and African Studies, Methodist Missionary Society Archive, Transvaal correspondence, Allcock to Noble, 7 March 1928.

78. 'Progress in the training of Bantu nurses', *S. Afr. Outlook* (Jan. 1934), 3.

79. See, for example, *Missionary Herald* (June 1935), 268 (Dec. 1935), cover.

80. *Missionary Herald* (Sept. 1930), 351.

10

'Dangerous motherhood': maternity care and the gendered construction of Afrikaner identity, 1904–1939

Marijke du Toit

Introduction

Feminist historians have long criticized medical histories of child-birth for ignoring its social context. In the rich literature on childbirth and its management published over the last two decades a variety of themes have been explored. A major concern has been to trace the transformation of childbirth as a female-dominated affair to a medical event controlled by men. Scholars have also looked specifically at women's role in maternity care. Thus American studies have explored 'the social relationship between women and their birth attendants, midwifery as a female institution, childbirth and female bonding'.[1] But partly because women who promoted the transformation of childbirth into a medical event were seen as mere appendages of a male-controlled system, their activities received less attention.[2]

In South Africa, social historians have so far neglected to examine women's experience of childbirth. Afrikaans women's active participation in the making of Afrikaner nationalism has likewise been hidden from history.[3] None the less, female Afri-kaner nationalists campaigned for the provision of maternity care for poor Afrikaans-speakers, and launched their own maternity care projects. A study of their efforts is doubly important: both to render women's role in nationalism visible and to make clear their active participation in the medicalization of childbirth.

The Afrikaans rural poor and maternity care, 1880–1930

In 1930, M. E. Rothmann suggested that Afrikaner mothers had hitherto neglected to consider their own interests: 'the mothers themselves have seldom yet, at least in our country, considered their own condition and position together'.[4] Appearing in the Afrikaans journal *Eendrag* (*Unity*), the official publication of the *Afrikaanse Christelike Vroue Vereniging* (the Afrikaans Christian Women's Organization, hereafter ACVV), Rothmann's message was directed at a specific audience. For the past twenty-six years the ACVV had practised a racially and linguistically defined philanthropy. The Afrikaner women at the head of this Cape-based organization had proclaimed their commitment to a burgeoning nationalist movement; through its social work the ACVV aimed to rescue poor whites for the benefit of the *volk* (people).[5]

As a leading member of the ACVV since the early 1920s, Rothmann was conscious that the organization's past efforts had not only involved material support for white, Afrikaans-speaking families, but also a specific focus on women. But for Rothmann, programmes that taught females the skills of motherhood were no longer adequate. She argued that 'birth conditions have never yet been examined . . . the mothers have not yet thought to investigate conditions of motherhood'.[6] Rothmann herself had spent the preceding year researching this topic. When collecting the life histories of women from across the South African countryside, she had questioned them extensively about childbirth and maternity care. It was no accident that Rothmann had only recorded the experiences of white, Afrikaans-speaking poor women and not those of black women. Her research was for the Carnegie Commission of Enquiry, which was specifically aimed at gauging the extent and causes of poverty amongst whites. This study had been largely prompted by nationalist fears of the economic decline of a crucial political constituency of white Afrikaans-speakers who formed the majority of poor whites. For some three decades, Afrikaner nationalists had increasingly expressed concern about the rapid growth of a rural underclass of landless and marginalized whites, and the migration of large numbers of mostly unskilled whites to towns and cities. The Carnegie Conference of 1932 provided the impetus for a series of *volks-kongresse* (people's congresses) in the 1930s, where nationalists developed programmes for the solution of the 'poor white problem'.

Rothmann's investigation showed that, in rural areas, Afrikaans poor whites' experience of childbirth had changed, but slowly. The women she interviewed often had smaller families than did their mothers. Still, families were often large and pregnancies tended to follow in quick succession. Contraceptives were virtually unknown in rural areas. When Namakwaland parents were questioned about their use in 1938 'one and all expressed surprise at hearing that such a thing existed'.[7] The interviewers probably asked the wrong question, although women familiar with abortifacients would hardly have passed their knowledge on to male sociologists. Abortion was practised widely enough to prompt the passing of legislation in 1928 specifically forbidding professionally untrained midwives from inducing or aiding 'abnormal . . . miscarriages'.[8] However, most women did not have the option of terminating pregnancy without often serious danger to their health.[9]

Childbirth was also a difficult and even traumatic experience for many women in the rural Cape. An old woman's telling description of transition from girlhood to married life in the late nineteenth century applied to many of her later counterparts: 'then I laid aside the yoke of wood, and put on the yoke of iron.'[10] She was a wage-labourer's daughter from the North-western Cape, who had worked on the land and cared for younger siblings until marriage to a nomadic farmer, which had brought additional burdens. Her husband had no land and soon gave up farming for wage labour; their nomadic life-style dictated the circumstances in which fifteen children were born. At one time

> she had not even a tent, a 'piece of tent', underneath which she sheltered. Her husband was away digging wells, far away . . . in the evening she became ill, and in the night when the little one slept she gave birth to a child. She just took him where he lay, bound and cut, wrapped him and left him next to her on the bed. She was too faint from exhaustion and hunger to do more and lay there till morning. There was no food in the house.[11]

Land ownership was a crucial determinant of the extent and nature of women's productive and reproductive labour. During the late nineteenth and the first decades of the twentieth century, patterns of land ownership amongst rural Afrikaans-speakers changed significantly. The combined effect of the growth (albeit slow and uneven) of market-oriented farming, rising land prices, and recurrent drought pushed many Afrikaans-speakers into a rural under-class. By the 1910s, many Afrikaans families barely subsisted on farms which had become smaller as each generation subdivided the land. Others eked out a meagre and precarious existence as sharecroppers. Those who had lost even this toe-hold on the land roamed the countryside with their goats and sheep looking for pasture to rent. By the 1920s, many erstwhile landowners and sharecroppers who had not yet moved into towns were wage-earning labourers.

In the Eastern Cape of the late nineteenth and early twentieth century, and in the province's arid northern districts until the 1930s, white Afrikaans families often harnessed all available family labour. Girls from families that owned little or no land often did domestic chores at home as well as work on the land. For the most part, all but the poorest stopped herding cattle, ploughing fields and digging wells after marriage: having and caring for children now dominated their lives.[12]

Even in the 1930s, professional birth attendants were hard to come by, for rich and poor alike, in the Cape's more isolated northern districts. Many women were tended by mothers or mothers-in-law, others engaged 'old women' who charged for their services. But their class positions were also crucial determinants of access to help during childbirth: whether women could rely on family networks, 'lay' midwives or qualified doctors for help often depended on access to land. Neeltjie de Wit, who married the owner of a small farm in the Little Karoo in 1908, and had the first of four children a year later, always had 'good help . . . always had an old black midwife, neighbours nearby, sisters-in-law'.[13] Women who were often on the move, whether married to nomadic farmers, wage-labourers or sharecroppers were less likely to have access to the skills of older family members, and were often too poor to afford 'old women's' services. Anna van der Westhuyzen, who married a shepherd in 1901, had painful memories of childbirth. She was alone when she gave birth to six of her nine children, 'husband in the veld, children at school, all alone'. She wanted assistance ('if only I could have had!') but could not pay the £1 for an aya's services.[14]

Moreover, in the Northern Cape and the Karoo, where women's work extended beyond arduous domestic labour of isolated homesteads to farming with goats, it was hardly possible to take time off after a birth. Rothmann's cryptic notes hinted at impoverished women's painful experience of pregnancy and childbirth whilst working to survive. A nomadic farmer's wife who lived in tin shacks on rented fields was chronically ill after the birth of twelve children and five miscarriages. She rarely rested for more than five days after giving birth, and after miscarriages 'seldom even lay down'.[15] In the more economically developed districts of the Cape, the poorest women also combined hard work with constant pregnancies. A woman from the Little Karoo, who was married to a shepherd, probably suffered less than her mother who had twenty-one children, most of whom had died young ('Ma still lay in bed when already they died'). But her nine children were also born in harsh circumstances. One child was born while she looked after cattle, 'under a wagon close to town'. She gave birth to others on sackcloth 'behind a bush, or in a hut or a tent'.[16]

As late as the 1930s, many Afrikaans women in the rural interior of the Cape still regarded birth as a 'natural' event that only rarely called for the intervention of professionals. In 1929 a woman from tiny Soebatsfontein in the North-western Cape explained her preference for female 'lay' doctors to Rothmann: 'I'll be frank madam, I'm afraid of a hospital and I am also afraid of a doctor. I don't just let people touch me: also not strip me naked. Our old wisewomen don't do that, no, they treat one properly.'[17]

Annie Nolte, the daughter of a road inspector and 'lay' midwife from a hamlet in the Northern Cape, married a road-worker who squatted on government land. She was tended by a nurse when her first child was born. But when her second baby was due in 1934 she did not think it worth the trouble:

> My second son, when he was born, then I just got me a granny from the hills. And she came and helped me and in just no time everything was done. Very quick. Very easy. Oh well, you know, those days we were not so refined that we actually needed a hospital – I never got into a hospital. I don't know such a thing.[18]

Magriet Abel, married to a railway employee in Upington when her first child was born in the same year, was emphatic about the trust women had in lay midwives. Birth was a natural event that rarely warranted the attention of doctors:

Oh, had lots of trust in the midwives, and they lost very few babies, and I remember there used to be a Dr. Galgut, a Jew, and he used to work very willingly with Mrs. Davis. He said she gave him tips that he, he never knew . . . he always came when Aunt Lenie called him, then he came, because then he knew there was a problem. But there wasn't a problem with her every day. I don't know whether there were fewer problems – but, well, you know, birth was a dead natural thing. It was a dead natural thing.[19]

But Abel's description of birth as *doodnatuurlik* (dead natural) was perhaps more appropriate than she intended, given the high mortality rates in the countryside of the 1930s. Old folk remedies testified to views of childbirth as holding special dangers for women. As an elderly Namaqualand woman remembered in 1929

In those days women were more careful than now; [their mothers] always warned against the danger of the seventh day, the ninth day and the twenty-second day after the birth.
The birth of the first child of the wife of a farm labourer in the Little Karoo was traumatic.
Woman only stayed for the birth, husband was stupid, as was the woman, she did not even say one should use a warm pot, the afterbirth did not come, did not bandage, became swollen, septic.[20]

The attentions of midwives steeped in local tradition were in fact often inadequate and even dangerous. In the early thirties, Northern Cape midwives still believed that washing a woman before ten days after childbirth was dangerous. Also, 'the umbilical cord must not be cut before the afterbirth comes (which sometimes take hours) otherwise it will 'be pulled inside'; so it is sometimes tied to the patient's leg'.[21]

When, in 1929, her daughter went into labour, Aunt Miena from the North-western Cape was familiar with the uses of a 'warm pot':

Aunt: When I arrived the child was already born; the mother was still on the floor, but the child was already

born. Then I helped them there but the afterbirth would
not come.

Interviewer: And what remedies did Aunt use?

Aunt: Well, I did not known about honey then; now they
say it is such an expelling thing. But we made her drink
other things. And four times I made her sit on a warm pot
with a little brandy in it, but I was frightened because she
bled so. Then the doctor was sent for, and he came and
took it away.[22]

Of course, women's preferences for midwives were not
unrelated to higher fees charged by doctors. As Rothmann's
Carnegie research suggested, economic necessity often dictated
that women only turned to doctors as a last resort. Even so, as
Aunt Miena's story suggests of the isolated rural poor in the
1920s, and as Abel and Nolte's stories suggest of the respectable
poor in the 1930s, many women now accepted that the medical
men had superior skills to be called on in case of difficulties.
However, during these years Afrikaans women's experience of
childbirth were not only shaped by changing attitudes amongst
the rural poor: middle-class women's ideas of proper medical
care were as important.

Reconstructing motherhood: Afrikaner women and the management of childbirth, 1928–1939

When Rothmann called on 'Afrikaner mothers' to pay attention
to inadequate maternity care in 1930, she knew that this was not
a new area of interest for Afrikaans women. Since their inception after the South African war, Afrikaans women's organizations had addressed themselves to the care of parturient
women. However, their approach to this issue changed over the
years, and Rothmann's initiative represented a further, significant shift.

At first, childbirth was not a public issue. The ACVV's welfare
work meshed with private forms of sociability, and help for
parturient women was extended in the privacy of homes. Typi-
cally, local ACVVs paid doctors' fees and provided parturient
women with food or clothes. But from the late 1910s, projects
that dealt specifically with maternity care were launched. The

ACVV's northern sister organization, the South African Federation of Women (together with others such as the Transvaal
Women's National Party) who argued that Afrikaans women
living in rural districts were often tended by inefficient 'lay'
midwives, established a training school for midwives under contract to work in rural areas.[23] From the mid-1920s, a few local
ACVVs also collected funds for the establishment of maternity
clinics with qualified staff. The hitherto private experience of
childbirth was therefore slowly becoming a public issue.

But women's reproductive needs hardly featured, when,
from the mid-1920s, nationalist efforts to alleviate poverty
amongst rural whites focused on health conditions. An extensively publicized *volksgesondheid* (people's health) campaign
emphasized high infant mortality rates amongst the Afrikaans
poor, but not inadequate maternity care. Children's health was
portrayed as women's particular responsibility; their ignorance
was supposedly a root cause of inferior health amongst Afrikaans children. Female Afrikaner nationalists agreed that 'the
future of our people is in the hands of the mothers', and
publicly urged Afrikaans women's organizations to 'educate the
rural population in the field of hygiene'.[24] These organizations
aimed for 'the spiritual and material progress of the *volk*': their
participation was crucial to the success of an educative campaign that meshed information about health with nationalism.

The ACVV promptly heeded the call. At its congress in 1925,
rural branches were urged to form *volksgesondheid* committees;
these would work to improve medical care and nutrition for
Afrikaans children. From 1928, when state funding for welfare
projects was transferred from financially hard-pressed local
authorities to provincial bodies, the ACVV's project grew
rapidly.[25]

Child-care was not the only concern of the ACVV's health
projects. In 1929 Rothmann interrupted her research for the
Carnegie Commission on birth conditions amongst the white,
Afrikaans-speaking poor in the countryside to visit a northern
branch. She explained that while the government was
interested in children's health and other nursing schemes, the
ACVV's new health policy differed from the government's in
that it focused on maternity care.[26] According to Rothmann, an
in- tegral part of the ACVV's *volksgesondheid* programmes was the
establishment of maternity clinics. At the same meeting, she
encouraged the women to organize for better conditions.[27]

Rothmann's project differed in scale from the local initiatives of the past decade: she urged health committees across the Cape to employ midwives. A more significant departure, however, was her insistence that maternity care merited government funds. The ACVV's executive now argued that the provision of adequate maternity care for poor whites would serve state interests. It was also convinced that the success of its programmes was of crucial importance to Afrikaner nationalism.

Afrikaans women's increased concern with the provision of maternity care in rural areas was crucially linked to changing attitudes towards childbirth and medical care. This was influenced by the growing monopoly of medical science in the care and definition of women's reproductive needs. Economic transformation in the late nineteenth century, together with the support of a more interventionist state, and rapid developments in medical science had facilitated the consolidation of a well-paid medical profession in South Africa, and its increasingly successful competition against 'lay' healers. Frequent articles by specialists – and general practitioners' exchange of 'interesting cases' in the 'Clinical notes' column of the *South African Medical Record* – suggest that medical men in the towns and cities practised obstetrics more frequently and enthusiastically from the early 1920s. By the mid-1920s, the increasing reluctance of doctors to 'give Nature a fair chance' prompted debates about the pros and cons of the new interventionist approach to gynaecology and obstetrics.[28]

But most doctors agreed that childbirth could only be properly managed by formally trained attendants. Correspondents warned of the dangers of 'vaginal examinations by untrained women' who paid not 'the slightest attention to asepsis'.[29] Writers also emphasized that, given the rareness of 'labours which can be accurately described as normal in every respect', midwifery required 'the long training and experience of a well-educated person'.[30]

While their black, poor and rural counterparts were hardly touched by the medicalization of childbirth, white middle-class women in the larger towns increasingly engaged medical men rather than midwives. Doctors' complaints in the mid-1920s that 'the status of the untrained [women] is rising'[31] probably reflected their increased competition with 'lay' healers rather than any real threat posed by the latter. Medical men had a steady clientele who could afford steep doctors' fees, and reported that patients no longer objected to surgical procedures.[32] With the relative comfort of anaesthesia and the (at first dubious) merits of newfangled instruments, perceptions of 'naturalness' were slowly replaced by obstetricians' notions of pregnancy and childbirth as pathological and thus warranting the active interference of medical science.

Rothmann's attitude towards childbirth suggests that ACVV members were also absorbing medical science's redefinition of women's reproductive experience. She certainly thought of pregnancy in terms of illness. If some of the more distressing cases fully warranted Rothmann's descriptions of 'illness on the veld', she also described uncomplicated childbirth in similar terms: 'In the evening she became ill, and in the night . . . she gave birth to a child'. Or, as she sadly noted of a Namaqualand woman shouldering the double burdens of farm work and child-care, 'all the milking and the cattle were in her hands. She had to tackle it, whether ill or healthy, pregnant or not. Pregnancy could not be seen as illness'.[33]

But given older perceptions that reproduction held dangers for women, and endless folk remedies for treatment, the crucial difference between this and older attitudes was perhaps not so much the emphasis on illness. The new element was rather the conviction that doctors and nurses bolstered by medical science, rather than wisewomen backed by herbalists' lore, should treat women in labour. At least some women supported the ACVV demand that the state should subsidize maternity clinics for poor whites with specific reference to their own experiences. Thus, a correspondent to *Die Burger* in 1925 argued 'as a mother of three children, who had the privilege of always having the services of a skilled doctor and nurse', that poor Afrikaans women should also be treated by trained midwives.[34] Rothmann herself had professional help for the birth of her first child. Significant numbers of the women who helped formulate and execute ACVV policy undoubtedly had similar experiences; certainly most branches were run by the wives of doctors, teachers and ministers of religion.

However, that middle-class women's notions of adequate maternity care were influenced by the medical establishment only partly explains why female Afrikaans-speakers wanted the Afrikaans poor treated by qualified midwives. Medical men were not alone in attempting to redefine and supply women's reproductive needs. While female philanthropists absorbed medical science's views of maternity care, they also sought to mould women's experience of childbirth to their own particular concerns. Efforts to relieve Afrikaans women of painful and dangerous childbirth experiences were inextricably linked to nationalist aims.

Much of the new interest in maternity care coincided with the idealization of motherhood in Afrikaner nationalism. Given that women were important as reproducers of the *volk*, it is perhaps not surprising that female Afrikaner nationalists now focused on an aspect of women's reproductive needs. Such nationalist sympathies also explain why women did not simply organize for the replacement of 'lay' midwives with qualified birth attendants. From the late 1910s, the nationalist press increasingly voiced fears about Afrikaans-speakers being 'lost' to the *volk* as poverty pushed them into close proximity with blacks. Female Afrikaner nationalists, intent on maintaining (or establishing) notions of racial purity amongst their poorer sisters, were also concerned that many midwives were black. The Women's Federation's own explanation of its decision to launch a training programme for midwives was deeply racist:

The League [for Afrikaans Mothers] and its work . . . is the direct result of the complaint of a white woman from the backveld of Lydenburg, who in the hour of her greatest need had no other succour other than that of a Kaffir woman. Her case was typical of thousands in our country.[35]

In the Cape, the few women who questioned nationalists' prevalent conviction that high infant mortality rates should primarily be combated with campaigns to improve women's knowledge of child-care echoed such sentiments. As 'Nurse' asked readers of *Die Burger*,

Has one of our great learned Ministers ever asked if something has been done to erect free maternity hospitals for our poor Afrikaans women? Has our Minister of Health ever made an enquiry and asked how many midwives there are in our small towns and our districts? So many of our poor women must get help from Hotnot women who are so filthy, that is why so many little ones are taken from us. Our Afrikaner women are not yet Kaffirs who can manage like animals.[36]

Nationalist convictions were also central to the *volksgesondheid* policy developed by Rothmann in the late 1920s. Like the small-scale projects of the previous decade, hers was motivated by the racial exclusiveness of Afrikaner nationalism. And yet her support for state-funded maternity care requires more careful consideration. In fact, a sophisticated set of ideas about women's place in the 'poor white problem' lay at the heart of the ACVV's new policy. In large part, it was Rothmann herself who formulated, publicized and implemented these ideas. Her views about the need for state-funded maternity care merit closer analysis.[37]

Rothmann's travel diary of 1928 reflected an acute awareness of women's subordinate role in Afrikaans communities. Encounters with the careworn women who attended her meetings in isolated rural areas confirmed that 'life is hard for a woman'. They also suggested that to organize women around their own needs would be difficult: 'the women, instead of standing together to make life easier for themselves, would rather stand together to make life easier for the children and the men'.[38] Rothmann wanted women to organize around their reproductive needs (and officials to recognize that those needs merited attention). But considered together with other, more widely publicized motivations for state involvement in maternity care, suggestions that women should prioritize their own interests appeared contradictory. In fact, Rothmann's concern to relieve women of painful and life-threatening experiences meshed with middle-class notions of women's nurturing and socializing roles, and nationalist beliefs of their place in the *volk*.

Like the advocators of *moederkunde* (mothercraft) in the *volksgesondheid* programmes of previous years, Rothmann was convinced that mothers were the linchpins.[39] In her final report she elaborated on 'the importance and indispensability of the mother as a home and social educator, that is as inculcator of the social sense in the child'.[40] But while her ideas were firmly rooted in the gendered notions of earlier *volksgesondheid* projects, she was also convinced that educative programmes would not suffice. At the root of women's inadequate performance as mothers were material conditions in an economically backward and socially stratified countryside. The burden of work on the wives of share-croppers and labourers, together with lack of proper care during pregnancy and childbirth, meant they could not be good mothers. She later summarized her findings in a memorandum to the

214

Secretary of Public Health on the need for maternity care:

> I came upon a spoor that led me to one of the basic causes
> of social regression . . . This was the fact . . . that the
> mother is the first shaper of the citizen; furthermore, that
> she is an extremely important shaper; and that a lack of skill
> in shaping can cause a people untold damage . . .
> . . . it became clear that the work of mothers in such areas
> was so overburdening that it reduced their life expectancy. If
> one generation of mothers after another had lived in such
> areas under what was really a deathly pressure, it was under-
> standable that they as mothers would become less effective
> educators; they were too tired . . .[41]

This was the context for her concern with birth conditions: her
conviction that maternity care was crucially important for
Afrikaner nationalism, and merited state funding. Hardship
during pregnancy and childbirth, she argued, adversely affected
'the quality of the woman, as producer and raiser of the child'.[42]
'Dangerous motherhood' called for action not only because
women's lives and health were under threat, but also (and more
importantly) because the *volk* itself was endangered. By providing maternity care, the ACVV would help fashion Afrikaans
women into the nurturers and educators that Afrikaner
nationalism needed:

> needy mothers . . . cannot help themselves – but the
> children still come; motherhood is still claimed of the
> mothers. To their own deadly danger. We women must
> think and make plans to take motherhood out of danger.
> We are a people; we have a task and a calling: we need
> good citizens; and without healthy, courageous mothers it
> is impossible to get good citizens.[43]

In fact, Rothmann sometimes argued that it was because
maternity care for the poor offered opportunities for social
upliftment that women were interested in this issue. Her memorandum to the Department of Public Health encapsulated
crucial aspects of the reasoning behind the ACVV's maternity
projects for the 1930s:

There is such a strong social aspect to the question of

maternity care for the poor that it is only natural that women hold on to it. It is extremely useful social work, not only because of health considerations, but also because it is so *ad feminam*. I wonder whether there is one time in the life of the normal woman . . . when she is as susceptible to guidance and sympathy as when she lies in the maternity bed. The good nurse can then teach her lessons that penetrate easily and deeply; she is dependent and receptive. In the proper maternity hospital, especially when it is simply furnished, she learns how good cleanliness and order are, and how essential; she considers her own matrimonial and domestic situation; she asks for and gets advice; where else shall she get authoritative advice about such vitally important matters? . . . Above all, when the poor-mother has been for fourteen days the object of studied care, and has not – as is the case at home – had to worry about serving others, she gets the impression that she as mother is worth the trouble of being treated in this way. That is a valuable lesson for her as educator . . .[44]

If the major theme underlying many feminist accounts of the chronology of birth management is that of control,[45] this picture of ignorant *armmoeder* (poor-mother) meeting knowledgeable nurse suggests that nationalist concerns gave the South African version of the 'reproductive takeover' a peculiar twist. For many feminist historians of childbirth in America and Europe, the central issue has been its transition from a predominantly female affair to a medical event controlled by male professionals.[46] Thus Oakley argues that although the trained personnel who first replaced 'lay' midwives were mostly women, their skills were 'defined predominantly in relation to the expertise and omniscience of the male professional'.[47] While this analysis is broadly applicable to a South Africa where the medical profession was a powerful patriarchal institution, a primary focus on male over female hierarchies cannot adequately explain the ACVV's venture.

Rothmann's description signals a crucial change in the social relationship between parturient women and birth attendants. While familiar women – their social equals or inferiors – helped them in their own home, rural women may often have retained a measure of control. Relations with 'lay' midwives were informed by ties of friendship, family and community. Annie

Nolte explained: 'the one woman helps the other. One is a granny and the other isn't'.[48]

Even so, solidarity between women was undercut by divisions of race and class. Rothmann's personal recollections pointed to racial divides: 'in my time in my town, [I had] to make do with the help of a coloured "Granny Annie"... through lack of any other'.[49] Moreover, when women were tended by midwives who practised their skills for economic survival, the extent of female solidarity must often have been limited by their different social standing. And feminist scholars have correctly warned against romanticizing the lay midwife as a 'persecuted female protoprofessional'.[50] Rothmann's horror stories are a powerful antidote to any such temptation. The wife of a nomadic farmer in the North-western Cape, attended by an elderly, half-blind midwife, could hardly have had a sense of 'control' during childbirth:

> When Mrs S arrived there, Mrs D lay on the floor, her feet half outside the door ... the child was born, lay covered to one side 'already quite limp'. The umbilical cord was cut off, about five inches long, and tied off with a knot, there was a whole puddle of blood. The mother lay helplessly, instructing Aunt Hessie [the midwife] as to where she must get further necessaries for the child.

In Rothmann's scenario, the 'lay' midwife was replaced by a professionally trained nurse, firmly in control of a 'decent little maternity clinic'. Here the crucial change in the management of childbirth was not the establishment of male control: rather, 'lay' midwives were replaced by women who had absorbed middle-class and nationalist notions of women's place in society.

In fact, that childbirth was still *ad feminam* was of central importance to Rothmann. The special bond created between participants in this intimate and exclusively female experience made for a unique educational opportunity. The parturient woman, rendered dependent and helpless at a crucial point in a life that centred on motherhood (and 'not her normal self' as Rothmann explained elsewhere) was receptive to the advice of a nurse schooled in this vocation.

That ties of community should still inform their relationship was also important for the success of this nationalist scheme: nurses had to be Afrikaans-speakers and, if possible, work in their own district. But if language and culture bound them together, it did so within the new hierarchy. In the nurse's eyes, the patient's reproductive function and her poverty were inseparable: she was what Rothmann called an *armmoeder* (poor-mother) in need of education and guidance. As such, she was the passive 'object of *informed* care'; an educated, professionally trained woman gave 'guidance and . . . *authoritative* advice' (my emphasis).

The professional midwives employed by the ACVV, then, had a role that extended beyond mere medical duties. As an advertisement placed by a Western Cape branch indicated, the duties of midwives and nurses employed by the ACVV included home visits and instruction. They were expected to have qualifications in midwifery and to have experience of general nursing.[51] Successful applicants were 'girls . . . who must help with organising the country',[52] who were to be used for 'national service'.[53] In even more explicitly nationalist terms, Rothmann explained why Van Wyksdorp should employ a nurse by pointing to 'the regression of the Afrikaner people and what is necessary to invigorate them again'.[54] *Gesondheidskommittee* (health committee) rules specified that nurses must be Afrikaans-speaking;[55] it is significant that the advertisement was placed in *Die Kerkbode*, the official publication of the Dutch Reformed Church. For Rothmann, English speakers had no place amongst the Afrikaans poor.[56] Appropriate candidates for work involving the social upliftment of the poor should ideally have 'respectable' backgrounds; if not actually middle-class, they were ideally to have absorbed middle-class notions of a proper upbringing.[57]

From *armmoeders* to *volksmoeders*? Implementing the ACVV's maternity care programmes

To what extent was the ACVV able to realize its plans? Did birth attendants and women in labour forge bonds that transcended differences of social standing, and that created new possibilities for shaping the identities of poor Afrikaans women?

Rothmann was only too aware of the obstacles she faced in moulding the ACVV's health programmes according to her concerns. At first, funding for maternity care could only be obtained in a roundabout way, because state officials only subsidized nurses' salaries when it was 'directed at child care'.[58] And as Rothmann soon discovered, doctors, when threatened with the loss of fee-paying patients, were not always sympathetic to the idea that women needed specialized care.[59]

Women from rural villages and farms were still suspicious of modern medicine, and did not always receive with enthusiasm the ACVV's plans to have their trusted midwives replaced by professional nurses. 'The people are so attached to the old midwives', Rothmann noted after addressing a meeting in Namaqualand on the need for improved maternity care.[60] Rothmann was convinced that local participation was crucial for successful organization.[61] But middle-class women's conviction that they could improve women's conditions was not always shared by their poorer counterparts. If harsh experiences of childbirth among impoverished Northern Cape women spurred Rothmann to action, their (and their menfolk's) apathy frustrated her.[62]

By 1936 the ACVV could report that their petitions for more substantial state subsidies had been successful. However, branches who could now afford to employ nurses were unable to do so. A major obstacle to the success of the ACVV's project was their failure to find suitable nurses. Throughout the 1930s the ACVV agitated without success for the training of more nurses. Nurses were in short supply in South Africa and – more pertinently for an organization that wanted to employ Afrikaans-speaking whites – the country had few training facilities. Training schools for midwives were private and profit-making. Nursing schools were also 'either profit-making concerns or semi-voluntary public hospitals verging on bankruptcy'.[63] Their apprenticeship systems of training exploited probationer nurses as cheap labour and kept numbers as low as possible. By the end of the 1930s, the ACVV still employed a relatively small number of health workers in rural areas. The situation would only improve after the Second World War, when the state channelled large amounts of funds into public health.[64]

While the state made no significant intervention, the ACVV arranged for the state-sponsored training of a limited number of midwives at a maternity hospital in Cape Town. By committing students to working for rural ACVVs, the organization aimed to ensure at least a limited supply of midwives for their project. But the ACVV still experienced difficulties in getting nurses and midwives to work in the countryside. If city maternity and general hospitals exploited and overworked their female staff, the isolated and primitive conditions of rural employment were also unattractive. This was daily life for a Karoo nurse in 1927:

> she rides on horse-back to her cases, and often has to spend three or four hours a day in the saddle when she goes to the more distant farms, but she is all the time on duty and on call, Sundays included . . . twice in the month she has been here her day off has been spoilt by her being urgently called out to a case.[65]

In Upington in the 1930s, the district nurse did not even have a horse at her disposal. Having no transport at her disposal she was forced to walk, often miles, which 'wore her feet out'.[66]

More pertinently, employment in the countryside was often uncertain, and payment low. A midwife in Namaqualand, who found that the health committee employing her could not afford to pay and that she had to survive on a partial government subsidy and sporadic fees from patients, wrote a desperate letter:

> I did not know what to do. But now I have decided to nurse for a while more with the subsidy of £30 a year, because I do not see another way how the ACVV can manage to appoint a nurse here. The different bodies that are responsible for the money are just as poor except for the divisional council. Everything is so uncertain that I am scared. Now I want to ask you kindly to please use your influence to raise the subsidy if the Department gives me £5 per month I can treat more poor cases.[67]

In terms of the training scheme for midwives, branches that recommended candidates also had to provide employment for them. But ACVVs in the rural backwaters were often too poor to comply. It was precisely in these areas that medical services for women were least developed: 'we find that the least amount of local effort always coincides with the greatest need'.[68] A graduate from the ACVV's midwifery course was told

> that there is more than enough need for your services in Namaqualand, but that the question of maintenance is the

difficulty; that the people can pay very little. Then there still remains the possibility, before you have to take recourse to Cape Town, that our Executive can give you a small monthly allowance for a year, to get you going. Our idea was to give you £1 per case, not exceeding £36 for the year. But it can only last for the first year . . . With best wishes, and appreciation of your courage to serve your people . . .[69]

Rothmann was well aware that many women, less eager to sacrifice their interests for *volksdiens* (service to the people), preferred the low but regular wages of urban hospitals.[70]

Faced with such difficulties, was the ACVV able to employ the women – imbued with middle-class and nationalist ideals – so crucial to the success of their schemes? Middle-class women were certainly entering the nursing profession in the early thirties, even if some rapidly exchanged careers for marriage. But given that the ACVV's course was subsidized, and the relatively low salaries of midwives, most applicants were probably from struggling rural or small-town families. The ACVV's executive stressed the need to screen candidates carefully, and local branches were encouraged to recommend 'deserving girls'. Head office sometimes disagreed with the motives of branches in recommending candidates. The former was primarily interested in educating Afrikaans-speaking midwives who could contribute to the social upliftment of poor whites; the latter saw the opportunity to help impoverished young women towards employment.[71] Some working-class women who had the requisite schooling did surmount the final hurdle of the ACVV's scrutiny and obtained loans to train. One woman, however, was refused admission to a midwifery course when the ACVV learned that she did not have quite the right skin colour, but a 'touch of the tarbrush'.[72]

A number of nurses employed by the ACVV measured up to expectations. Some even helped found branches and organize activities.[73] But the performance of others was disappointing.[74] Problems stemmed partly from the ACVV expecting nurses to perform a 'national service' by providing care at low fees; nurses were at least as concerned with making a living. Even reliable staff did not always share the organization's ideals. But when nationalist convictions overrode medical concerns, a local ACVV had sufficient power to make doctors comply. A Western

Cape branch refused to allow women to bear illegitimate children in their clinics; single mothers could apparently not be *volksmoeders*. Rothmann reported with some satisfaction that the ACVV had forced medical staff to comply:

> the other night our little Afrikaans doctor was very angry with us. The magistrate sent him to the birth of an unmarried case; poor people, six miles from town; he wanted to bring the girl in to us . . . we refused, and he was annoyed and angry. This was the third application for an illegitimate child in this first year; and the branch took a firm decision. I agree, because the clinic is meant for the poor sharecropper and farmhand's wife, and it really offers them a chance for upliftment. If we also sheltered the wild swallows, we would not get the virtuous and deserving. So we are digging in our heels. But believe me, doctors and nurses get annoyed and extremely angry with us when we also want to have a say.[75]

The attitudes of the ACVV's executive and local branches to 'lay' midwives illustrate the uneven penetration of the organization's programme into the countryside. Poor women certainly patronized the ACVV's clinics in increasing numbers from the late 1920s.[76] But ten years later isolated branches still struggled to break women's trust in 'lay' midwives.[77]

While the ACVV petitioned the state to extend its control over midwives with no formal training,[78] it differentiated between those midwives who clung to old practices in 'pure ignorance' and others who had doctors' approval. After some efforts to raise funds for a 'small hospital' with trained staff, a northern branch settled for a maternity clinic where they employed an 'excellent, although untrained nurse',[79] also a member of the ACVV. But head office's approval of this scheme was not too surprising. Unlike other midwives with no formal training, she was not taught her skills by 'lay' midwives. Regarded as 'more sort of a professional',[80] she started to practise while still in her twenties and soon worked with medical men.[81] As her daughter recalled, 'My mother was never trained for a nurse. She just caught the babies, and after a while she was so skilled . . . she worked among doctors, and she even had a little clinic where she took in the women'.[82]

In Upington, where the ACVV employed no nurse until the

1940s, the ACVV still made use of 'lay' midwives. Magriet Abel's recollections show how the organization's help meshed with more informal networks of mutual aid. The midwife

> was always there with the babies and went every day, again cared for the women, and then the ACVV gave, and also the neighbours. Oh those days we helped each other a lot, you know, you also knew more about each other's needs because there was, there was more mutuality and lots of visiting and so on. If the Mrs., I don't want to mention her name, if she has a baby, then Tant Lenie let us know there's a baby at Anna's again, then the one would send soup and the other . . .[83]

The midwife was also called when a struggling farmer's wife came to town to have her baby in the house of Aunt Lou, the attorney and local ACVV's president:

> there was a woman, they had so many little babies, and they were rather distinguished people, they were now, they were now white poor people, you understand. A very decent family, there's still some of them left around here. And she had so many little babies, then she always went to Aunt Lou – I think she went to Aunt Lou for three of her babies. And then she'd just stay there, and she just ate there, and Mrs Davis went to her, that's for the birth . . .[84]

That black midwives should be replaced by white nurses was implicit in the ACVV's scheme. However, racist attitudes from local ACVVs was sometimes tempered by a more cautious approach from the executive. In 1935 a rural branch asked what legal steps it could take against 'black girls who attend to white women'. Head office cautioned that the branch should not act against midwives simply because of their skin colour:

> Now I want to give you some serious advice: I don't think you should approach the matter along the lines of colour. A nurse is trained or untrained; competent or not. And in case of lack of training or capability one can take concerted action. Where an incompetent, unsuitable or unclean white woman does the work we would do the same, not so?[85]

Head office agreed that 'we must give preference to the white nurse' and suggested that 'coloureds' should be 'trained for work amongst their own people'. But in the absence of trained workers, it defended women's rejection of an 'inferior white' in favour of a 'thorough coloured' midwife as reasonable.

Conclusion

Feminist studies of childbirth and its management have successfully challenged gender-blind histories of obstetrics. But accounts that focus on efforts by men to establish control over women cannot adequately explain the reasoning behind the ACVV's maternity care projects. The campaigns launched by Afrikaner women during the 1920s and 1930s show that medical men were not alone in attempting to redefine and supply women's reproductive needs. The ACVV's leaders certainly absorbed medical science's views of maternity care. But they sought to mould women's experience of childbirth to their particular concerns. Efforts to relieve Afrikaans women of painful and dangerous childbirth experiences were inextricably linked to nationalist aims. The 'imagined community' of Afrikaner nationalism was cross-class and racially exclusive. Afrikaans women's organizations' interest in maternity care for poor whites coincided with mounting concern amongst nationalists that the fast growing numbers of poor, Afrikaans-speaking whites would merge with a black working class. This motivated the women's organizations to replace black 'lay' midwives with white Afrikaans-speakers. Rothmann's more ambitious project of 1928 was also motivated by nationalist-inspired concern about the 'poor white problem'. However, hers was a more sophisticated set of ideas about women's role in the solution to it. In Rothmann's eyes, Afrikaans mothers were central to efforts to reconstruct the 'Afrikaner' family amongst the poor. The ACVV's clinics were to play an important role in female nationalists' efforts to fashion Afrikaans poor whites into 'Afrikaners'.

For years, the leading women in the ACVV had recognized that they could best reach the poor through personal contact. While the ACVV conducted public campaigns, its main contribution to the construction of Afrikaner identity took place in the privacy of homes. Rothmann was likewise aware that *armmoeders* could best become *volksmoeders* in the intimate context of childbirth. The success of Rothmann's project depended on a change in the social relationship between parturient women and birth attendants. But here the crucial change was not that described in feminist accounts of the 'reproductive takeover': the establishment of male control over parturient women. In Rothmann's scenario, 'lay' midwives were replaced by women who had absorbed middle-class and nationalist notions of women's social role. In fact, female solidarity was to help build the cross-class, linguistically and racially exclusive 'imagined community' of Afrikaner nationalism.

Many feminist historians of childbirth and its management have used gender as the primary category for analysis. Their framework often seems blind to the presence of hierarchies other than that of men over women. This study of female Afrikaner nationalists' efforts to shape the gendered identity of poor Afrikaans-speakers demonstrates that a more complex analysis is necessary. And a feminist study of maternity care that acknowledges women as historical subjects must ask whether – and why – women promoted the medicalization of childbirth.

For the ACVV, childbirth was *ad feminam*: an event that should ideally be controlled by women. Rothmann complained that impoverished women would not organize for themselves. And yet the ACVV subordinated women's particular interests to those of class. Improved maternity care was necessary because impoverished women were suffering and dying, but the women who mattered were white and Afrikaans. 'Dangerous motherhood' called for action because the *volk* was endangered: the shift to maternity care was above all for nationalist, not feminist reasons.

Acknowledgements

I am indebted to Helen Bradford for her profuse and insightful comments, and detailed editing of this paper. Andries du Toit provided translations from the original Dutch and Afrikaans.

Notes

1. N. S. Dye, 'Review essay: history of childbirth in America', *Signs*, 6 (1980), 98.
2. Dye provides a comprehensive review of historical studies of

childbirth in the United States published in the 1970s. More recently, J. Murphy-Lawless has provided an interesting critique of feminist studies of the medicalization of childbirth in her article 'The silencing of women in childbirth or let's hear it from Bartholomew and the Boys', *Women's Internat. Forum*, 11 (1988), 293–9. Murphy-Lawless observes that, from the early 1970s, 'the struggle for power in the birthplace has been presented in feminist writing as one between women practitioners and the emerging profession of male midwives, with the latter gradually gaining control at the expense of the former' (p. 294). Most scholars seem to agree with A. Oakley that 'professional' midwives and nurses were appendages of a male-controlled medical hierarchy, and have not probed women's reasons for promoting the transformation of childbirth into a medical event. A. Oakley, 'Wisewoman and medicine man: changes in the management of childbirth', in J. Mitchell and A. Oakley (eds) *The Rights and Wrongs of Women* (London, 1976), 18.

3. In South African historiography 'Afrikaner' commonly refers to Afrikaans-speaking whites in general. While some revisionist scholars have challenged nationalist and liberal notions of organic nationalism with studies of the construction of an Afrikaner identity, most have retained this usage. Used in this way, however, the term 'Afrikaner' obscures the constructed nature of Afrikaner nationalism, and perpetuates the myth of a monolithic Afrikaner tribe or nation. I have used 'Afrikaner' to refer specifically to those Afrikaans-speakers who came to see themselves as belonging to the racially and linguistically exclusive imagined community of Afrikanerdom. When reference is made to 'white Afrikaans-speakers' or 'white Afrikaans women', skin colour and linguistic background – rather than membership of a specific political or ethnic group – is indicated.

4. M. E. Rothmann, 'Gevaarlike moederskap', *Eendrag* (1930), 22.

5. The original Afrikaans is used where no English translation exists for Afrikaans words that encapsulate central aspects of Afrikaner nationalism. Afrikaans terms for midwives translate with some difficulty. Until the 1940s, Afrikaans-speakers often referred to midwives as '*ou vrouens*' or 'old women'. The more respectful *doktorsvrou* ('doctor-woman') and *groot vrou* ('big woman') seem best translated as 'wisewoman'.

6. Rothmann, 'Gevaarlike moederskap', 22.

7. P. W. Kotze, *Namakwaland: 'n Sosiologiese Studie van 'n geïoleerde gemeenskap* (Cape Town, 1943), 69.

8. Cape Archives (hereafter CA), ACVV collection, A1953, (V)olume 2/3, (F)ile 8, 'Regulations for persons practising as midwives', 1928.

9. H. Bradford, '"Her body, her life": a hundred years of abortion in South Africa', unpublished paper delivered at Conference on Women and Gender in South Africa, February 1991.

10. University of Stellenbosch Document Centre (hereafter USDC), M. E. Rothmann Collection (hereafter MER), (file) 55.M.3, 'Aantekeninge oor besoeke aan gesinne in Namakwaland', p. 8.

11. USDC, MER, 55.M.3, 'Aantekeninge oor besoeke aan gesinne in Namakwaland', 1929, p. 8.

12. USDC, MER, 55.M.3, (district) Klaarstroom, p. 6; USDC, MER, 55.M.3, Prins Albert, pp. 1–62; M. E. Rothmann, *The Mother and Daughter of the Poor Family* (Stellenbosch, 1932), 197.

13. USDC, MER, 55.M.3, Prins Albert (case no.) 8, p. 30.

14. USDC, MER, 55.M.3, Klaarstroom (case no.) 1, pp. 3–6. 'Aya' refers to a black servant or nanny but could also mean black midwife. The white Afrikaans-speakers quoted in the text often referred to older black women in general as 'aias', the implicit assumption being that they were servants or of inferior status.

15. USDC, MER, 55.M.1.K.7, Rothmann (letter to) Mrs Conradie, 25 Oct. 1931.

16. USDC, MER, 55.M.3, Prins Albert 14.

17. USDC, MER, 55.M.3, Garies 6, p. 35.

18. Interview with A. Nolte by M. du Toit, 19 July 1990.

19. Interview with M. Abel by M. du Toit, 17 July 1990.

20. USDC, MER, 55, M.3, Prins Albert 1, 9; USDC, MER, 55.M.3.2, Garies.

21. USDC, MER, 55.M.1.K.7, Rothmann, Conradie, 25 Oct. 1931.

22. USDC, MER, 55.M.3, Garies 31, p. 46.

23. C. Searle, *The History of the Development of Nursing in South Africa, 1652–1960* (Cape Town, 1965), 350; *Eendrag,* 2 (1938), 1.

24. *Die Burger* (17 March 1925), 9.

25. Searle, *Nursing in South Africa,* 256; *Die Huisgenoot* (18 Sept. 1925), 45; USDC, MER, 55.M.1.K.11, A. Geyer, Rothmann, 16 April 1929.

26. CA, A1953, Kenhardt, 26 Oct. 1929.

27. CA, A1953, Kenhardt, 26 Oct. 1929.

28. W.H. Maxwell, 'The use of forceps', *J. Med. Ass. S. Afr.,* 2 (14 July 1928), 343–4. Also, for example, O.J. Curry, 'Uterine displacements', *S. Afr. Med. Rec.,* 21 (28 July 1923), 326–9; D.H. Wessels, 'Conservative treatment in gynaecology', *S. Afr. Med. Rec.,* 24 (13 March 1926), 108–11; T. Trail, 'Treatment of puerperal fever', *S. Afr. Med. Rec.,* 24 (13 March 1926), 106–8; J.A. du Toit, 'Two interesting cases', *J. Med. Ass. S. Afr.,* 2 (12 May 1928), 240–1. (The *South African Medical Record* was re-named the *Journal of the Medical Association of South Africa* in 1927, when it also became affiliated to the British Medical Association. The new journal also incorporated the *Medical Journal of South Africa.*)

29. K. Bremer, 'Vaginal examinations by untrained women', *S. Afr. Med. Rec.,* 23 (8 Aug. 1925), 347. See also the correspondence that followed this article: (12 Sept. 1925), 395–6, (14 Nov. 1925), 495–6; K. Bremer, 'Applied evolution', *J. Med. Ass. S. Afr.,* 2 (14 April 1928), 171–6.

30. J. Bruce-Bays, 'The doctor, the midwife and the patient', *J. Med. Ass. S. Afr.,* 2 (14 April 1928), 177.

31. Bremer, 'Vaginal examinations', 347.

32. Wessels, 'Conservative treatment', 109.

33. M. E. Rothmann, USDC, Carnegie papers, 55.M.3, Garies 36.

34. 'Vrouesake', *Die Burger* (17 Jan. 1925), 6.

35. *Die Boerevrou* (Jan. 1926), 12.

36. *Die Burger* (7 Jan. 1925), 8.

37. In addition to her widely publicized contribution to the Carnegie Report, Rothmann wrote prolifically on the need for state-funded maternity care and the nature of the ACVV's projects. Until the late 1930s she was centrally involved in formulating the ACVV's policy on health care. She managed virtually all head office's correspondence with government officials, and until 1934 she personally assisted with the implementation of projects in rural areas.

38. CA, A1/2/1, Aug. 1928.

39. USDC, MER, 55.M.l.K.ll, Rothmann, A. Geyer, 4 May 1929.

40. Rothmann, *Mother and Daughter*, 175.

41. CA, A1953, 2/3, F9, Rothmann, Secretary of Public Health, *c.* 1939.

42. USDC, MER, 55.M.l.K.ll, Rothmann, A. Geyer, 4 May 1929.

43. Rothmann, 'Gevaarlike moederskap', 24.

44. CA, A1953, 2/3, F9, Rothmann, Secretary of Public Health, *c.* 1939.

45. Dye, 'History of childbirth', 98.

46. Murphy-Lawless, 'The silencing of women in childbirth', 294.

47. Oakley, 'Wisewoman and medicine man', 18.

48. Interview with A. Nolte.

49. CA, A1953, Al/1/1, 31 May 1935.

50. Dye, 'History of childbirth', 99.

51. CA, A1953, A1/2/1, May 1928.

52. CA, A1953, V2/9, F116, Rothmann, M. Laubscher, 3 Dec. 1936.

53. CA, Dutch Reformed Church, ACVV Collection, V21, 2/4/1, 3 March 1936.

54. CA, A1953, Add 1/14/3/1/1/1, Van Wyksdorp, 16 March 1935.

55. CA, A1953, A1/2/1, July 1928.

56. CA, A1953, V2/29, F116, Rothmann, M. Luckhoff, 5 April 1939 (although Luckhoff had no problems with the candidate: letter 15 April 1935).

57. CA A1953, Al/1/1, A. Geyer, M. Luckhoff, 12 May 1934.

58. USDC, MER, 55.M.l.K.7, Rothmann, J. H. Conradie, 25 Oct. 1931.

59. USDC, MER, 55.M.l.K.7, Rothmann, J. H. Conradie, 25 Oct. 1931.

60. CA, A1953, A1/2/1, Aug. 1928.

61. USDC, MER, 55.M.l.K.7, Rothmann, J. H. Conradie, 25 Oct. 1931.

62. USDC, MER, 55.M.l.K.7, Rothmann, J. H. Conradie, 25 Oct. 1931.

63. Searle, *Nursing in South Africa*, 254.

64. Searle, *Nursing in South Africa*, 254–7.

65. CA, A1953, A 1/1/1, J. M. Buckton, Rothmann, 27 Dec. 1927.

66. Interview with M. Abel.

67. CA, A1953, Al/1/1, J. Preis, Rothmann, 6 Dec. 1935.

68. CA, A1953, Al/1/1, Rothmann, M. Thompson (Secretary, Department of Public Health), 12 Nov. 1934.

69. CA, A1953, Al/1/1, Rothmann, Miss Faul, 29 Nov. 1934.

70. CA, A1953, Al/1/1, Rothmann, M. Thompson, 1934; A1953, Al/1/1, Rothmann, 2 July 1935.

71. CA, A1953, Al/1/1, Rothmann, Mevr. Pellissier, 2 July 1935.

72. USDC, MER, 55.M.1.K.ll, reply scribbled on letter from Rothmann to A. Geyer, 25 April 1932.

73. CA, A1953, V2/9, F116, Rothmann, M. Laubscher, 3 Dec. 1936.

74. CA, A1953, Al/2/1, July 1928; CA, A1953, Al/1/1, A. E. Le Roux, Rothmann, 22 Oct. 1935.

75. USDC, MER, 55/66/169, Rothmann, A. Geyer, 5 Nov. 1941.

76. Rothmann, 'Gevaarlike moederskap', 24.

77. CA, A1/2/4, 1937.

78. CA, A1953, V2/3, F9, 13 March 1939.

79. CA, A1953, A1953, Al/2/1, Oct. 1928.

80. Interview with M. Abel.

81. Interview with M. Abel.

82. Interview with A. Nolte.

83. Interview with M. Abel.

84. Interview with M. Abel.

85. CA, A1953, Al/1/1, Rothmann, S. J. de Leew, 31/5/1935.

11

'That welfare warfare': sectarianism in infant welfare in Australia, 1918–1939

Philippa Mein Smith

Infant mortality rates fell remarkably in northern and western Europe between the 1870s and 1950. European peoples outside Europe, including Australia and New Zealand, were also affected by the infant mortality decline. From the late nineteenth century, in a common pattern, infant mortality 'drop[ped] like a stone'.[1] There were considerable disparities, however, in the timing and course of the transition to lower rates between and within countries.

In the 1880s infant mortality in the Australian colonies began to fall from a rate of over 120 deaths per 1,000 registered live births. From the turn of the century, when the Commonwealth of Australia was created, it declined steeply. Infant mortality in New Zealand began to decline from the 1870s from a lower level, of just over 100 deaths per 1,000 live births. The differing rates of infant mortality in the two countries persisted into the 1920s, when the New Zealand rate of 40 deaths per 1,000 attracted world attention (the equivalent Australian rate in 1925 was 53).[2] Until surpassed by Sweden in 1950, New Zealand possessed the lowest infant mortality rate in the world. The record set by New Zealand challenged Australia's reputation as a healthy country, particularly in the 1920s, when infant mortality was increasingly becoming the yardstick by which the campaign to save lives was measured. (See Figure 11.1.)

The result was an infant welfare movement which was sectarian in character,[3] and shaped by intense belief systems conveyed by charismatic figures. Foremost amongst these was Dr Frederic Truby King, the New Zealand child health authority. In the 1920s, his personal contribution as an itinerant

Figure 11.1 The yardstick: infant mortality decline in Australia and New Zealand, 1870–1950

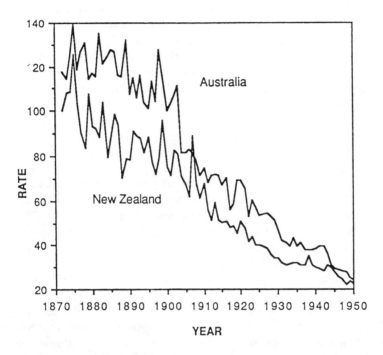

Sources: Australian Bureau of Statistics, *Demography Bulletins; NZ Vital Statistics* (various issues).

ideologue manifested itself in making Australia a battleground for the contradictions inherent in his ideas. The battle waged over the ideas he tried to promote not only reveals differences between childrearing rules in New Zealand and Australia, where attitudes were more casual, but also illuminates the special character of the Australian movement. As Meckel has found for the United States, infant welfare programmes were as much the products of competition as of consensus.[4] Some upright middle-class professional people, many of whom had had their receptiveness deepened by imperialist and pronatalist beliefs, were attracted to Truby King's ideas, while others preferred their own programmes. It was characteristic of the Australians that they refused to adhere to one scheme.[5]

231

The formation of Australian infant welfare schemes

Much infant welfare work in Australia was shaped by demographic change, and the emphasis the Great War placed on the sanctity of new life.[6] In Australia and New Zealand, the decline in infant mortality coincided with reduced marital fertility, which reached its nadir in the Depression of the 1930s. Recently, demographers have linked the fall in infant mortality to a wider 'health transition', fitting together changes in fertility and mortality and their perceived causes.[7] Contemporaries, however, did not share this favourable view; they responded with alarm to the fall in the birth rate and to what they perceived as high infant mortality. This was despite the fact that New Zealand had the lowest infant mortality rate in the world by the 1890s and Australia shared second place with the Scandinavian countries.[8] State support for infant welfare was shaped by public concern over the falling rate of population growth and by the 'white Australia policy' of filling the 'empty' spaces and retaining white dominance of the continent.[9] Medical moralists, nationalists and imperialists connected the decline in the birth rate in white countries of the empire with the problem of infant mortality and presumed low replacement rates. Indeed, the fertility decline was turned into an imperial concern that exemplified racial decadence. Infant mortality was seized upon as the key to the twin problems of natural increase and 'national efficiency', or the nation's future productivity. Such anxieties were responsible for the 1903–4 Royal Commission on the Decline of the Birth Rate and on the Mortality of Infants in New South Wales, which marked a shift in emphasis from the environment to a 'new public health' that focused on the mother and on the child.[10]

Another factor motivating state support for infant welfare schemes was the emerging enthusiasm for public health measures. In Australia, as in the United States and Britain, perceptions of infant mortality developed in phases, influenced by developments in germ theory.[11] Health interventions altered accordingly, and reflected the general shift in the public health movement, moving from efforts to improve sanitation, to purifying milk, to educating mothers in the care of their babies.

These shifts were evident in the tentative beginnings of the Australian infant welfare movement between 1904 and 1914. During these years, France, the United States and Britain provided the models. Sydney's first scheme, begun in May 1904, followed the English model of home visiting by a lady sanitary inspector. In 1908 a private school for mothers was opened on the initiative of the National Council of Women, and in 1914 these two ventures merged to form the first three baby clinics in New South Wales. New South Wales was distinguished by early state involvement, with strong support from the Labor government. From 1908, other states took a variety of initiatives. Queensland and Victoria established 'milk institutes' in Brisbane and Melbourne, which aimed not only to supply clean milk to infants, but also to educate mothers, whereas in South Australia the Adelaide School for Mothers, opened by women's private efforts, focused on education. In practice, by 1910, most states operated some form of 'mothercraft' schooling. The real spur to infant welfare services, however, arose when administrators were stirred by the losses of the Great War into putting their weight behind the movement. As one commentator stated, wartime economic and political priorities meant that 'The hope of Australia lies in healthy living babies, fewer dead babies, stronger children, and a fitter race ... Population means power. The nation that has the babies has the future'.[12]

In Australia the effective formation of the infant welfare movement dates from 1918 with the establishment of the Victorian Baby Health Centres Association in Melbourne and the Royal Society for the Welfare of Mothers and Babies in Sydney. The latter was intended to prevent overlap among groups competing for funds to reduce infant mortality, and to secure Sydney's medical profession a controlling interest, including interest over the state baby clinics.[13] While 'mothercraft' generally dominated the type of services offered, the schemes were shaped according to state politics. In 1918 Queensland's Labor government, following the example of New South Wales, set up four baby clinics. Funding came from the revenue of the state lottery, which also paid for the preferred public maternity hospitals opened in the 1920s.[14] In Victoria, a non-Labor state, baby health centres were opened by women's voluntary initiatives from 1917. In 1918 they ob- tained a £1 for £1 subsidy from the state government to cover half the salary of each nurse and to assist with running costs. City councils provided buildings and the other half of the salary bill. The support of municipal councils ensured that the centres in Victoria would be varied in style and instruction and flourish irrespective of which government was in power. In Victoria many of the aims and objects of the infant welfare movement were borrowed from New Zealand, but were simplified and softened in tone by the removal of references to the 'duty' and 'lofty view' of motherhood.[15] In the less populated states, the Adelaide School for Mothers had three attached infant welfare centres by 1919, and Tasmania two, but Western Australia, while providing a maternity hospital, had no centres until the 1920s.[16]

In response to demand, measures to improve mothers' behaviour, which had begun in the capital cities, began to spread to middle-class suburbs in the 1920s, and to the countryside in the 1920s and 1930s, helped by the community spirit of the Country Women's Association. None the less, the Australian infant welfare movement was scattered and piecemeal – owing largely to the country's size – and there were considerable differences between the states in the nature and timing of initiatives. Under Australia's federal constitution, the states retained power over health, with the exception of quarantine. Lacking federal involvement in infant welfare until the late 1930s, mothercraft institutions varied according to the distinctive features of their state and their founders. Australia not only had less co-ordination at the national level than the United States, but also contrasted strikingly with New Zealand, a small country noted for its intensive and tightly organized scheme.

The 'gospel' according to Truby King

It was into this varied Australian scene that New Zealand's Dr Frederic Truby King entered in 1919. A controversial media idol of his generation, in 1907 Truby King and his wife had founded the New Zealand Society for the Health of Women and Children, which had earned the appellation 'Royal' for its 'systematic pioneering educational health mission'. All over the world the society had spawned offshoots that followed Truby King's clockwork rules for training babies.[17] The Plunket Society, as it was popularly known, was named after Lady Plunket, the wife of the New Zealand Governor-General, just as Australian milk institutes were named after state governors' wives. The Society set up not only rooms or centres, but also Karitane hospitals (the first one began in the Truby Kings' beach cottage); these were spectacularly sited havens run along the lines of sanatoria, for the education of mothers and nurses in scientific feeding, and for the care of babies with feeding difficulties.[18] The models for this New Zealand infant welfare society came from Britain, France and the United States. While the concept of the infant welfare nurse was English Dr Pierre Budin's promotion of breastfeeding in France impressed Truby King, as did American infant feeding rules; and he also gained ideas from other European countries.

Truby King was fiery, with a compelling presence, and a driving ambition. A wizened bent figure, he was a small man, blinded in the left eye by a tubercular infection which had left his face lopsided. On platforms he dazzled audiences with graphs and entranced them with his musical delivery. When he died in 1938 the Bishop of Wellington said in a funeral eulogy that he had the 'eyes . . . of a visionary, almost of the fanatic'.[19] His wife Isabella Millar, dux of Edinburgh Ladies College, supported his career with her talents and devotion, writing his baby columns in the New Zealand newspapers.[20] The couple adopted a daughter, Mary, who in later years worked for their cause. Truby King's appeal to the public to fulfil the 'duty of . . . Health and National Efficiency' arose from years of experience; from 1889, he had dealt with disturbed and handicapped people as superintendent of the Seacliff Mental Asylum near Dunedin.[21] His work in mental health informed his ideology of mending haplessly misshapen lives, and his baby routines were, in part, an outcome of observing the feeding and weight gain of young animals on the asylum farm at Seacliff.

Three points about his rules invited controversy in Australia. First, there was one guide, 'God and the laws of Nature', and it was his code that enshrined natural law.[22] Disease resulted from immorality; a healthy race was the reward for true morality. A baby reared according to Truby King's twelve rules, who was breastfed for the first nine months, given water (boiled), put out in the fresh air, dressed in 'non-constrictive' clothing, bathed and dressed quickly (no dawdling), given massage (not cuddles, but 'muscular exercise and sensory stimulation'), kept warm, taught regularity of all habits, drilled in cleanliness, whose mother *learnt* mothering and how not to 'spoil' her baby, would follow the Ten Commandments.[23]

Second, 'The problem of right and wrong feeding and nutrition in early infancy', as he summarized it for Australians, was 'the main determinant of the health and fitness of the being

Plate 11.1 Dr Truby King outside Karitane Hospital, Melrose, Wellington, *c.* late 1920s

throughout life', and largely determined 'the fate of the race'.[24] Truby King espoused early twentieth-century medical opinion, that high rates of infant death resulted from incorrect feeding. Improper feeding often resulted from overfeeding; demand feeding was also implicated. Mothers therefore had to be persuaded to feed 'in the natural way':[25] the central edict of the infant welfare movement. But this 'natural' mothering was in practice most unnatural, as mothers had to feed at strict times with a strict amount if they were to avoid overfeeding and indigestion and the sequel of diarrhoea.

'Nature's milk recipes' also set the standard for the bottle-fed baby, who was at risk of being 'built out of the wrong stuff'. For the artificially fed, Truby King prescribed a single choice: 'humanized milk', that is, cows' milk modified to resemble as closely as possible the milk of the average healthy mother. According to Truby King, scientific mothers bore a moral duty to prepare the best substitute for the milk 'specially designed . . . . by the Creator'.

> Whale's-milk for the Baby-whale,
> Rabbit's-milk for the Baby-rabbit,
> Cow's-milk for the Calf, and
> 'Mother's-milk' for the Baby.[26]

Mothers who fed their babies cows' milk, Truby King instructed a Sydney audience in 1919, made their babies 'conform to a standard God Almighty had made for the cow'.[27] Such flagrant violation of the laws of nature could only be expected to result in divine punishment: diarrhoea.

Feeding humanized milk, before Truby King co-opted the term, was also known as percentage feeding, because it entailed adjusting the percentages of protein, fat and sugar in cows' milk to the averages in human milk. Either the cows' milk was diluted with water to reduce the protein content, and milk sugar and fat added, or the cream was left to rise, skimmed off, and then diluted and sweetened. Truby King acquired this idea from the Americans Dr Thomas Morgan Rotch, the first Professor of Paediatrics at Harvard University, and Dr Luther Emmett Holt of Columbia University's medical school in New York, whom Apple terms the 'Boston school'.[28] Emmett Holt, the leading authority at the turn of the century, proved to be the principal source of Truby King's catechismal method. After 1908 the New

Plate 11.2 Poster in support of Truby King's promotion of breastfeeding, illustrating the hazards of bottle-feeding, 1917

Source: *Maternity and Child Welfare*, 1, 4 (1917).

Zealander neglected to acknowledge as Holt's the rule not to 'let 10 o'clock in the morning pass without getting [baby's] bowels to move'.[29]

Australian doctors were quick to dismiss Truby King as a synthesizer of contemporary, and at times outmoded, medical beliefs. Customarily inclined to the view that the United States experience was more relevant to that of urban Australia, they had experimented with percentage feeding since the 1890s but most had abandoned it by the 1910s as unnecessarily complicated. Truby King, however, had turned humanized milk into a celebrated part of his personal catechism.[30] Australians, such as Dr Helen Mayo of the Adelaide School for Mothers, advocated less rigid rules and thought that babies did well on 'almost any food'.[31] This posed problems, as Truby King built his reputation on the principle that the country with the best infant mortality rate provided the model for others to follow. Convinced that he and the Plunket Society were responsible for New Zealand's noble record, he assumed that his regimen should be adopted by others. How significant then was Truby King's influence and following in Australia?

Truby King and the sharpening of sectarian conflict

Truby King is one of New Zealand's more problematic gifts to the world. In 1925 he complained in Sydney that Australians did not 'want to learn anything from New Zealand', but he was none the less widely influential.[32] In the 1920s he attempted to make his country a model for Australia, heedless of the constraint that New Zealand, as the country with the best performance, could only be followed if the conditions which had spelled success in New Zealand were equally present in Australia. It was natural to argue, as the Australians did, that the differences between the two countries meant that what worked well in small New Zealand cities 'would not work in the big cities of the mainland like Melbourne'.[33] This reasoning gained added force when infant health leaders disagreed in their prescriptions. The potential for dispute between Truby King and his Australian counterparts multiplied with personality and generational conflicts and doubts about rivals' competence. The Australian authorities could not ignore Truby King, a noted proselytizer, who captivated the press and, above all, women. 'I wish he would go back to his little island and stay peacefully on his hill top', Dr Vera Scantlebury Brown, the Director of Infant Welfare for the State of Victoria, lamented in 1929, just as the press welcomed the 'champion baby-saver' yet again to Sydney.[34]

In the 1920s Australia and New Zealand were still colonial, in different ways. Australia, with its numerous population of Irish descent, powerful trade unions and well-organized Labor Party, and with a strong egalitarian, anti-authoritarian ethos, harboured rather more suspicion of imperial intentions. New Zealand, smaller, with a more homogeneous Anglo-Scottish population, was bound to the *imperium* and less assertive, unless in the imperial interest. New Zealand's proud record of the lowest infant mortality rate in the world was not sufficient for Australians to invite New Zealand instruction. Truby King had first to become a world authority. In 1918–19 he completed his wartime service by establishing the Mothercraft Training Centre (Karitane hospital) for the Babies of the Empire Society in London, and appeared as an imperial figure at an international Red Cross meeting at Cannes.[35] 'When Great Britain wanted guidance', it seemed, 'she sent for Truby King'.[36] In fact his erstwhile patron Lady Plunket summoned him to England. Lady Munro Ferguson, the wife of the Australian Governor-General and sister of Lady Plunket, invited Truby King to Australia on his way home from London.[37] The prophet's ventures in both hemispheres demonstrated that he had devotees at the highest imperial levels. He charmed the imperial elite into rearing by his routines; and because the Duchess of York was patron of the London Mothercraft Training Centre, even the little Princess Elizabeth, a child of the 1920s, was advertised in Sydney's press as a Truby King baby.[38]

Truby King made at least ten trips to Australia between 1919 and 1931. Although some visits were fleeting, they always caused a stir. His first tour, at the end of 1919, coincided with concern to rebuild the peoples depleted by war and lately ravaged by influenza. From Perth to Sydney he proclaimed the familiar slogan that the 'great wastage of manhood, womanhood, and also infant life caused by the war must be made good'; it was 'lamentable' that babies were not always welcome. There had been a progressive decline in physical efficiency, caused by the fall in the bearing and nurture of infants. With 'all the . . . enthusiasm of a missionary preaching a new gospel', he pronounced that lowering the infant mortality rate by the proper care of children was women's work, 'the only work in which they were immeasurably ahead of men'.[39] Australian infant welfare organizers welcomed Truby King for this propaganda; he articulated better than they could the issues of efficiency and women's place in the home.

The apparent success of the New Zealand scheme, however, provoked disputes as to whether the Plunket System was the best in the world and ought to be adopted in its entirety. Infant mortality had been falling in New Zealand from the 1870s; but the Plunket Society benefited from having been founded in 1907, a bad epidemic year, indeed the very year that marked the end of severe fluctuations in the infant mortality curve caused by epidemics. By the time Truby King arrived in Australia in 1919, the New Zealand rate for that year was just over half of its rate in 1907. Deaths from infant diarrhoea fell faster still, from a recorded total of 336 for the years 1908–10 to 87 by 1917–19. In Dunedin in 1918, not one child under 2 died of diarrhoea.[40] To the Australian press, ignoring the local decline, it seemed that such dramatic results could only be explained by the activities of the Plunket Society.[41]

It could only be a matter of time, the faithful believed, before Truby King converted Australia. The Melbourne *Sun* splashed this headline after Truby King's visit in 1923:

N.Z. Babies Survive
But Many of Vic.'s New Natives Die Before One Year . . .
If We Had The Plunket System Here Our Little Ones
Would Live.[42]

Truby King's competitors had other ideas. Australians had to 'work out [their] own salvation', said Dr W. F. Litchfield of the Royal Society for the Welfare of Mothers and Babies, even if, state by state, beginning with New South Wales, they did despatch doctors and nurses across the Tasman, to discover faults in the New Zealand system, and if there was 'anything more than a mere name in Truby King'. Australia had 'more to teach than to learn' from him.[43]

Truby King's own performances in Australia show his movement and his opposition to have been intensely sectarian, and embodied in charismatic leaders. The contradictions inherent in his ideas enabled disciples and rivals to preach slogans and practices to suit their own obsessions. Dr Vera Scantlebury

Brown had the task of placating the hostility between the Victorian Baby Health Centres and the Truby King-ites, who formed their own society in 1920; exasperated, she attributed 'infant welfare troubles' the world over to those desiring 'notoriety' who 'rush into it because it is such a popular subject and such an easy way to make a name'. It attracted '*cheap* natures' prepared to neglect the cause to gain a following.[44] Truby King proved himself the archetypal charismatic figure by asserting that the differences between the sects were fundamental and irreconcilable.[45] He wanted 'petty' differences 'sunk' between the rival societies in Sydney and Melbourne, yet drove deeper the 'gulf' that he had helped to create by his dogmatic insistence on 'uniform, consistent, authoritative advice', that is, on Australia's conversion.[46] An economic motive could be identified in his behaviour, as it reduced competition and made his code more distinguishable from others. 'Many people . . . appear to have fallen under the glamour of his perfervid utterances', complained the New South Wales Labor Minister of Public Health in 1925, and 'accept them as the inspired gospel of the latter day prophet'.[47]

Professional rivalries were at the core of the conflict. Competition among doctors was inevitable in a rising profession, especially from the medical establishments in Sydney and Melbourne who scorned Truby King as a 'free lance'.[48] The detail of the New Zealand scheme, especially in nurse training, appealed to politicians and reformers keen to learn from a system in working order, but they soon regretted having Truby King as a consultant because he and his devotees believed that the New Zealand system was the only way forward. Today it is Truby King's name that is associated with the prescription of 'feeding and sleeping by the clock', fashionable in the 1920s, for the very reason that his was the most elaborate version of the rules promulgated by the movement to 'save the babies' and to 'keep well babies well'. Australians, too, exhorted mothers to breastfeed for eight or nine months or to bottle-feed safely using modified, rather than humanized, cows' milk. Regularity was an imperative for success in baby care.[49] But Truby King, perhaps because his own life was erratic and nocturnal, expressed his doctrine as a set of 'hard and fast rules' that ostensibly were easy for mothers to follow. His Australian opponents spurned such rules, defending the baby as an individual and 'not a machine with standardized parts'. The

Australians allowed for flexibility and mother love, permitting a mother to pick up the baby when it was upset. Truby King's methods, represented as cheap and simple, were in practice complicated, and humanized milk was expensive. Mothercraft, following his system, accentuated class distinctions; its elaborateness meant that mothers needed resources and education if they were to keep to the rules.[50]

These issues surfaced in Truby King's battle with the English authority Dr Eric Pritchard, who, as leader of the voluntary infant welfare organizations in England, was a key figure in London during the First World War. Clearly he was not someone to be crossed by a colonial upstart. Pritchard, too, owed a debt to Emmett Holt and promoted breastfeeding. But he sought (allegedly) simpler ways of bottle-feeding than the Truby King method, which he rejected as irrelevant for the urban poor. Worse, Pritchard's baby, adapted to London's slums, ate less than the golden mean in Truby King's feeding table, and the divine British standard was challenged. The conflict begun in Britain came to a head in Australia.[51]

The battle over humanized milk and protein

In Victoria the Baby Health Centres were loyal to Pritchard and ambivalent towards Truby King. In Sydney, the hostile forces were gathered in the Royal Society for the Welfare of Mothers and Babies. Both groups were more relaxed about feeding rules. Even today they are more easy-going on this subject than the Plunket Society's former allies in Australia. They fought the Truby King-ites on the issue of artificial feeding, and in particular the use of humanized milk. Part of the dispute centred on Truby King's emulsion. Forever perfecting his method, after the war he copied Pritchard in concocting an emulsion of fats and oils to replace top milk in his recipes. Although the emulsion kept well, which made bottle-feeding safer, its content astounded Australians. As Queensland's Director of Infant Welfare, Dr Alfred Jefferis Turner, quipped, 'to call anything "humanised milk" which has been modified by the addition . . . of peanut oil, is surely a strange use of language'.[52] The president of the Royal Society for the Welfare of Mothers and Babies was even less polite: 'The woes of Sir Truby King are like those of the anti-Fascisti in Italy', he contended in 1925, 'mainly due to oil, not castor oil in this case but cod-liver, with a liberal addition of peanut and cotton-seed'.[53] This seemingly inconsequential detail illustrated the extremes attained by sectarian controversy. The emulsion, while it did not create the rift in the infant welfare movement, certainly helped to perpetuate it in New South Wales. In 1925 Sir Truby King, newly-knighted and without, on this occasion, the temperate influence of his wife, astonished Sydney when he asserted that he had sent a ship-ment of the emulsion at the order of the New South Wales government in 1922, of which the Royal Society had refused to take delivery. The consignment was in fact unsolicited and the Sydney Society sent it back because the New Zealand 'Kariol' attracted a 40 per cent duty, inflating its cost to double that of the local product.[54] This posed a quandary for Elizabeth McMillan, the society's Matron, who had trained with Truby King in London and had held the coveted post of matron at the Dunedin Karitane Hospital in 1921. As the daughter of Sir William McMillan, she belonged to Sydney's business and political elite. Deprived of an important ingredient, Matron McMillan, determined to prepare humanized milk to Truby King's recipes, was caught surreptitiously bottling the New Zealand emulsion which she had obtained from New Zealand for herself and was dismissed for this, along with other insub-ordinate acts.[55] Amid public outcry, she departed with the Governor's wife in tow and launched her own Australian Mothercraft Society (Plunket System), a 'misnomer' to her rivals, to spread the true faith 'throughout the Common-wealth'.[56]

The dispute raised bigger issues. According to the Victorians and Sydney's Royal Society, 'humanizing' milk, by reducing the protein to make it more digestible and adding milk sugar and fat, did not suit Australians or the Australian climate. Protein triggered the fiercest debate. The protein argument had a long and tangled history which was punctuated by Truby King's visits. He led the 'low' protein or humanizing school, while the 'high' protein faction, for whom Pritchard was a mentor, was headed by Melbourne's paediatricians. In their view, Truby King became more 'violent' over high and low protein as he grew older, more passionate and more dogmatically outspoken.[57]

His Spencerian argument never faltered: nature adjusted the proportion of protein to the rate of growth of the progeny of a species. It was 'scarcely . . . accidental' that cow's milk contained nearly three times as much protein as human milk and that a calf grew three times as fast as a baby; excessive protein overtaxed the digestive organs, poisoning a child, stunting its growth, and causing diarrhoea and 'obstinate constipation'.[58] His outbursts over protein became legendary. On bad days he would roar, 'God put 1.4 per cent protein into breast milk, and I tell you that anyone who gives a baby more than 1.4 per cent protein is blaspheming God Almighty'.[59] Recalling one occasion when he 'held forth for nearly two hours', Scantlebury Brown retorted that 'he could do things his way if he liked and slash and bang . . . but . . . I would do things my way'.[60]

The clash reflected the differences in the Australian and New Zealand climates and babies' physical responses to summer heat. Truby King's competitors asserted that since the percentages in humanized milk had to be balanced, 'low protein' meant 'high fat'. In hot weather Australian children succumbed to digestive upset if given the rich New Zealand diet. One Melbourne general practitioner decided that a cross, sleepless and underweight baby, fed to Truby King's recipes and vomiting between meals, was 'having too much fat'. He prescribed the forbidden Nestlé's milk, with fatless broth.[61] The answer for Australians who disliked fat was dried milk formulae such as Glaxo or Lactogen, patent foods, or lactic acid milk, fashionable in the United States; these were anathema to Truby King because of their high protein content.[62] It was a dispute which had little secure experimental work to draw on. If some doctors chose low protein, their small charges developed fat intolerance; if other doctors ordered strong, high-protein feeding, constipation ensued. Most Australians settled for high protein with the ritual it demanded, on the pot, and its reduced risk of underfeeding. To obtain the portion of amino acids found in mothers' milk, the bottle-fed baby, they asserted, needed more protein than those being breastfed; the curd of cow's milk was deficient in this.[63]

The argument over protein exemplifies how medical ideas responded to the decline in infant mortality. As fewer babies died from diarrhoea, overfeeding ceased to be a rationale for baby rules. In the 1920s and 1930s preoccupations switched from overfeeding to underfeeding, a change which was itself influenced by the Depression. The protein debate was an outcome of the fall in infant mortality, and showed the way in which doctors belatedly acknowledged that the problem had changed.

By the 1920s 'prematurity' had replaced diarrhoea as the major killer and neonatal mortality dominated infant mortality statistics, while surveys during the Depression revealed undernourishment in pre-school children. The Australian solution was high protein. From the late 1920s Dr Hilda Kincaid, the medical officer in charge of child welfare for the City of Melbourne, promoted high protein for growth and building up resistance, and her colleague, Dr Kate Campbell of the Victorian Baby Health Centres, gave high protein feeds to premature babies. As more babies survived infancy, the infant welfare movement expanded its coverage to include both the new-born and the pre-school child, who needed protein for growth, yet risked undernourishment; in the Depression high protein seemed safer.[64]

The protein argument is complicated. Impure milk was a dangerous ingredient in any recipe, and in an Australian summer, Dr Margaret Harper, who trained Sydney's infant welfare nurses and medical students, warned that the New Zealand regimen was safe only when 'good fresh milk' was obtainable and could be kept 'clean and cool'.[65] Australians had earlier abandoned as foolhardy the top milk method popularized by Truby King, where the mother left the milk to stand, or set, for up to 5 hours in warm weather. One doctor had treated four babies for diarrhoea in one morning as a result of mothers trying to humanize milk.[66] In New Zealand milk went 'sour'; in Melbourne it went 'bad', Stella Allan ('Vesta', of the *Argus*) told readers. Blaming the effect of heat on milk for her own baby's bout of diarrhoea in her first months in Melbourne, she advised women to 'consult our own baby doctors'. She observed that Truby King worked in 'much easier conditions', especially in cold Dunedin.[67]

The conflict illuminates the haphazard state of the milk supply. Even where it improved slowly as a result of better sanitation, babies were still in danger from dirty dairies and faulty distribution, and, indirectly, because mothers were induced to wean infants on to anything other than liquid milk. One-fifth of Melbourne's milk in the 1920s was of grade A quality, an improvement since 1900, but, even when the transport of milk to the city took only an hour, it still arrived up to 10 to 15 degrees Fahrenheit warmer than the daily temperature.[68] There was no compulsory bacterial standard and the milk in the householder's 'billy' or jug was readily adulterated, as one

Sydney father discovered when he caught the milkman at the tap in the garden.[69]

The dispute also reveals that not everybody thought pasteurization was a good thing. Victorian authorities supplied raw milk packed in ice for babies and the advice in all states was to boil milk.[70] Truby King, on the other hand, advocated home pasteurization, as practised by his nurses in Melbourne. Immediately the morning milk arrived the mother was to heat it to 155°F, maintaining that temperature, with the aid of a thermometer, for 5 to 10 minutes before cooling it rapidly in a muslin-draped jug. She was to repeat the procedure four times in 24 hours.[71] This can have been no easy task on a wood stove or coal range. We may ponder, too, the effects of heating milk at too low a temperature or of pasteurizing milk that was already too old.

There would have been no debate had the dairy lobby not blocked pasteurization and opted instead for an expensive tuberculin-tested system, which ensured that the milk supply continued to endanger health. Without the help of compulsorily pasteurized milk in Melbourne, or of bottled milk in Sydney, mothers had to be extra careful over their babies and food until the 1950s. It was also only in the 1950s that large numbers of Australian households obtained refrigerators. Truby King's opinions about milk merely emphasize that the milk supply played little part in the Australian infant mortality decline.[72]

Although Truby King was initially admired for his appeal to the well-to-do, Australians saw themselves as more sympathetic than he was to the needs of the individual baby and of the mother in the home. Their pragmatism would not allow them to agree on one scheme, as they opposed 'over scientific fussiness which insists on measuring and sterilizing everything'.[73] Often they settled on a simple half-water, half-milk mixture because this seemed 'about right'. To the New Zealand school, this was 'slipshod'. What began as a medical contest grew to be a clash of patriotisms, in which Truby King damned 'with bell and candle everything Australian'.[74]

Truby King's contribution to Australian infant welfare work

The extent of Truby King's influence and following in Australia remains to be considered. In New South Wales and Victoria,

Truby King seemed ubiquitous, with his photograph in his centres, his books and emulsion, his admirers, and the invective which reverberated even when he was at home.[75] But the extent of his following across the country was insignificant. By the 1930s there were more than a dozen infant welfare associations in Australia, counting the New South Wales and Queensland systems of baby clinics, with a major mothercraft association in every state other than Queensland.[76] Truby King Societies, of which there were four – two in Victoria, one in New South Wales and one in South Australia – were in a distinct minority. They could not compete against the much older dominant mother-craft institutions such as South Australia's Mothers' and Babies' Health Association, and, least of all, against services established by Labor governments.[77] Truby King's nurses, especially those trained in New Zealand or London, proved to be his keenest disciples; his leading nurses in Australia were to work, he told them, 'in the spirit of Florence Nightingale'.[78] To Scantlebury Brown, the Karitane-trained nurse Sister Maude Primrose was the 'primary cause of disturbance' in infant welfare in Victoria, because of her role since 1917 in campaigning for the Plunket System.[79] Truby King's nurses were welcomed in Tasmania but largely confined to country towns in South Australia, while in Adelaide, Sydney and Melbourne they weighed babies in department stores. Significantly, it was in non-Labor Victoria that, by any institutional count, Truby King enjoyed his largest following: in 1930, 10 per cent of the 134 infant welfare centres in Victoria aligned themselves to the Society for the Health of Women and Children (Plunket System), and 60 per cent to the Victorian Baby Health Centres. While the Victorians' share remained unchanged, that of the Truby King-ites increased over time to 14 per cent of 220 centres by 1939–40. The re-maining centres, deterred by the 'welfare warfare', stayed independent and under local council control.[80] Sectarianism, then, flourished where there was diversity, and also bred diversity.

Truby King nurses and societies were recognized and funded in Victoria but outlawed in New South Wales. Being outcast from the public system severely limited the extent of Truby King's following in Sydney, because devotees had to rely solely on their own resources.[81] Personalities as well as political structures helped shape these different outcomes. In Victoria, Scantlebury Brown overcame the hostility from the Truby

King-ites that so upset her by setting state standards and state examinations for infant welfare nurses from 1927. Bent on team work, she invited the matrons of the training schools to dinner, and held Christmas parties for the nurses. She charmed local councillors and appeased local general practitioners in the Victoria area, opened centres in her children's school holidays, and everywhere won people over with her humanity and unpretentious interest in them.[82] Her conciliatory attitude was not matched in New South Wales, where Truby King's outbursts provoked responses that helped to ensure his nurses remained excluded from baby health centres. Dr E. Sydney Morris, the first Director of Maternal and Baby Welfare, never forgave Truby King for criticizing the New South Wales movement in the 1920s and for his promotion of the Plunket System 'as the only method which could bring salvation to the State'.[83] Morris's hostility was important because he led the New South Wales Public Health Department for a quarter of a century. The methods of the Truby King-ites, he alleged, were a divisive influence and created disharmony.[84]

None the less, to explore the messianic missionary flavour that Truby King gave to the movement assists us in understanding the strength of claims made by its leaders and the conviction that these could carry with other people. Australia became a battleground in the period in which the infant welfare movement directed its efforts at infant mortality; as in other countries, the preoccupation was with feeding, especially artificial feeding. The perceived importance of the issues hotly contested in the 1920s faded with the fall in infant mortality, and as responsibility for health services transferred under modernizing government departments to the welfare state.

That there was competition serves to illuminate a basic characteristic of the Australian movement: there was no one scheme. But the sectarianism proved to be one of many problems to be overcome and which, in being overcome, shaped its various identities. Consider the Australian problem of distance: in Victoria from 1924 to 1934 infant welfare clinics were transported by train to remote locations, as they were in South Australia in the 1930s. Travelling baby health centres (motor caravans) and sisters driving baby Austins followed, as did correspondence schemes as communications improved. The ways in which difficulties in general were overcome affected the nature of services provided as these had to adapt to local conditions.

Truby King failed in his bid to convert Australia. His efforts showed that methods effective in one country were not necessarily applicable in another. But he was widely influential. One of his achievements was to make New Zealand a model in the 1920s in the training of the infant welfare movement's nurses. At the first 'Tresillian' mothercraft home, established by Sydney's Royal Society in 1921 with Matron McMillan in charge, wickerwork Plunket cots remain lasting symbols of his influence. Nurse training in Victoria, too, owed a debt to New Zealand, but the backing of the churches proved more important as church babies' homes became infant welfare and mothercraft training schools. Truby King's position as Director of Child Welfare served as a catalyst for the appointments of Directors of Infant Welfare (in New South Wales, Maternal and Baby Welfare) in three states, while his censure drove Australians to establish their own standards. Like Truby King, the Australians borrowed from America, Britain and France, and shaped their own infant welfare movement.

To borrow from everywhere does not preclude initiation of one's own methods. Truby King was a synthesizer, and so were Australian infant welfare authorities. This is how health and social policies are often made. Australians initiated their own schemes, drawing on what they perceived to be the best knowledge available. By the 1920s they were influenced not only by the New Zealand model but by infant feeding developments in the United States, and some were paying attention to child psychology. The infant welfare entities that Australian authorities created were less particular and less detailed in their procedures than the rules of Truby King, and that is how Australians wanted them; in an era of system, his rivals scorned 'system' and opted for a greater emphasis on variety and individuality.

Despite hostility and resistance, Truby King enjoyed extraordinarily widespread exposure in Australia, which lasted into the 1950s, through women's magazines, newspapers and radio. His creed was spread by his nurses and by his adopted daughter, Mary Truby King, one of the first Truby King babies (in her feeding, at least) who moved to Sydney in 1929. Her book, *Mothercraft*, described motherhood as a joy rather than as a duty and made Truby King's message more Australian.[85]

Elsewhere, I have considered the effectiveness of the movement, suggesting that little weight can be placed on its claims, by showing temporal and spatial mismatches between the patterns of decline in infant mortality rates and the movement's spread and coverage. Further, no assessment can be made of the contribution of infant welfare schemes without considering mothers, and the complexity of mothers' practices belies any simplistic claims. The infant welfare movement was itself part of the 'health transition' and capitalized on rapid demographic changes.[86] The sectarianism in Australia that Truby King aroused, while seemingly inconsequential, was a product of the more intensive attention given to babies. Through his system, Truby King, or the 'fairy godfather of babies', as a Sydney newspaper called him, made the issue of mothers and babies visible and important.[87] He put them on the agenda in terms of expenditure, both through his invective and through his broad appeal. Truby King's real significance lies in the way in which he raised political and public awareness about the value of life and health. The conclusion that follows from the Australian evidence is that he affected mortality by stirring up anxiety about standards of motherhood rather than through his methods.

Acknowledgement

Portions of this chapter appeared in an earlier form in P. Mein Smith, 'Truby King in Australia: a revisionist view of reduced infant mortality', *NZ J. Hist.*, 22 (1988), 23–43.

Notes

1. E. van de Walle, 'How do we define the health transition?', in J. Caldwell, S. Findley, P. Caldwell, G. Santow, W. Cosford, J. Braid, D. Broers-Freeman (eds), *What We Know About Health Transition: The Cultural, Social and Behavioural Determinants of Health*, Health Transition Series no. 2, vol. 1, Australian National University (Canberra, 1990), xiv. In the Antipodes, the infant mortality rate was a European construct, as it was measured to exclude Aborigines and Maoris.

2. One example is R. M. Woodbury, *Infant Mortality and its Causes* (Baltimore, 1926), ch. 8.

3. The headline 'That welfare warfare' appeared in the *Daily Telegraph*, Sydney, 8 Nov. 1925.

4. R.A. Meckel, *Save the Babies: American Public Health Reform and the Prevention of Infant Mortality 1850–1929* (Baltimore and London, 1990), 9.

5. See Lady Munro Ferguson to Truby King, 15 April 1919, 5 May 1919, 31 July 1919, Plunket Society (PS) AG7/127/923, Hocken Library, Dunedin.

6. For the impact of the Great War on Canadian infant welfare work, see ch. 5 by Cynthia Comacchio.

7. Caldwell *et al., Health Transition.* The average completed size of the white Australian family more than halved from six children in the 1870s to 2.4 children by the 1930s. L. Ruzicka and J. C. Caldwell, *The End of Demographic Transition in Australia* (Canberra, 1977), 26.

8. T. A. Coghlan, *The Wealth and Progress of New South Wales 1900–01* (Sydney, 1902), 1007.

9. M. J. Lewis has made this point in 'The "health of the race" and infant health in New South Wales: perspectives on medicine and empire', in R. Macleod and M. J. Lewis (eds), *Disease, Medicine and Empire: Perspectives on Western Medicine and the Experience of European Expansion* (London, 1988), 301–15, and '"Populate or perish": aspects of infant and maternal health in Sydney, 1870–1939', unpub. Ph.D. thesis, Australian National University, 1976.

10. The commission is the subject of N. Hicks, *'This Sin and Scandal': Australia's Population Debate 1891–1911* (Canberra, 1978).

11. cf. Meckel, *Save the Babies,* 5.

12. Advertisement for New South Wales' first baby week, 'Long live King baby?', *Sunday News,* Sydney, 24 March 1920.

13. For the Sydney medical profession and maternity services, see ch. 2 by Milton Lewis.

14. W. Selby, 'Maternity hospitals and baby clinics', in J. Pearn and M. Cobcroft (eds) *Fevers and Frontiers* (Brisbane, 1990), 197–212.

15. Victorian Baby Health Centres Association (VBHCA), *1st A/R* (1918–19).

16. On Western Australia, see A. Davis, 'Infant mortality and child saving', and M. A. O'Hara, 'Child health in the interwar years, 1920–1939', in P. Hetherington (ed.) *Childhood and Society in Western Australia* (Perth, 1988), chs 11 and 12.

17. 'Vesta', 'A school for mothers. The New Zealand scheme', *Argus,* Melbourne, 19 Sept. 1917, 12.

18. Royal New Zealand Society for the Health of Women and Children (RNZSHWC), *A/Rs,* Central Council, Hocken Library.

19. *Dominion,* Wellington, 14 Feb. 1938. A. Jefferis Turner remarked on his 'great driving power', in 'Experiences in preventive medicine', *Med. J. Aust.,* 12 Nov. 1938, 810.

20. For biographical details, see M. Truby King, *Truby King the Man* (London, 1948), and P. Mein Smith, 'Isabella Truby King', in C. Macdonald, M. Penfold and B. Williams (eds) *The Book of New Zealand Women* (Wellington, 1991), 354–6.

21. F. Truby King, *The Story of the Teeth and How to Save Them* (Auckland, 1935, first pub. 1917), 3.

22. Truby King, draft letter to *Argus,* n.d. (Feb. 1923), PS AG7/127/923.

23. Truby King, *Feeding and Care of Baby* (London, 1910, 1913, 1917). On Truby King's code of motherhood, see E. Olssen, 'Truby

King and the Plunket Society: an analysis of a prescriptive ideology',
NZ J. Hist., 15 (1981), 3–23.

24. Truby King to ed., *Argus,* 17 Feb. 1923, file courtesy of St Kilda
City Council.

25. Truby King, *The Feeding of Plants and Animals* (Wellington,
1905), 6.

26. Truby King, *The Components of Various Milks,* bound with *Natural
Feeding of Infants* (Dunedin, RNZSHWC, 1917).

27. *Sydney Morning Herald,* 18, 19 Dec. 1919; *Daily Telegraph,* 19 Dec.
1919. Royal Society for the Welfare of Mothers and Babies (RSWMB),
Press Cuttings, 11/1, Sydney.

28. R. D. Apple, *Mothers and Medicine: A Social History of Infant
Feeding, 1890–1950* (Madison, Wis., 1987), ch. 2.

29. Truby King, *Feeding and Care* (1917), 62, and *The Expectant
Mother, and Baby's First Month* (Wellington, 1916), 37; cf. L. Emmett
Holt, *The Care and Feeding of Children* (London, 1906, first pub. 1894).

30. RSWMB, *A/Rs* (1923–25). W.F. Litchfield spoke for his colleagues in his dismissal of percentage feeding as an 'unnecessary
refinement', *Australas. Med. Gaz.,* 27 Dec. 1913, 581.

31. H. Mayo, *Med. J. Aust.,* 21 Nov. 1925, 600.

32. *Daily Telegraph,* 20 Oct. 1925, RSWMB, 11/2.

33. W. G. Cuscaden, City of South Melbourne, *Health Officer's Report*
(1918–19), 3.

34. V. Scantlebury Brown, Diary B4, 12 Feb. 1929, 73, Melbourne
University Archives; *Sunday Times Pictorial,* 17 Feb. 1929; *Guardian,* 2
July 1929, RSWMB, 11/2.

35. RSWMB, *1st A/R* (1918–19), 3, RSWMB, 4/1; *Daily Telegraph,* 17
Dec. 1919, RSWMB, 11/1; 'Welfare of infants. Great expert's visit', PS
AG7/127/923; M. Truby King, *Truby King the Man,* chs 24–6.

36. J. Hume Cook to ed., *Argus,* 4 May 1923.

37. Lady Plunket to Truby King, 1917, King Family Papers, MS
1004, F 4, Alexander Turnbull Library, Wellington; Lady Munro
Ferguson to Truby King, 15 April 1919, 5 May 1919, 31 July 1919, PS
AG7/127/923. The sisters, Victoria and Helen, were daughters of the
Marquess of Dufferin and Ava, a former Governor-General of Canada
and Viceroy of India. Lady Plunket was Queen Victoria's god-
daughter.

38. *Sunday News,* 20 March 1927; *Sunday Telegraph Pictorial,* 13 May
1928, Australian Mothercraft Society (AMS), Newspaper Cuttings,
Sydney.

39. *Argus,* 2 Dec. 1919, 7, 5 Dec. 1919, 6; *Una – The Journal of the
Royal Victorian Trained Nurses' Association,* 30 Dec. 1919, 310; *Sydney
Morning Herald,* 18 Dec., 19 Dec. 1919, RSWMB, 11/1; 'Welfare of
infants. Great expert's visit', PS AG7/127/923.

40. *Appendices to the Journal of the House of Representatives,* 1923, H-31,
25, Wellington.

41. *Sydney Morning Herald,* 29 Nov. 1919; *Sunday News,* 30 Nov. 1919,
RSWMB, 11/1; *Argus,* 2 Dec. 1919, 7.

42. *Sun,* n.d. The leaders of the Society for the Health of Women
and Children of Victoria, J. W. Springthorpe, L. Levy and J. Hume

Cook, assumed Plunket would become the 'accredited Australasian system', circular letter, 14 Dec. 1922, Footscray City Council, H/6.

43. W. F. Litchfield *et al.*, RSWMB, General Council, *Minutes,* Report B (unexpurgated version), 6 Jan. 1920, also 12 Feb. 1920; RSWMB, *A/R* (1924–5), 16.

44. Scantlebury Brown, Diary B8, 8 Dec. 1929, 21–2.

45. E.g. Truby King, *Trans. Australas. Med. Cong.*, Supp. to *Med. J. Aust.*, 12 July 1924, 481, 485.

46. *Argus,* 20 Oct. 1925, 10, 21 Oct. 1925, 30. He replaced 'consistent' by 'systematic' in Truby King, Mental Hospitals Department, Wellington, to Town Clerk, Footscray, 23 Nov. 1925, Footscray, H/6.

47. *Daily Telegraph,* 27 Oct. 1925; *Herald,* 27 Oct. 1925, RSWMB, 11/2.

48. J. W. Springthorpe, Diary 12, 26 Dec. 1927, Diary 13, 5 Dec. 1929, Diary 14, 28 July 1930, State Library of Victoria, and RSWMB, General Council, *Minutes,* 6 Jan. 1920, Report B, discussed attitudes to the mere doctor from Dunedin.

49. M. Peck, *Your Baby: A Practical Guide to Mothers and Nurses,* Melbourne, *Woman's World,* 1929, 23.

50. Examples include S. Harrison, *Med. J. Aust.*, 6 Dec. 1919, 479; Royal Commission on Health (RCH), Evidence of A. Jefferis Turner, 18 June 1925, q.18791; Peck, *Your Baby,* 33, 37, 51. K. M. Reiger discusses the paradox in the more lenient Australian codes of teaching mothers to be natural mothers, in *The Disenchantment of the Home: Modernizing the Australian Family 1880–1940* (Melbourne, 1985).

51. See E. Pritchard, 'Some practical points in the management of breast-feeding', *Archs Ped.*, March 1913, 164–78; *idem, Infant Education* 2nd edn (London, 1920); *idem, The Physiological Feeding of Infants and Children* 4th edn (London, 1922); Truby King, *A Plea for the Drawing Up . . . of Simple Reliable Consistent Standards for Guidance in the Rearing of Normal Infants,* Victoria League Imperial Health Conference, 20 May 1914.

52. Jefferis Turner, *Med. J. Aust.*, 12 June 1926, 670, RCH, Evidence, 18 June 1925, q.18796.

53. *Daily Telegraph,* 8 Nov. 1925, RSWMB, 11/2. Australians opposed vegetable oils because they believed them to be an inferior source of vitamins. M. Harper, *The Parents' Book,* Sydney, RSWMB, 1926, 41.

54. *Daily Telegraph,* 25 Oct. 1925; *Sydney Morning Herald,* 23 Oct. 1925, RSWMB, 11/2. Innes-Noad to Truby King, 18 May 1922, PS AG7/128/931; RSWMB, *Minutes,* 8 June 1922, 12 July 1922, 4/1.

55. RSWMB, *Minutes,* 17 Oct. 1922 to 27 Feb. 1923, 4/1; *Evening News,* 19 Feb. 1923; *Sydney Morning Herald,* 23 Feb. 1923, RSWMB, 11/1.

56. E. McMillan to Town Clerk, Footscray, 19 Nov. 1925, Footscray, H/6; *Labour Daily,* 16 July 1927, RSWMB, 11/2.

57. Scantlebury Brown, Diary B6, 25 July 1929, 29.

58. Truby King, *NZ Med. J.*, 6 (Nov. 1907), 75–7, 86, and 20 (Feb. 1921), 34, 45–8; *Feeding and Care* (1917), 111.

59. K. Campbell, Session 1, *Jubilee Conference on Maternal and Child*

Health, April 1976; W. Kapper, Interview with Dame Kate Campbell, n.d. (1976), Scantlebury Brown Papers.

60. Scantlebury Brown, Diary B6, 25 July 1929, 29.

61. V. H. Wallace, Patient History Cards, 17/1, Melbourne University Archives.

62. In the 1920s, the work of the Chicago paediatricians appeared more suited to Australian tastes and temperatures. On the 'Chicago school', see Apple, *Mothers and Medicine.*

63. F. N. Le Messurier, *Med. J. Aust.,* 21 Nov. 1925, 603–7; Scantlebury Brown, *Med. J. Aust.,* 8 Jan. 1927, 42–6.

64. H. Kincald, *Med. J. Aust.,* 16 Aug. 1930, 224; K. Campbell, *Med. J. Aust.,* 28 April 1934, 557–60. Also H. Mayo, draft paper, Mayo Family Papers, PRG 127/7/3, Mortlock Library, Adelaide.

65. Harper, *The Parents' Book,* 45.

66. RCH, Evidence of A. Jeffreys Wood, 10 Feb. 1925, q.2097.

67. 'Vesta', *Argus,* 9 May 1923. Allan was a New Zealander.

68. RCH, Evidence of Jeffreys Wood, 10 Feb. 1925, q.2097, W. Kent Hughes, 11 Feb. 1925, q.2233–4.

69. Information courtesy of H. Macnab, June 1988.

70. A. Jeffreys Wood, 'The care of milk in the home', *Health,* April 1923, 105–8; Scantlebury Brown, *A Guide to Infant Feeding* (Melbourne, 1929), 18; A.P. Derham, 'Lectures to nurses on infant feeding', no. 6, Children's Hospital, 1931, A.P. Derham Papers, 5/2/1, Melbourne University Archives.

71. M. J. Ward to ed., *Age,* 3 Dec. 1920, PS AG7/128/931; Nurse Tucker to Town Clerk, Footscray, 16 Nov. 1922, Footscray, H/9; Truby King, *Feeding and Care,* 20, 23, 28.

72. This finding supports that of M. J. Lewis on Sydney, in 'Milk, mothers and infant welfare', in J. Roe (ed.) *Twentieth Century Sydney: Studies in Urban and Social History* (Sydney, 1980), 193–207.

73. Dr A. Elizabeth Wilmot, former Director of Maternal, Infant, and Pre-School Welfare, interview with P. Mein Smith, Melbourne, Sept. 1985. Quotation from A. P. Derham, 'Lectures', 1931, Derham Papers, 5/2/1.

74. A. Purcell, *The Australian Baby* (Melbourne, 1928), 80–1 (Matron Purcell ran the VBHCA training school). For patriotic beliefs, see the *Bulletin,* 5 Nov. 1925.

75. Scantlebury Brown, Diary B9, 13 Feb. 1930, 94; Conference of . . . AMS with Director-General of Public Health . . . , 16 May 1930, Papers relating to the history and recognition of the Australian Mothercraft Society (Karitane), 1925–59, 2/8566.1, Archives of NSW.

76. Wendy Selby has kindly informed me that Queensland did have a mothercraft association, formed in 1931 when the Labor Party was briefly out of office, but it remained unimportant because the long-serving Labor government disliked outside interference. See Selby, 'Maternity hospitals and baby clinics'.

77. The Adelaide School for Mothers became the Mothers' and Babies' Health Association in 1927. The four Truby King societies were the Society for the Health of Women and Children of Victoria (1920), the Australian Mothercraft Society (1923), the Truby King League of

Victoria (1931) and the Truby King Mothercraft League of South Australia (1934); the last was begun by Mary Truby King. Their records are held, respectively, at the Tweddle Hospital, Melbourne; Karitane, Sydney; the National Library of Australia, and Mortlock Library, Adelaide.

78. Society for the Health of Women and Children, 1922–6, Footscray, H/6.

79. Scantlebury Brown, Diary B9, 8 Feb. 1930, 87.

80. Victoria, Commission of Public Health, *Reports of the Director of Infant Welfare.*

81. The Australian Mothercraft Society ran fifteen clinics, in addition to the Karitane hospital, whereas there were 221 public baby health centres in New South Wales in 1940.

82. Scantlebury Brown, Diaries; C. James (daughter), interview with P. Mein Smith, Melbourne, 12 Sept. 1985.

83. Director-General of Public Health to Accountant, 14 May 1926, 2/8566.1, Archives of NSW.

84. Morris was Director-General of Public Health from 1934 to 1952. His persistent objections are recorded in 2/8566.1, Archives of NSW.

85. M. Truby King, *Mothercraft*, Sydney, 1934. From Sept. 1934 her articles were published in the *Australian Women's Weekly.*

86. P. Mein Smith, 'Infant welfare services and infant mortality: a historian's view', *Aust. Econ. Rev.*, 1 (1991), 22–34; *idem*, 'Reformers, mothers and babies: aspects of infant survival, Australia 1890–1945', unpub. Ph.D. thesis, Australian National University, 1990, esp. ch. 7.

87. *Sunday Pictorial*, 17 Feb. 1929.

12

The costs of modern motherhood to low income families in interwar Britain

Elizabeth Peretz

> Each child under two should have one pint of milk a day,
> and a teaspoonful of Cod Liver Oil three times a day
> except in hot weather. If this cannot be afforded the
> doctor at the local Infant Welfare Clinic will see that it is
> provided free.[1]

This piece of advice was one of the thousands of prescriptions
for modern motherhood aimed at poor mothers in the 1920s
and 1930s. The author of these directives believed that, although the advice would cost money to follow, where necessary
the state (the local authority) would provide for what were then
called 'necessitous cases'. Evidence discussed below suggests the
author's confidence was misplaced. Mothers who wished to
follow the advice had no guarantee that the state would provide
if they could not meet the expense. Services and treatment
nationally prescribed were not always available locally. Where
they were provided, sometimes free to the necessitous, the maze
of standards and procedures, different scales of assessment and
methods of calculating net family income could bar applicants,
leaving them to shoulder the guilt of a sickly baby, or go without
some necessity themselves.

In the commercial world of the interwar period, fashions in
motherhood and infancy offered new and promising market
possibilities. Medical, dietary, and general prescriptions for
healthy childhoods were disseminated by experts who found an
easy target amongst families concerned for their children's
welfare. The numbers of nurses and consultants involved as
specialists in childrearing and maternity care expanded, and
the incomes and consulting rooms of general practitioners were

swelled by pregnant mothers and their infants.[2] Hospital delivery became increasingly common in these years; the percentage of women having their babies in maternity wards rose from 15 per cent in 1927 to 25 per cent in 1937, and 54 per cent in 1946.[3] Increasingly, the cheaper domiciliary midwife was advised only for 'safe' and 'normal' deliveries.[4] The number of infant welfare clinics in England and Wales increased from 842 in 1916 to 3,145 in 1937. By 1937 there were 5,350 health visitors in Britain, a large part of whose work was to give childrearing advice in the home.[5]

Modern methods of childrearing: the cost to the family

Both at the time and subsequently, substantial claims have been made for the success of the maternity and child welfare movement in Britain, although others have challenged the legitimacy of the assertions.[6] Less prominence has been given to the question of the cost of these services to low income families who followed the advice prescribed. Lewis and Macnicol argue that among the reasons for the lack of economic aid to mothers during this period was an avoidance of the minimum wage issue, and a concentration on the growth of professional bodies rather than the duties of the state towards mothers and children. The Women's Co-operative Guild and the Children's Minimum Council were amongst the most prominent bodies promoting family allowances (state grants to aid poor families in raising their children) before the Second World War.[7] This section looks at how much the advice and admonition on childrearing pouring from all quarters to poor mothers eroded the meagre budgets of low income households, through the purchasing of cots, prams, layettes, and proprietary foods, attendance at clinics, and payment for hospital deliveries.

One significant outcome of the maternal and child welfare movement, as it developed in Britain, was the promotion of a viable commercial market in medical services, patent foods, infant clothing and nursery equipment. Health visitors, medical officers, and volunteers in infant welfare centres distributed advice on pregnancy and childrearing in urban working-class districts and in villages. This was substantially the same advice as that given to women in middle-class districts by general practitioners and nannies or nursery nurses. Primarily educational in their aim, these centres were to be used in three ways, as was stressed in a pamphlet produced by the British Medical Association in 1921:

(a) for educational, advisory, and preventive work; (b) for treatment of actual disease in infants; (c) for the provision of food and clothing or other material goods when necessary or desirable.

None the less the association went on to claim that

Nearly all the witnesses agreed that it was detrimental to the interests of the work to encourage the opinion that the Centre is a place to bring babies when they are ill . . . [and] the gratuitous supply of artificial food and dried milk has proved detrimental to the best interests and influence of the Centres. The people who go to them mainly for what they can get very cheaply or for nothing are not as a rule the kind of people who value or will benefit from the educational work of the Centre.[8]

By becoming committee members and volunteers in maternity and child welfare centres, middle-class mothers, who were converts to the new ideas, spread modern motherhood amongst labouring and working-class women in the towns and countryside. Then, as now, fashions in what was good for a baby, or what promoted good health, were liable to change; faith in chocolate and cocoa in the years in and after the First World War gave way to a belief in the health-giving properties of milk and butter in the late 1930s. Each succeeding fashion had its advocates.[9] Most advice cost money to follow. Advisers were aware of this, and numerous ways were devised of reducing the expense for low income families. In many clinics patterns and material for the prescribed 'layettes' were sold at cost price. Parents were encouraged to make cots from orange boxes (see Plate 12.1), whilst patent foods and medicines were bought in bulk and distributed at cost price.[10] Special grants were also available to low income families, through which local authorities provided services free to those in need. The Ministry of Health would reimburse local councils up to 50 per cent of costs incurred in this way. The policy of only giving services and goods free to those who 'needed' help created great administrative problems, and a system of grants that was very uneven. As Titmuss argued,

> Before the war, it was often believed by many people who did not use the statutory health services that provision was free of charge. This was not so; for local authorities had the power (and sometimes the duty) to recover what they could from the people who were helped. In consequence, there grew up a bewildering variety of means tests covering a large range of services. Apart from unemployment and health insurance, at least twenty tests were in common use by the local authorities. Nearly all these tests were based on different income scales, and often the same authority employed for no good reason different tests for the various services it supplied.[11]

Clearly, if these means tested grants helped the people who needed them, they would have ameliorated some of the problems; if appropriate grants had been readily available, low

Plate 12.1 The model nursery at Silverdale Girls' School, Newcastle-under-Lyme

Source: *Mother and Child*, 1 (Nov. 1930), 306, in Bodleian Library.

income families would have been put to no extra expense by the modern methods, and not inconvenienced by them. However, a popular image in the interwar period was of a respectable working-class family scrimping and saving to pay for what experts told them would promote their children's health, which suggests that new methods became a significant item on family budgets.

Eve Garnett explored this theme in a children's book written about a small town dustman's family of the 1930s. The book met with much acclaim when it was originally published in 1937, and was greeted with equal popularity when it reappeared in 1956 in the midst of great enthusiasm for the newly created National Health Service. The book was based on notes and real memories of the minutiae of East End life in 1930s London. In the book, the council paid for the children's stay in an isolation hospital when they had scarlet fever, but the family had to pay for the convalescent holiday and the strengthening medicine for the children, which caused real hardship. This was testified to by a conversation between the parents:

> Mrs Ruggles: 'You'd best realise it's savin' up for doctors' and chemists' bills we've got to be afore we thinks of anything else. Peg and Jo's got to be fed up with malt-and-oil when they comes out, and Jo's that pulled down the doctor says as six weeks in the country'll barely set him up.

Later, as Mr Ruggles worked out the costs of convalescence, 'Four pounds, nine shillings, and sixpence, Rosie', he announced to his wife at last, 'just for the fares and keep'. Finally, when his 12 year old daughter, Kate, dropped the malt- and-oil she thought,

> Oh, how dreadful! The precious malt-and-oil – an extra large jar too, to last all the holiday – *a whole 8 shillings and 6 pence worth*! What would Mum say? And what would Peg and Jo do without it? – probably get ill – get measles again – perhaps die this time – a second attack so soon.[12]

A social survey carried out in the 1940s on the real costs of maternity outlined the other hidden costs in addition to midwifery fees. The survey team concluded that the average working-class family in their sample (families of all the babies born in one week during the spring of 1946) spent around £32 on each first baby, whilst agricultural families spent £22. This included expenditure on equipment, clothes and housework, which could not be covered by the national insurance grant of 30s. to 40s. paid to those families with a parent in work. Although costs might have increased over a decade, and expectations may have risen, most items on the following list of expenses for mothers in 1946 were also urged on mothers in the 1930s: 'pram, cot, bath, blankets, rubber sheets, napkins (at least 26), vests, night-gowns, dresses, knickers, matinee coats, bootees, leggings, gloves, bonnets and shawls.'[13] This was merely the original outlay for a straightforward birth. Complications could increase the expense and so could infant ill health. Added to this was the cost of food and medicines advised to safeguard the infant's health.

Infant welfare clinics and health visitors were key promoters of modern methods in childrearing practices, but mothers were also exposed to changing ideas from a variety of other national and local sources. Advice columns on childrearing appeared in national and local newspapers and women's magazines; advertising hoardings urged patent products to safeguard children's health; and health programmes were broadcast on the radio. Special childrearing books and magazines were produced, with a wide circulation and multiple reprints. *The Mothercraft Manual,* for instance, which first appeared in 1923, had sold over 263,000 copies by 1948.[14]

Modern methods were fashionable. An Oxford informant, who disliked the infant clinic because she saw it as unhygienic, and was suspicious of health visitors as 'do-gooders', remembered magazine articles on child welfare being passed from hand to hand in her street. The local chemist, rather than the health visitor, answered her queries. None the less, this informant was modern in her methods. Married to a milkman with an income of under 30s. a week, she struggled to obtain a pram, a cot, patent foods, and to pay for visits to the general practitioner. The childrearing advice carried with it a threat. Ignore it and jeopardize your family's health; follow modern methods and win peace of mind. This same informant still blamed herself for the fact that one of her children was frail and suffered from colic, which she linked to the fact that she had failed to continue to take pills recommended by a medical officer at the antenatal clinic. The pills had been recommended because she was thought to be lacking in calcium, but she could not afford to replace the pills when the first course ran out.[15]

Poverty: the national and the local problem

The expense involved in following advice, and the effects this had on the budgets of low income families, varied from area to area and was determined by levels of wages, rent and unemployment. Such costs need to be set in their local context, and will be discussed below. On a national scale, however, there is abundant evidence that many families in the 1930s survived on poor diets, and that those families with young children were particularly at risk. These families, who found it hard or impossible to buy adequate clothing, had great difficulties meeting extra demands on the family purse. A number of detailed studies of family budgets from these years show that many families did not have enough money to sustain protein levels necessary to maintain health.[16] In 1934 Boyd Orr estimated that

> so far as the evidence goes, it suggests that people living at the economic level of the dole are living near or below the threshold of adequate nutrition. The number at this economic level must run to nearly 20% of the population, somewhere in the neighbourhood of ten millions.[17]

In 1938 Pringle similarly claimed that it was the lack of money available to housewives, rather than bad household management, that caused nutritional problems in families. According to a key study by Brockington, large families with very young children were particularly at risk of falling below the adequate nutritional standards.[18]

As the nutritional surveyors found, local, rather than national, surveys of families are the best way of establishing what was happening in poor families. The four areas to be explored here have been chosen for their differences, especially economic ones: Oxford, a prosperous university town; Oxfordshire, a large county with a scattered population; Tottenham, a borough on the boundary of Greater London; and Merthyr Tydfil, a sprawling town in the depressed South Wales mining valleys. Geographically, Tottenham was a compact residential area, dominated by light industry on the outskirts of London, covering 4 square miles; Oxford City was an old county and university town built in a star shape around a flood plain and the surrounding hills, covering some 12 square miles; Oxfordshire County covered 736 square miles of Cotswold upland, Thames Valley floodplain, and undulating countryside, with a primarily agricultural population living in small market towns and villages; and Merthyr Tydfil, a mining community, covered 16 square miles of precipitous narrow mountain valleys. As Table 12.1 shows, for the years 1921 and 1931 these areas had varied populations, birth rates, and numbers of infants under the age of 4. Politically and culturally, the areas also differed greatly from each other, as will be outlined below.

There were stark contrasts between the areas in terms of prosperity and rates of unemployment. As Table 12.4 indicates, Oxford had a remarkably low level of unemployment; not more than 5 per cent of the population were unemployed during the worst years of the Depression, while in Merthyr Tydfil the rate reached 60 per cent in some years.[19] There were also marked differences in wage levels. Many workers in Oxford brought home wages of between £2 and £4 per week, while agricultural workers in Oxfordshire earned on average between 32s. and 37s. a week. In Merthyr Tydfil the majority of household incomes were 29s. 6d. or less. Tottenham families, with high London wages, might have been expected to be more prosperous. In 1932, however, Llewellyn Smith estimated that 7.8 per cent of Tottenham's population was living in poverty.[20]

Wherever they were based, families struggled to feed themselves. Even in prosperous Oxford family incomes were diminished by high overheads; rent could be as much as 20s. a week, and there were the additional costs of travel, heating and insurance. In the 1930s when many workers flooded into Oxford, overcrowding and homelessness became a grave problem, and rent charges increased significantly. A young family of five relying on one income even in Oxford could slip below the malnutrition line. In 1939 the nutritionist Boyd Orr told an Oxford audience that a family of five could not be adequately nourished on less than 20s. 6d. a week.[21] Families in Merthyr Tydfil would have found this even harder. Housewives in Oxfordshire would have had less difficulty than their Merthyr Tydfil counterparts following instructions given by a travelling Women's Institute exhibition in 1934, which showed how to cook wisely for a family of five with only 20s. 3d. to spend on food per week.[22]

Table 12.1 A comparison of population, birth rate, infant death rate, and the number of children aged 4 or under in Merthyr Tydfil, Tottenham, Oxford County Borough and Oxfordshire in 1921 and 1931

	Year	Population	Area in square miles	Children aged 4 or under		Birth rate	Infant deaths per 1,000 births
				No.	% of population		
Merthyr Tydfil	1921	80,116	16	8,413	10.50	27.5	90
	1931	71,108		5,350	7.52	15.9	105
Tottenham	1921	146,711	4	13,434	9.16	22.8	67.9
	1931	157,772		11,455	7.26	14.1	52.9
Oxford County Borough	1921	67,290	12	3,720	5.52	16.47	36.4
	1931	80,539*		5,265	6.53	15.04	44.4**
Oxfordshire	1921	122,325	637	10,912	8.92	19.8	55.9
	1931	129,082		9,465	7.33	15.8	30.7

* Oxford County Borough, area, and population extended after 1929 under the Local Government Act.
** 1931 was an abnormal year for Oxford County Borough, the trend otherwise continued downwards.

Sources: Census figures and MOH A/Rs for the respective areas.

While the four areas examined differed greatly socially and economically, the local evidence bears out national claims that many families were malnourished, and were unable to afford the extra claims on the household budget. The need for grants and free services was evident.

Local variations in 'scales of eligibility' for free maternity and infant welfare provision

Voluntary groups coping with need across Britain were keenly aware of the problems of poverty and its effects on child health in the 1930s, and the importance of grants and free services. In 1932, the Save the Children Fund investigated the help given by local authorities and charities to families with babies and young children.[23] The survey focused on nineteen towns. Table 12.2, taken from this research, shows the disparity in existing provision, even between three neighbouring authorities in South Wales. This raises the question as to whether these differences were caused by a variation in the real need of the various towns. A comparison of the unemployment figures in these towns, however, suggests that 'need' would have been fairly constant. Despite this parity, however, free milk and food was most abundant in the town with the least unemployment.

Throughout Britain, local authority help for families in need varied greatly. In the late 1930s, Miss Burt of the Midwives Board carried out detailed research under the auspices of the Population Investigation Committee, which uncovered wide differences in scales of eligibility for midwifery services, foods and treatment for mothers and infants. The research, not published until 1943, showed that families could not rely on the availability of free services. Some of the blame for this was laid at the government's door. For instance, even though payment for midwifery care was not required in necessitous cases, families were pressured to 'remit part or the whole of the fee. There is no definition of "necessitousness", and the Ministry of Health has, so far as we know, given no guidance on this point.'[24]

In 1939, Ford, a social researcher from Southampton University, exposed the enormous variations which existed across Britain. His plea was for standardization and co-ordination in the offering of free services. Ford found authorities offering

Table 12.2 Provision of free milk and meals to infants, expectant
mothers and children in 1931 in three South Wales communities

	Rhondda	Pontypridd	Merthyr Tydfil
Population	141,346	42,717	71,480
Unemployment	40.7%	58.3%	53.3%
Nos of free school meals provided	4,065	0	1,006
Amount spent on free milk at clinics	£11,061	£900	£2,935*
Children found to be subnormal as regards nutritional status	329	301	453

* For expectant mothers and infants under 1 year.
Note: Only very rough estimates can be made of the numbers receiving the
meals and the milk; 20 children might have received free meals in the Rhondda
and 4 in Merthyr, if each child had 5 meals a week for 40 weeks a year. In the
Rhondda, 1,000 children and expectant mothers could have received 365 pints
of milk costing 3d. per pint. The numbers of children cited here may reflect
more about the assiduity of medical officers and the measures they implemented
than the real numbers of children who were in need.
Source: Save the Children Fund, *Unemployment and the Child* (London 1932).

eleven or more services free on seven different scales for calculating need. These scales might include the income of the head
of the family alone, or of all the household; they might make
allowances for rent, travel, meals at work, or none of these
things; they might be based on a simple rate per capita, or on a
local sliding scale. Ford argued that these differences had resulted from the scales, 'Having been drawn up at different dates,
and under different circumstances of financial ease and public
mood'.[25] The legislation covering scales of eligibility was
permissive, and each local authority negotiated each scale for
each service separately with the Ministry of Health as the
occasion arose. The Ministry of Health offered suggestions to
local authorities about what services should be offered and
about the scales of eligibility for services. These were also drawn
up at different times, in varying financial circumstances. Guidelines to local authorities on eligibility for free milk, for instance,
changed over the years, being more generous before 1922 and
in the late 1930s, when the government was less restricted.
During the Depression, guidelines were more stringent. The

only constant message from the Ministry was that, wherever possible, authorities should 'pay special regard . . . "as to whether particular services were or were not likely to be remunerative, either at once or in the near future"'.[26] This was not very encouraging to families in need.

Services and scales of eligibility in Tottenham, Oxford, Oxfordshire, and Merthyr Tydfil

The considerable variation in services and material help offered by the state, through local authorities and charitable agencies is testified to by the experience of those who lived in Merthyr Tydfil, Oxford, Tottenham, and Oxfordshire. In each area there was great disparity in the services offered to mothers and children and in the scales of eligibility for free provision to low income families. Councils provided free instruction through medical officers, health visitors, and clinics. Some advice cost nothing to follow, but where it necessitated seeking medical treatment, a special diet, or simple remedies the families were expected to pay, unless they applied for help and could prove eligibility. Calling in a general practitioner for a medical emergency during domiciliary midwifery was the only situation in which the council would immediately pay for a service and reclaim later. This procedure was a statutory one which provoked complaints; all the authorities discussed here found it hard to reclaim. Some of the Councils could only reclaim the expenses in as few as 10 per cent of cases.

Of the four councils, Tottenham was the one which offered most services, and the most generous scales. Maternity and child welfare provision and school health services (all public, none voluntary) were the crown of civic pride in Tottenham. This may be attributable to the fact that the borough escaped the worst of the Depression and had a strong Co-operative Labour presence and a dwindling charitable middle class throughout the interwar period. In 1920, Tottenham Council boasted four infant clinics, a minor ailments clinic, an eye clinic, an orthopaedic clinic, a dental clinic, two antenatal clinics, a cot centre (residential nursery) and a day nursery. Mothers could be prescribed meals, milk (1 pint per day for expectant mothers and children under 5), hospital delivery, home helps, or convalescence for themselves or their children.

Table 12.3 A comparison of the maternity and infant welfare services offered by local authority and voluntary sectors in Merthyr Tydfil, Tottenham, Oxford County Borough and Oxfordshire in 1937

	Merthyr Tydfil	Tottenham	Oxford County Borough	Oxfordshire
Infant welfare centres	8	4	14	12
Antenatal clinics	1	2	2	0*
Postnatal clinics	0	2	0	0
Gynaecological clinics (including birth control)	0	1	1	0
Day nurseries	1	2	1	0
Artificial sunlight treatment	1	1	0	0
Dental clinics	1	2	1	0
Maternity hospitals	1	2	2	1
Minor ailments clinics	1	2	1	0

* In 1935, antenatal work in Oxfordshire was contracted to general practitioners by the local authority.
Source: MOH *A/Rs* from the relevant areas.

All advice was free; all treatment, care, or goods could be obtained free including milk, Virol, and cod liver oil and malt. In addition, many goods were available at cost price through the clinics, including paper patterns and materials for layettes and infant clothing. By 1937, midwifery and obstetric services, a gynaecological clinic which also gave birth control advice, nursery schooling and infant hospital treatment had been added to the list of local authority facilities. The maternity and child welfare services were well advertised. Elaborate health weeks were held each year, with competitions, talks and posters. Access was easy. Clinics were open every day except Sunday in one part or another of this geographically compact borough; health visitors routinely asked the maternity and child welfare sub-committee for free or reduced rate items for mothers, which the committee decided upon at its monthly meetings.[27]

The 1919–20 scale of eligibility for free milk was 7s. 6d. income per head where there were five in the family (parents with children under 14 years). If a family of five could show that only 37s. 6d. was coming into the household each week, they

Plate 12.2 Poster for Tottenham Infant Welfare Centre, from 'Health Week', 29 November to 3 December 1937

Source: Bruce Castle Museum, Mary Evans Picture Library.

were eligible for free services. The gross income could be more than this, because several discounts were allowed. Only 50 per cent of income from lodgers and children aged over 14 (after discounting the first 12s.) was seen as household income, and rent, insurance, fares to and from work, and expenses for child-care could be deducted.[28] This could mean that a family on a respectable wage of nearly £3 a week could be eligible for several pounds' worth of help.

In 1921 the Ministry forced Tottenham to tighten its scale.[29] Only rent and insurance were allowed as deductions. Although the level of eligibility was still 37s. 6d. for a family of five, a family needed to be poorer to qualify. There was still a good take-up of the free milk provided: 300 to 400 recipients a week in the 1930s, and an expenditure of £3,000 to £4,000 per annum. Expendi- ture on milk in Merthyr Tydfil amounted to £2,935 in 1931. Tottenham's eligibility scale for free midwifery, which accorded with that of the Ministry in 1937, was different from its milk scale: income 12s. per head for a family of five (60s. total), less rent only, counting only one-quarter of the state maternity benefit as income.[30] The cost of the day nursery in 1928 was 'minimum 6d., increases 1d. for every 1s. – above 10s. of weekly income, less rent'. Even where access to free services was en-couraged, as it was in Tottenham, the system was extremely complicated, and eligibility for one service did not guarantee eligibility for another.

In Tottenham, parents could find themselves chased up and threatened by the National Society for the Prevention of Cruelty to Children (NSPCC) if they had not followed the proferred advice. In 1938, the report of Tottenham's School Medical Officer praised the NSPCC for 'ensuring treatment and cleanli-ness in those cases where parents fail to act on the advice given by members of the school medical staff'. The NSPCC increas-ingly took on a new role in the 1930s, of following up and legally threatening families who did not follow the clinics' health prescriptions.[31]

Merthyr Tydfil County Borough Council was Labour dominated through much of the interwar period, and might therefore have been expected to have the same level of service as Tottenham, and to have provided the same ease of access to free services. In comparison to Tottenham, however, it had a restricted maternity and child welfare service. In 1920 there were four infant clinics (entailing up to 4 miles' walk for a mother and her baby to attend) and a minor ailments clinic. By 1937 there were, in addition to the above, clinics for dental and orthopaedic care, a maternity wing provided by the local authority hospital, borough midwives, an artificial sunlight clinic and antenatal clinics. Cod liver oil was also available free on production of an unemployment card, as was milk (1 pint per day for an infant under 1 year and expectant mothers in the last 2 months of pregnancy).[32]

From February 1923 to July 1937 the council set the scale for free milk for mothers and children in a family of five at 7s. per head net income after deduction of rent (35s.). Up to June 1937 the scale for free midwifery was 10s. per head net income after the deduction of rent (50s.) for a family of five (including the unborn baby). In 1937 midwifery care cost 25s.. Those who had their babies in the infirmary were charged 42s., but costs were considerably higher when complications arose. In 1927, the council allowed Nellie Brown to pay off her midwifery bill of £30 8s. in monthly instalments of 2s.[33] The application procedure for obtaining free milk was so simple that it drew complaints from the Ministry of Health; a mother had only to show her husband's unemployment card at the clinic to obtain free milk for herself in the last 2 months of pregnancy, and for her infant up to the age of 1.[34]

Merthyr Tydfil, which was nationally designated a depressed area, attracted some charitable help which effectively increased the availability of goods and services. This included a nursery school, set up by the Save the Children Fund in the 1930s, offering places at 1s. a week; the provision of free Marmite, Ovaltine and Colactol by the National Birthday Fund for the years 1934–7; and free holidays, courtesy of the Pearsons Fresh Air Fund and the Eastbourne Round Table.[35] However, for poverty-stricken families the charitable sources were sporadic 'windfalls', available one year and not necessarily the next.

While Merthyr Tydfil and Tottenham had Labour Councils, the Oxford and Oxfordshire Councils were dominated by Liberals and Conservatives. In Oxfordshire, to be eligible for free milk, the income for a family of five was raised from 29s. (with allowance for rent) to 30s (with no allowances for rent) in 1932.[36] In prosperous Oxford, the scale was substantially worse than in Tottenham or Merthyr Tydfil. In Oxford in 1931 a mother of a family of five could only obtain 1 pint of free milk daily in the last 3 months of pregnancy or for her infant up to the age of 1 if she proved that she had an income of less than 38s. 4d. No deduction was made for rent, but a deduction of up to 9d. per day was made for meals at work.[37]

The only service common to all four local authorities was the provision of health visitors. In Oxford and Oxfordshire there were fewer services, and a heavier reliance on the charitable voluntary sector. Domiciliary midwifery in the countryside and infant welfare in the city were almost exclusively organized by charitable groups 'under the licence' of the local authority. Yet, as demonstrated below, the power relations between local authorities and the voluntary sector were not necessarily straightforward.[38]

Oxford's services were formed during the period 1905–22, with the help of the Medical Officer of Health (hereafter MOH), four influential women from the infant welfare association (the dons' wives Mrs H. A. L. Fisher, Mrs A. L. Smith, Mrs Prichard, and Mrs J. Wells) and the voluntary hospital, the Radcliffe Infirmary.[39] By 1921 Oxford council was paying towards a weekly sick baby clinic at the Radcliffe Infirmary, free treatment for babies at the eye hospital and beds for necessitous maternity cases in the Radcliffe Infirmary. There were eight voluntary association infant welfare clinics, and four local authority health visitors who worked closely with untrained volunteer health visitors. By 1937 there was a dental clinic, a birth control clinic, two clinics for mothers both before and after birth, and twelve infant welfare centres, which by this time had been taken over by the local authority. Ten health visitors were also in service in 1937, but untrained voluntary visitors no longer appeared to be used. In Oxford, free help was hard to obtain throughout the period. From 1919, milk orders were available, and vitamins for necessitous cases also became available in 1937. The vitamins, however, had to be obtained from a special clinic for cases of hardship, and the arrangement for procuring free milk was tortuous. First, the MOH visited the home, then details of incomes were checked with employers before an order could be obtained. The milkman had to be paid before a claim could be made. Reclaiming the money involved travelling to the town hall offices with the relevant card. Home helps, obstetric aid, and midwifery were also available through the council, but were used less frequently than would be suggested by the size of the population.[40] The clinics, run by dons' and other local professionals' wives, sold milk, Virol, material, patterns, and cod liver oil at cost price.

In Oxfordshire, in 1920, there were four infant clinics, five health visitors, and four county midwives. By 1937, the council had employed a voluntary midwifery service and general practitioners to provide an antenatal service, offered maternity beds through an arrangement with Oxford's Radcliffe Infirmary and other voluntary hospitals, and had a nominal arrangement with an obstetrician for difficult cases. Free milk, hospital treatment for infants, home helps, confinement costs, and travel costs for treatment were available through the health committee, which sat only once a quarter. Few mothers had services or goods free in Oxfordshire. Table 12.4 starkly shows the differences experienced by mothers in financial and material need in the four areas.

What were the reasons for such differences? Webster has argued that there were economic reasons; councils in depressed areas had difficulties raising their rates and did not have

Table 12.4 A comparison of charges for maternity services in Merthyr Tydfil, Tottenham, Oxford County Borough and Oxfordshire in 1937

	Merthyr Tydfil	Tottenham	Oxford County Borough	Oxfordshire
Midwife	25–30s.	42s.	35 – 42s.	25s.
Maternity beds (1 week)	42s.	63–84s.	98s. 7d.	98s. 7d.
Dentist	?	6d.	?	?
Artificial sunlight treatment	?	1s.	None	None
Tonsils	?	5s.	?	42s.
Convalescence (1 week)	None	10s.	None	None
Day nursery (1 week)	1s.	6d.	?	None
Income scales for claiming free milk	35s.	37s. 6d.*	38s. 4d.	30s.
Average weekly income	29s.	40 – 80s.	40 – 80s.	32 – 37s.
Unemployment	60%	7.8%	5%?	5%?

'None' means no service was provided.
* Allowance made for rent, meals, fares, child-care.

Sources: Minute books of MCW Sub-committee; MOH *A/Rs*; H. Llewellyn Smith (ed.) *The New Survey of London Life and Labour*, vol. 3 (London, 1932).

enough money to cope with local needs. National grants in these circumstances were hard to obtain because in the 1920s they had to be matched with local money.[41] In Merthyr Tydfil the relatively poor service was partly attributable to the sheer lack of money within the council. Merthyr Tydfil was an expensive council to run even in prosperous times; digging drains and building roads and houses on steep valley sides over coal shafts was not cheap. Spending on these services competed with the provision of maternity and child welfare facilities. The men and women making up the Labour majority wanted more money to be given to families, so that they could buy the goods and services they wanted, rather than being reliant on a variety of means-tested narrowly prescribed goods and services. This might partly explain why milk provision was the one large item on the council budget, representing a basic and safe addition to the household income that could be used at the mother's discretion. Maternal and child welfare was seen to be the patronizing domain of the Liberals and Conservatives in this area and was scorned by the Labour working-class wives, who were proud of their households and maternal ability.[42] Medical services provided free on an insurance basis to miners' families, not just mothers and infants, minimized the need for the council to provide outpatient and screening clinics such as those established in Tottenham.

Tottenham's relatively good services and generous scales were connected with the prosperity of the borough, but other factors played an important part. 'The future' had a high profile in this outer London borough; the two successive MOsH for Tottenham, Dr Kirkhope and Dr Hogben, both fought hard for a good preventive health service for mothers, infants, and children, but they would not have succeeded without the matching enthusiasm of their councillors from the Co-operative Labour Party and the Low Church 'Brotherhood'. Nor would they have succeeded if there had been a powerful charitable presence in the area. The strong local Women's Co-operative Guild offered little competition to the teaching they offered in infant clinics. Many of the mothers attending were new to the area, starting a fresh life in one of the two London County Council housing estates. Tottenham was, therefore, an ideal ground for spreading the new scientific methods, and for providing them free where necessary.[43]

Oxford and Oxfordshire were both prosperous enough

authorities to have provided full services and to have encouraged poorer mothers to claim as much gratis as they needed. Part of the explanation for the poor services and the relative absence of takers for free services was rooted in political attitudes and power dynamics rather than economic circumstances. Both councils were dominated by Conservatives and Liberals who also sat on the committees of voluntary organizations in the city and the county. Both councils regarded local authority services as the expensive option, to be used only when voluntary organizations and public assistance had failed. Victorian ideals of self-help featured in discussions about services and scales of eligibility. In 1933, for instance, the maternity and child welfare sub-committee in Oxford debated whether mothers should pay to attend infant welfare clinics so that they would appreciate them more. Such a debate would have been unthinkable in Tottenham or Merthyr Tydfil.[44] The contrasts in provision and attitudes between these four authorities are clearly shown in Tables 12.4 and 12.5. While the figures

Table 12.5 Comparing the budgets for maternity and child welfare as a whole, milk in particular, and the take-up of free milk in Merthyr Tydfil, Tottenham, Oxford County Borough and Oxfordshire in 1937

	Merthyr Tydfil	Tottenham	Oxford County Borough	Oxfordshire
Estimated budget for maternity and child welfare	£7,825	£15,214	£4,895	£5,500
Money spent on milk and cod liver oil	£4,900	£2,780	£800*	?
Estimated individuals in receipt of free milk at any one time†	1,094	800–900	235	?

* No numbers available for 1937. In 1938, £825 was spent on milk and preparations, and £5,649 16s 3d was spent on maternity and child welfare as a whole. The £800 is therefore a rough estimate based on this.
† All the figures in this column are estimated from monthly reports in the minutes of the maternity and child welfare sub-committees. I have assumed from the evidence that many families received milk for several months.
Sources: Minutes books of MCW sub-committees; Treasurers Reports, Council Minutes of all the relative areas.

are based on estimates, they show predictably that Tottenham had the highest level of involvement in maternal and infant welfare and spent the largest sum on free services.

Conclusion

The four local authorities discussed here confirm the existence of material want in contrasting areas of Britain, and show the different priorities these areas attached to scientific motherhood. The labyrinthine procedures to obtain help must have put off many potential applicants. Mothers on a low income in Tottenham appear to have been better served in every way than their counterparts in Oxfordshire or Merthyr. Advice on modern methods was freely available to mothers at all income levels through clinics, health visitors, magazines, chemists, or the radio. Appetites were whet, and anxieties raised. Material support, or help in kind, to ensure families on a minimum wage would not go without the prescribed cod liver oil or convalescent treatment, was less forthcoming. The national maternal and child welfare movement, refracted through local attitudes and conditions, provided mothers with very different messages, services and help. Only in Tottenham did poor families not face the risk getting poorer if they followed the new prescriptions.

Conditions in the 1990s are beginning to echo those of sixty or seventy years ago. A recent national report has revealed that

> one in five parents said they had gone hungry in the last month, December 1990, because they 'did not have enough money' to buy food. Forty-four per cent of the parents said they had gone short of food in the last year to ensure that other members of the family had enough. One in ten children under five had gone without food in the last month because of lack of money.[45]

In these circumstances, taking a child to the clinic would involve a bus ride, and thus the loss of half a day's wages on top of paying the fares. For those families who might lose another meal in the search for childrearing advice from the professionals, such obstacles would impose a serious deterrent.

Acknowledgements

I would like to thank Lara Marks, Hilary Marland, Valerie Fildes and Charles Webster for their help and support in preparing this chapter.

Notes

1. Association of Maternity and Child Welfare Centres, 'Food Budgets for the Family' (1932), Leaflet no. 41.

2. J. Lewis, *The Politics of Motherhood* (London, 1980); A. Digby and N. Bosanquet, 'Doctors and patients in an era of National Health Insurance and private practice, 1913–1938', *Econ. Hist. Rev.*, 2nd series, XLI (1988), 74–94.

3. Lewis, *Politics of Motherhood*, 120; L. Marks, 'Irish and Jewish women's experience of childbirth and infant care in East London 1870–1939: the responses of host society and immigrant communities to medical welfare needs', unpub. D.Phil. thesis, University of Oxford, 1990, ch. 6. See also ch. 3 by Lara Marks, esp. Table 3.2.

4. E. Peretz, 'A maternity service for England and Wales: local authority maternity care in the inter-war period in Oxfordshire and Tottenham', in J. Garcia, R. Kilpatrick and M. Richards (eds.) *The Politics of Maternity Care* (Oxford, 1990), 30–46.

5. MOH *A/R* (1936–7) (London, 1937).

6. This is a debate of long standing. One of many contemporary writers who attributed the fall in infant mortality to the infant welfare movement was G. Newman, *The Building of the Nation's Health* (London, 1939). For more recent claims of the success of the movement, see D. Dwork, *War is Good for Babies and Other Young Children* (London, 1987). More critical assessments of the infant welfare movement which dispute its success are Lewis, *Politics of Motherhood*; C. Webster, 'Health, welfare and unemployment during the depression', *P & P*, 109 (1985), 204–30.

7. J. Macninol, *The Movement for Family Allowances 1918–45* (London, 1980); Lewis, *Politics of Motherhood*.

8. 'The value of maternity and child welfare work in relation to the reduction of infant mortality: Report of the Medico-Sociological Committee of the British Medical Association', BMA Pamphlet, 1921.

9. E. Peretz, 'Infant welfare in Oxford between the wars', in R. Whiting (ed.) *Oxford and its People* (Manchester, forthcoming).

10. E. Peretz, 'The professionalization of childcare', *Oral Hist.*, 17 (1989), 22–8.

11. R. M. Titmuss, *Problems of Social Policy* (London, 1950), 154.

12. E. Garnett, *Further Adventures of the Family From One End Street* (London 1937, repr. 1956), 30, 37, 60.

13. Royal College of Obstetricians and Gynaecologists and the Population Investigation Committee, *Maternity in Great Britain* (Oxford, 1948), 107–36, p. 124.

14. M. Liddiard, *The Mothercraft Manual* (London, 1st edn 1923, 7th edn 1930). Other examples include F. Truby King, *Feeding and Care of Baby* (London, 1st edn 1910, 11th repr. 1923); A. M. Hewer, *Our Baby* (Bristol, 1st edn 1891, 20th edn 1932).

15. Interview by E. Peretz with Mrs Eldred, Oxford, 1985.

16. C. M. M'Gonigle and J. Kirby, *Poverty and Public Health* (London, 1936); J. Boyd Orr, *Food, Health and Income* (London, 1936); F. Brockington, 'The influence of the growing family upon the diet in urban and rural districts', *J. Hyg.*, 38 (1938), 40–61; A. M. N. Pringle, *An Enquiry into Malnutrition*, based on an investigation carried out in 1938 by The Ipswich Committee against Malnutrition.

17. Boyd Orr, *Food, Health and Income*, 190–1.

18. Pringle, *An Enquiry into Malnutrition*; Brockington, 'The influence of the growing family upon the diet'.

19. E. Peretz, 'Regional variation in maternal and child welfare between the wars: Merthyr Tydfil, Oxfordshire and Tottenham,' in D. Foster and P. Swan (eds) *Essays in Regional and Local History* (Hull, 1992).

20. H. Llewellyn Smith (ed.) *The New Survey of London Life and Labour* (London, 1932) vol. 3, 403–4.

21. *Oxford Times*, 14 Feb. 1939.

22. *Oxford Times*, 26 Oct. 1934.

23. Save the Children Fund, *Unemployment and the Child* (London, 1932).

24. E. Grebenik and D. Parry, 'The maternity services before the war', *Agenda* (1943), 133–46, p. 135.

25. P. Ford, *Incomes, Means Tests and Personal Responsibility* (London, 1939), 22.

26. Save the Children Fund, *Unemployment and the Child*, 32.

27. Tottenham material derived from MOH *A/Rs* (1919–39); *Minute books* of MCW sub-committee, and miscellaneous publicity material in Tottenham archives at Bruce Castle, Tottenham.

28. Tottenham, *Minute books* of MCW sub-committee, 13 Oct. 1920.

29. Tottenham, *Minute books*, 7 June 1921.

30. Tottenham, *Minute books*, 21 April 1937.

31. Tottenham School MOH *A/R* (1938).

32. Merthyr Tydfil MOH *A/R* (1937).

33. Merthyr Tydfil, *Council Minutes*, Public Health Section, 28 June 1927.

34. Interview by E. Peretz with Mrs V. Evans, Merthyr Tydfil, 1987.

35. Peretz, 'Regional variation'.

36. Oxfordshire Public Health Committee, *Minute book*, 9 July 1932.

37. Peretz, 'A maternity service', 30–46.

38. Peretz, 'Infant welfare'.

39. Oxford County Borough MOH *A/Rs*.

40. Barnett House Survey Committee, *Social Services in the Oxford Region* (Oxford, 1938), vol. 1; Oxford County Borough, *Minute books* of MCW sub-committee, 1919–39.

41. Webster, 'Health, welfare and unemployment'.

42. Peretz, 'Regional variation'.

43. Peretz, 'Regional variation'.

44. Oxford County Borough, *Minute books* of MCW sub-committee, signed 14 June 1933. The person who wished for charges to be made, Dr Collier, asked her colleagues 'What are the *right* mothers [for the centres]? Those who are anxious to help themselves or those who wish to throw their responsibility for parenthood on the rates?'

45. National Children's Home, *Poverty and Nutrition Survey* (London, 1991), 1–16.

Bibliography

The works listed are restricted to those concerned with maternal and infant health and welfare from 1870 to 1945. Works on the related subjects of midwifery, childbirth, birth control, child health, demographic change, and the development of health services have not been included. For references to non-English language works not included here, see *Current Work in the History of Medicine.*

Africa

Beinart, J. M. (1992) 'Darkly through a lens: changing perceptions of the African child in sickness and health, 1900–45', in R. Cooter (ed.) *In the Name of the Child: Health and Welfare, 1880–1940,* London and New York, 220–44.

Gaitskell, D. (1981) 'Female mission initiatives: black and white women in three Witwatersrand churches, 1903–1939', unpub. Ph. D. thesis, University of London.

Hill, A. K. (1985) *Population, Health and Nutrition in the Sahara: Issues in the Welfare of Selected Western African Communities,* London.

Hunt, N. R. (1988) '"Le bébé en brousse": European women, African birth spacing and colonial intervention in breast feeding in the Belgian Congo', *Internat. J. Afr. Hist. Stud.* 21: 401–32.

Longmore, L. (1954) 'Infant mortality in the urban African: the African attitudes towards it on the Witwatersrand', *S. Afr. Med. J.* 28: 295–8.

Maclean, C. M. U. (1966) 'Toruba mothers: a study of changing methods of child-rearing in rural and urban Nigeria', *J. Trop. Med. Hyg.* 69: 253–63.

Moyo, E. (1973) 'Big mother and little mother in Matabeleland', History Workshop pamphlet, Oxford.

Searle, C. (1965) *The History of the Development of Nursing in South Africa, 1652–1960,* Cape Town.

Unterhalter, B. (1982) 'Inequalities in health and disease: the case of mortality rates for the city of Johannesburg, South Africa, 1910–1979', *Internat. J. Health Serv.* 12: 617–36.

Asia

Chandrasekhar, S. (1955) 'Some observations on infant mortality in India: 1901–1951', *Eug. Rev.* 46: 213–25.

Chaudhuri, N. (1988) 'Memsahibs and motherhood in nineteenth-century colonial India', *Vict. Stud.* 31: 517–35.

Chen, P. C. Y. (1985) 'Child health in Malaysia: 1870–1985', *Med. J. Malaysia* 40: 165–76.

Davanzo, J. and Habicht, J. P. (1986) 'Infant mortality decline in Malaysia 1946–1975: the role of changes in variables in the structure of relationships', *Demography* 23: 143–60.

Ferrer-Franco, I. (1957) 'Hospitals run by women doctors: the maternity and children's hospital', *J. Am. Med. Women's Ass.* 12: 17–19 (Manila, the Philippines).

Foll, C. V. (1958) 'The perils of childhood in Upper Burma', *J. Trop. Pediat.* 4: 122–6.

—— (1959) 'An account of some of the beliefs and superstitions about pregnancy, parturition and infant health in Burma', *J. Trop. Pediat.* 5: 51–9.

Kunhikannan, N. K. (1920) 'Infant feeding in Burma', *Indian Med. Gaz.* 55, 265–6.

Lindenbaum, M. J. (1983) 'The influence of maternal education on infant and child mortality in Bangladesh', unpub. paper, International Centre for Diarrheal Disease Research, Bangladesh.

Manderson, L. (1982) 'Bottle feeding and ideology in colonial Malaya: the production of change', *Internat. J. Health Serv.* 12: 597–616.

—— (1987) 'Blame, responsibility and remedial action: death, disease and the infant in early twentieth century Malaya', in N. Owen (ed.) *Death and Disease in Southeast Asia*, Singapore, 257–82.

—— (1989) 'Political economy and the politics of gender: primary health care in colonial Malaya', in P. Cohen and J. Purcall (eds) *The Political Economy of Primary Health Care in Southeast Asia*, Bangkok, 76–94.

Moriyama, Y. (1987) 'History of health care for mother and child in Japan', *Asian Med. J.* 30: 7–19.

Richell, J. (forthcoming) 'A life's sources: elements in Burmese historical demography 1775–1940', in P. Xenof (ed.) *South East Asian Demographic History*, Ann Arbor, Michigan.

—— (forthcoming) 'Determinants of demographic change in Colonial Burma', unpub. Ph.D. thesis, School of Oriental and African Studies, University of London.

Tilak, H. V. (1966) 'Evolution of maternity and infant welfare in Bombay and other parts and an ideal pre-natal service', *Indian Practit.* 19: 135–9.

Australia

Aden, J. (1982) 'Octavius Beale reconsidered: infanticide, baby farming and abortion in New South Wales, 1880–1939', in Sydney

Labour History Group, *What Rough Breast? The State and Social Order in Australian History*, Sydney, 111–29.

Davis, A. (1983) 'Public policies towards motherhood and infant care in Western Australia, 1900–1922', unpub. BA Honours diss., University of Western Australia.

—— (1988) 'Infant mortality and child saving: the campaign of women's organizations in Western Australia, 1900–1922', in P. Hetherington (ed.) *Childhood and Society in Western Australia*, Perth, 161–73.

Deacon, D. (1985) 'Taylorism in the home: the medical profession, the infant welfare movement and the deskilling of women, *Aust. & NZ J. Sociol.* 21: 161–73.

Durey, M. (1982) 'Infant mortality in Perth, Western Australia, 1870–1914: a preliminary analysis', *Stud. West. Aust. Hist.* 5: 62–71.

Lewis, M. J. (1976) '"Populate or perish": aspects of infant and maternal health in Sydney, 1870–1939', unpub. Ph. D. thesis, Australian National University.

—— (1978) 'Obstetrics: education and practice in Sydney, 1870–1939', *Aust. & NZ J. Obstet. & Gynaecol.* 18: 161–8.

—— (1979) 'Sanitation, intestinal infections and infant mortality in late Victorian Sidney', *Med. Hist.* 23: 325–38.

—— (1980) 'Hospitalization for childbirth in Sydney, 1870–1939: the modern maternity hospital and improvement in the health of women', *J. Roy. Aust. Hist. Soc.* 66: 199–205.

—— (1980) 'Milk, mothers and infant welfare' in J. Roe (ed.) *Twentieth Century Sydney: Studies in Urban and Social History*, Sydney, 193–207.

—— (1980) 'The problem of infant feeding: the Australian experience from the mid-nineteenth century to the 1920s', *J. Hist. Med.* 35: 174–87.

—— (1982) 'Some infant health problems in Sydney, 1880–1939', *J. Roy. Aust. Hist. Soc.* 68: 67–73.

—— (1988) 'The "health of the race" and infant health in New South Wales: perspectives on medicine and empire', in R. MacLeod and M. Lewis (eds) *Disease, Medicine and Empire. Perspectives on Western Medicine and the Experience of European Expansion*, London and New York, 301–15.

Mein Smith, P. (1988) 'Truby King in Australia: a revisionist view of reduced infant mortality', *NZ J. Hist.* 22: 23–43.

—— (1990) 'Reformers, mothers and babies: aspects of infant survival, Australia 1890–1945', unpub. Ph. D. thesis, Australian National University.

—— (1991) 'Infant welfare services and infant mortality: a historian's view', *Aust. Econ. Rev.* 1: 22–34.

O' Hara, M. A. (1988) 'Child health in the interwar years, 1920–1939', in P. Hetherington (ed.) *Childhood and Society in Western Australia*, Perth, 174–86.

Reiger, K. M. (1982) 'Women's labor redefined: child bearing and rearing advice in Australia 1880–1930', in M. Bevege, M. James and C. Shute (eds) *Worth her Salt: Women at Work in Australia*, Sydney, 72–83.

—— (1985) *The Disenchantment of the Home: Modernizing the Australian Family 1880–1940*, Melbourne.

Schlomowitz, R. and McDonald, J. (1991) 'Babies at risk on immigrant voyages to Australia in the 19th century', *Econ. Hist. Rev.* 44: 86–101.

Selby, W. (1990) 'Maternity hospitals and baby clinics', in J. Pearn and M. Cobcroft (eds) *Fevers and Frontiers*, Brisbane, 197–212.

Thearle, M. J. (1985) 'Infant feeding in colonial Australia 1788–1900', *Aust. Paediat. J.* 21: 75–9.

Britain and Ireland

Allan, P. and Jolley, M. (eds) (1982) *Nursing, Midwifery and Health Visiting Since 1900*, London.

Armstrong, D. (1986) 'The invention of infant mortality', *Sociol. Health & Illn.* 8: 211–32.

Aykroyd, W. R. and Kevany, J. P. (1973) 'Mortality in infancy and early childhood in Ireland, Scotland, and England and Wales, 1871 to 1970', *Ecol. Food Nutr.* 2: 11–19.

Ballard, L. M. (1985) '"Just whatever they had handy": aspects of childbirth and early childcare in Northern Ireland, prior to 1948', *Ulster Folklife* 31: 59–72.

Beaver, M. W. (1973) 'Population, infant mortality and milk', *Popul. Stud.* 27: 243–54.

Behlmer, G. K. (1977) 'The child protection movement in England, 1860–1890', unpub. Ph. D. thesis, University of Stanford.

Buchanan, I. H. (1980) 'Infant mortality and social policy: the eugenists and the social ameliorators, 1900–1914', *Soc. Soc. Hist. Med. Bull.* 27: 5–8.

—— (1983) 'Infant mortality in British coal mining communities, 1880–1911', unpub. Ph. D. thesis, University of London.

—— (1985) 'Infant feeding, sanitation and diarrhoea in colliery communities, 1880–1911', in D. J. Oddy and D. S. Miller (eds) *Diet and Health in Modern Britain*, London, 148–77.

Dally, A. (1982) *Inventing Motherhood. The Consequences of an Ideal*, London.

Davies, C. (1982) 'The G. P. and infant welfare in the interwar years', *Soc. Soc. Hist. Med. Bull.* 30–31: 9–12.

—— (1988) 'The health visitor as mother's friend: a woman's place in public health, 1900–14', *Soc. Hist. Med.* 1: 39–59.

Davies, M. L. (ed.) (1915) *Maternity: Letters from Working Women*, repr. London 1978.

Davin, A. (1978) 'Imperialism and motherhood', *Hist. Workshop J.* 5: 9–66.

Dwork, D. (1987) *War is Good for Babies and Other Young Children: A History of the Infant and Child Welfare Movement in England 1898–1918*, London and New York.

—— (1987) 'The milk option: an aspect of the history of the infant welfare movement in England 1898–1908', *Med. Hist.* 31: 51–69.

Dyhouse, C. (1978) 'Working-class mothers and infant mortality in England, 1895–1914', *J. Soc. Hist.* 12: 248–67.

Fildes, V. (1992) 'Breastfeeding in London, 1905–19', *J. Biosoc. Sci.* 24: 53–70.

Fox, E. (1991) 'Powers of life and death: aspects of maternal welfare in England and Wales between the wars', *Med. Hist.* 35: 328–52.

Gittins, D. (1977) 'Women's work and family size between the wars', *Oral Hist.* 5: 84–100.

—— (1982) *Fair Sex. Family Size and Structure 1900–1939*, London.

Hardyment, C. (1983) *Dream Babies: Child Care from Locke to Spock*, London.

Higginbotham, A. (1985) 'The unmarried mother and her child in Victorian London 1834–1914', unpub. Ph. D. thesis, University of Indiana.

Kendall, I. (1979) *Mothers and Babies First?: The National Insurance Maternity Grant in Historical and International Perspective*, ed. by J. Streather, London.

Kerr, C. (1979) 'The politics of married working class women's health care in Britain, 1918–1939', unpub. Ph. D. thesis, University of Sussex.

Lane-Claypon, J. E. (1920) *The Child Welfare Movement*, London.

Lee, C. H. (1991) 'Regional inequalities in infant mortality in Britain, 1861–1971: patterns and hypotheses', *Popul. Stud.* 45: 55–65.

Lewis, J. (1980) *The Politics of Motherhood: Child and Maternal Welfare in England, 1900–1939*, London.

—— (1980) 'The social history of social policy: infant welfare in Edwardian England', *J. Soc. Pol.* 9: 463–86.

—— (1986) 'The working-class wife and mother and state intervention, 1870–1918', in J. Lewis (ed.) *Labour and Love: Women's Experience of Home and Family 1850–1940*, Oxford, 99–120.

—— (1990) 'Mothers and maternity policies in the twentieth century', in J. Garcia, R. Kilpatrick and M. Richards (eds) *The Politics of Maternity Care: Services for Childbearing Women in Twentieth-Century Britain*, Oxford, 15–29.

Lodge, M. (1986) 'Women and welfare: an account of the development of infant welfare schemes in Coventry 1900–1940 with special reference to the work of the Coventry Women's Cooperative Guild', in B. Lancaster and T. Mason (eds) *Life and Labour in a Twentieth Century City: The Experience of Coventry*, Coventry, 81–97.

Lomax, E. (1972) 'Advances in pediatrics and in infant care in nineteenth century England', unpub. Ph. D. thesis, University of California.

Loudon, I. (1986) 'Deaths in childbed from the eighteenth century to 1935', *Med. Hist.* 30: 1–41.

—— (1986) 'Obstetric care, social class and maternal mortality', *Br. Med. J.* ii: 606–8.

—— (1987) 'Puerperal fever, the streptococcus and the sulphonamides 1911–1945', *Br. Med. J.* ii: 485–90.

—— (1991) 'Some historical aspects of toxaemia of pregnancy. A review', *Br. J. Obstet. & Gynaecol.* 98: 853–8.

McKee, E. (1986) 'Church-State relations and the development of

Irish health policy: the mother-and-child scheme, 1944–53', *Irish Hist. Stud.* 98: 159–94.

McLeary, G. F. (1933) *The Early History of the Infant Welfare Movement*, London.

—— (1935) *The Maternity and Child Welfare Movement*, London.

—— (1945) *The Development of British Maternity and Child Welfare Services*, London.

Macfarlane, A. and Mugford, M. (1984) *Birth Counts: Statistics of Pregnancy and Childbirth*, 2 vols, London.

Marks, L. (1990) 'Irish and Jewish women's experience of childbirth and infant care in East London 1870–1939: the responses of host society and immigrant communities to medical welfare needs', unpub. D. Phil. thesis, University of Oxford.

—— (1990) 'A comparative study of Irish and East European Jewish married women's work and motherhood in East London 1870–1914', *Polytechnic of North London, Irish Studies Centre Occasional Papers Series* 2: 5–32.

—— (1990) '"Dear Old Mother Levy's": the Jewish Maternity Home and Sick Room Helps Society 1895–1939', *Soc. Hist. Med.* 3: 61–88.

—— (1991) 'Medical care for pauper mothers and their infants: poor law provision and local demand in East London 1870–1929', unpub. paper, University of Essex.

—— (1992) '"The luckless waifs and strays of humanity": Irish and Jewish immigrant unwed mothers in London 1870–1939', *Twentieth Cent. Br. Hist. 3.*

—— (forthcoming) *Outsiders and Insiders: Jewish Woman's Experience of Childbirth and Infant Care in East London 1870–1939*, Oxford.

Marland, H. (1992) 'A pioneer in infant welfare: "The Huddersfield Scheme", 1903–1920', *Soc. Hist. Med.*

Munro Kerr, J. M. (1933) *Maternal Mortality and Morbidity*, Edinburgh.

Munro Kerr, J. M., Johnstone, R. W., and Phillips, M. H. (eds) (1954) *Historical Review of British Obstetrics and Gynaecology, 1800–1950*, Edinburgh.

Newman, G. (1906) *Infant Welfare: A Social Problem*, London.

Newsholme, A. (1935) *Fifty Years in Public Health*, London.

Oakley, A. (1984) *The Captured Womb: A History of the Medical Care of Pregnant Women*, Oxford.

Pamuk, E. R. (1988) 'Social class inequality in infant mortality in England and Wales from 1921 to 1980', *Eur. J. Popul.* 4: 1–21.

Parton, C. (1983) 'The infant welfare movement in early twentieth-century Huddersfield', *JORALS* 3: 69–77.

Peretz, E. (1989) 'The professionalization of childcare', *Oral Hist.* 17: 22–8.

—— (1990) 'A maternity service for England and Wales: local authority maternity care in the inter-war period in Oxfordshire and Tottenham', in J. Garcia, R. Kilpatrick, and M. Richards (eds) *The Politics of Maternity Care*, Oxford, 30–46.

—— (1992) 'Regional variations in maternal and child welfare between the wars: Merthyr Tydfil, Oxfordshire and Tottenham', in D. Foster and P. Swan (eds) *Essays in Regional and Local History*, Hull.

—— (forthcoming) 'Infant welfare in Oxford between the wars' in R. Whiting (ed.) *Oxford and its People*, Manchester.

Prochaska, F. K. (1989) 'A mother's country: mothers' meetings and family welfare in Britain, 1850–1950', *Hist.* 74: 379–99.

Riley, D. (1981) 'The free mothers: pronatalism and working women in industry at the end of the war', *Hist. Workshop J.* 11: 59–118.

—— (1983) *War in the Nursery*, London.

Roberts, A. E. (1975) 'Feeding and mortality in the early months of life: changes in medical opinion and popular feeding practice, 1850–1900', unpub. Ph. D. thesis, University of Hull.

Roberts, E. (1984) *A Woman's Place: An Oral History of Working-Class Women 1890–1940*, Oxford.

Rose, L. (1986) *The Massacre of the Innocents: Infanticide in Britain 1800–1939*, London.

Ross, E. (1986) 'Labour and love: rediscovering London's working-class mothers, 1870–1918', in J. Lewis (ed.) *Labour and Love: Women's Experience of Home and Family 1850–1940*, Oxford, 73–96.

Smith, F. B. (1979) *The People's Health, 1830–1910*, London.

Thane, P. (1991) 'Genre et protection sociale; la protection maternelle et infantile en Grand Bretagne, 1860–1918', *Genèses* 6: 73–97.

Urwin, C. and Sharland, E. (1992) 'From bodies to minds in childcare literature: advice to parents in inter-war Britain', in R. Cooter (ed.) *In the Name of the Child: Health and Welfare, 1880–1940*, London and New York, 174–200.

Wall, R. (1976) 'Infant mortality in the 1890s', *Loc. Popul. Stud.* 17: 48–50.

Watterson, P. A. (1986) 'The role of the environment in the decline of infant mortality: an analysis of the 1911 census of England and Wales', *J. Biosoc. Sci.* 18: 457–70.

—— (1987) 'Environmental factors in differential infant mortality decline in England and Wales circa 1895 to 1910', unpub. Ph. D. thesis, University of London.

—— (1988) 'Infant mortality by father's occupation from the 1911 Census of England and Wales', *Demography* 25: 289–314.

Webster, C. (1982) 'Healthy or hungry thirties?', *Hist. Workshop J.* 13: 11–29.

—— (1985) 'Health, welfare and unemployment during the depression', *P & P* 109: 204–30.

Winter, J. M. (1979) 'Infant mortality, maternal mortality, and public health in Britain in the 1930s, *J. Eur. Econ. Hist.* 8: 439–62.

—— (1982) 'Aspects of the impact of the First World War on infant mortality in Britain', *J. Eur. Econ. Hist.* 11: 713–38.

—— (1983) 'Unemployment, nutrition and infant mortality in Britain, 1920–50', in J. M. Winter (ed.) *The Working Class in Modern British History*, Cambridge, 232–305.

—— (1986) *The Great War and the British People*, London.

Wohl, A. S. (1983) *Endangered Lives: Public Health in Victorian Britain*, London.

Woods, R. I., Watterson, P. A. and Woodward, J. H. (1988–9) 'The causes of rapid infant mortality decline in England and Wales, 1861–1921', pts I and II, *Popul. Stud.* 42: 343–66, 43: 113–32.

Wright, P. W. G. (1988) 'Babyhood: the social construction of infant care as a medical problem in England in the years around 1900', in M. Lock and D. R. Gordon (eds) *Biomedicine Examined*, Dordrecht, 299–329.

Canada

Abeele, C. R. (1987) '"Nations are built of babies": maternal and child welfare in Ontario, 1914–1940', unpub. Ph. D. diss., University of Guelph.

—— (1988) '"The infant soldier": the Great War and the medical campaign for child welfare', *Can. Bull. Med. Hist.* 5: 99–119.

—— (1988) 'The mothers of the land must suffer: maternal and child welfare in rural and out-post Ontario', *Ontario History*, 183–206.

Arnup, K., Lévesque, A. and Pierson, R. R. (eds) (1990) *Delivering Motherhood: Maternal Ideologies and Practices in the 19th and 20th Centuries*, London and New York.

Burtch, B. E. (1987) *Midwifery Practice and State Regulation*, Ottawa.

Cliche, M. A. (1991) 'Christian morality and sexual double standards – unwed mothers at Misericorde-Hospital in Quebec City 1874–1972', *Histoire Sociale – Social History*, 24: 75–125.

Kealey, L. (ed.) (1979) *A Not Unreasonable Claim*, Toronto.

Lewis, N. (1982–3) 'Creating the little machine', *BC Stud.* 56: 44–60.

Portier, B. de la (1974) *Au service de l'enfance: l'Association Québécoise de la Goutte de Lait 1915–1965*, Quebec.

—— (1976) 'La protection de l'enfance au Canada français du XVIIIe siècle jusqu'au debut du XXe siècle', *24th International Congress for the History of Medicine*, Budapest, 1974, acta 1976, vol. 1, 157–71.

Strong-Boag, V. (1982) 'Intruders in the nursery', in J. Parr (ed.) *Childhood and Family in Canadian History*, Toronto, 160–78.

Strong-Boag, V. and MacPherson, K. (1986) 'The confinement of women: childbirth and hospitalization in Vancouver, 1919–1939', *BC Stud.* 69–70: 142–75.

Stuart, M. (1989) 'Ideology and experience: public health nursing and the Ontario child welfare project, 1920–25', *Can. Bull. Med. Hist.* 6: 111–31.

Sutherland, N. (1976) *Children in English Canadian Society*, Toronto.

France

Ariès, P. (1962) *Centuries of Childhood*, London.

Fuchs, R. G. (1984) *Abandoned Children: Foundlings and Child Welfare in 19th Century France*, Albany, NY.

—— (1987) 'Legislation, illegitimacy and poverty: child abandoning mothers in 19th century Paris', *J. Interdisc. Hist.* 18: 54–80.

—— (1988) 'Rich man, poor women: Paul Strauss and the politics of motherhood in Third Republic France', paper presented at the Pacific Coast Branch of the American Historical Association.

—— (1990) 'Preserving the future of France: aid to the poor and pregnant in 19th century Paris', in P. Mandler (ed.) *The Uses of Charity: The Poor on Relief in the Nineteenth Century Metropolis*, Philadelphia, 92–123.

Fuchs, R. G. and Knepper, P. E. (1989) 'Women in the Paris Maternity Hospital: public policy in the nineteenth century', *Soc. Sci. Hist.* 13: 187–209.

Laberge, A. F. (1991) 'Mothers and infants, nurses and nursing: Alfred Donne and the medicalization of childcare in 19th century France', *J. Hist. Med.* 46: 20–43.

McDougall, M. L. (1983) 'Protecting infants: the French campaign for maternity leaves, 1890s–1913', *French Hist. Stud.* 13: 79–105.

Offen, K. (1984) 'Depopulation, nationalism and feminism in fin-de-siècle France', *Am. Hist. Rev.* 89: 648–76.

—— (1987) 'Women and the politics of motherhood in France, 1920–1940', European University Institute, Florence, working papers, no. 87/293.

Rollet, C. (1981) 'Infant feeding, fosterage and infant mortality in France at the end of the 19th century', *Population, Selected Papers* 7: 1–14.

Schneider, W. H. (1986) 'Puericulture, and the style of French eugenics', *Hist. Philos. Life Sci.* 8: 265–77.

Sussman, G. D. (1975) 'The Wet-Nursing business in nineteenth-century France, *French Hist. Stud.* 9: 304–28.

—— (1982) *Selling Mother's Milk: the Wet-Nursing Business in France 1715– 1914*, Urbana, Ill. and London.

Theband, F. (1986) *Quand nos grand-mères donaient la vie: la maternité en France dans l'entre deux guerres*, Lyon.

Germany

Imhof, A. E. (1981) 'Unterschiedliche Säuglingssterblichkeit in Deutschland 18. bis 20. Jahrhunderert – Warum?', *Z. Bevölkerungswiss.* 4: 343–82.

Kintner, H. J. (1982) 'The determinants of infant mortality in Germany from 1871 to 1933', unpub. Ph. D. diss., University of Michigan.

—— (1986) 'Classifying causes of death, during the late nineteenth and early twentieth centuries: the case of German infant mortality', *Hist. Meth.* 19: 45–54.

—— (1988) 'Explaining infant mortality declines: the case of Germany from 1871 to 1925', *Popul. Index*, 54: 476.

—— (1988) 'The impact of breastfeeding patterns on regional differences in infant mortality in Germany, 1910', *Eur. J. Popul.* 3: 233–61.

Knodel, J. (1968) 'Infant mortality and fertility in three Bavarian villages: an analysis of family histories from the 19th century', *Popul. Stud.* 22: 297–318.

—— (1982) 'Child mortality and reproductive behaviour in German village populations in the past: a micro-level analysis of the replacement effect', *Popul. Stud.* 36: 177–200.

Knodel, J. and Walle, E. van de (1967) 'Breastfeeding, fertility and infant mortality: an analysis of some early German data', *Popul. Stud.* 21: 109–31.

Koonz, C. (1986) *Mothers in the Fatherland: Women, the Family and Nazi Politics*, New York and London.

Taylor Allen, A. (1985) 'Mothers of the new generation: Adele Scheiber, Helene Stocker, and the evolution of a German idea of motherhood, 1900–1914', *Signs* 10: 418–38.

Thieme, G. (1984) 'Disparitäten der Lebensbedingungen: Persistenz oder Raum-Zeitlicher Wandel?', *Erdkunde*, 38: 258–67.

Wegmann, H. (1990) 'Mütterschulung in Kaiserin Auguste Victoria Haus zwischen 1910 und 1930', *Schriftenr. Gesch. Kinderheilk. Arch. - Berlin* 7: 91–110.

Latin America

Radbill, S. X. (1954) 'Historical notes on child hygiene in Latin America', *Atti del XIV° Congresso Internazionale di Storia della Medicina*, Romme and Salerno, vol. 2, 3–7.

Yankauer, A. (1966) 'An historical analysis of programs for the reduction of early childhood mortality in Latin America', *J. Trop. Pediat.* 12: 26–31.

The Low Countries

Bande-Knops, J. *et al.* (1989) 'History of prenatal care in Belgium', *Biol. Neonate* 55: 150–4.

Daalen, R. van (1985) 'The start of infant health in Amsterdam: medicalization and the role of the state', *Neth. J. Sociol.* 21–22: 126–39.

Galen, J. van and Mevis, A. (1980) 'Zuigelingenzorg in Oost–Brabant, 1918–1940', in N. Bakker *et al.* (eds) *Een Tipje van de Sluier. Vrouwengeschiedenis in Neder- land*, Amsterdam, vol. 2, 73–83.

Haas, J. H. de (1956) *Kindersterfte in Nederland: Child Mortality in the Netherlands*, Assen.

Haas, J. H. de and Haas-Posthuma, J. H. de (1967) '75 jaar zuigelingen-strfte 1892–1967', *Maandschr. Kindergeneesk.* 35: 184–202 (Dutch with English summary).

Hofstee, E. W. (forthcoming) 'Births, infant diets and infant mortality: their regional differentiation in the nineteenth century', in R. M. Smith (ed.) *Regional and Spatial Demographic Patterns in the Past*, Oxford.

Bibliography

De Knecht-van Eekelen, A. (1984) *Naar een Rationele Zuigelingenvoeding. Voedingsleer en Kindergeneeskunde in Nederland 1840–1914*, Ph.D. thesis, University of Nijmegen, Nijmegen (Dutch with English and German summary).

—— (1986) 'Towards a rational infant-feeding: the science of nutrition and paediatrics in the Netherlands 1840–1914', in J. Cule and T. Turner (eds) *Child Care through the Centuries*, Cardiff, 153–64.

Lesthaeghe, R. J. (forthcoming) 'The breast-feeding hypothesis and regional differences in marital fertility and infant mortality in the Low Countries during the nineteenth century', in R. M. Smith (ed.) *Regional and Spatial Demographic Patterns in the Past*, Oxford.

Lieburg, M. J. van and Marland, H. (1989) 'Midwife regulation, education, and practice in the Netherlands during the nineteenth century', *Med. Hist.* 33: 296–317.

Marland, H. (1992) '"A woman's touch": women doctors and the development of health services for women and children in the Netherlands 1879–c. 1925', in H. Binneveld and R. Dekker (eds) *Sickness and History in the Netherlands*, Hilversum.

—— (forthcoming) 'The guardians of normal birth: the debate on the standard and status of the midwife in the Netherlands around 1900', in E. Abraham (ed.) *Successful Home Birth: The Dutch Obstetric Model*, Amherst, MA.

Poppel, F. van (1983) 'The relationship between socioeconomic position and infant and childhood mortality in the Netherlands in the period 1850–1940', in *International Population Conference Manila 1981*, Liège, vol. 5, 649–89.

—— (forthcoming) 'Religion and health: Catholicism and regional mortality differences in 19th-century Netherlands', *Soc. Hist. Med.*

Pruijt, M. (1989) 'Roeien, baren en in de arbeid zijn. Vroedvrouwen in Noord-Brabant, 1880–1960', in M. Grever and A. van der Veen (eds) *Bij ons Moeder en ons Jet. Brabantse Vrouwen in de 19de en 20ste Eeuw*, 's-Hertogenbosch, 122–42.

Spoorenberg, J. (1981) 'De opvoeding van arbeidersvrouwen. Zuigelingenzorg in Amsterdam 1903–40', unpub. diss., University of Amsterdam.

—— (1984) 'Bakerpraat of doktersadvies? Arbeidersvrouwen en zuigelingenzorg in Amsterdam tussen 1900 en 1914', in A. Angerman et al. (eds) *Een Tipje van de Sluier. Vrouwengeschiedenis in Nederland*, Amsterdam, vol. 3, 78–95.

Vandenbroeke, C., Poppel, F. van and Woude, A. M. van der (1983) 'Le développement séculaire de la mortalité aux jeunes âges dans le territoire du Bénélux', *Ann. Démog. Hist.* 257–89.

—— (forthcoming) 'Infant and child mortality in Belgium and the Netherlands: their long-term development', in R. M. Smith (ed.) *Regional and Spatial Demographic Patterns in the Past*, Oxford.

Vroede, M. de (1981) 'Consultatiecentra voor zuigelingen in de strijd tegen de kindersterfte in Belgie vóór 1914', *Tijdschr. Gesch.* 94: 451–60.

New Zealand

Brookes, B. (1991) 'Aspects of women's health, 1885–1945', in L. Bryder (ed.) *A Healthy Country: Essays on the Social History of Medicine in New Zealand*, Wellington, 149–64.

Donley, J. (1986) *Save the Midwife*, Auckland.

Griffiths, S. (1984) 'Feminism and the ideology of motherhood in New Zealand 1896–1930', unpub. MA thesis, University of Otago, Dunedin.

Mein Smith, P. (1986) *Maternity in Dispute. New Zealand 1920–1939*, Wellington.

—— (1986) 'Mortality in childbirth in the 1920s and 1930s', in B. Brookes, C. Macdonald and M. Tennant (eds) *Women in History: Essays on European Women in New Zealand*, Wellington, 137–55.

Milne, L. S. (1976) 'The Plunket Society: an experiment in infant welfare', unpub. BA (Hons) essay, University of Otago, Dunedin.

Olssen, E. (1981) 'Truby King and the Plunket Society: an analysis of a prescriptive ideology', *NZ J. Hist.* 15: 3–23.

Parkes, C. M. (1991) 'The impact of the medicalisation of New Zealand's maternity services on women's experience of childbirth, 1904–1937', in L. Bryder (ed.) *A Healthy Country: Essays on the Social History of Medicine in New Zealand*, Wellington, 165–80.

Parry, G. (1982) *A Fence at the Top: The First 75 Years of the Plunket Society*, Dunedin.

Woodbury, R. M. (1922) *Infant Mortality and Preventive Work in New Zealand*, Washington, DC.

Russia

Dunn, P. P. (1974) '"That enemy is the baby": childhood in Imperial Russia', in L. de Mause (ed.) *The History of Childhood*, New York, 383–405.

Ransel, D. L. (ed.) (1978) *The Family in Imperial Russia: New Lines of Historical Research*, Urbana, Ill.

—— (1988) *Mothers of Misery: Child Abandonment in Russia*, Princeton, NJ.

Waters, E. (1987) 'Teaching mothercraft in post-revolutionary Russia', *Aust. Slav. E. Eur. Stud.* 1: 29–56.

Scandinavia

Backer, J. E. and Aggenaes, O. (1966) *Infant mortality in Norway, 1901–1963*, Oslo (Norwegian with English summary).

Brändström, A. (1984) '"The loveless mothers": infant mortality in Sweden during the nineteenth century with special attention to the parish of Nedertorneå', unpub. Ph. D. thesis, University of Umeå (Swedish with English summary).

—— (1988) 'The impact of female labour conditions on infant mortality: a case study of the parishes of Nedertorneå and Jokkmokk, 1800–96', *Soc. Hist. Med.* 1: 329–58.

Brändström, A., Broström, G. and Persson, L. A. (1984) 'The impact of feeding patterns on infant mortality in a nineteenth century Swedish parish, *J. Trop. Pediat.* 30: 154–9.

Högberg, U. (1985) *Maternal mortality in Sweden*, Umeå University, medical diss., new series no. 156, Umeå.

Högberg, U. and Bröström, G. (1985) 'The demography of maternal mortality – seven Swedish parishes in the 19th century', *Internat. J. Gynaecol. & Obstet.* 23: 489–97.

Högberg, U. and Wall, S. (1986) 'Secular trends in maternal mortality in Sweden from 1750–1980', *Bull. WHO* 64: 79–84.

—— (1986) 'Age and parity as determinants of maternal mortality – impact of their shifting distribution among parturients in Sweden from 1781–1980', *Bull. WHO* 64: 85–91.

Högberg, U. *et al.* (1986) 'The impact of early medical technology on maternal mortality in late 19th century Sweden', *Internat. J. Gynaecol. & Obstet.* 24: 251–61.

Lithell, U.-B. (1981) 'Breastfeeding habits and their relation to infant mortality and marital fertility', *J. Fam. Hist.* 6: 182–94.

—— (1981) *Breastfeeding and Reproduction: Studies in Marital Fertility and Infant Mortality in 19th Century Finland and Sweden*, Uppsala.

—— (1988) 'Childcare – a mirror of women's living conditions: a community study representing 18th and 19th century Ostrobothnia in Finland', in A. Brändström and L.-G. Tedebrand (eds) *Society, Health and Population During the Demographic Transition*, Umeå, 91–108.

Matthiessen, P. C. (1965) *Infant Mortality in Denmark 1931–1960*, Copenhagen.

Rosenberg, M. (1989) 'Breastfeeding and infant mortality in Norway 1860–1930', *J. Biosoc. Sci.* 21: 335–48.

Trolle, D. (1963) 'Perinatal maternal mortality in the Maternity Hospital in Copenhagen throughout 200 years', *Dan. Med. Bull.* 10: 240–4.

Southern Europe

Bellacicco, A. and Maravalle, M. (1974) 'On the fundamental variations in infant mortality by region from 1863 to 1961', *Genus* 30: 203–23 (Italian with French and English abstract).

Breschi, M. and Bacci, M. L. (1986) 'Saison et climat comme contraintes de la survie des enfants. L'expérience italienne aux XIXe siècle', *Population* 41: 9–35, 1072–4.

Garcia-Gil, C. *et al.* (1989) 'Epidemiological appraisal of the active role of women in the decline of infant mortality in Spain during the twentieth century', *Soc. Sci. Med.* 29: 1351–62.

Guidi, L. (1986) 'Parto e maternità a Napoli: carità e solidarietà spontanee, beneficenza instituzionale (1840–1880)', *Sanità Sci. Storia* 1: 111–48.

Herring, D. A. and Sawchuk, L. A. (1986) 'The emergence of class differentials in infant mortality in the Jewish community of Gibraltar, 1840–1929', *Coll. Anthropol.* 10: 29–35.

Ramos, E. (1971) 'Evolución de la mortalidad de los niños en Valencia desde 1860 a 1920', *Med. Esp.* 66: 45–54.

Savona-Ventura, C. (1991) 'Reproductive performance on the Maltese Islands during the Second World War', *Med. Hist.* 34: 164–77.

Sawchuk, L. A. *et al.* (1985) 'Evidence of a Jewish advantage: a study of infant mortality in Gibraltar, 1870–1959', *Am. Anthropol.* 87: 616–25.

United States

Antler, J. and Fox, D. M. (1976) 'The movement toward a safe maternity: physician accountability in New York City, 1915–1940', *Bull. Hist. Med.* 50: 569–95.

Apple, R. D. (1980) '"To be used only under the direction of a physician": commercial infant feeding and medical practice, 1870–1940', *Bull. Hist. Med.* 54: 402–17.

—— (1986) '"Advertised by our loving friends": the infant-formula industry and the creation of new pharmaceutical markets, *c.* 1870–1910', *J. Hist. Med.* 41: 3–23.

—— (1987) *Mothers and Medicine: A Social History of Infant Feeding, 1890–1950*, Madison, Wis.

Bogdan, J. (1978) 'Care or cure? Childbirth practices in nineteenth-century America', *Fem. Stud.* 4: 92–9.

Breckinridge, M. (1952) *Wide Neighborhoods. A Story of the Frontier Nursing Service*, New York.

Brenner, M. H. (1973) 'Fetal, infant and maternal mortality during periods of economic instability', *Internat. J. Health Serv.* 3: 145–59.

Cheney, R. A. (1984) 'Seasonal aspects of infant and childhood mortality: Philadelpia, 1865–1920', *J. Interdisc. Hist.* 14: 561–85.

Chepaitis, J. B. (1968) 'The first federal social welfare measure: the Sheppard-Towner maternity and infancy act, 1918–1932', unpub. Ph. D. thesis, University of Georgetown.

Condran, G. A. and Karamarow, E. (1991) 'Low child mortality in the United States in the early twentieth century: an examination of a Jewish immigrant population', *J. Interdisc. Hist.* 22: 223–54.

Cone, T. E., Jr. (1976) *200 Years of Feeding Infants in America*, Columbus, Ohio.

—— (1979) *The History of American Pediatrics*, Boston.

—— (1985) *History of the Care and Feeding of the Premature Infant*, Boston.

Dwork, D. (1977) 'The child model (or the model child?) of the late nineteenth century in urban America', *Clio Medica* 12: 111–29.

Dye, N. S. (1980) 'Review essay: history of childbirth in America', *Signs*, 6: 97–108.

—— (1983) 'Mary Breckinridge, the Frontier Nursing Service and the introduction of nurse midwifery in the United States, *Bull. Hist. Med.* 57: 485–507.

—— (1987) 'Modern obstetrics and working-class women: the New York Midwife Dispensary, 1890–1920', *J. Soc. Hist.* 20: 549–64.

Dye, N. S. and Smith, D. B. (1986) 'Mother love and infant death, 1750–1920', *J. Am. Hist.* 73: 329–53.

Edwards, M. (1984) *Reclaiming Birth: History and Heroines of American Childbirth Reform*, Trumanburg, NY.

Ehrenreich, B. and English, D. (1978) *For Her Own Good. 150 Years of the Experts' Advice to Women*, New York.

Ewbank, D. and Preston, S. H. (1990) 'Personal health behavior and the decline in infant and child mortality: the United States, 1900–30', in J. Caldwell, S. Findley, P. Caldwell, G. Santow, W. Cosford, J. Braid, D. Broes-Freeman (eds), *What We Know about Health Transition. The Cultural, Social and Behavioural Determinants of Health*, Canberra, vol. 1, 116–49.

Golden, J. (1984) 'From breast to bottle: the decline of wet nursing in Boston, 1867–1927', unpub. Ph. D. diss., University of Boston.

—— (1988) 'From wet nurse directory to milk bank: the delivery of human milk in Boston, 1909–1927', *Bull. Hist. Med.* 62: 589–605.

Halpern, S. A. (1988) *American Pediatrics: the Social Dynamics of Professionalism, 1880–1980*, Berkeley, Calif.

Hoffert, S. D. (1989) *Private Matters: American Attitudes Towards Childbearing and Infant Nurture in the Urban North 1800–1860*, Urbana, Ill.

Jones, K. W. (1983) 'Sentiment and science: the late nineteenth century pediatrician as mother's advisor', *J. Soc. Hist.* 17: 79–96.

King, C. R. (1991) 'The New York maternal mortality study: a conflict of professionalisation', *Bull. Hist. Med.* 65: 476–502.

Klos, S. F. (1992) *Reform Initiatives in American Maternal Health Service, 1900–1940*.

Kobrin, F. E. (1966) 'The American midwife controversy: a crisis of professionalization', *Bull. Hist. Med.* 40: 350–63.

Ladd-Taylor, M. (1986) *Raising a Baby the Government Way: Mothers' Letters to the Children's Bureau, 1915–1932*, New Brunswick, NJ.

—— (1988) '"Grannies" and "spinsters": midwife training under the Sheppard-Towner Act', *J. Soc. Hist.* 22: 255–75.

—— (1991) 'Hull House goes to Washington: women and the Children's Bureau', in N. S. Dye and N. Frankel (eds) *Gender, Class and Reform in the Progressive Era*, 110–26, Lexington, Ky.

—— (forthcoming) *Mother-Work: Women, Child Welfare and the State 1890–1930*, Urbana, Ill.

Leavitt, J. W. (1986) *Brought to Bed: Childbearing in America, 1750 to 1950*, New York and Oxford.

Lentzner, H. R. (1987) 'Seasonal patterns of infant and child mortality in New York, Chicago and New Orleans: 1870–1919', unpub. Ph. D. diss., University of Pennsylvania.

Lesser, A. J. (1985) 'The origin and development of maternal and child health programs in the United States', *Am. J. Publ. Health.* 75: 590–8.

Levenstein, H. (1983) '"Best for babies" or "preventable infanticide"? The controversy over artificial feeding of infants in America, 1880–1920', *J. Am. Hist.* 70: 75–94.

Litoff, J. B. (1978) *American Midwives: 1860 to the Present,* Westport, Conn.

—— (ed.) (1986) *The American Midwife Debate: a Sourcebook of its Modern Origins,* Westport, Conn.

Longo, L. D. and Thompsen, C. M. (1982) 'Prenatal care and its evolution in America', *Proceedings of the Second Motherhood Symposium,* Madison, Wis.

McMillen, S. G. (1990) *Motherhood in the Old South: Pregnancy, Childbirth, and Infant Rearing,* Baton Rouge, La. and London.

Meckel, R. A. (1985) 'Protecting the innocents: age segregation and the early child welfare movement', *Soc. Serv. Rev.* 59: 455–75.

—— (1990) *Save the Babies: American Public Health Reform and the Prevention of Infant Mortality 1850–1929,* Baltimore and London.

Mooney, M. P. (1983) 'Milk to motherhood: the New York milk committee and the beginning of the well-child programs', *Mid-America* 65: 112–34.

Murphy-Lawless, J. (1988) 'The silencing of women in childbirth or let's hear it from Bartholomew and the Boys', *Women's Internat. Forum* 11: 293–9.

O'Donnell, J. (1990) 'The development of a climate for caring: a historical review of premature care in the United States from 1900 to 1979', *Neonatal Network* 8: 7–17.

Pact Brickman, J. (1978) 'Mother love – mother death: maternal and infant care: social class and the role of government', unpub. Ph. D. diss., City University of New York.

Pottishman Weiss, N. (1974) 'Save the children: a history of the Children's Bureau, 1903–1918', unpub. Ph. D. diss., University of California, Los Angeles.

Preston, S. H. and Haines, M. R. (1991) *Fatal Years: Child Mortality in Late Nineteenth-Century America,* Princeton, NJ.

Quiroga, V. A. M. (1986) 'Female lay managers and scientific pediatrics at Nursery and Child's Hospital, 1854–1910', *Bull. Hist. Med.* 60: 194–208.

—— (1989) *Poor Mothers and Babies: a Social History of Childbirth and Child Care Hospitals in Nineteenth Century New York City,* New York.

Radosch, P. F. (1986) 'Midwives in the US – past and present', *Population Research and Policy Review* 5: 129–45.

Rothman, S. M. (1981) '"Women's clinics or doctors' offices": the Sheppard-Towner Act and the promotion of preventive health care', in D. J. Rothman and S. Wheeler (eds) *Social History and Social Policy,* New York, 175–201.

Sandelowski, M. (1984) *Pain, Pleasure, and American Childbirth: From the Twilight Sleep to the Read Method, 1914–1960,* Westport, Conn.

Schaffer, R. G. (1991) 'The health and social functions of black midwives on the Texas Brazos Bottom, 1920–1985', *Rural Sociology* 56: 89–105.

Schmidt, W. M. (1973) 'The development of health services for mothers and children in the United States', *Am. J. Publ. Health* 63: 419–27.

Wilkie, K. E. and Moseley, E. R. (1959) *Frontier Nurse: Mary Breckinridge,* New York.

Woodbury, R. M. (1926) *Infant Mortality and its Causes,* Baltimore.

West Indies

Searle, C. (1960) 'Infant and early childhood death rates over the last hundred years in the negro population of Antigua, West Indies', *Br. J. Prev. Soc. Med.* 14: 185–9.

Uttley, K. H. (1959) 'The epidemiology of puerperal fever and maternal mortality in Antigua, West Indies, over the last hundred years', *J. Obstet. & Gynaecol. Br. Emp.* 10: 240–4.

Comparative and International

Beekman, D. (1977) *The Mechanical Baby: a Popular History of the Theory and Practice of Child Rearing,* London.

Block, G. and Thane, P. (eds) (1991) *Maternity and Gender Policies: Women and the Rise of European Welfare States 1880–1950,* London.

Cooter, R. (1992) *In the Name of the Child: Health and Welfare, 1880–1940,* London and New York.

Fildes, V. (1986) *Breasts, Bottles and Babies: A History of Infant Feeding,* Edinburgh.

—— (1988) *Wet Nursing: A History from Antiquity to the Present,* Oxford.

—— (1988) 'The history of breastfeeding to c. 1920', *Breastfeeding Review* 13: 8–13.

—— (1991) 'Breastfeeding practices during industralisation, 1800–1919', in F. T. Falkner (ed.) *Infant and Child Nutrition Worldwide: Issues and perspectives,* Florida.

Haines, M. R. (1985) 'Inequality and childhood mortality: a comparison of England and Wales, 1911, and the United States, 1900', *J. Econ. Hist.* 45: 885–912.

Imhof, A. E. (1984) 'Säuglingssterblichkeit im Europäischen Kontext, 17.20. Jahrundert. Ueberlegungen zu einem Buch von Anders Brändström', *Newsletter no. 2 from the Demographic Data Base,* Umeå.

King, J. and Ashworth, A. (1987) 'Historical view of the changing pattern of infant feeding in developing countries: the case of Malaysia, the Caribbean, Nigeria and Zaïre', *Soc. Sci. Med.* 25: 1307–20.

Klaus, A. C. (1986) 'Babies all the rage: the movement to prevent infant mortality in the United States and France, 1890–1920', unpub. Ph. D. diss., University of Pennsylvania.

—— (1992) *Every Child a Lion: The Origins of Infant Health Policy in the United States and France 1890–1920,* Ithaca, NY.

Koven, S. and Michel, S. (1990) 'Womanly duties: maternalist politics and the origins of welfare states in France, Germany, Great Britain, and the United States, 1880–1920', *Am. Hist. Rev.* 95: 1076–108.

Loudon, I. (1988) 'Maternal mortality: 1880–1950. Some regional and international comparisons', *Soc. Hist. Med.* 1: 183–228.

—— (1991) 'On maternal and infant mortality 1900–1960', *Soc. Hist. Med.* 4: 29–73.

—— (forthcoming) *Death in Childbirth: An International Study of Maternal Care and Maternal Mortality, 1800–1950,* Oxford.

Oakley, A. (1976) 'Wisewoman and medicine man: changes in the management of childbirth', in J. Mitchell and A. Oakley (eds) *The Rights and Wrongs of Women,* London, 17–58.

Schmelz, U. O. (1971) *Infant and Early Childhood Mortality among Jews of the Diaspora,* Jerusalem (Institute of Contemporary Jewry, The Hebrew University).

Shorter, E. (1982) *A History of Women's Bodies,* New York.

Smith, R. M. (forthcoming) 'Explaining spatial differences in infant mortality: environmental and behavioural effects', in R. M. Smith (ed.) *Regional and Spatial Demographic Patterns in the Past,* Oxford.

Teitelbaum, M. S. (1971) 'Male and female components of perinatal mortality: international trends, 1901–63', *Demography* 8: 541–8.

Torres, A. and Reich, M. R. (1989) 'The shift from home to institutional childbirth: a comparative study of the UK and the Netherlands', *Internat. J. Health Serv.* 19: 405–14.

Index